W9-DDI-459

ECONOMIC RELATIONSHIPS AMONG STATES

By the same author

BRITAIN AND CHINA

NATIONALITY AND WEALTH

CONFLICT AND PEACE IN THE MODERN
INTERNATIONAL SYSTEM

THE CONTROL OF THE SEABED

INTERNATIONAL AGENCIES: The Emerging Framework of
Interdependence

TYPES OF INTERNATIONAL SOCIETY

THE UNITED NATIONS: How it Works and What it Does

SOCIALISM WITHOUT THE STATE

A HISTORY OF THE UNITED NATIONS:
Volume 1: The Years of Western Domination, 1945–1955

THE MANAGEMENT OF THE WORLD ECONOMY

ECONOMIC RELATIONSHIPS AMONG STATES

A Further Study in International Sociology

Evan Luard

St. Martin's Press   New York

337
L926

© Evan Luard 1984

All rights reserved. For information, write:
St. Martin's Press, Inc., 175 Fifth Avenue, New York, NY 10010
Printed in Hong Kong
First published in the United States of America in 1984

ISBN 0–312–23514–3

Library of Congress Cataloging in Publication Data

Luard, Evan, 1926–
  Economic relationships among states.

  Includes index.
  1. International economic relations.   I. Title.
HF1411.L79   1983   337   83–3293
ISBN 0–312–23514–3

Contents

Introduction: The Economic Dimension in International Society

This volume is the second of a trilogy devoted to the study of 'international society'. The three volumes represent an attempt to study the behaviour of nations on a sociological basis: that is, through analysis of individual societies of states, each having many of the characteristics of smaller-scale societies – a regular pattern of relations among their members, established forms of intercourse, a system of stratification, traditional institutions, norms of conduct, acknowledged procedures for resolving disputes, even sometimes an embryonic system of authority.

The basis of this approach was set out in the first volume of the trilogy, *Types of International Society* (New York, 1976). That book sought to analyse the main characteristics of a succession of historical 'societies' of states, from the multi-state system in ancient China 2500 years ago, the Greek city-state system, the age of dynastic states in mediaeval Europe, the age of religious wars, the age of sovereignty, the age of nationalism, to the international community as we have known it in recent times. The study sought to examine the characteristic 'ideology' of each of these societies (the distinctive beliefs among the member-states concerning the nature of international society and appropriate relationships within it), the varying motivations governing state actions, the means used to procure those ends, the different types of stratification measuring status among states, the various sets of roles adopted within each society, the prescribed norms of conduct, and the international institutions characteristic of each.

That study was concerned principally with political and military relations, which in most ages have determined the character of each society. The economic dimension within each society was discussed only incidentally, as one factor among many. But any approach that terms itself sociological must clearly be very much concerned with economic influences. For – without necessarily accepting the more enthusiastic expositions of the view that economic relationships determine all others – few would deny that they are at least a vitally important factor within all social systems, including international societies.

It is thus somewhat perplexing that, within the still embryonic discipline of international relations, the study of the economic relations of states has, until recently, played so little part. This is, no doubt, partly for the simple reason that those who write about international relations are usually political scientists by training, and claim little knowledge of economic affairs. Yet this reticence displays either an excessive modesty, in its implication that those untutored in the mysteries of economics are unlicensed to express themselves even on the remoter fringes of that subject, or an excessive preoccupation with the traditional concerns of international relations, demanding a stern refusal to be distracted into a tributary stream regarded as marginal in importance.

Writers on international relations have not, of course, totally overlooked the economic factor. There is scarcely a book on the subject which does not devote a few paragraphs, or even a chapter, to economic aspects of international relationships; and there have been a number of studies of 'political economy' in the contemporary world. Yet it is none the less the case that these relations have rarely been regarded as a central concern of the discipline, and there are few books in the field that deal exclusively, or even mainly, with economic relations and their effect on international relationships generally.

This is the more surprising because, in the study of domestic politics and domestic political systems, the importance of economic questions has, at least since the time of Comte and Marx and others of their age, been widely recognised. Many (including many who are not 'Marxists') have seen them as a central, if not the crucial, variable on which all else is based. If economic considerations have been recognised as so dominant in political life within states, why have they not been accepted as being so between them?

The contention that political life is determined by economic factors, like many other political theses, easily lends itself to exaggeration and distortion. The thesis was perhaps particularly persuasive in the age when it was born – the early nineteenth century – because that was an age of especially powerful economic forces, when a new industrial age came into being, when political systems, in some countries at least, had begun to provide a greater degree of political power for the emerging capitalist elite, and when the great mass of working people, while deprived of political power, were only too visibly brutally subordinated to the economic forces dominating society. There have been many other ages, probably the majority, in which the prime concern, of peoples and governments alike, was not with economic affairs at all: when people were more preoccupied, for example, with the practice of religion, the distribution of political power or the system of justice. Yet it is difficult to deny that, in all ages, economic concerns, the desire of one group to extend its economic power, and to secure still greater wealth and so status for itself, the concern of rival groups to compete with each other for trade or wealth, above all the demand of less privileged groups to free themselves of their dependence and to obtain a greater degree of equality in economic circumstances, have been political factors of the highest importance. And any reputable social scientist would wish, in examining a domestic society, to include a full examination of the economic forces that are so powerful in their effect.

Should not equal importance then be attributed to economic factors as an influence on the relations of states? That certainly seems a hypothesis worth exploring, and is one of the questions which this study seeks to examine. It is clear that there have been certain periods of history when economic considerations had only a small impact on the working of international society. When economic contacts between states were anyway only tenuous, they were unlikely to be normally the main influence on policy; and in many earlier ages it has been the competition for military or political power among states that has driven them to rivalry or war, rather than conflicting economic interests. During the age of dynasties, in the late Middle Ages, inter-state relations were largely devoted to dynastic ambitions and disputes; except in one or two rare cases, economic factors played only a small part in promoting conflict (even the beginning of the Hundred Years War, sometimes quoted as an example of the contrary, is not really so: economic conflict was then an *effect* and not a cause of a war which emerged primarily from the dynastic ambitions of Edward III). Similarly, in the age of religions between 1559 and 1648, inter-state relations were dominated above all by religious beliefs and religious rivalries, and economic factors, then too, were only marginal. In modern times, as economic relations among states have intensified, they have played a more significant role than before in influencing their relations, but they have still rarely been the major cause of war among states.[1]

None of this, however, proves that economic factors have been unimportant in influencing relations among states. For even if they have not been the dominant concern in influencing inter-state relations, or the main cause of war, they may have had a significant and independent importance of their own. Economic relations have, in fact, normally been a quite separate dimension in the dealings of states amongst themselves. Just as individuals in their everyday personal affairs are not *primarily* concerned with economic relationships, yet none the less recognise that they have a special importance of their own, both for themselves and for those with whom they deal, so too among states: largely independently of their normal everyday relations with each other – concerned with the competition for power or the control of territory – states have at the same time been engaged in economic relationships as well, which have at times become of overwhelming importance and have had usually at least an influence on other relationships. The changing role these economic relations have played, the different forms they have taken, and the reasons for the differing external economic policies pursued, are at least worth examination.

There is one respect in which the economic relations of states differ wholly from their political or military relations. The latter are undertaken almost exclusively by governments. But economic relations are undertaken partly by governments and partly by private individuals and organisations. The actions of each will affect the other. The activities of individuals, and the transactions they can undertake abroad, are directly affected by the policies of their government and the agreements which that government makes with other states. Conversely, the policies pursued by governments will normally (though not always, as we shall see) be directly related to the economic interests and aims of their own nationals in relation to other states. We are dealing here, therefore, with the relations, not of governments alone but of entire states with each other.

International economic *policies* are mainly government policies: in promoting trade, in concluding economic agreements, in imposing tariffs and other forms of restriction. But the economic relations undertaken by private individuals – merchants, bankers, importers, investors – dealing direct with individuals, firms and organisations in other states, often represent the main substance of economic relations between states: a substance which governmental action merely influences and adjusts. We are concerned with both types of transaction; and we must distinguish clearly the differing objectives of governments and of individuals, and the methods employed by each, as well as their influence on each other.

To some extent there will be an identity of interest between the two. The private trader, in promoting his own personal profit, will indirectly be profiting the state as a whole – and so even the government of that state. Conversely, the government of a state, conscious of this fact, is concerned to promote not only the economic interests of the state as such, but also of the various sections of its peoples. Sometimes they need to choose between one section of the population and another; the economic policy designed to help the farmers may harm the consumer, the policy that protects one industry may harm another. But a direct conflict of interest between rulers and governments, on the one hand, and populations as a whole on the other, is unusual.

Yet a division of interest can exist. The government may be concerned in its dealing with foreign states to promote its own revenues and its own economic power (for example, through taxes on exports and imports, or by creating monopolies for particular firms and enterprises); and this may not always serve the economic interests of its people generally. Conversely, private interests, especially economically powerful sections of that population, may have interests quite different from those of their governments: for example, in earning profits and creating employment abroad rather than at home. In examining policy towards other states, we have to bear carefully in mind the distinction between the aims and interests of different groups and those of governments.

A government's policies in the economic field may be influenced sometimes by factors that are not economic at all but political or diplomatic. This is another reason why, while a government's external economic policies will usually be designed to assist at least some part of its own population, it may sometimes pursue policies which conflict with their interests. When Louis XI banned the export of grain to the Low Countries in 1470–80, to bring pressure on Burgundy, he may have served his own political interests but he damaged the interests of the land-owners and the peasantry of France, and the economic interests of France itself. When the export of strategic goods to Communist countries was prohibited by Western governments after the Second World War, they may have promoted the political interests of their states, but only at the expense of the interests of the exporters of those products and their workers. Whether the state as a whole benefited from the policy in either case, even though many of its people lost, is a question of judgement. The essential point is that, as these examples show, states on the one hand, and the individuals within them on the other, have interests that are sometimes quite distinct. Each undertakes actions in the economic field, sometimes independently of each other. Both types of action affect economic relations with other states and the individuals within them; but the actions which each undertakes in its own interest will not necessarily be of benefit to the other.

The interests of the state may conflict still more with those of *particular* groups and individuals. Because they are not able, alone or even in groups, to protect their interests abroad without the aid or support, or at least the acquiescence, of their own government, individuals seek to mobilise the state on their behalf. Just as within states individuals find that it is through *collective* action that they can best protect and promote their own interests – for example, in guilds, trade unions, trade associations, companies or political parties – which have a strength on which the individual cannot call, so too in international economic relations the individual finds that he can pursue his own interests best through collective action. Here the state is the collective body which can best promote those interests. So all seek to ensure that the state makes use of its special power on their own behalf: and their aim is, ideally, to bring those in authority to see their group interests as the interests of the state.

Within each state different individuals and groups will have differing success in ensuring that the state represents their interests effectively. How far they succeed in achieving this – and the degree therefore, to which individual interests are promoted by the collective action of the state – is one of the important questions which we shall need to study. But everywhere we shall see take place a *collectivisation of interests*. Through that process, a single body, the state, is used to promote the collective interests of the groups exercising power within each country.

Even more important than the differing capacity of individuals and groups to influence their own state, however, is the differing capacity of *states* to make their collective interests effective in their relations with other states. A militarily powerful state may be able, for example, to promote the interests of all its citizens more effectively than one which is not so strong. So too may one that is economically powerful. What will determine the economic welfare of the individual citizen, therefore, is partly his own success in ensuring that his government recognises and promotes his own interest, and partly the success of his government in securing national interests in its relations with other states. Each of these are factors which we shall want to examine in the study which follows.

Economic relations between states, and what influences those relations, are therefore just as much a matter of concern to international sociology as economic relations within states may be to the sociology of smaller societies. In both cases, such a study is concerned not only with material relationships but also with the social conceptions, social attitudes and social doctrines which brought about such relationships. Thus just as, in our earlier study, we found there was special importance in a factor which we described as 'ideology' – the concepts, assumptions, expectations concerning inter-state relations and the types of behaviour to be expected or tolerated within a society of states – and which we saw had a crucial influence on international relationships, so we shall find in examining economic relations among states the importance of a form of *economic* ideology, a theory or 'doctrine' about economic relations, which comes equally to influence the economic behaviour of states. Just as the ideology within states – 'capitalism' or 'communism' (or more often particular versions of each) – may govern the economic relations established there, so a particular international doctrine may govern economic relations within a society of states. Another subject that will concern us, therefore, is the changing character of these 'doctrines' and the different types of economic relationship associated with each.

In other words, we are interested in economic relationships as part of the wider relationship among states in each age; and we are concerned especially with the role economic relations play in establishing a particular kind of political and social order among states.

1 Doctrine

Human actions are swayed, in most fields of activity, by a few relatively simple conceptions and underlying beliefs. These are usually instilled at a relatively early age and become assumptions that cannot readily be disregarded. The beliefs may be rarely articulated or never even thought about at all. They are part of a customary framework of thought that is taken for granted, never questioned, and becomes the starting-point on which action is based.

Economic systems are often rooted in such simple assumptions. If it is believed that human nature is selfish and mercenary, it will be assumed that only powerful incentives, in the form of the profit motive and high differentials in income, will motivate people to successful economic activity. If it is assumed that they are co-operative and selfless, it will be concluded that an economic system based on co-operation rather than personal gain may work most successfully. If it is taken for granted that a single ruler or a few wise men, an omniscient bureaucracy or an all-wise political party, know best what is right for the nation as a whole, it will be assumed that economic activities too should be minutely regulated by the powers that be, rather than left to the hazards of individual activity and a free market. Conversely, if it is believed that the best government is the least government, and that if left to their own devices men will establish a natural balance of interest between them, the presumption will be against government interference in the economic activities of citizens.

Most people would not admit, and may not be aware, that they are influenced in their attitudes to political and economic questions by a few simple assumptions of this kind. They may be able to find reasons to justify their preference for one belief or slogan rather than any other – in 'competition' rather than 'co-operation', a 'free market' rather than 'socialist planning', 'monetarism' rather than 'Keynesianism'.

Few readily believed in other words, that they are slaves to some defunct economist. But the fact that they can find such reasons does not prove that they have escaped those influences. The defunct

1

economist, unseen and unknown, may mould the thoughts of those who never even knew of his existence.

In international society a similar process takes place. The type of economic relationship established with other states may result from simple inherited assumptions about the way to secure national prosperity. Very often, as we shall frequently see in the pages that follow, the assumptions that govern the international economy are related to those that prevail concerning the domestic economy. In a crude sense, a general belief in a free market and free trade at home will lead to a belief in a free market and free trade abroad. A general belief in detailed regulation of the domestic economy and widespread intervention by the government of the day will lead to a corresponding assumption concerning foreign economic relations. A belief in the need for restrictive monetary policies at home will create a corresponding belief abroad. And so on. It is with the character of this underlying doctrine, the way it emerges and the way it influences the economic policies of states towards each other, that we shall be concerned in this chapter.

From where does the underlying 'doctrine' derive? Sometimes it may be genuinely the creation of some great thinker of the time. The ideas expounded in Adam Smith's *Wealth of Nations*, for example (though foreshadowed by some other writers), transformed the economic thinking, domestic and international, of his day. But usually, even in those cases, the doctrine becomes widely *accepted* only because it corresponds to some widely felt need or interest of that age. The *Wealth of Nations* was not deliberately written to promote the interests of any particular group, class or nation, but to expound what Adam Smith saw as the most rational way of running a national (and indeed an international) economy. But the fact that it acquired such huge influence, the fact that it came to be quoted so widely, and so approvingly, by many – and especially by the merchants of the following age – reflected the fact that, whatever the motives which caused it to be written, it corresponded with the interests of a powerful force within society, in this case the commercial classes generally as well as with the national interests of Britain as a whole. However it was intended, therefore, it became, in effect, the underlying ideology of the age of commercialism that followed.

In other cases, there has existed no single work that can be said to represent the carefully reasoned ideology of the economic society in question. The ideology then represents nothing more than a set of assumptions, each one widely held but rarely discussed. The economic beliefs of the seventeenth and early eighteenth centuries, subsequently bundled together and labelled as 'mercantilism', are of this kind. Many writings and actions of that day reflected these beliefs; many others take them for granted. But there is no universally acknowledged text or source from which they flowed (indeed, some doubt if there was any single set of beliefs at all). The doctrine is merely the amalgam of the most widely held assumptions of the age.

Sometimes such a doctrine stems merely from existing *practice*. There is no single work expounding the doctrine of the mixed economy today (though possibly the writings of Keynes come closest to this). Yet the doctrine of the mixed economy, that is of a regulated capitalism, in one form or another, for long governed the thinking of large parts of the western world. And in this case too it influenced attitudes towards the international economy as much as to national economic life: when a *managed liberalism* was the ruling creed within states, it was between them too (see pp. 36–48).

We shall be concerned, then, in this chapter with examining some of the general economic conceptions of this kind in each age and the way they influenced foreign economic policy. We shall seek to trace the changing social forces in each age and their effect on the doctrine prevailing at a particular time. And we shall consider how far the emergence of a particular doctrine at a particular period corresponded to the deeply-held needs of particular states, or at least of an economically powerful interest-group within them.

PROVISION AND POWER (1300–1600)

During the later Middle Ages, the dominant economic power, between states as well as within them, was that of the princes. The power wielded by the ruler in the political sphere, which was almost total, was reflected in a comparable absolutism in the economic field. The doctrine of monarchical power, as laid down in the writings of Bodin, Machiavelli and Hobbes, expressed a reality that was economic as well as political.

It was seen as the nature of royal power that it was, in this field as in others, absolute and often arbitrary. It could thus be used to impose drastic restraints on the normal course of economic activity. The concept of a 'free market' had no existence in such an age, whether in domestic or in international economic relations. The assumption everywhere was that economic activity, even more perhaps than other aspects of life, required careful regulation. In the towns this regulation had long been undertaken, in very detailed fashion, by the gilds and the town governments they dominated. Now it was undertaken at national level by kings: to secure adequate supplies, to maintain stable prices, to restrict entry to particular trades. The rulers of the period, national or civic, regulated the smallest details of economic life. They established minimum and maximum prices; maximum interest rates; minimum, but more often maximum wages. The exact details of methods of production and precise standards for the final products were specified. Entry into particular crafts was rigidly controlled, and the number to be trained and the type of training laid down. The days and locations of markets and access to them were regulated. All trade between certain towns was to be undertaken along particular routes or in particular markets. Over agriculture, the source of most necessities of life, equally elaborate regulations, setting out the crops to be grown, or the obligation to cultivate on pain of forfeiture, were decreed.[1] The guiding principle throughout the age, in economic as in other matters, was one of *autocratic regulation*.

This principle of autocratic regulation was applied equally to foreign economic relations. So total bans might be suddenly imposed on trade with a certain country: as when Edward III suddenly cut off trade with Flanders in 1336, or Louis XI banned the export of grain to the low countries in 1470. Artisans of particular kinds were forbidden to emigrate, as were textile workers from France, Flanders and other areas. New duties or export taxes were now imposed, now abandoned; English wool taxes were changed almost yearly in the fourteenth century. Total prohibitions of imports from particular areas, or exports of particular kinds, were suddenly introduced, or as suddenly abandoned, for diplomatic as much as economic reasons. Autocratic regulation was applied even to the field of personal consumption. Statutes were passed that women were not to wear certain types of lavish material, nor to adorn themselves with certain kinds of jewels, such as pearls, which were regarded as luxurious. The number of guests who could be invited to weddings or christenings was restricted, and even the number of courses that could be served to them. The size of the dowry a father could give when his daughter married was limited, as were the presents a husband could give to his bride.[2] These controls too had their effect on foreign economic policies. In Barcelona in 1422, the importation of fur, woollen and silk fabrics 'for sale or wearing' was forbidden, and the entire population had to wear the simpler clothes made locally. Similar laws restricting the imports of luxuries were passed in other states. Foreign merchants, such as the Lombards in England, were blamed for bringing useless luxuries to the country, and their activities sometimes halted for these reasons. Dislike of extravagant sumptuary display combined with resentment at foreign traders taking gold from the country to cause controls on their activity. So the desire to curb conspicuous consumption was the cause of restrictions on foreign trade.

Imports of essentials, on the other hand, were positively promoted. One of the economic doctrines of the day was the belief in the policy of 'plenty' or 'provision'. The famous textbook on royal rights and duties, *De Regimine Principium*, asserted that 'it was the duty of a ruler to ensure that the community was supplied with what was necessary for its sustenance'.[3] This was, as Machiavelli pointed out, a teaching not only of duty but also of prudence, since the ruler who failed to feed his people might well expose himself to revolution. The policy of the rulers was often, therefore, in contrast to the objective in most other ages, to welcome imports and discourage exports. The Hanseatic merchants in London, for example, though resented by some of their direct competitors in England, were welcomed by the king and by most other classes, and on these grounds were accorded extensive trading privileges, including some not enjoyed even by their English competitors. They were welcomed because they could satisfy certain essential needs of the consumer which could not be satisfied in any other way. In Norway, the Hanseatic traders were well regarded, for similar reasons. So were the Venetians in Byzantium and the Lombards in France. All over Europe rulers, in thinking of trade, thought in terms of ensuring supplies rather than winning exports. Exports might even be forbidden, to retain supplies at home.[4]

A second element in the thinking of this period was a concern to *capture* trade, seen everywhere as a source of revenues. The traditional revenues of early mediaeval times – domanial dues, the profits of justice, markets, feudal aids, and so on – were declining or defunct. There were no taxes on incomes or production. The obvious target for taxation was the activity through which money principally changed hands: trade. To win trade to a town or market brought gains of three sorts: it could satisfy the local need for goods, it could bring trade to local merchants, and it could bring revenues to the ruler, or the town government, that taxed the trade. Thus a major aim was the capture of trade that could bring these benefits. For France, for example, the establishment of the fair at Champagne, which brought together traders from Flanders in the north and Lombardy in the south, brought not only prosperity to a considerable part of the country but also revenues for the king. But the aim was manifested above all in the establishment of 'staples': towns through which trade throughout the area was compelled to pass.[5] So, for example, Vienna compelled all south German merchants wishing to trade to east Europe to dispose of their wares in Vienna, after which Viennese merchants would take them further. King Wenceslas of Bohemia demanded that strangers who stayed in the city for five days were not to carry their goods any further but must sell them there. English merchants trading to Iceland were forced to pass through Bergen (which compelled them to sail in the opposite direction to their destination). Venice compelled all the trade to Ragusa to pass through Venice. These are only a few examples of an almost universal phenomenon of the time. Trade was forcibly directed to particular markets to the benefit of those who controlled them. Foreign traders and foreign states were seen as *prey*, to be fleeced by the rulers for the benefit of himself or his state.

A third element in the prevailing economic ideas was the attitude to gold. Domestically, gold was seen very simply as a source of wealth; indeed, as wealth itself. The Estates General of France declared that 'money is to the body politic what blood is to the human body, so any loss has to be made good'. Internationally, one of the major concerns of rulers and their advisers was to conserve and increase the stock of gold and silver in their countries and especially in their own royal coffers. Here too, autocratic regulation was in this age the means employed: direct controls to safeguard the stock of bullion.[6] Sometimes its export was totally prohibited. Sometimes merchants were obliged to hand to the Crown whatever gold or silver they gained through trade abroad. Richard II in England simply forbade anybody to go abroad except nobles, merchants and the king's soldiers; and in this way minimised the drain of gold. The Count of Flanders, even more simply, had all travellers passing through his territory bodily searched to ensure that they took no precious metals out of the country.

A fourth feature of mediaeval economic doctrine was the concern of the ruler in his economic policies to safeguard or increase the power and security of his state: the so-called 'policy of power'.[7] As the Middle Ages progressed, this came to be of increasing importance in the minds of most princes: Francis Bacon, for example, spoke of Henry VII 'bowing the ancient policy of this Estate from consideration of Plenty to consideration of Power'. For this aim too, autocratic regulation provided a simple remedy. Rulers would simply prohibit altogether the export of anything of military value. Export of all metals, horses, saltpetre, arms, shipping and other goods was often banned. Conversely, special steps were taken to secure the *supply* of strategic materials, especially the so-called 'naval goods' – pitch, timber, hemp, and so on. Special assistance was given for the local production of saltpetre, armaments and strategic materials. Special measures were taken to promote shipbuilding and the use of native ships. Richard II's Navigation Act, the first of a long series extended until the mid-nineteenth century, was designed to strengthen England's military strength by promoting and protecting native shipbuilding, a measure subsequently copied by other states. Sometimes the eating of meat was prohibited at particular periods (the so-called 'political lent'): this would increase fish-eating, and so assist the fishing industry and promote naval power. Special obligations were placed on traders for strategic ends: in Edward IV's reign in England, all merchants importing goods from Venice were required to bring four bowstaves with them for every ton of other goods they bought. So, once more, rulers used the method of autocratic regulation to control economic activity and promote the military power of states.

During the late Middle Ages, therefore, international economic policies reflected the ideas governing the domestic economy. Foreign economic relations, like other aspects of the economy, were controlled by autocratic means: by embargoes and decrees, arbitrary levies and impositions. The measures adopted often depended on the whim of the ruler. His motives were often not economic but political, as where exports were suddenly cut off for foreign policy reasons. And in so far as the ruler was concerned with economic benefits, these were often the economic benefits not for his people but for himself: above all his desire for revenues. Export duties and prohibitions, monopolies, taxes or tolls: these were imposed, sometimes with little regard for their effect on trade or production, because they could provide greater sources of income for the ruler himself, who, with his immediate advisers, alone controlled economic policy. So the economic conceptions and the economic practices of the age reflected its political concerns: above all the demands of power and the provision of supplies.

THE WAR OF MONEY (1600–1750)

From about the beginning of the seventeenth century onwards – the exact date of transition varied from one state to another[8] – the ruling concern of governments in their economic relations with other states began to change.

In almost every state, the dominant political force remained the ruler. But rulers were no longer concerned only with personal power or dynastic rights. They increasingly identified themselves with the state they ruled. Even when their power remained absolute, as in France, they now delegated substantial parts of it to the great ministers, such as Richelieu, Mazarin and Colbert; and these in practice often now exercised a greater direct influence on policy than did their masters. And even more than these, they cherished the aim to strenghten and expand the power of their own state. This objective – state-building – became the dominant concern, in foreign as much as domestic policy.

These aims were reflected in economic policies. Other states were now seen not as prey, still less as friends or partners, but as *rivals*: fellow nations under fellow rulers who must be checked in their pretensions to equality. This concept of *rivality* was a central feature of the age, economically as politically. There was no disposition to concede that states could share common, or even mutual interests. The assumption everywhere was that what one nation gained must be taken from another.

The achievement of political power must thus involve winning ascendancy over other states. Everywhere power was seen as a finite quantity; as it was increased for one, it must inevitably decrease for another. This was expressed in the concept, characteristic of the age, of the 'balance of power': an idea which became widely aired from the end of the seventeenth century onwards. In a pamphlet entitled 'Europe's Catechism', for example, which appeared in 1741, it was declared that 'when any Potentate has arrived at an exorbitant Share of Power', the rest should 'league together in order to reduce him of his undue Proportion of it'. The implication was that there existed in the world a fixed quanity of 'power'; and this must be carefully rationed out to ensure that no one nation got too much of it.

In economic relations, a precisely similar attitude was shown in the concept, equally widespread and equally discussed, of the 'balance of trade'. Here too, the amount of international trade available was generally regarded as a fixed quantity; so that, if one nation wanted more, it must win it at the expense of others. Colbert, for example, in many ways the archetypal figure of this age, declared commerce 'to be a perpetual and peaceable war of wit and energy, among all nations . . .

Each nation works incessantly to have his legitimate share of commerce or to gain an advantage over another nation';[9] and he accused the Dutch of the desire 'to acquire the trade of the whole world into their hands . . . and to rob other nations of the same'[10] (an aim which he himself whole-heartedly reciprocated). In consequence, he believed, 'trade causes perpetual strife, both in time of war and in time of peace, between all the nations of Europe, to decide which of them shall have the greatest share'.[11]

This concept of competition for a limited quantity of trade, though much derided in the age that followed, was not, in the circumstances of the age, as foolish as it is sometimes made to appear. Purchasing power, in an economy still largely on a subsistence basis, was genuinely limited, and the amount of the mainly luxury goods then traded internationally – sugar, tobacco, wine, spices and some textiles (in addition to naval goods) – that could be sold in Europe could not be expanded indefinitely.[12] As Colbert himself put it: 'The discovery of new trade is very uncertain . . . And even if it did occur, it would not bring about new consumption of necessaries or luxuries. At the most it could make it easier for one nation rather than another to attract those goods which are already consumed and which constitute a part of the consumption of all Europe.'[13] Certainly, whether the belief was rational or otherwise, it was generally held and influenced policy. Thus nations did not merely, as in other ages, compete for trade by competing to *create* it. They competed to secure for themselves a larger proportion of the finite quantity thought to be available. And they were all the more delighted if, in winning trade for their own nation, they were damaging another. Colbert and other French leaders, for example, made no secret of their hope of ruining their rivals, above all the Dutch, by depriving them of the commerce they had dominated for so long. So Colbert wrote to his master, exulting that France 'is flourishing not only in itself, but also by the want which it has inflicted upon all neighbouring states. Extreme poverty appears everywhere. There is only Holland which still resists and its power in money decreases visibly.'[14]

The same concept of competition for a limited quantity was held above all in relation to money. Here too, it was commonly believed, there existed a relatively fixed stock of bullion available in the international (that is, the European) economy. It had, of course, been hugely increased by imports of precious metals from America; but that flow was now less, and in any case caused only a marginal variation from year to year. The nations of Europe were, therefore, according to the doctrine, engaged in mutual contest for the stock of money now circulating within the continent: in other words, there was, as Colbert put it, a 'war of money'. 'I believe this principle will be readily agreed to,' he declared, 'that it is only the balance of money in a state that makes a difference in its greatness and power'.[15] One of the advantages of the limited availability of specie, in the eyes of the age, was that the state which succeeded in securing more would not only enrich itself but also weaken others. So Colbert pointed out that, 'there being only a given quantity of money which circulates in all Europe ... one cannot succeed in increasing it ... without at the same time taking the same quantity from other states, a fact which causes the double elevation which has been seen to progress notably in the last few years, ... the one augmenting the power and greatness of your Majesty, the other abasing that of his enemies and those who are jealous of him'.[16] This was not an idea confined to the French. So in England too, only a little less exultantly, John Locke declared that 'riches do not consist of having more Gold and Silver, but in having more in proportion than the rest of the World or than our Neighbours, whereby we are enabled to procure for ourselves a greater Plenty of the Conveniences of Life than comes within the reach of Neighbouring Kingdoms and States, who, sharing the Gold and Silver of the World in less proportion, want the means of Plenty and Power and so are Poorer'.[17] So here too the doctrine was one of relativity: as in the case of trade and power, it was not the absolute quantity but the balance which counted. As the German cameralist (financial adviser), P. W. von Hörnigk, put it, 'whether a nation be today mighty and rich or not depends not on the abundancy of its powers or riches, but principally whether its neighbours possess more or less than it. For power and riches have become a relative matter.'[18]

This doctrine of rivalry, a struggle among states to acquire the best possible share of a limited quantity of assets, was extended even to the field of shipping. Since trade itself was limited in quantity, states must compete to ensure that as much as possible was taken in their own ships, if necessary at the expense of others. To quote Colbert again: 'The commerce of all Europe is carried on by ships of every size, to the number of 20,000, and it is perfectly clear that this number cannot be increased, since the number of people of all the states remains the same, and consumption likewise remains the same ... The Dutch fight at present, in this war [of commerce], with 15,000–16,000 ships ... the English with 3000 to 4000 ships ... the French with 500 to 600. These two last cannot improve their commerce save by increasing the number of their vessels, and cannot increase this number save from the 20,000 which carry all the commerce, and consequently by making inroads on the 15,000 to 16,000 of the Dutch'.[19] There thus took place a competition for shipping, as for money and trade: by building, purchasing and financing it. This was designed to ensure not only that as much as possible of native merchants' trade was conducted in native ships, but at the same time that in time of wars, which occurred with great regularity in this age, enough ships were available to fight them.

Thus the ideas that dominated the domestic market were translated to the international economy. The interests of the nation were seen like those of the individual merchant: it needed to trade, and not only to trade but to trade at a 'profit' – that is, to bring in a surplus of money. This belief, that the main aim of the state was to increase its share of trade, money and shipping, was, of course, primarily that of the monarchs and their ministers, the dominant figures of the age. But it was a belief which accorded well with the interests of the rising merchant class too. The direct influence that class had on state policy was in most states limited (see p. 72; the United Provinces and to a lesser extent England were partial exceptions). It was the ministers, not the merchants, that made the merchants' concern with trade and profits that of the nation. But it was the traders and those associated with them who mainly spread the doctrine in writing (it was indeed because the conceptions of merchants prevailed that the name 'mercantilist' was attached by Adam Smith to the whole bundle of policies pursued in this age).[20]

Many of the most ardent and best known proponents of the new doctrines were themselves merchants. In England, for example, Mun, Child, Misselden, North and Defoe, among the most trenchant and influential writers on the subject, were either themselves merchants or had merchant connections.[21] The merchants were inevitably, in general, the supporters of policies which benefited them. But it would be a crude distortion to suggest that states adopted such policies simply because of the interests or inclinations of the merchants. They were not, in most of the states, particularly powerful: certainly not in France which pursued those policies most single-mindedly. The statesmen of the day followed the policies they did because they thought they benefited the state, not because they helped the merchants. Everywhere now it was the interest of the state – rather than the interest of the rulers or of ordinary people – which was regarded as the ultimate end of policy. The achievement of the merchants is that the belief emerged that the policies which favoured them best promoted the interest of the state.

The merchants quite directly helped to bring about one significant change in doctrine. The mediaeval concern to win a greater stock of treasure from other states than was lost to them persisted. But it now came to be recognised that this did not necessarily require draconian controls over the movement of bullion, or other measures of direct regulation. The same object, it began to be seen, could be secured through the development of foreign trade, so long as a 'balance of trade' that is, an export surplus, was always maintained. Not surprisingly, those merchants engaged in foreign trade were particularly eloquent on behalf of this view. It was expressed in the very title of Mun's famous work, *England's Treasure Through Forreign Trade*. That book was mainly designed to defend the trade to the East Indies (in which Mun was engaged), previously often condemned for the loss of bullion it entailed, on the grounds that the final outcome, after re-exports had occurred, was to bring a net gain of bullion to the state. As Mun himself put it: 'All nations which have no mines of their own are enriched with Gold and Silver by one and the same means ... which is the Ballance of their forreign Trade'.[22] This view came to be reflected in policy. The strict controls of the age of autocratic regulation were abandoned. In England, the prohibition of the export of specie was lifted in 1663; and a similar relaxation soon followed in other countries.[23]

The prevailing doctrine thus held that the most important single means of promoting state interests was the expansion of foreign trade. But there was a peciliarity in the approach to foreign trade of this period. Selling was everywhere regarded as superior to buying. This followed automatically from the overriding concern with the 'balance of trade'. The benefit which trade brought in securing needed goods for the consumer, and so promoting the general welfare, was scarcely regarded. Trade was not seen as a series of transactions from which, since it was willing on both sides, both parties must benefit equally. The mentality of the salesman everywhere prevailed. So it was that Mun declared 'We must ever observe this rule: to sell more to strangers yearly than we consume of theirs in value'. So Charles Davenant, also a merchant, declared: 'It is the Interest of all Trading Nations, whatsoever, that their Home Consumption should be little, ... and that their own Manufactures should be sold at the Highest Markets and send Abroad: since by what is Consumed at Home one loses only what another gets, and the Nation in General is not at all the Richer: but all Foreign Consumption is a Clear and Certain Profit.'[24] And so Becher, the German cameralist, who as a state official was more obviously concerned about the trade balance, could put it still more bluntly: 'It is always better to sell goods to others than to buy goods from others, for the former brings certain advantage and the latter inevitable damage.'[25]

Another new feature of the thinking of the day was the belief in the need to mobilise the state in the winning of trade abroad. New strategies were adopted for this purpose. The old-fashioned staple – the city market through which all trade had to pass – was abandoned. The capture of trade occurred now rather in the acquisition of colonies: these were then reserved for the traders of the home country. Colonies were a new type of captive market: and the home country was the staple for all their trade. They were seen at this stage not so much as a source of raw materials (except for a few strategic goods) but of any commodities that could be traded profitably. As Montesquieu declared, 'the end of their establishment is not the foundation of a town or a new empire but the extension of commerce'. To Colbert, the colony 'seemed a natural corollary to certain kinds of commerce, a base for the operation of companies in different areas, a source of goods for trade, an overseas extension of the power, the population and the resources of France'.[26] And with the increasing involvement of the state in administration, what had been trading settlements increasingly became colonies, in which commercial interests were buttressed by the sovereign power of the state so that the state's interests could be safeguarded there. In 1650, Cromwell's parliament declared that colonies are 'and ought to be subordinate to and dependent upon England . . . and subject to such laws and orders as are or shall be made by the Parliament of England'.

A final element in the thinking of the day was the belief that state action was required to strengthen industry at home: to help the balance of trade and specie and to build up the self-sufficiency which most governments desired, for strategic as well as industrial reasons. The new power of the great ministers was mobilised to that end. In France, Colbert 'wished to see France producing all the minerals, manufactured goods, naval stores and luxury articles, as well as all the agricultural products, that she consumed. He did not wish to ban all imports, but he believed in reducing them by tariff and by direction of consumption.'[27] Frederick the Great pursued a similar policy in Prussia. In other words, duties were now imposed not just for revenue as in the Middle Ages, but for protective purposes. Walpole in England, at the beginning of the eighteenth century, for the first time established an overtly protective tariff, to deter imports and to assist domestic industry. In Germany, the cameralists advised their rulers about the measures needed to promote native industry, and so to assist tax revenues. Bounties were given to promote exports or import saving. Everywhere the aim of protection was not so much to promote employment but to improve the balance of trade and so increase the stock of money in the country. As Colbert put it, the effort is 'to prevent money from going out, by means of the establishment of all sorts of manufactures, and of everything necessary for use in life; and to make it come in by means of all sorts of commerce and by facilitiating the export of all our goods and manufactures.'[28]

Perhaps the supreme characteristic of the thinking on international economic relationships in this age therefore was the idea of rivalry: of competition for a limited quantity of available trade, money, shipping, colonies, even human skills (skilled artisans were deliberately lured from one nation to another and conversely often forbidden to emigrate). In this competition, other nations are seen as enemies and competitors, never as partners. Success by one's own nation would lead to the abasement of others (this was one of the advantages of success). So Colbert, in extolling the war of money within Europe congratulated his master that he had 'already conquered Spain, Italy, Germany, England and some others, in which he had caused great misery and want, and by despoiling them he had enriched himself'.[29]

The same invisible barrier which the ideology of sovereignty created in the political sphere, sharply dividing one state from another and so determining the character of their political relations,[30] dictated equally the character of their economic relations. While tolls and other barriers *within* states were gradually removed, tariffs and other protective measures were erected *between* them, to create a series of separate national pools of economic activity. Each state felt it could promote its interests best by means of national policies to promote its own balance of trade, its own balance of bullion, even though each knew that all could not succeed in this simultaneously. And because state interests were overriding, merchants too, in pursuing their own private profit, had always to declare (like Mun in his famous book) that their activities were promoting not only their own welfare but also the power and prosperity of the state to which they belonged: by winning from other states a greater share of the limited quantity of trade, treasure and economic welfare held to be available within the world economy as a whole.

COMPARATIVE COST AND COMPETITIVE
COMMERCE (1750-1870)

From around 1750, a new age emerged, with new assumptions and a new doctrine about economic relationships among states. The new assumptions reflected changes in technology and the resulting changes in the economic interests of states. The industrial revolution, then beginning to affect many countries, but above all Britain, altered the character of trade and relative economic power. It also changed social structures. The growing commerical class, gradually beginning to acquire a significant political influence in some states, became a more dominant force and caused the economic objectives of states to be seen in a different light.

Other nations were no longer seen simply as prey, to be attracted to local markets where duties and imposts could be levied, as in the Middle Ages; nor as rivals, competing for trade and precious metals, as in the previous age. They increasingly began to be seen above all as *markets*, in which the products of the newly developing industry could be sold. As in other ages, particular nations – in this case Britain above all – were especially affected by the new opportunities and so had a special interest in disseminating the doctrine which maximised them. But as in other ages, too, though the new ideas reflected the interests of particular classes and particular countries, they eventually affected the thinking, the attitudes and the actions of all alike.

There had already been some anticipation of the new ideas. The Dutch had, over the previous century, enjoyed some of the same commercial and industrial predominance that Britain was to enjoy in the age to come. They had possessed a more advanced manufacturing capability than any other European state; and, being poor in raw materials but rich in sea-craft and commercial enterprise, had developed the most flourishing trading connections of any state of Europe (and therefore the world). It was thus in the Netherlands that criticisms of the rigidities which resulted from the massive state intervention of the previous period began: long before a similar reaction manifested itself in Britain and, eventually, other states. Already in the early seventeenth century, John de Witt, in his memoirs, advocated the ending of bounties for export and of taxes on imports, the abolition of all monopolies, and the maximum freedom for manufacturers and traders to get on with the task of creating and exchanging wealth.[31] Similar voices began to be raised elsewhere. North, the English writer and businessman, in his *Dicourse upon Trade* of 1691, advocated complete freedom of trade and attacked all measures of protection, such as those existing at that time against oriental textiles and between England and France: 'it is peace and industry and freedom that bring trade and wealth and nothing else'. Others with trading interests, such as Davenant and Child, also called for liberalisation, at least in some respects: 'Trade was by its nature free', the former declared. 'Laws to give it Rules, ... are seldom advantageous to the Public.' The French writer, Boisguilbert, at the beginning of the eighteenth century called for a freeing of commerce, not only within nations but between them, to increase the wealth of all. And a little later the French *économiste*, Quesnay, declared: 'Maintain complete liberty of commerce, for the regulation of interest and external trade most certain, most precise and most profitable to the nation and to the state consists in full liberty of competition.'

So there was already, well before the end of the previous period, a reaction from the general belief in interventionism by governments to promote state purposes. When, from the middle of the eighteenth century, London replaced Amsterdam as the main financial centre of Europe, and Britain became the strongest manufacturing and commercial power of the continent, it was her writers and statesmen who began to declare most eloquently the advantages to be derived from a freer trading system. Such ideas reflected the views felt increasingly insistently by the merchants and manufacturers themselves, conscious of the expansion of trade which, they believed, awaited them if they were less constricted by the restraints then subjecting them. Already in 1701, representatives of the principal commercial towns of France had declared in a memorandum their view that commerce could perform its task of supplying reciprocal needs and wants more effectively if generally freed from all restraints apart from modest duties. Now more numerous, more prosperous and more influential than before, the manufacturing and commercial classes increasingly demanded more freedom to pursue their own businesses. The new ideas, though disseminated by writers on 'political economy', reflected the views and attitudes of the merchant community with whom they were often closely in touch. Adam Smith was certainly conscious of the views of this kind held among the Glasgow merchant community he knew.[32] And his writings, the most powerful and original expression of the doctrines of the new age, reflected views that were increasingly widely shared among the rising business community.

Once again, the ideology of domestic economic life was spread to the international economy too. The watchword of the French physiocrats, '*laisser-faire, laisser-aller*', was now increasingly applied to trading relations among states as well. Indeed, it was in the field of foreign trade that the new demand for greater freedom most strongly manifested itself.

The first major new idea was the concept that there could exist a *community* of interest, instead of a conflict of interest in economic relations, between states as between individuals. The assumption of a fundamental rivalry among states, which was so typical of the age before, was now replaced by the acceptance that there could be mutuality of interests; and this too came to be applied among states as among individuals. Already in 1752, at the very beginning of this period, David Hume wrote in his essay, *Jealousy of Trade*: 'I shall therefore venture to acknowledge that not only as a man but as a British subject I pray for the flourishing commerce of Germany, Spain, Italy and even France itself. I am at least certain tht Great Britain and all those nations would flourish more did their sovereigns and ministers adopt such enlarged and benevolent sentiments towards each other'. This idea, that one nation could benefit from the prosperity of others, was a revolutionary one, wholly contrary to the concepts of Colbert and others in the age before. Since that age had assumed that there existed a limited quantity of international trade for which nations must compete, it followed automatically that the gain of one was the loss of another. The new doctrine began now to assume that the total quantity of trade might be expanded, and that all could benefit from it together.

There emerged therefore the idea of a general harmony of interests, a natural economic order which operated between states as well as within them. The French physiocrats expressed a belief in a 'natural and substantive order' of society which could best be attained by the removal of artificial controls on industry and trade. Adam Smith raised this conception of a harmony of interests, among states as among individuals, to be the central idea of his own economic theories which were to become so influential. This new concept even affected the statesmen of the age. Thus Eden, later to negotiate the treaty reducing trade barriers between Britain and France, declared in 1778 that it was 'now well understood that the flourishing of neighbouring nations in their trade is to our advantage'. Gradually, the new approach affected even popular thinking. So the British MP, Sir H. Parnell, speaking in the British parliament in 1826, supported the abolition of the previous mercantilist restrictions on the export of machinery, on the grounds that 'the use of that machinery would enable other countries to increase their wealth, and we should ultimately derive a proportionate benefit from such an increase'. And twenty years afterwards, Cobden supported the repeal of the Corn Laws on the grounds that only if Britain provided a market for the exports of other nations could they in turn afford to buy British manufactures.

A second new idea was related to this. There could be a common interest not only between nations (or individuals), but also between nations (or individuals) and the whole community to which they belonged. Self-interest and public interest could be one. Abroad as much as at home, the merchant, in pursuing his own profit, would also secure the profit of the whole community. For he would be guided by Adam Smith's famous invisible hand, which would lead him to 'promote ends which were no part of his intentions': that is, the benefit of the community. The nation equally, seeking to expand its trade in foreign markets, would further the interests of foreign nations, and the international community generally, as well as of itself. The merchant nation, like the individual merchant in his own community, would promote a more efficient division of labour between states, and so increase the prosperity of all. Each state would contribute most to the common good by producing what it was best equipped to produce. As Adam Smith put it: 'if a foreign country can supply us with a commodity cheaper than we ourselves can make it, better buy it off them with some part of the produce of our own industry, employed in a way in which we have some advantage.[33]

This meant that far from seeking self-sufficiency, as believed in the previous age, a nation should be sometimes prepared deliberately to make over to other countries branches of industry and commerce in which it was less well qualified by nature. Thus Ricardo argued that England would benefit by importing food instead of trying to grow all its own: 'There would always be a limit to our greatness while we were growing our own supply of food: but we should always be increasing wealth and power whilst we obtained part of it from foreign countries and devoted our manufactures to the payment of it.'[34] Each nation, by excelling in those areas where it was best equipped to excel, would contribute most to the common good. In pursuing its own advantage it would procure advantage for other nations too.[35] Ricardo, normally regarded as the inventor of this theory of comparative advantage, believed that if there was no interference by government in the freedom of manufacturers and traders, they would concentrate on producing and selling what they could produce most cheaply in comparison with the producers and merchants of other areas: that is, where their comparative advantage was greatest. Some things might still be imported even if they could be produced more cheaply at home, if the profit from home production was less than in the areas where the comparative advantage was greatest.[36] In this way all would offer each other the goods they were best equipped to produce.

These ideas became the ideological foundation for free trade policies. They appealed particularly to countries well equipped with materials, capital and skills. For if the doctrine were accepted, such nations might largely monopolise the most advanced industries, where they had the advantage, while others might be condemned more or less permanently to more backward types of production. It is thus not surprising that the doctrine appealed most strongly to a nation such as Britain which, because of its technological start, could be expected to be in the former situation. Britain was capable of producing more cheaply than other nations a number of products in high demand elsewhere: above all cotton goods, iron and coal. Such a nation was certain, so long as governments did not place artificial barriers in their way, to be assured of flourishing markets abroad. The doctrine of comparative advantage, therefore, and of non-intervention by governments, corresponded not only with apparent economic good sense but with British national interests. This does not mean that it was propounded so eloquently by British writers only for that reason. But it is perhaps not entirely coincidental that the writers who employed this argument were mainly British by birth and that it was in Britain that the theory was most widely disseminated.[37]

The third of the new ideas of this age, which followed automatically if both the others were accepted, was that all trade was good in itself. While foreign trade had previously been desired only as a means to an end – a favourable balance, an improved stock of bullion, national power, or the chastening of rivals – now it was seen as an automatic means of promoting human welfare. All trade between individuals must make both parties richer, since both exchanged what they valued less for what they valued more. Trade between *states* must equally benefit both parties for the same reason: for it would, according to Adam Smith, produce a more efficient international division of labour.

All three of these theories – in a mutuality of interests among states (rather than a conflict), in public benefit from private profit (whether of states or individuals), and in the positive value of all trade – were radical departures from the conceptions of the age before. All, therefore, took time to become accepted. Even in Britain, there remained a strong attachment to traditional views: partly because it took time for mentalities to adjust to new concepts, and partly because even in a single country interests were not uniform – farmers in England, and particular types of manufacturer, might continue to gain from protection, while others benefited from freer trade. But in time all three were increasingly widely accepted. All three pointed to the removal of trade barriers.

On the basis of these theories, trade with other countries was seen in a different light. The preoccupation with the 'balance of trade' was now abandoned or at least modified. Of course, the concern for an overall balance could not be altogether forgotten: no nation could sustain a prolonged drain of bullion, in this age any more than in the previous one. But at least the stronger nations, especially Britain, no longer fussed, as they had before, with the exact balance with each individual country (especially when, like Britain, they had no reason to fear that the overall balance would be altogether disadvantageous).[38] Adam Smith had declared that 'nothing could be more absurd than this whole doctrine of the balance of trade'; and he and other writers were particularly scornful of the idea of trying to achieve a balance in each trade separately. So in the debate on the Eden treaty of 1786, the former Prime Minister, Shelburne, now Marquis of Lansdowne, rejoiced that the 'old calculations', so much called in aid by the opponents of the treaty, had now been 'exploded', and 'the idea of estimating the balance of each trade was given up'. Lord Grenville, early in the next century, denounced the concept of the balance of trade as a 'doctrine so antiquated and so proscribed by all men of enlightened views that it was only fit for the Dark Ages'.[39] And in 1817, Henry Brougham, intoxicated by the new ideas, presented a motion to the House of Commons, deploring the fact that, although the 'old mercantile system has long been exploded', the effects of 'this extirpated heresy are interwoven with our whole commercial policy'; and declaring it 'absolutely necessary to enter upon a careful but fearless revision of our whole commercial system'.[40]

The attitudes and actions of statesmen were directly influenced by the new theories.[41] The writings of Adam Smith were well known to many of the politicians of his own day, not only in England but also abroad. Shelburne and Pitt, the two British prime ministers who in the 1780s initiated a series of negotiations with foreign states to promote international trade, culminating in the Eden treaty with France in 1786, were followers of Adam Smith and strongly influenced by his views: Pitt explicitly acknowledged Smith as his master. Bulow, the Prussian Minister of Finance, who was responsible in the next century for abolishing innumerable internal tariff barriers in Prussia and for establishing a liberal outer tariff for the whole kingdom (and, indirectly, for the low outer tariff of the Zollverein), was an ardent admirer of Smith and his views. The new doctrine, in other words, was not one for economic theorists and writers only, but one which deeply penetrated the thinking of those responsible for policy.

Gradually, the legitimacy of the free trade idea began to be increasingly generally accepted. The manufacturing interests were everywhere attracted by the new beliefs. More persuasive to them than abstract calculations about maximising the general welfare was the argument that the effect of a lowering of barriers would be a reduction in food prices, and therefore in the wages they would need to pay. There was still a widespread belief in the 'iron law of wages'. According to this, wages could never rise above subsistence level. Thus lower food prices must mean not a higher standard of living for all, but lower wages. The industrialist's costs would therefore be reduced and he could expand his sales still further. This argument was widely used by free traders in Britain as showing the advantage which Britain would gain by abandoning the Corn Laws and reducing tariffs.[42] Liberalisation was, of course, also commended in the interests of consumers generally (the first time that consumers had been seriously considered in the determination of foreign trade policy since the Middle Ages). So Adam Smith complained that, under the so-called mercantile system of the previous age which he denounced so strenuously, the 'interest of the consumer is almost constantly sacrificed to that of the producer; and it seems to consider production and not consumption, as the ultimate end and object of all industry and commerce'.[43] And even after his time, in the arguments of the publicists, the advantages of freer trade and cheaper imports were still seen mainly from the point of view not of the consumer, but of the producer and manufacturer, who should enjoy lower labour costs as a result.

There was another reason put forward at this time for freeing trade. This was the general belief in a glut of goods. The development of industrial capacity had indeed created a new situation. The new factories were able to produce very large numbers of goods at relatively low cost; and they did so normally before it was known that a market existed for them. While in the previous era goods had been produced in order to trade, to meet a particular market requirement, now they were just produced, after which a market had to be found for them. In the previous era, moreover, many consumer goods had to be sought abroad – textiles from India, sugar and spices from the East, tobacco from America and the West Indies – but now the main consumer goods were increasingly manufactured at home in the factories of Manchester and elsewhere. Yet the home market alone was not adequate to absorb them. It was thus essential to find new markets abroad which would absorb the 'surfeit' of goods and of capital that was now emerging. In the view of some, this made necessary a new programme of colonisation, or of settlement of existing colonies (as was demanded by writers like Wakefield). Industrialisation made such colonies essential to provide the markets which expanding industry required (as well as an outlet for population and 'superabundant' capital). Colonies came to be seen, therefore, in the new economic thinking, not so much as a *source* of materials or trading profits, as in the previous age, but as an outlet for surplus population, goods and capital.

There was yet another change in doctrine. In the previous era, as we saw, economic policies were seen as instruments in a kind of war. The new doctrine was often proposed as a means of promoting peace. Even in the 1770s, when the first tentative efforts were being made by Shelburne and Pitt to liberalise trade, this argument was used. Eden, the chief British negotiator of the trade treaty with France of that name, declared that such an agreement 'might perhaps remove many prejudices . . . and I have no hesitation in saying that in my opinion a peace is good in the exact proportion that it . . . recognised the great principle of free trade'.[44] In the next century, these arguments were expressed more strongly. The free trade movement presented itself as concerned as much to promote international harmony and concord as a more flourishing business between states. So Cobden wrote that 'free trade is God's diplomacy, and there is no other certain way of uniting people in bonds of peace'.[45] And he wrote to a friend in 1842 that free trade agitation and the peace movement were 'one and the same cause . . . The efforts of the peace societies, however laudable, can never be successful so long as the nations maintain their present system of isolation. The colonial system can never be got rid of except by the indirect process of free trade which will gradually and imperceptibly loosen the bonds which united our colonies to us by a mistaken notion of self-interest. Free trade, by perfecting the intercourse and securing the interdependence of countries one upon another, must inevitably snatch the power from the government to plunge their people into wars.'[46] J. S. Mill saw increased trade as the source of progress as well as peace: 'it may be said without exaggeration that the great extent and rapid increase of international trade, in being the guarantee of the peace of the world, is the great permanent security for the uninterrupted progress of the ideas, the institution and character of the human race'.[47] Even Gladstone saw the Anglo–French commercial treaty of 1860 as having averted a real risk of war with France. There is no reason to suppose that there was anything hypocritical about such claims. Even at the most cynical it could be held that, to flourish, commerce required peace; and it was not altogether implausible to believe that (as Henry Kissinger and others were to maintain in a later age) trade could create a nexus of common interests that might restrain governments from war. History, however, seemed less convinced about the relationship: for between 1815 and 1914, the only major European conflicts took place precisely in the short period between 1854 and 1878 when free trade was at its apogee.

In many different ways, therefore, economic international relations were seen in a new light in this age. Trade was not necessarily a bitter contest with other nations, each competing to acquire the maximum share of a limited quantum. It could be of mutual benefit to all, and might be increased to the advantage of both parties. The restraints which governments had imposed on it for centuries were not an aid but an artificial barrier: they should, as far as possible, be removed so as to secure the most rational possible division of labour. Activity that profited the individual would equally profit the community to which he belonged; and the individual nations that could produce most econom-ically the goods that other nations wanted should therefore (like the individual who could best produce the goods that other men wanted) be enabled to sell their goods as freely as possible to those who wanted to buy. For a time the new doctrines came to be generally adopted in this age, and by nations of varying economic circumstances. But it is not perhaps surprising that they were adopted most speedily and most enthusiastically by those states, classes and individuals that had most to gain from them.

THE EXPORT OF PROGRESS THROUGH THE EXPORT OF CAPITAL (1870–1914)

Around 1870, changes in the structure of European and North Ameri-can society transformed the way in which economic relations among states were conceived and conducted.

The relatively simple capitalist system which had emerged during the industrial revolution, with fairly small-scale manufacturing enterprises, under proprietors who, even if they had to borrow a part of the funds they needed, retained a dominant control over the way the enterprise was run, began to be replaced by a more complex form of organisation. The principle of the joint-stock company, which had existed for trading purposes for years, was widely extended into industry. Somewhere around 1850, in most countries of Europe, such companies had been given legal personality; and from 1856 in Britain, and a little later elsewhere, the principle of limited liability relieved the shareholder of responsibility for the debts of his own company. This innovation itself symbolised the new power of the shareholders: a privileged form of usurer was created, who was accorded the right to the profits of his enterprise, but was protected against meeting its losses in case of failure. As industry grew larger, it became more dependent on external capital. The dominant place in the economy increasingly came to be taken by the capitalist in the true sense; the lender, the provider of capital, on whom industry depended. This was, above all, the banker and the bondholder. The dominant figure in the economy was no longer the enterpriser, the mill-owner or inventor, but the financier who provided the cash: no longer the Arkwright, the Stephenson or the Bessemer, but the Rockefeller, the Morgan and the Carnegie. In seeking remunerative uses for their capital, the bankers and shareholders were following the doctrines of the leading economists. As Jevons put it, 'the general demand for capital makes it possible to obtain interest continually on the smallest amount. Hence capital not immediately required should always be lent.'[48]

This advice affected the international economy equally. Here too there was a 'general demand for capital' which made it possible 'to obtain interest continually'. There was a seller's market in capital. It was now the lender of funds, even more than the trader, that became the dominant figure, and the main innovative force. International investment for the first time became a factor comparable to international trade in importance in economic relations. Internationally, too, the lenders were often bankers: Rothschilds, Barings, Schroders in Britain, the Deutsche Bank and the Dresdner Bank in Germany, the Credit Lyonnais and Societe Generale in France – active not only in meeting the immediate necessities of bankrupt governments elsewhere, but also in assisting and encouraging them to new ventures; to make their economies less 'backward', by investment in railways and tramways, in gas and electricity, in mines and plantations. And just as in the domestic economy the other archetypal figure, besides the banker, was the shareholder, lending the funds that industry required and winning increasing control over the industrial enterprise in the process, so in the international economy it was the bondholder, lending to governments at fixed interest, varying according to the credit each could command; and, there too, gradually winning for themselves an increasing measure of control over their debtors' economies. In this way, it was felt, the rapidly growing class of rentiers brought progress to benighted lands beyond the seas. So the governments of the most developed countries became increasingly concerned to protect the interests of the lenders of funds who were their own nationals; determined to ensure that they secured the return that had been promised them; and willing, when necessary, to demand and win direct control over the economies concerned – or at least over their financial mainsprings – to guarantee that return. And so, all over the world, in Latin America as in the Near East, in North Africa as in the Far East, governments of the undeveloped world became increasingly dependent for their survival on the lenders into whose debt they increasingly fell (see p. 227 ff.).

Traders had already begun to cast their eyes to the more distant (and more dependent) territories beyond the seas for profits. The agricultural and industrial depression that began soon after 1870 made manufacturers and exporters see salvation in those regions. Large-scale imports of grain from the US, and of meat from South America and Australia, made possible by advances in steamships and refrigeration, brought a serious agricultural depression in Europe, which in turn was followed by a more general depression of prices lasting until almost the end of the century. The newly developed manufacturing industry, in Belgium, Germany and other parts of west Europe, demanded higher tariffs, to protect it from imports, above all from Britain, but also from each other.

So the underlying philosophy changed once more. The whole doctrine of free trade which had prevailed for almost a century before was now eroded. The protectionist ideas of Friedrich List acquired more influence than the liberal ideas of Adam Smith. The west European countries, which over the past two decades had in turn followed Britain in adopting more liberal policies, from the early 1870s began to revert to protectionist sentiments. France, which had been a liberal trading country under Napoleon III, raised duties on some industrial products in the early 1870s. Germany sharply raised her tariffs, on both industrial and agricultural products, in 1879, and later increased them again, in 1890 and 1902. Russia raised her already high tariff in 1877, 1881–2, and again in 1890–1. The US, which had never adopted the free trade doctrine but had raised her tariffs consistently from the beginning of the century, now raised them still higher in the McKinley tariff of 1890 and the Dingley tariff of 1897. Even in Britain, the call for 'tariff reform', though not yet heeded, began to be increasingly loudly proclaimed. The idea of a mutuality of interests, that the sharing of markets with neighbours might provide outlets for surplus products to both parties, which had dominated in the previous age, was increasingly abandoned.

Instead, a new doctrine arose. In place of the markets that were increasingly closed in Europe, it was held, new ones were now required, further afield. For all this time, while markets were being reduced through depression at home and tariffs abroad, industrial capacity was increasing. This made it the more important, it was generally believed, to find new markets elsewhere. The obvious place to find them was away beyond the seas. A constant theme of European industrialists, and therefore of their governments, was the need to find new markets in the colonies; even to find new colonies that would *become* new markets. So the influential French writer, Beaulieu, wrote in 1874: 'The most useful function which colonies perform is to supply the mother country's trade with a ready market to get its industry going and maintain it, and to supply the inhabitants of the mother country, whether as industrialists, workers, or consumers, with increased profits, wages or commodities.'[49] So Jules Ferry, the French premier, speaking in the French parliament in 1885, declared: 'The colonial question is for countries like ours, which are by the very character of their industry tied to large exports, vital to the question of markets . . . From this point of view the foundation of a colony is the creation of a market.' And in 1877, the Bordeaux Chamber of Commerce wrote to the Ministry of Finance: 'Experience has proved that France, whose overseas exports are held back by ever-increasing competition, must find in colonies inhabited by her own nationals guaranteed markets for her primary and industrial products.'[50]

So colonisation – or at least the extension of economic activity further afield – was the new watchword. It was frankly accepted that the search for colonies was at least partly motivated by the search for markets, which the revived protectionism made more necessary. In 1890 Jules Ferry, now no longer prime minister, wrote: 'Colonial policy is the daughter of industrialisation . . . If Europe had been able to establish something like a division of industrial labour between the manufacturing countries . . . Europe would not have to look outside its own boundaries for markets for what it produced. The protective system is a steam-engine without a safety valve unless it is balanced and supported by a sensible and serious colonial policy ... New masses of consumers must be made to arise in other parts of the globe, otherwise we shall put modern society into bankruptcy ... Colonial policy is an international expression of the external laws of competition.'[51] Everywhere colonies meant trade. Salisbury declared in 1886 that Britain might be forced to annex territories abroad to preserve trading outlets. Joseph Chamberlain put the idea at its simplest when he stated: 'The Empire is commerce'; and he later justified the British colonial expansion in Africa on the grounds that otherwise 'the greater part of the continent would have been occupied by our commercial rivals who would have proceeded to close this great commercial market to the British empire'. Spokesmen for other European countries expressed similar views. The German writer Fredrich Fabri, enthusiastically answering the title of his book, *Does Germany Need Colonies?* in 1879, pointed to the new markets and new fields of investment that colonies could provide, and even indicated the particular territories – Samoa, New Guinea, Madagascar, Formosa, North Borneo, for example – which Germany should appropriate to that end (several of which Germany shortly proceeded to acquire): 'We are convinced beyond doubt that the colonial question has become a matter of life or death for the development of Germany. Colonies will have a salutary effect on our economic situation as well as on our entire national progress.' Even American writers were not unaffected by the prevailing concern for new markets in the under-developed world: 'For the means of finding new productive employment for capital, it is necessary that the great industrial countries should turn to the countries which have not felt the pulse of modern progress ... The United States cannot afford to adhere to a policy of isolation while other nations are reaching out for the command of these new markets ... New markets and new opportunities for investment must be found if surplus capital is to be profitably employed.'[52]

This last concern – the need for new investment opportunities – was another aspect of the new doctrine. In a world of emergent capitalism, it now became a powerful motive among the lending states. In a Europe in depression, there was insufficient scope for investment. There was thus an increasing inclination to look to lands beyond the seas, whether colonies or 'semi-colonies' (that is, dependent countries not formally colonised), not only as convenient trading outlets but as the answer to the problem of the 'surfeit of capital' at home and the 'declining rate of profit', so widely deplored, that had resulted.

The need for outlets abroad for this purpose was widely asserted by European commentators, financiers and statesmen. Already in 1866, Beaulieu had written of the far better opportunities for profit abroad: 'The same capital which will earn 3 or 4 per cent in agricultural improvements in France, will bring 10, 15 or 20 per cent in an agricultural enterprise in the United States, Canada, La Plata, Australia or New Zealand.' He noted that sums invested in building new railways in France would earn only 2 or 3 per cent but in new countries could earn 10 or 20 per cent.[53] Jules Ferry wrote in 1890: 'Surplus capital engaged in industry not only tends to diminish the profits of capital but also tends to raise the wages ... Europe can perhaps be thought of as a business concern which sees the volume of its business declining over a certain number of years.'[54] American writers took the same view. As one wrote, 'American investors are not willing to see the return on their investments reduced to the European level. Interest rates have already declined here within the last five years. New markets and new opportunities for investment must be found if surplus capital is to be profitably employed ... Whether this policy carried with it the direct government of groups of half-savage islands may be a subject for argument, but upon the economic side of the argument there is but one choice – either to enter by some means upon the competition for the employment of American capital and enterprise among these countries, or to continue the needless duplication of existing means of production and communication with the glut of unconsumed products ... and the steadily declining return upon investments which this policy will invoke.'[55]

This advice was gratefully accepted. With declining opportunities at home, European investors not only sought but obtained huge new fields for investment abroad. In the 40 years after 1870, overseas investment increased many times. British foreign investment, by far the largest, quadrupled: from nearly a billion pounds in 1873 to nearly 4 billion in 1914. By this time, it equalled about a quarter of the national wealth.[56] French foreign investment tripled in the same period, and by 1914 was about one-sixth of total national wealth.[57] By 1914, the income from British investments abroad had reached the huge proportion of 10 per cent of national income of all kinds: a ratio never seen before and never to be seen again. The proportion reached about 6 per cent in France and 3 per cent in Germany. The effect was that the national income of the European countries came to depend crucially on the success, and the security, of foreign lending.[58] Governments increasingly competed with each other to win the opportunities to invest. Foreign policies became much concerned with that struggle. In Tunis, Turkey, Egypt, China, Latin America and elsewhere, consuls and ambassadors of the Western powers vied with each other to offer loans to foreign governments, so putting these already over-dependent governments still further in their debt. As Walter Bagehot admitted, the industrial states 'press upon half-finished and half-civilised communities incalculable sums: we are what the money-lenders are to students of Oxford and Cambridge'. They did this, of course, in the confident assumption that such activities were as much in the interest of the receiving countries as those from which the capital came. It was a part of the 'civilising mission' to bring progress to the backward, which the European had so generously undertaken.

A related feature of the doctrine of the day was the stress on the sacred duty of debtors to repay, and the right of creditors to enforce this. Once again this reflected ideas held in the domestic economy. Just as the dominant lenders *within* the developed countries – the monied classes and institutions – were able to use or change the legal system to place the highest possible value on the repayment of debt (filling the prisons, for example, with unhappy debtors and defaulters), so within the international society the powerful lending states were able to ensure that an equal importance was placed on the international repayment of debt. The importance of that principle justified the right to use every form of pressure, including the use of armed force, if necessary, to secure repayment. 'International law' laid down (at least as expounded in the dominant states) that such actions were justifiable. The right of 'reprisal' included the right to use armed force to secure repayment of debts.[59] In an age of bondholders, the security of investments inevitably became a primary concern. In general, the countries from which the investments came were militarily powerful states: those to which they went were militarily weak. On a whole series of occasions, Western governments employed either the threat or the actual use of force to ensure that the impoverished governments of lesser countries should meet their obligations. The British occupation of Egypt in 1882 was largely undertaken to ensure financial conditions in Egypt which would guarantee repayment to British and other foreign bondholders. The French government undertook a naval expedition to the island of Mytilene to impose the repayment of debt by the Ottoman sultan to financiers under French protection. Britain and Germany together sent a naval expedition against Venezuela in 1902 to demand and secure an undertaking to repay debts to their nationals. In 1908, Holland sent a squadron to seize two Venezuelan vessels as an act of 'reprisal' for non-payment. Such actions reflected the character of the international society as a whole: the only international society in history where armed force was used for debt-collection.

Such problems of enforcing repayment were, of course, avoided in areas fully under the sovereignty of the more advanced powers: that is, in colonies. Trade and investment alike inspired a new interest in the acquisition of colonies. A new ideology justifying colonisation emerged. It was increasingly believed that the more 'advanced' countries had a new role and mission, even a duty, to bring progress and enlightenment to more backward regions, by introducing them to the joys of civilisation and Western capitalism. So the European nations, with great self-sacrifice, took on their shoulders the 'white man's burden', under which they bound their sons to exile, 'to seek another's profit and wish another's gain'; or in the French view, undertook a 'mission civilisatice' that impelled them to bring enlightenment and progress to the backward lands. It was on these grounds that Gladstone, himself once an anti-colonialist, eventually rejoiced at the entry of Germany among the colonial powers, declaring 'God speed to her: she becomes our ally and partner in the execution of the great purpose of Providence for the advantage of mankind'.[60]

Jules Ferry proclaimed the duty of the 'superior races' in 'civilising the inferior races': 'is it possible to deny,' he asked, 'that it is good fortune for the unhappy populations of equatorial Africa to fall under the protectorate of the French nation or the English nation?'[61] King Leopold of the Belgians, personally responsible for some of the most appalling exploitation of the age, persuaded himself that his concern was 'to open to civilisation the only part of our globe where it has not yet penetrated, to pierce the darkness which envelops whole populations, a crusade worthy of this century of progress'.[62] Others – Dilke, Seeley and Froude in England, Beaulieu in France, Fabri and others in Germany – justified colonialism on more self-interested grounds, seeing the colonial empire as a source of materials, as a field of emigration, and above all as a foundation for national greatness. A whole literature emerged to show the blessing which European economic and political penetration would bring to the people it overwhelmed.

In the previous age, Disraeli and Bismarck had each declared that there was little economic benefit to be had from colonies (though each went on to acquire them), while Gladstone had looked forward confidently to them all becoming free quite soon. That assessment altered drastically in this age. Colonies were now seen as profitable, new markets it was important to dominate (see pp. 141–2). By 1900, whole new colonial empires had been acquired. Most of the world outside Europe and the Americas had by then been placed under colonial or semi-colonial rule. In the 50 years before 1914, almost the whole of Africa, most of the Pacific, and much of south-east Asia, were parcelled out among the major powers, while other countries, such as China, Persia, Turkey and Egypt, were placed under a 'semi-colonial' domination that was little different. According to one calculation, the proportion of the world's land surface occupied by Europeans increased from 35 per cent in 1800 to 84.4 per cent in 1914.[63] New colonial powers – Germany, Italy, Belgium – now joined the traditional colonial powers of Britain, France, Portugal and the Netherlands. Between 1870 and 1900, the British Empire increased by half as much again in land area and by a third as much again in population.[64] Motives were not exclusively to do with trade and investment. Strategic considerations, above all the desire not to be outdone by others, were a major factor – perhaps the most important of all. Even so, the desire to win markets (or at least to avoid being excluded from markets by others) was undoubtedly a major part of the motivating force behind the new imperialism.[65]

Colonies were the most attractive type of market, for both trade and investment, because they were captive areas totally under the control of the developed nation with goods and capital to export. The metropolitan power could use its authority to keep out rivals. It was never concealed that the purpose of control was to promote the interests of that power, even if it conflicted with that of the colony. Thus Britain, in managing the Indian economy, had no compunction in preserving a huge and expanding market for British industry, even though this allowed the traditional Indian textile industry to be destroyed. France, in managing the economies of Algeria and Indo-China, was concerned with promoting the trading opportunities of French businessmen rather than with the welfare of local producers. Colonial powers resolutely refused protective duties to local industries against their own exports to the colonies, even though they normally accorded precisely such protection to their own industry at home. At the same time, home industry was given a privileged position in colonies, both for trade and investment, against that of other industrial countries. There was not usually a return to full-scale monopoly for the colonial power, such as existed in the seventeenth and eighteenth centuries: enough of the doctrine of free trade had persisted to prevent this. But there was no hesitation in establishing a position of preference for the home trader and manufacturer that was little different. The easiest way to do this was simply to assimilate the colonial territory to the tariff system of the mother country; the home manufacturers thus had the same advantage against foreign manufacturers as they had in their own territory. So, for example, France assimilated Senegal and Gabon to her own tariffs in 1877, Algiers in 1884, Indo-China in 1887, Madagascar in 1897 and Tunis in 1898; and so eventually almost monopolised exports there.[66] Japan, as soon as she became a colonial power, applied her own tariffs to her possessions: for example in Formosa, Korea and Sakhalin. The US assimilated Puerto Rico and Hawaii after she took them from Spain, and established preferences in her own favour in the Philippines, Guam and the Virgin Islands. Italy established preferential tariffs to her own advantage in her African colonies. Even in the Congo, though theoretically the open door was, at international insistence, applied (with a 10 per cent import tax applied to all nations), in practice the monopolies and concessions for Belgian industry created by King Leopold established an equally preferential system. Britain, almost alone, did not (at this time) establish preferential duties in her own favour; but this was because she alone was able to establish a considerable commercial dominance without them.

Such policies brought immediate and visible benefits to the trade of the colonial power. The US supplied only 8 per cent of the imports of the Philippines in 1900; but by 1913, after preferential tariffs had been introduced, the figure rose to 45 per cent. Puerto Rico bought 40 per cent of its imports from the US in 1899, but 90 per cent twenty years later. France, with the help of her differential tariffs, supplied between 60 and 80 per cent of the imports of Algeria, Tunis, Madagascar and other territories. But even without overt discrimination of this kind, dominance could be obtained. Britain supplied nearly 80 per cent of the imports of Nigeria and over 50 per cent of those of India, even without the aid of preferences, because of her competitive power and her overwhelming presence as the colonial power. France dominated the imports of Morocco, where she enjoyed no preferences, almost as effectively as those of Tunis, where she did.[67]

There was, therefore, a general belief that colonies and semi-colonies (such as China, Persia, Turkey, the Balkans, Central America and other areas where economic domination was acquired without sovereignty) might provide the markets to sustain industrial growth in

Europe.[68] This belief in the economic potential of colonies and semi-colonies was based often on totally unrealistic conceptions of the opportunities they could provide. Thus Stanley, the explorer, addressing the eager merchants of Manchester, made their mouths water with his calculation that, if European civilisation and Christianity could only teach the natives of the Congo area to put on cotton clothes – at least on Sundays – this shoud lead to the sale of '320 million yards of Manchester cotton cloth' since 'there are 40 millions of people beyond the gateway of the Congo, and the cotton spinners of Manchester are waiting to clothe them'.[69] If only they could be induced to wear such clothes in the week as well, the amount of cloth required would amount to £26 million sterling a year. There was endless talk of the 400 million consumers of China who, it was widely believed, were eagerly waiting to buy cotton shirts from Manchester. These fabulous opportunities were widely regarded as fully sufficient justification (though not the only one) for the retention of colonial power. As Sir Frederick Lugard, later governor of Nigeria, put it in his book *The Rise of our East African Empire* (1893): 'As long as our policy is one of free trade, we are compelled to seek new markets; for old ones are being closed to us by hostile tariffs ... It is inherent in a great colonial and commercial empire such as ours that we go forwards or backward ... We are accountable to posterity that opportunities which now present themselves of extending the sphere of our industrial enterprise are not neglected, for the opportunities now offered will never occur again.'[70] Few doubted that the opportunities so made available amply justified the cost and labour of acquiring and ruling such territories. Sir Harry Johnston, explorer and administrator, reckoned up the tally in respect of West Africa that: 'Since we have begun to control the political affairs of parts of West Africa and the Niger basin, our annual trade with those countries, rendered secure, has risen from a few hundred pounds a year to about 10 million. This is sufficient justification for our continued government of these regions and their occasional cost to us in men and money.'[71]

Paradoxically, while the major powers were taking control of large overseas territories where they secured economic dominance for themselves, lip-service was still widely paid to the idea of free economic competition all over the world. This mirrored the doctrine of free competition, widely accepted for the domestic economy. Just as at home the age of monopolies, internal tolls and special trading rights was at an end, abroad the age of monopoly trading, bounties and special privileges was in theory over. The principle of 'non-discrimination' was widely proclaimed. This was reflected in the widespread adoption of the 'most favoured nation' clause. Treaties of navigation and commerce were concluded among most of the leading states, under which they undertook to grant each other trading rights, and especially customs duties, equivalent to the most favourable granted to any other country. As the adoption of the principle became almost universal, and countries began to apply for the first time a relatively uniform set of customs duties and trading rights in place of the special rates and privileges offered in earlier ages, the idea of a free and equal international trading system began to emerge.

At the same time, the idea developed that, so far as possible, the world trading system should be shielded from the interventions of governments. Its working should be to a large extent automatic and self-regulating. This automaticity was seen most clearly in the arrangements made for facilitating payments between states and freeing them from control by governments. Through the establishment of the gold standard in the early 1870s, for the first time a single international measure of value was created. Since each country pegged its currency to gold (and to gold alone) at a fixed rate, all were fixed in relation to each other as well. This created something like a single, automatically operating world economy. Individual economies were regulated by their relationship to this, rather than by the independent actions of their own government. If a country had an adverse balance of payments, which would therefore lead to a loss of gold, its central bank would need to raise interest rates and restrict credit; while the country in surplus would relax credit and lower interest rates. This would lower economic activity and the volume of imports in the former and increase them in the latter, so leading to a righting of the balance. Such a system could be operated by central banks applying relatively automatic procedures. Governments interfered with the process hardly at all. This accorded with the prevailing economic ideas calling for minimum intervention by governments in the working of the economy.

There was another way in which the international economy reflected prevailing economic doctrine. The most typical doctrine of the period was that of marginal utility; once called the 'economics of the rentier class'. Economic life was now analysed, not, as in the previous age, in terms of the production process itself and the input of labour, land and capital which might be required, but in terms of the subjective preferences of those who purchased, and so influenced production decisions. The central figure of the production system was now the person with money in his hand; and just as his valuation of the final utility to himself of alternative products would determine prices, so his judgement of the benefit to himself of alternative investments, on the basis of their marginal productivity, would determine the ideal distribution of capital, both within states and between them. The assumptions were of an inter-connected world, in which investment could be undertaken freely from one territory to the next without inhibition, and in which its value and distribution would depend exclusively on 'economic', not at all on political, factors. This was held to be as much in the interest of the receivers as the givers. On this basis the banker and bondholder, the doctrine maintained, performed a vitally important economic function since they distributed capital; and for this service it was to them that the main profit for investment should go, not to those who provided the labour or the land. The income which the rentier derived was justified on the basis of the 'abstinence' which he was held to have undergone (regardless of the insignificant sacrifice in practice required of the investor of ample means) or the 'risk' he ran (regardless of the assurance powerful governments provided). The same doctrine could be applied internationally as well. There too, the provider of capital was seen as the main benefactor of mankind, the main source of progress and development throughout the world, to whom adequate financial return had to be assured if his services were to be secured.

In this age, therefore, with a vast increase in the lending of money and in the influence of the money-lending class, new ideas emerged about economic relationships among states. Investment increasingly was seen as the main agent of progress. It was believed to be in the interests of states that they should borrow heavily, whether for construction of railways and public utilities, or for public expenditure generally and the repayment of debt, even if this brought them increasingly under the financial tutelage of a few European states. It was seen as natural that economies of the most backward states should fall, therefore, under the domination and even the direct control of wealthier and more successful ones. The latter, conversely, would benefit from the creation of *substitute* markets, for both trade and investment, to replace the sagging markets of Europe. So, it was held, diverted by new barriers from the markets of their neighbours, they should now devote their attention to establishing commercial and financial dominance in the more distant and more dependent territories beyond the oceans. And a whole new doctrine, proclaiming the benevolent and progressive character of such an enterprise, was developed to justify these changes.

THE END OF LAISSER-FAIRE (1914–50)

The outbreak of the First World War ushered in a new age, in economic, as in all other international relationships. In the age that followed, new social forces emerged, which increasingly acquired control of economic decision-making within states and transformed economic relations between states. As a result, new economic doctrines developed which affected both the way in which governments organised domestic economic affairs and the way they conducted their economic relations with other states.

The most dramatic and conspicuous change was the huge increase in the role of governments in economic affairs. There developed a new belief in intervention by the state: deliberate government action to remedy the increasingly apparent deficiencies in the working of the market; in some cases to control and administer whole sections of the economy; even occasionally to run the entire economic system. Faith in *automatic* processes – in the 'free market', in trade generated by private traders according to the principles of comparative costs, in investment distributed by business on the principle of the marginal productivity of capital, in the automatic adjustment of payments imbalances by the mechanism of the gold standard – so widely cherished in the previous age, now suddenly declined. Increasingly deliberate intervention by national governments in all these processes was felt necessary. As a result, the internationalism which had marked both the doctrine and the practice of economic relations in the previous age (despite the nationalism so evident in political relationships) was now more and more replaced by autarchic motives, a concern for the national, rather than the international economy: national balances in trade and exchange, national reserves, national production and above all national levels of employment.

The increase in the level of government intervention was first manifested at the moment the period began: during the First World War. Everywhere, governments assumed comprehensive powers: to control shipping, railways and other communications, to maintain trade and exchange controls, to safeguard supplies of food and raw materials, to control rents and housing, to direct labour, to ensure adequate production and supply of coal and other fuels, to organise production of armaments and other essential instruments of war:[72] in other words they adopted the 'war socialism' which even Churchill, for all his wholly unsocialist views, at this time demanded. During the twenty-year peace that followed (after a brief and abortive attempt to restore the pre-war economic system), intervention increased still further. In domestic economic affairs, governments began to regulate on an unprecedented scale: to control the banking system, to control the use of foreign exchange, to regulate trade and payments, to introduce public works schemes, and in many other ways. In one or two cases, this control went much further. In the Soviet Union, from 1917 on, the entire economy was taken into the hands of the government. In Germany and Italy, a very large measure of government control of the economy was introduced. Even in Sweden, the US and other capitalist countries, government economic action, designed to counter depression, was seen on a scale never known before. When war broke out once more in 1939, controls of a still more universal and comprehensive kind were imposed, in the effort to concentrate every available ounce of national effort in winning the new armed struggle.[73] And even after that war was ended, widespread controls were maintained in the era of destruction and shortages that immediately followed.

Economic theory both reflected and encouraged this trend. Like economic practice, it was increasingly sceptical of the notion that the unrestrained forces of competition and 'free enterprise' automatically operated in the public interest, either domestically or internationally. The possibility of 'imperfect competition', leading to distortions of the system and bringing excessive advantages to some groups at the expense of others, was increasingly widely acknowledged. Above all, the only too evident crises by which the system was beset – unprecedented industrial conflict both before and after the First World War, followed by the worst depression in world history in the early 1930s – made it evident that the old theories of the Manchester school had failed and that new ones were now required. This new ideology appeared above all in the writings of Keynes. Already in 1924, Keynes had declared, in his essay of that name, the 'end of laisser-faire'. He asserted that the capitalist system now needed modification and regulation. Governments would now be required to make a 'coordinated act of intelligent judgement ... on the scale on which it is desirable that the community as a whole should save, the scale on which these savings should go abroad in the form of foreign investments, and whether the present organisation of the investment market distributed savings along the most materially productive channels'. There was need for 'deliberate control of the currency and of credit by a central institution'. In other words, what was required was 'improvement in the techniques of modern capitalism by the agency of collective action'.[74] And ten years later, in his still more influential *General*

Theory of Employment, Interest and Money, he advocated more sweeping measures of 'demand management', control of credit, fiscal policy and public works, designed to compensate by public action for the over-saving, under-consumption, and resulting under-employment of the private sector. Keynes was not alone in these concepts. Many other economists of the age proposed ways in which capitalist economies might need to be managed to make them stable and self-sustaining.[75] And the increasing number of socialist inclination advocated a far wider degree of government intervention than that advocated by Keynes.

One of the most widespread manifestations of the new approach to economic affairs was the reverence everywhere paid to the concept of 'planning'. Because, it was now conceded, the sum of self-interests did not necessarily add up to a sum-total comprising the public interest, guidance by public authorities was required to secure the maximum benefit for all. In the words of Keynes, 'the world is not so governed from above that private and social interests always coincide. It is not a correct deduction from the principles of economics that enlightened self-interest always operates in the public interest ... Experience does not show that individuals, when they make up a social unit, are always less clear-sighted than when they act separately.'[76] The necessity of planning economic activity, rather than leaving it to the chance decisions of producers and consumers, was first explicitly recognised during the First World War. The effective prosecution of the war effort was believed to require detailed planning of all economic activity. Later, during the world depression, it was again widely held that only a new effort by governments to plan and direct economic activity could recreate vigorous economic growth and restore employment. During Roosevelt's New Deal, there was a widespread disposition to look to 'planning' as the answer to all problems. Roosevelt himself spoke, only a few months after his inauguration, in the second of his famous fireside chats, about the need for 'a partnership in planning between government and business'.[77] Harold Ickes, one of the prophets of the New Deal, declared that 'with the vanishing of the physical frontier, the necessity of a rational national plan has become more and more apparent'.[78] Other prominent New Dealers, such as Tugwell and Moley, were even more committed to the need for planning. In other capitalist societies too, the goal of a 'planned economy' increasingly came to be taken for granted. It was accepted even by some Conservatives: Winston Churchill in 1930 declared that 'it is increasingly admitted every day that the State should interfere in industry'; while a few years later Harold Macmillan could write that 'planning is forced upon us not by idealistic reasons but because the old mechanism [of market forces] is no longer adequate'. In socialist economies above all, the ideal of the comprehensive planning of economic development was taken even further – as manifested above all in the Five Year Plans introduced in the Soviet Union.

The increased faith in the role of government brought with it an increased faith in the part to be played by bureaucrats. In the previous age, the role of civil servants in economic affairs had been limited. In general, economies had been allowed to run themselves, and the number of bureaucrats concerned with economic affairs had been small. In 1910, the total number of civil servants employed in the British Treasury was about 130, and the number of the entire British civil service was 55,000 (excluding industrial civil servants). By 1930 these figures had risen to 300 and 111,000 respectively, and by 1950 to 1370 and 433,000. Moreover, it was not merely the increase in the numbers of civil servants that mattered: it was the increase in their influence. Because governments were intervening over economic affairs far more than in any earlier age, they relied far more on the expert advice of central banks, treasury officials and other advisers to guide them on such matters. With the dramatic growth in government intervention in the economy, coupled with the increasing dependence of governments on bureaucratic advice, with the increasing complexity of administration, economic events were now more and more determined by the beliefs, attitudes and decisions of individual civil servants, rather than those of businessmen or even of politicians.

Once again the ideas that dominated the domestic economy were extended to international economic relationships. Here too, it was widely held, especially after 1931, activity needed to be planned. The allocation of exchange for expenditure abroad, the amount of foreign investment to be allowed, the value of imports to be permitted, the exports to be promoted, currency parities, all of these, which only a few years before had been, directly or indirectly, the net outcome of myriad decisions by individual businessmen and consumers, were now carefully planned: to be determined by rational and deliberate decision, rather than left to the vagaries of the markets. Here too, it was held, public intervention might be necessary – in this case international intervention – to help to redress disequilibria, especially in payments and rates of inflation, within the international economy. And these ideas finally secured their full expression in the negotiations of 1944–5, in which Keynes himself played a leading part, to set up a wholly new international monetary system, no longer based on the automatic mechanism of the gold standard, but relying on deliberate and rational decisions on an international basis to provide credit on certain conditions to individual governments, to undertake 'surveillance' of exchange rates and currency flows to maintain the stability of the system. In the international economy also, therefore, there was now less faith in the automatic beneficence of the free market and of the invisible hand, an increasing belief in the need for regulation and intervention of many kinds, a new faith in 'planning' and 'management' of economic forces, and in the role of bureaucrats in undertaking this. Here, too, there was no longer a willingness to submit to the blind forces of economic competition, an increasing desire for governmental action to control these forces. In that process, many of the basic assumptions taken for granted in the previous age, about economic relations between states, were now abandoned.

Perhaps the most fundamental feature of the previous trading system had been the gold standard, that symbol of automaticity, non-intervention, and a stable economic system. While it had been slow in operating, it could be relied on eventually to correct the imbalances in the system and restore equilibrium without any action by governments. Already in the First World War, that buttress was temporarily abandoned. The dislocation of economic contacts, the less sure availability of gold, the need for independence from outside forces, caused most countries to abandon the gold standard (in other words, they ceased to undertake to exchange their currency for gold at a fixed rate). But the presumption was always that the system would be restored after the war.[79] After the war, however, stocks of gold were still less than before 1914. A number of countries had by now adopted the 'gold exchange standard', under which they held in their reserves, instead of gold, claims on other countries which remained on the gold standard – mainly the US and, after 1926, Britain – in the form of currency, bank deposits or securities. Thus it was some time, despite repeated exhortations from many sources, before the long-heralded return to gold and convertibility took place. A number of important countries, including France and Britain, returned to the gold standard temporarily from 1925 onwards; but most were obliged to leave it again in 1931, and all except the US by 1936.

As a result, a totally new international monetary system came into being, in which gold ceased to act as before, as the measure by which currencies were linked to each other at a stable parity and as the mechanism which, in theory at least, ensured the stability of the whole system. Governments now wished for greater freedom to choose the parity of their own currency. Most, in abandoning or rejoining the gold standard, devalued or adopted some new parity. New currencies altogether, with a deliberately chosen exchange rate, were introduced in the Soviet Union in 1922 (the chervonetz), and in Germany in the following year (the rentenmark); with the supply carefully limited to prevent inflation and maintain the parity. Governments were no longer prepared to tolerate the slow and deflationary adjustment, at heavy cost to employment, that the gold standard demanded (though, as it turned out, levels of unemployment were in most countries far higher after the gold standard was abandoned than they had been while it operated). Exchange rates now were deliberately chosen by governments and maintained by market operations in foreign exchange, so the level of economic exchanges could be manipulated rather than left to the severe discipline of the gold standard. Roosevelt himself epitomised the change, in the message he sent to the International Economic Conference in London in June 1933, announcing the devaluation of the dollar: he then took pride in the fact that the 'old fetishes of so-called international bankers' were being replaced by 'efforts to plan national currencies with the objective of giving to those currencies a continuing purchasing power which does not vary greatly in terms of the commodities and needs of modern civilization'. The basic transformation was, however, not simply the abandonment of gold. It was the conversion to the idea of *planned* money to replace the unplanned monetary movement of the previous age. Already in 1923, Keynes preached in his *Tract on Monetary Reform* a managed money supply determined by domestic needs rather than external constraints;[80] and he pursued the theme later in his *Treatise on Money.* Sir Basil Blackett produced a book, *Planned Money*, that is known to have influenced Roosevelt and Col. House at the beginning of the New Deal.[81] This idea of money management was increasingly extended to the international field. The agreement between the US, Britain and France of 1936 (by which France finally abandoned the gold standard once more), in which they undertook to pursue certain policies designed to maintain monetary stability, can be seen as the beginning of the *international management* of money: a strategy that was to be attempted more extensively in the age that followed.[82]

With the new idea of managed money, went *managed interest rates.* One of the effects of the gold standard in the previous age had been that interest rates were not fully under the control of national governments. For they were to be determined rather by international than by national factors: domestic credit was adjusted according to the external pressures on the gold reserves caused by fluctuations in the balance of payments, rather than by the needs of the domestic economy. In Britain, the leading financial state of Europe, the base interest rate, on which all the other rates on the money market, and so the whole domestic economy, depended, had not been determined by the government or a government department at all, but by a wholly autonomous central bank; and this institution was itself composed not of domestic bankers (who might have been especially concerned about the effect of interest rates on the domestic economy) – these were not represented at all – but by merchant bankers, who dealt in international investment and the acceptance of international bills of exchange, and whose main concern was with the international economy. In this system, the level of domestic activity was a residual resulting from the need to maintain relative price levels and avoid an outflow of gold. In the period after 1914, governments were no longer so willing to see interest rates left to international forces that were indifferent to such vital objectives as the domestic level of employment. Increasingly, the effect of interest rates in determining levels of investment (on the assumption, later to be questioned, that investment decisions were strongly affected by the cost of borrowing) was considered their most important function. Keynes, for example, already in the 1920s, and especially in his *General Theory*, held that governments should seek to control the rate of interest and should keep it low at a time of unemployment as a means of re-stimulating demand. The adoption of strict exchange controls, which followed the abandonment of the gold standard, meant that interest rates could now be more easily adjusted to purely domestic needs. Cheap money policies were widely pursued to promote investment and employment. In Britain, the bank rate was held at 2 per cent for years after June 1932, and after the Second World War was held at 3 per cent for similar reasons. In the US, Democratic administrations similarly believed strongly in the duty of government to use their influence to keep down rates of interest. This new conception of the role of interest rates, the belief that they should be controlled by governments for domestic purposes, transformed their role in the international economy. They no longer served as a signal to guide funds from those economies which needed to deflate to those which required to grow. Exchange controls, protection and other methods served to insulate one economy from another. Investment funds were now attracted more by the hope of appreciation in one country or fear of a depreciation elsewhere; and this intensified the search for strict exchange controls to insulate each economy. The nationalisation of interest rates, therefore, still further intensified the breakdown of the international economy and replaced it with a series of carefully managed national economies.[83]

With managed money and managed interest-rates went *managed trade*. Increasing disequilibrium in trade and payments brought a new belief in artificially created and controlled exchanges of trade: through bilateral and barter agreements rather than the enterprise of individual businessmen.[84] One effect of the abandonment of an international economy and of a free market system was the rejection of the principle of non-discrimination in economic relations as this had developed in the previous century. The principle itself was not of ancient vintage. Until the late eighteenth century at least, discrimination in trade was widespread, and indeed normal. Governments and rulers chose for themselves their economic partners, and what concessions were made to which in exchange for what privileges in return. But from the time of Adam Smith there had been a concern to abandon artificial distortions of this kind. The main instrument of non-discrimination had been the most-favoured-nation clause. This had been, in the first place, not an act of generosity, in which concessions were prodigally and unversally bestowed on all and sundry; but a defensive mechanism by which one government would ensure that any concession made by another government to a rival would be accorded equally to itself. As a result, the clause had been inserted in trade agreements of every kind until, towards the end of the nineteenth century, it had come to be regarded as almost unquestioned that concessions offered by one state to another should be extended indiscriminantly to all offering a similar undertaking in return. Now, after the First World War, that assumption was challenged once more. Bilateral arrangements, and even barter deals, became widespread. The east and central European countries, with the special economic difficulties and unstable finances of new and small states, from the beginning undertook a large proportion of their trade under special arrangements of this kind. But after the crisis of the early 1930s, most governments resorted to discriminatory arrangements, under which a particular partner or group of partners were given concessions not granted to other states. The open international economy was replaced by a series of trading and currency blocks, associations based on political as much as on economic principles. Even Britain, the arch-apostle of a free and non-discriminatory trade, now, under the Ottawa agreement of 1932, entered into special arrangements for 'imperial preferences' with fellow members of the

British Empire, under which the parties granted each other reciprocal concessions not accorded to others (which did not prevent Britain from vetoing an attempt by Holland, Belgium and Luxembourg to enter into a customs union of their own at about the same time, or from joining with France in preventing a German–Austrian customs union). In addition, Britain undertook a large number of bilateral agreements with individual countries – Argentina, Denmark, Sweden, Norway, Estonia, Latvia, Finland, Lithuania and Iceland – which undertook to increase the proportion of their imports coming from the UK in return for a corresponding commitment by Britain.[85] Similar policies were adopted by other major powers. So Germany, from 1933 onwards, entered into an increasing number of bilateral and group arrangements especially with the governments of central and eastern Europe, under which a large part of her trade was governed by bilateral and barter arrangements of this type. France joined in the so-called 'gold block' with Italy, the Netherlands, Belgium and Switzerland. The US, traditionally a believer in an uncontrolled trading pattern, entered into twenty or thirty bilateral agreements between 1934 and 1938, offering special concessions, exceptions to the normal quotas, duties and other restrictions, or other arrangements to promote mutual trade. The entire commerce of the Soviet Union was undertaken by bilateral agreements, usually for barter, with chosen partners. And even after the end of the Second World War, for at least a decade, because of the dislocation of production, shortage of goods and foreign exchange, similar arrangements were continued everywhere for a number of years, only marginally liberalised by payments unions or other clearance arrangements. So for thirty years or more, the entire principle of non-discrimination that had been the basis of international trade during the previous period was placed in abeyance. The choices and decisions of bureaucrats and politicians, managing trade to promote national interests, rather than the free transactions of merchants, became the determining factors governing international commerce.

Fourthly, protection was everywhere re-established. Trade policies were now highly autarchic, geared above all to secure self-sufficiency. In the previous age, trade had been the province of traders. Government interference was regarded as an aberration. Though a substantial measure of protection had been restored from the late 1870s, the ideal of liberal trading practices was still widely accepted. In the new period, these aims were at first still cherished. In the major conferences that took place immediately after the First World War – at Brussels, Porte Rosa and Genoa – the aim of trade liberalisation, the removal of

controls, high tariffs and discrimination, was almost universally endorsed. But in practice, little progress was made in restoring the
pre-war system. In 1925, seven years after the war ended, tariffs were
still considerably higher than in 1913.[86] The US, despite her favourable trading position, raised her tariffs in 1921–2; raised them again in
1928; and in 1930, during the panic which followed the Stock Exchange crash of 1929 and consequent depression, introduced the still
more restrictive Hawley–Smoot tariff, the highest in US history. From
this period, higher tariffs began to be introduced everywhere, followed, after the international monetary crisis of 1931, by restrictions
of many other kinds: quotas, licences, import prohibitions, exchange
controls, monopolies, bilateral agreements and similar types of intervention. These seemed the surest and simplest means of preserving
exchange balances and safeguarding employment.[87] As a result of
these measures, trade itself declined sharply, and even after recovery,
revived less than production.[88] For governments everywhere, the
revival of domestic production and employment took precedence over
the revival of trade,[89] and the fact that the latter could help the former
was rarely recognised. The success of particular countries, above all
Germany, in restoring virtually full employment and a flourishing
economy by autarchic means, served still further to discredit the
traditional faith in a free international trading system. In short, it was
no longer assumed that international trade should be determined by
'comparative cost' or other purely economic criteria. Increasingly, it
was taken for granted that political as well as economic considerations
would determine the flow of trade between states.

Fifthly, investment as well as trade and money was managed and
nationalised. International lending declined. Governments were no
longer willing to allow available funds to move relatively freely from
one country to another. In the previous period, though, as we shall see,
access to capital markets had been to some extent controlled by
governments, usually for political reasons (see p. 185), this interfered
only quite marginally and somewhat erratically in the total flow of
funds across the world. The main constraints on lending were set by the
credit-worthiness of governments and the profitability of alternative
uses of capital; and in general, even if *borrowers* could not always
borrow when they wished, lenders could lend to the countries they
chose and for the purposes they chose.[90] In the new age, this was no
longer so. It was now not the borrowing but the lending of money that
was controlled. It was controlled partly for political reasons (so British
investment was primarily in the sterling area and German investment

in eastern Europe) but, above all in the interests of individual national economies. The main constraint was shortage of foreign exchange. Britain, which had been able to finance large-scale foreign lending in the previous period (as well as a deficit in trade) from surpluses on shipping, insurance and interest on previous loans, no longer earned such a large surplus; and what foreign lending was possible had to be concentrated mainly among sterling area countries, which had special access to the London market. The US at first suffered few difficulties of this kind, and became in the 1920s by far the largest lender, especially to Germany and other West European countries, but this flow too was reversed from 1928 onwards. During the 1930s, capital movements and even short-term lending were still more strictly controlled. So international lending, like trade and interest rates, was increasingly *managed* for national purposes.

A final new feature of the international economy in this period, which almost all the other developments reflected, was the conviction that economic events, whether domestic or international, could be *controlled*. It was no longer necessary, it now seemed, for mankind to submit blindly and helplessly to ineluctable and uncontrollable economic forces. The trade cycle, for example – whether in the form of the familiar 7–9 year cycle from boom through depression to boom again, or of the less familiar longer cycle, which some now claimed to detect over thirty or forty years – had previously been seen as an act of God, or at least as the net result of myriad decisions by individual consumers and producers, which could not be influenced, or even accurately foreseen, by governments. Now governments presumed to influence, even to counter this cycle. Some of the actions taken by the Swedish, German, US and other governments in the 1930s were designed explicitly to counteract the trade cycle, even possibly to overcome it altogether. And some of the economic writings of the day – notably but not exclusively those of Keynes – sought to show the dynamics which made this both necessary and possible. This was only the most manifest example of the new hubris, the new faith in the human mastery of economic forces.[91] Domestically, it was shown not only in the devotion to 'planning' already described, but in the sudden realisation of the capacity of the tax system and social services to undertake large-scale redistribution among populations. Internationally, the belief in planning was seen in the endless succession of international conferences designed to guide and co-ordinate the actions of individual governments in directing their own economies: though few of these led to effective action to resolve the problems, they indicated a quite new belief that human initiatives might successfully confront economic forces hitherto totally untamed.[92]

Most of these changes in the way the international economy was perceived and in the international policies pursued reflected a single major trend above all others: the increasing disposition to concentrate attention on the immediate needs of the *national* economy rather than on the health of the international economy as a whole. This reflected in part the nationalism of the age, or at least a narrow domestic viewpoint, as seen, for example, in the isolationism of the US and the independent national approaches of the West European states. It reflected partly the growth of national bureaucratic machines, which had acquired both the power and the ability to influence the working of national economies and had been trained to look at problems only from a national standpoint. Public opinion too was little concerned with the economies of other countries. The widespread anger at high levels of unemployment, for example, was directed almost exclusively at levels of unemployment at home, not abroad, and few tears were shed if the measures needed to remedy the former made the latter worse. Even the businessmen and bankers who, with their interests spread across the world, had previously often injected a wider international viewpoint, now saw their interests focused above all within their own economies. In the first months of the New Deal, an influential article in the *Saturday Evening Post* declared that 'the first problem is that of mending the internal economy of nations, each one to find out how to balance its own budget, re-employ its own people, restore its own solvency'. It is known that this article impressed and influenced Roosevelt; and similar ideas affected most governments. This was indeed the philosophy of the time.[93] Until individual economies were restored, it was felt, there was no hope of restoring the world economy as a whole. Thus national controls were placed on trade, exchange movements, exchange rates and interest rates. Even the movement of people, previously allowed to take place freely, letting millions of people migrate within and between continents, was now for the first time rigidly controlled to suit national interests. Autarchy, especially after the slump of the early 1930s, became the universal prescription of the age.

In other words, a wholly different set of beliefs about the way national economic policies towards the outside world should be conducted now developed. It was no no longer accepted that, either domestically or internationally, spontaneous economic forces, based on the individual decisions of consumers and producers, automatically worked for the greater public good. On the contrary, it was widely held that it was necessary for governments to intervene, through regulations, controls, 'planning' of all kinds, to influence those forces. For the international economy too, there was no faith in automatic mechanisms, such as the gold standard, as means to regulate levels of inflation and activity on the basis of balance of payments pressures; and a new faith in the deliberate actions of governments, including their ability to set their own exchange rates to suit their own purposes (as France did in 1926, Britain in 1931 and the US in 1933). Interest rates were seen now primarily in national terms, in the light of their effect on investment and activity at home, rather than as an instrument for protecting reserves. Investment abroad was increasingly controlled by governments, to protect foreign exchange or to promote national interests, political as well as economic. Even trade was seen in terms of its capacity to threaten or promote employment at home, rather than as a means of securing a sensible division of labour in the world economy; and as a result, protection and bilateralism were taken to limits never seen in any earlier period. The main economic decisions were no longer taken by traders, bankers or bondholders, involved in an international economy, but by national decision-makers, ministers and bureaucrats, concerned about national ends but with little regard for international consequences. Under their auspices wholly new assumptions, a quite new doctrine, governing international economic exchanges emerged.

AN INTERNATIONAL ECONOMY (1950–80)

In the age that followed, the structure of economic society changed once more.

The most important development was the destruction of distance, which affected economic life as everything else: money, trade and investment now flowed across national borders far more easily than ever before. In consequence, in both the public and private sector, the most important economic forces became transnational ones. In previous ages, international economic transactions had mainly been undertaken by forces firmly based in one state even though operating in another. There now emerged forces that were not based firmly in any particular state, but operated impartially in many. As in the previous age, bureaucrats and businessmen remained the significant figures: but it was now international bureaucrats and international businessmen who increasingly directed and dominated the international economy. In some cases, these were international officials running international organisations – the EEC, the OECD, the IMF and the World Bank, for example – whose function was no longer related to the interests of particular states but devoted to the management of the international economy as a whole. Still more important were the international bankers and businessmen, working in transnational undertakings, whose activities and interests also transcended the boundaries of any individual state, including even the powerful developed states in which they originated.

In this new environment, the ideas that had prevailed in the previous age were abandoned, and a new set of doctrines began to emerge. Domestically, the prevailing notion was of the 'mixed economy', in which basic services and industries, and overall financial control, were in the hands of the state, so providing a framework within which private forces undertook the bulk of economic activity. This was reflected in ideas about the international economy. There too, international bodies would provide the framework and the acknowledged principles within which private forces could best operate. So the belief in the need for each nation to seek its own salvation independently within a tightly enclosed national economic system, the faith in autarchy and bilateralism as a means to that end, were now once more abandoned. The idea of an international economy returned. But this was no longer an international economy that was automatic and undirected, as before 1914. The belief was now in a conscious and deliberate international effort to establish an ordered framework. The dominant concept was that of *multilateralism*, an idea quite new in this age. In all the principal areas of economic activity – trade, money and investment – it was now held, there should be joint decisions, to establish a jointly managed system based on commonly accepted principles. Multilateral organisations should be set up to implement this new system. While the national state would remain the principal focus of economic decision-making, in its international dealings it should operate always within a framework of international rules that were internationally devised. So in declaring an 'international economy' in his book of that name, Gunnar Myrdal, a foremost economist of the time who (himself heading a multilateral organisation) typified the new approach, stated that the means of achieving this was 'by means of bilateral or multilateral agreements between separate and sovereign states. The goal is always to approach a unified policy through these agreements, implying an international coordination of national policies and their application within each country for agreed precise purposes, so that they are directed towards a common goal.'[94]

This was the theory. But the multilaterism which emerged, quickly showed itself to be somewhat narrowly based. In practice, the states that joined in devising and managing the new system were a relatively small group: those that were dominant when the period began. It was mainly the already rich countries which created the new organisations and formulated the new rules. At the time the new system emerged, at the close of the Second World War, and in the years immediately afterwards, many poor countries were still under colonial rule, while the rest were without significant influence. It was therefore the advanced countries of Europe and North America – above all the US alone – that mainly devised the new economic system. And it is perhaps not surprising that the principles which underlay the new institutions were those which they themselves upheld and which corresponded best with the interests of their own countries and the dominant forces within them.

This was to be seen in each main area of international economic activity. In the field of trade, for example, an effort was quickly made to put into practice the new belief in multilateralism. Immediately after the Second World War, there was an attempt to set up an International Trade Organisation (ITO), embracing most of the nations of the world, within which trade problems would be looked at on a collective basis (though in accordance with the principles that the dominant countries favoured). That attempt itself failed, mainly because of differences among the rich countries themselves, but the search for a multilateral framework continued. A number of Western countries got together in establishing the General Agreement on Tariffs and Trade (GATT), designed to provide the framework for multilateral negotiations for tariff reductions and other forms of liberalisation: in other words, the trade questions which mattered most to the rich states. Membership was for long confined mainly to a relatively small group of developed countries. Though gradually the membership increased, so that after thirty years it included over half the international community, and though in time it began to become more attentive to the problems of poor countries, the underlying principles remained those established by the rich. And the series of 'rounds' or systematic negotiations which it implemented secured a far greater reduction of trade barriers between the rich countries themselves than between the rich countries and the poor or between the poor countries themselves.

In addition, the rich established a still more limited multilateral forum, confined to themselves alone, the OEEC (Organisation for European Economic Cooperation) and its successor OECD (Organisation for Economic Cooperation and Development) within which questions of trade and industry were considered solely among the industrialised states. These were the bodies that counted in settling most trade problems. With the birth of many new states, there was pressure for more comprehensive institutions: and eventually a new forum was established, UNCTAD (United Nations Conference on Trade Development), in which the poor countries held a voting majority, and which was therefore used by them for pressing demands for change in the system. But for long it had little effective influence.

The principles applied in this new trading system inevitably reflected the interests of the countries which dominated. The most important single principle was that of 'liberalisation'. As in the nineteenth century, it was the states that were economically most powerful which had the greatest interest in the opening up of markets. At first this was, above all, the United States (US). During and after the Second World War, the US had acquired an economic dominance greater than that enjoyed before by any single power. During that war, in the Atlantic Charter signed between Roosevelt and Churchill, she had secured recognition of the principle of 'the enjoyment by all states . . . of access on equal terms to the trade and to the raw materials of the world which are needed for their economic prosperity'. She negotiated mutual aid agreements with many of her allies, which included commitments on both sides to bring about the 'reduction of tariffs and other trade barriers'.

So the goal of liberalisation (in contrast to the autarchic aims of the pre-war period) became an important part of the doctrine of the age. Yet the liberalisation now undertaken was, in practice, a highly selective one. Few countries – not even the US herself – were willing to adopt anything like free trade. This could scarcely have been in the interest of developed countries, some of whose industries would have been highly vulnerable to competition from low-cost countries, especially in simple manufactures such as textiles and in agricultural products. Most, therefore, wanted to retain restrictions in those areas where they were vulnerable. The US from the beginning excluded agriculture from the general principle of liberalisation, and was joined in this by other high-cost producers in west Europe (only Britain, as a food-importer, was willing to see considerable reduction of agricultural protection, but was anxious to maintain the right to imperial preferences.) Most rich countries wished to retain protection of particular kinds, especially against imports from developing countries, and so invented new principles to govern international trade. They called for 'fair trade', 'orderly marketing arrangements', 'managed free trade', 'countervailing duties', 'safeguards' and other concepts to justify particular kinds of protection, primarily against poor countries (see p. 199). The new concept of 'liberalisation', therefore, was one which was given a special and highly selective meaning.

Another closely related element of the new doctrine was the principle of 'non-discrimination'. This was applied to trade and payments alike. During the inter-war period, the most-favoured-nation (m.f.n.) principle had largely lapsed through the growth of bilateral agreements and special relationships. Now a single uniform tariff rate was, in theory, supposed to be applied to all states alike, irrespective of the major differences in their economic circumstances. Mutual concessions were to be granted on the basis of 'reciprocity'. These principles were by no means favourable to poor countries. There could be little reciprocity between states whose economic conditions were totally different: between those that were dependent on imports for all except the simplest products and those which could be largely self-sufficient in almost every field (such as the US). The principle therefore mainly suited the more powerful states: for them it would result in the progressive opening, at little cost, of markets that might otherwise have remained closed, and would deter the establishment of arrangements between particular groups of states. Just as the principle of the 'open door' had been appealed to mainly by the strongest states in the nineteenth century, as a means to open up markets to them, so now the stronger states, above all the US, appealed to similar principles now. In negotiating the establishment of the ITO and the GATT, the US saw non-discrimination as inseparable from trade itself: 'the achievement of expansion of trade and the achievement of non-discrimination are the same thing,' the US delegate to the London conference on the ITO declared.[95] So, in negotiating a new system for civil aviation, the US, with by far the largest civil aviation fleet in the world, pressed for the 'five freedoms' which would have given her the greatest opportunities for winning traffic all over the world, including the right to pick up and land passengers in third countries through which the aircraft was passing. So, in the field of banking and investment, the US sought the greatest possible assurances of free capital movements,[96] a provision which most other countries wished to restrict, and later free trade in services. Conversely, in the field of shipping, where the strong countries were the traditional maritime powers – Britain, Norway, Greece and others – it was these who wished to maximise freedom of operation, while the US, weaker in this area, was willing to see a far greater degree of international regulation.[97] Non-discrimination, in other words, was a doctrine with greater attractions for the economically powerful than for nations likely to remain consumers.

So, here too, doctrines that found favour for the domestic economy were applied to the international economy too: liberalisation and non-discrimination were the international expression of the principles that governed the 'market economy' at home. In the same way, the doctrine of monetarism, which found increasing favour in the management of individual national economies, was increasingly applied to the world economy likewise. In theory, the international monetary system, like the trading system, was to be governed by multilateralism. Monetary questions were now to be tackled on a collective and no longer on a unilateral basis. As the British Chancellor of the Exchequer put it to the House of Commons in 1943 in describing the proposals for a new monetary system then being put forward: 'We want to secure an economic policy agreed between the nations and an international monetary system which will be the instrument of that system. This means that if any one government were tempted to move too far, either in an inflationary or deflationary direction, it would be subject to the check of consultations with other governments, and it would be part of the agreed policy to take measures for correcting tendencies to disequilibrium in the balance of payments of each separate country.[98] An international body would be established to take responsibility for the management or 'surveillance' of the world monetary system. It would use its resources to help member states to adjust their payments problems without resort to severe deflation, which would damage other countries and the international economy as a whole, by providing short-term assistance in return for undertakings that the necessary domestic policies would be undertaken to remedy the underlying imbalance. Even parities would no longer be changed unilaterally and without regard to the international interest, as in the inter-war period, but only after consultation with the international community. So here too a problem that had previously been tackled only on a unilateral basis was now to be approached collectively: under its Articles of Agreement, the new International Monetary Fund (IMF) was specifically to secure the 'multilateralisation' of payments. It was no longer sufficient to rely on national reserves, on nationally chosen parities and national adjustment policies. Reserves, parities and adjustment policy alike were to be internationalised. Eventually, even an international currency, the SDR (special drawing right) was to be established, to supplement the increasingly scarce supplies of gold and the unstable national currencies previously used as reserves.[99]

But again, it was a special form of multilateralism. It was a few rich countries which framed the new principles, and subsequently dominated the new institutions set up to apply them. A special voting system was created within the new monetary organisation to ensure that the economically powerful countries would have a dominant say. They were able to use that position to ensure that the organisation pursued the policies they favoured. For example, credit was granted to those in difficulty only in return for undertakings to undertake deflationary policies (instead of the expansionary policies the system was supposed to encourage). The issue of SDRs was strictly limited. A commitment to free market policies was demanded. But, in addition, the rich countries increasingly resorted to alternative arrangements, in which the poor states had no part at all. As instabilities began to appear, they were resolved not by consultation within the IMF as a whole, but by special arrangements made by the richer countries alone: in the organisation of a gold pool, in the so called Basle arrangement, in the General Agreement to Borrow among ten industrial states, in arrangements among their central bankers in the Bank of International Settlements (BIS). So, increasingly, the management of the system was undertaken not only by the IMF, embracing the whole international community, but only a small part of it; not only by the Group of Twenty (later Interim Committee) of the IMF, but by the Group of Ten developed states that met outside it; not only by the Executive Board of the IMF, which was supposed to decide its policy, but by the Group of Five particularly powerful states, which in the 1970s met independently to discuss monetary questions. Thus the 'multilateral surveillance' which was so much demanded came to be undertaken in practice by bodies that were dominated by the richer states.[100]

The way the system operated was still further transformed by the new theory of monetarism. In the inter-war period, the main domestic concern had been unemployment, and the dominant domestic doctrine had been demand-management and the creation of employment; so international monetary policy before the war and immediately afterwards – for example, the concern to keep up the price level, the demand for exchange controls, the tendency to competitive devaluation, the system of temporary credit to deficit countries created in 1945 – reflected this concern. After 1950, the main domestic concern was inflation, which now became more serious, both domestically and internationally, than in any earlier age. The new orthodoxy in domestic policy thus became the doctrine of monetarism, which held that the root cause of inflation was not excessive wage settlements or imperfections of competition, but the failure of governments in each country adequately to limit the supply of money. This affected international economic policies. In the international economy too, it was held, the greatest danger was an excess of money, leading to international inflation. The thinking and policy of the new international organisation operating in the field, the IMF, clearly reflected that concern. It established itself as the scourge and enemy of inflation in every shape and form, and became, both in its own decisions on credit creation and in its influence on individual governments, the powerful advocate of financial orthodoxy and deflationary policies. It sternly rejected alternative schools of thought, especially powerful in Latin America, which found other explanations of inflationary pressures and their significance for each economy. Its credit policies were not concerned, as many of its founders once hoped, to maintain the level of demand in the world economy as a whole and so sustain full employment as widely as possible, but only with granting immediate short-term help to countries in difficulties in return for strict promises of financial rectitude, involving normally a *reduction* of demand and strict control of the money supply. Above all, it rejected proposals that the new artificial currency created might be used as a means of increasing the purchasing power available to poor countries, and so sustaining world demand in a period of widespread employment, as financially irresponsible. Such proposals it held, reflected the doctrine of the previous age. Now internationally, as nationally, hard money policies became everywhere the norm.

But perhaps the most fundamental changes in the system concerned the nature and scale of international investment in this period. Here too there was an attempt, for the first time, to establish an element of multilateralism. Private movements of capital were now supplemented by a publicly organised system. Most investment remained in private hands. Yet it was now accepted that these private flows, for production and for profit, needed to be supplemented, as within states, by public investment for public purposes; for example, in cases where there might be little direct return and so little attraction for the private investor. The new concept of 'development assistance' for poorer countries emerged. This was to be used for similar purposes to the loans which many poor countries had raised in the money markets of rich states before 1914. They were, however, now raised on a government-to-government basis, and sometimes on concessionary terms. At the beginning, such loans were mainly bilateral. But increasingly, because of the reluctance of the donor countries to maintain such programmes, and the preferences of the receiving states for aid through international organisations, much assistance began to be provided by international institutions. At first, repayment at normal rates of interest was normally required, so that the transfer was scarcely charity. As time went on, loans for deferred terms or at low rates of interest, or outright grants, were increasingly made. In either case, the effect was that investment too – or a part of it – was multilateralised.

Here too, however, the multilateral system was less genuinely collective than might at first appear: since the rich countries made sure through the voting systems established in the main institutions concerned – the World Bank and its affiliate, the International Development Association – that (as in the IMF) ultimate power was in the hands of the rich states from whom most of the money came. It was they, therefore, that in practice determined the policies of the organisations and even decided to which countries loans could be made: they ensured, for example, that aid was cut off to such countries as Cuba and Chile when they offended against the rules which they themselves had laid down. So once more it was a kind of oligarchic control that was established. The distribution of international funds was again, as in the years before 1914, partly subject to political decisions, though now of an apparently multilateral body rather than the individual political decisions of particular governments.

The growth of multilateral investment was in any case not the main change which took place at this time. More significant was the huge increase in private investment and in attitudes towards it. The internationalisation of the economy had the effect that private companies increasingly looked abroad for investment opportunities. Foreign investment was now overwhelmingly direct investment, by large companies based in richer countries, in production facilities in other countries, rich and poor alike. Direct investment of this sort had been scarcely known in earlier ages. Now it proliferated. A new transnational world economy was being created.

The most important agents of this huge increase in foreign investment were the very large transnational corporations which developed at this time. These corporations were not usually 'multinational', though often described as such: they were mainly firmly based in a single state, especially the US. But their activities were dispersed among large numbers of countries all over the world. Though their activities were concentrated mainly in the developed states, they were also active among poor countries, where they were still more dominant since they represented a far higher proportion of total economic activity. They were particularly active in relatively high technology industries, which were anyway beyond the reach of poor states. In many cases, they possessed a semi-monopoly position, resulting from technological advance based on intensive and costly research and development, management skills, economies of scale, or proprietary knowledge,[101] advantages which were far more important than the availability and cheapness of the classical factors of production. US corporations predominated among them: of the top sixteen such companies in the mid-1970s, twelve were US firms, and of the top 200 over half were American.[102] By the scale of their operation (and in some cases their turnover was far greater than the national budget of many states) and the universality of their activities, such corporations began to be the dominant forces within the international economy. Yet they were not under the control of national governments. Because their operations were worldwide, because funds and products could be switched from one state to another according to the demands of the market, accounting could be adjusted so that tax losses occurred in high-tax states and tax liabilities in low-tax states. Thus they represented a totally new species within the world economy, effectively above and beyond the nation-state.[103]

For this very reason, the corporations were seen by some as the new benefactors of the human race, disinterested purveyors of investment funds, and so development, uncontaminated by national bias. They brought industry to countries which had little. They brought training for industrial workers. They brought a transfer of technology to countries which might otherwise have little chance of acquiring it. They brought a transfer of management techniques, of systems of organisation and of the attitudes required by successful economic growth. They brought foreign exchange. They brought exportable products and sometimes assured markets elsewhere. They operated mainly in new and fast-growing industries. Finally, they secured economies of scale which would not have been possible without transnational operation.[104]

To others, the corporations were a sinister and malign influence. It was complained that they took far more out of the countries where they operated, in remitted profits and markets foregone, than they put in. They encouraged patterns of consumption and of production that were quite inappropriate to the states in which they operated. They displaced native firms or deterred their development. They brought in their own managers from the home country rather than training locally engaged staff. They could evade tax obligations by juggling their prices and their accounts to their own advantage. They acquired a degree of economic power, in individual states and internationally, that no private groups ought ever to enjoy and which exceeded that of many national governments. Above all they benefited a few states – and primarily one – at the expense of many others, already disadvantaged, which became increasingly dependent economically on entities that were controlled many thousands of miles away, by those who had no genuine concern for the long-term welfare of their states or their peoples. The 'multinationals' were therefore widely seen as enemies, through which a new form of domination had emerged within the international economy, of a kind that had not been seen in any earlier age.

Thus, for many countries, the international character of the new economy had costs as well as benefits. And the economic doctrines by which it was justified – liberalisation, non-discrimination, convertibility, monetarism, freedom of investment – did not appeal equally well to all countries. Some sought to cut themselves off altogether from these powerful extraneous forces: through 'self-reliance' or 'delinking'. Others, seeing this as a passport to backwardness, demanded on the contrary that the international forces should be tamed and used to assist the economic purposes of poor countries. So Raul Prebisch, the guru of the developing world (another economist who headed an international organisation), declared that 'the idea was gaining ground that international financial cooperation should be increasingly channelled through multilateral conduits' and that 'it is of great importance to perfect mechanisms whereby the aims of multilateralism can be more effectively achieved'.[105] But it was a new kind of multilateralism that he and others demanded. Confronted with an international economic system which the rich had created in accordance with their own concepts, poor countries put forward a new doctrine. They called for a new international economic order (NIEO) which would implement a different set of principles. They demanded, for example, the principle of 'permanent sovereignty over natural resources', according to which each state had the right to control the resources of its own territory, even if owned by private interests elsewhere, including the right of nationalisation where appropriate, with or without compensation.[106] They demanded new trading principles which would acknowledge the special position of developing countries, including their right to enjoy special preferences and their right to impose trade restrictions related to their stage of development. They demanded an integrated programme of commodity agreements for the support of primary prices, including a 'common fund' to be used to finance such agreements, and the indexation of commodity prices to ensure that these retained their purchasing power in relation to industrial products. They defended the right of producing countries exporting raw materials to form their own producers' associations (comparable to that successfully established in the field of oil) and to concert their activities to regulate prices (while condemning 'restrictive business practices' for the same purpose among business organisations).[107] They laid down the duty of 'industrial adjustment' among the rich countries so that these would be able to make available markets in suitable fields, such as simple manufactures, to the exports of the developing countries. They even proclaimed a form of international socialism: the principle that certain resources, such as those of the sea-bed, of the celestial bodies and (in the view of some) the Antarctic, were the 'common heritage of mankind', which were jointly owned by all countries and from which all should draw benefits.

Such declarations had little impact on the world trading system. The rich countries showed little enthusiasm for the new principles. Marginal adjustments were made to take some account of this new alternative doctrine. Aid came to be given on softer terms, often as grants; general preferences in favour of all developing countries (rather than particular favoured geographical groups) were introduced by most developed states; debts were rescheduled or cancelled; a 'common fund' to help finance commodity agreements was, at least in principle, agreed. New institutions were established, in which the viewpoint of developing countries could be expressed more effectively; UNCTAD in the field of trade, the Interim Committee of the IMF in the field of money, and innumerable committees and agencies of the UN for many specialised topics. An organised dialogue on all such questions was launched. So multilateral debate brought some agreed changes for the benefit of poor states. But these were insignificant in effect. The so-called NIEO never came into being. The rich countries remained concerned mainly about their economic relations with each other. The multilateral discussions which counted were their own economic 'summits', outside the UN framework, in which poor countries were not represented at all. 'Global negotiations' were accepted only if they did not threaten the existing framework. The basic principles on which the international economy was based thus remained those acceptable to the rich states of the world.

This was therefore an international economic system different from any that had been seen before. With the shrinking size of the world and the abandonment of attempts at autarchy, national economies increasingly coalesced into a single international economy, in which transnational forces, both private and public, played an ever greater part. The concept of multilateralism, it was hoped, would make it possible to manage these complex forces. International systems of management were established in every field. As time went on, however, these became increasingly ill-equipped to cope with the problems that arose. Power within them was never evenly distributed. The rules they laid down were inappropriate in dealing with the problems of the majority of poor states, which had little share in framing them. And they could do little to cope with the inequalities in economic power and standard of living, which became increasingly marked and increasingly unacceptable to many states. Unemployment on a huge scale developed in many countries; which in turn produced a challenge to the new rules outlawing protection. Inflation became extremely high, not helped by periodic rises in the prices of some essential raw materials (though for most of the time the price of the manufactured products sold by the industrialised countries rose still faster); and variations in its rate brought the abandonment of the attempt to establish stable exchange rates. Above all, the huge increase in international transactions and in capital flows between states, much of it of a short-term character, which the new transnational banks and other corporations helped bring about, created major instabilities of a kind which national governments were increasingly unable to control. The new multilateral institutions were not yet capable of managing the still more powerful private economic forces which had now emerged within the international economic system.

2 Interest-Groups

In the last chapter, we considered the main ideas that have been held at different times concerning international economic relationships. In many cases, these ideas have reflected the interests of particular groups, or particular states, in each period. We now need to look in greater detail at the balance of influence within states in each of these periods; and to consider in particular how certain groups have been able to impose their own conception of national interest on the states to which they belonged: in other words, how the *collectivisation of interests* has been achieved within the international economy.

Ultimate decision-making power within states never operates in total isolation. However concentrated it may appear, it is always subject to pressures from outside. All those who may be affected by the decisions to be made seek, within the scope available to them, to exert influence on the decisions finally reached. Their long-term influence depends not so much on their effect on individual decisions; it depends on the ability to influence the ideas and concepts by which all are governed.

In international society, influence is still further divided: since authority there is dispersed among a number of centres, the interests concerned, rather than surrounding a single source of power, operate independently from each other, seeking to influence a number of different governments. Only occasionally do interest-groups, especially in modern times – international transport unions, the major oil companies, say – operate on an international basis, influencing a number of governments simultaneously. More often, similar interest-groups operate, in similar ways and to similar ends, separately within different states.[1] In this case, the important long-term effect is not on individual decisions, but on the expectations and assumptions within the system as a whole.

Among political scientists over the last half-century or so, it has been many times argued[2] that the essential political process within states consists in a constant interaction of influences of many kinds and from many sources, leading to arrangements and compromises between them, rather than in clear-cut disinterested decisions by governments or parliaments. These arrangements represent the outcomes which best reconcile the interests of the dominant groups. This theory, although it can be overdrawn, does take account of certain features of the political process within states which, in descriptions of purely constitutional processes, are often ignored. Within the international political system, the thesis has still greater attractions. For here, even more conspicuously, because there exists no supreme coercive power and no clear-cut political process, outcomes are usually the result of arrangements and compromises, a balancing of interests among the powerful, whether governments or groups, rather than of clear-cut actions or decisions by a single authority.

This is especially true in the economic field. Since wars are rarely fought primarily to secure economic objectives, economic agreements made between governments normally represent a deal of one sort or another, reached through a process of bargaining and mutual give-and-take rather than through the total coercion of one group by another. And the position adopted by each government in such negotiations normally reflects the interests of the various groups who have secured power within it: who have been able to make the state's purposes their own. In securing influence in their own state, such interests are able to influence the international economic system as a whole.

Regulation of the international economy has been, and is still today, even less advanced than that of the national economy. Joint decisions to change or modify the system as a whole are barely possible (though occasionally an inter-governmental agreement – to adopt the gold standard, to establish the IMF system, or to agree in the GATT never to raise tariffs – comes close to this). Because of this disorganised character of the international economy, because it evolves rather than is deliberately changed, there is even more scope than in national states for influence by groups and classes operating together in their own way to promote their own interests.

It is with the activity of such groups in influencing the action of their own governments, and therefore the international economy as a whole, that we shall be concerned in this chapter. The character and aims of these groups have varied greatly from one age to another. Still more has the influence each type of group has been able to exercise in each age. During the later Middle Ages, there existed one source of power that was outstandingly stronger than all others within each society: the rulers themselves, against whom all the groups, ministers and advisers, the big magnates and land-owners who paid them homage, the financiers and bankers who lent them money, the big merchants and tradespeople who engaged in commerce in the towns, the artisans and craftsmen of the cities, and the peasants in the countryside, each having a different and sometimes conflicting interest, were of little consequence. The influence each of these could exert on policy was limited, and for the most part the rulers took their own decisions to meet their own needs. In the following period, the influence of the king's ministers increased in relation to that of the sovereign himself; while that of the commercial classes, though stronger than before, was still limited. Only in the nineteenth century did the influence of the manufacturing and commercial classes increase significantly; an influence inevitably reflected in the international policies actually pursued. During the twentieth century, influence has been more deliberately and self-consciously organised: associations of manufacturers, traders, industrial workers, environmental groups, and many others exist for the express purpose of seeking to affect the decisions of governments. New techniques for swaying government departments and legislatures have been developed by such groups. Internationally too, a more elaborate organisation exists. Transnational corporations, international trade associations, international trade unions, operate in competition to secure their ends. Even governments today join in organised interest-groups: in the Group of 77 or in OECD, the Organisation of Petrol Exporting Countries (OPEC) or the International Energy Association (IEA). The same type of pluralist political system, comprising a constant interaction of rival groups, each seeking to compete for influence, that exists at the national level, now increasingly exists within international society too.

In the chapter that follows, we shall seek to examine the changing character of the main interest-groups concerned with international economic relationships which have been active in different economic ages; and to trace the ways they have tried to influence the policies of their own governments, or even the whole character of the economic society in which they lived, in the direction they desired.

MAGNATES AND MONEYLENDERS (1300–1600)

In the later Middle Ages, power was highly concentrated. At the apex of the social structure, dominant and isolated, stood the figure of the ruler.

Because of the power he enjoyed, it was the ruler who, with some advice, mainly determined the policies of the state. He was thus usually able to ensure that its economic policy reflected his own primary concerns. These did not necessarily conflict with those of the majority of his people.

As we saw, one of the main objectives of rulers, both in the kingdoms and in self-governing cities, was to ensure an adequate supply of food and other essentials for their peoples. This was clearly an interest shared between rulers and the community as a whole: it was because it was in the interests of the people that it was in the interests of the ruler. Similarly, in pursuing the policy of power – that is, in seeking to increase the kingdom's capacity for war – the rulers could be said to protect the interests of their people generally: at least in so far as that policy safeguarded their defence rather than encouraged them to useless foreign adventures. Even in undertaking economic measures directed against other states – cutting off essential supplies to them, sequestrating their merchants' goods, or engaging in trade wars (see pp. 162–5) – he could be said to pursue common purposes in so far as his subjects identified with those enterprises and felt their costs worth the benefits – in trading rights, indemnities or simple plunder – which resulted.

In many cases, however, the ruler's interest differed from those of some or all his peoples. His main concern at all times, in foreign as much as domestic economic policy, was to raise revenues. If the revenues were to be used for genuinely national ends, this too might be said to promote the interests of his peoples; though in varying degrees, according to the nature of the expenditures and the incidence of the tax. But if the revenues were to be used for conspicuous consumption by the court, or for useless and self-interested foreign wars, a clear-cut conflict of interests between himself and many of his population resulted. In such cases, only his chief ministers or the members of his court, that is those who shared his enjoyment or triumph in such activities, yet paid little of the price, could be said to share a clear common interest in them.

Because it was the ruler who exercised ultimate power, other interests could make themselves felt only at his discretion. He might consult with his immediate advisers on many issues. Often there was a great council or council of state, which would be convened before important decisions were made. If the assent of parliament was required for securing revenues, as in England, this too would need to be consulted on some matters of foreign economic policy: for example the taxing of trade. But on most such matters, usually other interests made themselves felt only so far as the ruler listened. Those interests were anyway often conflicting, and he had to make a choice. Measures that would benefit one section of the population would adversely affect others. Thus measures to attract foreign traders (such as those introduced by the English kings in favour of the Hanse) would favour the consumers, the importers (such as the merchants of Bristol) or those producing for export (from whom the Hanse bought), but would damage the interests of many local producers and the merchants who sold their wares. Similarly, the prohibition of exports of wool, such as were introduced in both England and France in the fourteenth century (mainly for diplomatic reasons) would help the local cloth-makers but harm the wool-growers (by reducing prices).[3] The choice made by the rulers between different groups depended on the circumstances of the day, the influence of particular groups and the whims of the rulers. But in general it can be said that the choice of the ruler in most cases was to favour the consumers (who represented the largest group in terms of numbers including politically powerful forces). Governments could not afford to neglect 'the protection of the interests of the consumer with his call for an adequate supply of low-priced goods of a reasonable quality. This policy reflected the common interest of courts, the landed nobility and the patriciates of towns. Its persistence in mediaeval economic history is perhaps due in the last resort to the fact that these classes, in kingdoms and local communities, were the rulers of the land.'[4]

Powerful groups, therefore, could influence the rulers. Another group whose views the rulers could not afford to ignore altogether was that of the great *magnates*, the large landholders, sometimes controlling substantial fiefdoms of their own. Where the king's power was weak, the goodwill of such mighty subjects was particularly important to them. Numerically they had a strong voice in the councils which advised the rulers. Most frequently in such discussions, they too represented the interests of the consumers. Both they and those who lived on their estates were dependent on imports brought by foreign merchants for part of their needs and they therefore normally opposed attempts to place greater restraints on the aliens. 'It was in part the nobility behind the throne who were responsible for a certain "liberalsm" in the early economic attitudes of rulers; for they created an atmosphere in which the merchant, from wherever he came, was a welcome customer and still more a welcome purveyor of those things which added variety to consumption and pomp to power.'[5] This attitude was shown in England by the support of the magnates for the foreign traders in the Magna Carta of 1215 and in their petition of 1258; and in France by the concern of that group to secure favourable trading opportunities for merchants from Italy.

A different type of interest-group was formed by the *foreign bankers*, on whom the rulers became so dependent for loans during much of this period. These in many ways shared the interests of the rulers: for their own prosperity depended on the continued prosperity of the ruler to whom they lent. But their interests were not identical. They had no interest in war, luxury or conspicuous consumption – perhaps the major and overriding preoccupation of the rulers themselves – since these inhibited the latters' capacity to pay their debts. Conversely, they had every interest in prudent financial administration: a matter to which most of the kings were profoundly indifferent. The financiers were in many cases transnational figures, who often had interests in several lands and might even be supporting more than one royal house. The two Lombard firms that financed Edward III in the early years of the Hundred Years War, also financed the King of Naples; the Fuggers supported both princes and Pope. In theory, such people might have secured huge influence through the financial leverage they wielded. By their decisions to grant or withhold loans they could virtually dictate the results of wars (or other important endeavours for which finance was required – Charles V bought his election to the Empire with funds which were largely supplied by the Fuggers, a fact of which Jacob Fugger did not hesitate to remind the Emperor after his election).[6] They did indeed win limited, short-term power in this way. Sometimes they were able to secure control of particular taxes or revenues as security for their loans (as the Italian bankers, Riccardi, did in the days of Edward I); they took in pawn some of the most precious belongings of the state or the church as a pledge for loans (five of the crowns of Edward III and his queen were in the hands of moneylenders in the early 1340s); and they sometimes held important personages as hostages, or even prevented a ruler from leaving a particular town, until a loan was paid.[7] But their ability to convert this short-term financial leverage into a wider influence was limited. It was limited mainly by the unscrupulousness of the rulers in ignoring their debts: Edward III virtually ruined the two Italian bankers who had financed him in this way. Thus they found themselves, like many other international creditors to the present day, more dependent on those to whom they lent than the latter were on them. Often, they were compelled to go on paying bad money after good indefinitely if they were to secure any return at all. 'Once a firm plunged deeply into financial business with a ruler withdrawal was difficult. To recover previous advances and safeguard ultimate chances of profits, the banker had to continue lending. If things were going badly with his princely client, he had to be helped more than ever ... Frequently the final results were catastrophic. Some princes could not ... resist the temptation of plundering and ruining perfectly solvent creditors as an alternative to repaying their loans.'[8]

A more important influence on policy was the *merchant class*, especially the larger merchants who acquired increasing economic and political power at this time. The more prosperous of these began to be represented in the king's councils.[9] Their voice was powerfully expressed in parliaments, where these existed.[10] In some cases, as in England, these wealthier merchants in time replaced the bankers as a source of finance for the rulers (in England they secured, in return, a monopoly in the export of wool for a number of years). In this way, a kind of symbiotic relationship between merchants and rulers developed. Gradually during this age, in some states at least, 'bourgeois interests (along with princely interests) gained in effectiveness at the expense of those of the nobility ... Merchants, financiers and entrepreneurs had become a permanent part of the social structure, had acquired some of the instruments for exercising influence over government policy and opinion, and in some places had obtained a hold over the instruments of government themselves.'[11]

But the interests of the merchants in foreign economic policy varied widely. Those that were exporters were concerned to promote their interest in foreign lands and to prevent state action likely to lead to restraints on their activities there. Usually, they recognised that this required reasonable treatment of alien merchants in their own countries. Thus, in the long conflict between the Hanse and England in the fifteenth century, though protectionist pressures were powerful at both ends (and ultimately in both cases prevailed), it was those merchants that travelled abroad that did most to resist the pressures at home: so the Hanse merchants in London called for a less restrictive treatment of English traders in Danzig; while the English merchants trading abroad, especially the Merchant Adventurers, favoured more liberal policies towards the Hanseatics in London.[12] Importing merchants also had an interest in freeing trade. Thus, in that same conflict the merchants of Bristol, who sold Hanseatic goods in that port, sought to resist the demands of the City of London for further restrictions against the Hanse; while the general traders in Cologne who sold

English cloth refused to support the Hanseatic League in its conflict with the English.[13]

On the other hand, the traders who competed with the foreigners, selling local produce of the same kind, were jealous of the foreign merchants and sought to have greater restraints imposed on them (especially when, as in England, Flanders and some other places, they themselves faced greater government levies than did the foreigners). As the influence of this group increased, the movement against foreign traders intensified. It was strengthened by the growth of alternative sources of supply, both at home and abroad, and by a growing nationalism in the sentiment of the ruling classes. In time, the foreign traders, far from being placed in a privileged position, found themselves saddled everywhere with heavier imposts and more severe restraints than the native traders. Conflicts intensified; their goods were impounded; occasionally they were expelled altogether.

The protectionism of this age, therefore, unlike those of the ages to come, was the creation of the traders rather than of the producers. The producers, whether peasants, craftsmen or artisans, usually had too little political power to bring about protection in their favour. Some had an interest in foreign trade, and even in favourable opportunities for foreign traders. The English wool-growers did better in the rare intervals (such as the middle of the fourteenth century) when foreign merchants, and not only the English ones, could purchase their products. Similarly the wine-growers in France, who sold wine to England, Flanders or the Hanse towns, and silk producers in Italy, whose fabrics were sold all across Europe, had an interest in free markets abroad and favoured policies that would not alienate unduly the governments of the countries to which they sold. Other producers had different interests. The restraints on exports of wool in England and France, which harmed the wool-growers, brought benefit to the cloth-makers in both countries;[14] and though the objective of such measures was often to damage a foreign ruler, in practice it frequently served to help domestic interests. Protection of local production of the kind that later became common was less necessary in this age. Most of the goods traded were specialist products not otherwise available where they were sold – Baltic furs, wax, hemp and timber, Italian silks and luxury goods, French wine and salt, English wool and unfinished cloths, Flemish cloth. These rarely represented a threat to native industries but were in much demand for consumers. Only where new industries were being introduced (such as silk production in France) did protectionism on behalf of producers (as against traders) begin occasionally to be introduced.

The great *mass of the population* had little immediate influence on policy. They had no representatives in parliament or in court to plead their cause. This does not mean that their interests were forgotten. As we have seen, one of the main concerns of the rulers was 'provision', the assurance of supplies to feed their people. The interest of most ordinary people was in securing the supplies which the foreign merchants brought. So it was that the cloth-workers of Gloucestershire came out in favour of the Hanse merchants when their privileges were threatened in 1468. In London, the poorer sections of the population were well disposed to the Hanseatic merchants who brought in cheap goods from abroad.[15] Occasionally, the dissatisfaction of the people at their economic condition would burst out in violent insurrections: as in Flanders in 1280 and 1340, in England in 1381 and in Florence in 1378-9, usually over food prices. Whether or not successful in the immediate sense, such uprisings served as warnings to rulers that the interests of the great mass of the population in economic policy could be forgotten only at their peril.

In this age, therefore, it was the interests of the rulers which ultimately prevailed. It was the interest of the rulers which dictated the policy of power. It was their believed interests which dictated the policy of bullionism. But they could not ignore the interests of their people as a whole; and as all of their people were consumers, in the final resort many of the policies were directed to protect the interests of consumers. Everywhere the consumer interest was dominant. It was shared by the royal courts, the great magnates and large sections of the wider population. Producer interests were, at national level, weakly organised. The policy of the rulers reflected that balance. In the final resort, the interest of the rulers in survival, and the interest of the bulk of their peoples in reasonably-priced supplies, determined the policies that were pursued.

MONARCHS AND MINISTERS (1600–1750)

In the age that followed, the balance of influence changed. The most obviously powerful force remained the ruler, his power in many cases more absolute than ever. Always at his shoulder, however, there now stood the great ministers who served him, and who exercised in practice, so long as they retained their master's favour, a still greater influence on policy. Such ministers as Richelieu and Mazarin in France, and Walpole in England, having responsibility for executive acts, exercised an authority more personal and detailed than did most of the sovereigns themselves. Beyond them were the lesser ministers, including those who had a special responsibility for financial matters or for foreign relations, whose influence could also be considerable. In a few countries, parliaments were able to make their voice felt on policy questions: in the United Provinces and Britain, these had some weight. There were the merchants, now increasingly numerous and increasingly organised in most countries, and often having their own means of exerting influence. Finally, there was the vast mass of the public, not normally articulate or vocal, yet a force at least to be reckoned with in every country, however autocratic the system of government. Each of these groups had its own interests which, while they sometimes coincided, were often in conflict.

There was no clear-cut division of interest between the sovereigns and the ministers who served them. Both shared one common purpose: the general objective of state-building, which was manifestly in the interests of each. If the state was prosperous and powerful, so too, generally speaking, would be the ruler, and almost equally glorious his ministers. Both therefore shared an interest in establishing a more efficient and productive economy at home, and a larger share of international trade abroad. Ministers identified with their master's success in achieving this. In Colbert's eyes, 'the object of economic statesmanship is to provide the monarch with the funds he needs for order and glory: to a large extent any increase in these funds must come from increases in the volume and circulation of cash, the only way to increase the tax-paying capacity of the population'.[16] The cameralists in Germany still more insistently impressed on their rulers their interest in a flourishing trade and industry. The strength and independence of the home economy became a primary interest of each, and foreign economic relations had to be subordinated to that end.

Conflicts of interest between monarchs and ministers could arise, however. One of the main interests of the sovereigns was still the raising of revenue. Their needs in this respect were even more pressing than in the previous age. The cost of administration, the cost of maintaining the royal court (including huge palaces, such as Versailles, the Louvre and Sans-souci), above all the cost of undertaking the continual foreign wars of the period, became greater than in any previous age. Ministers, however, had to enjoin continually the need for economy. Although the sources of revenue were greater than before, they were rarely enough; and financial necessity continued to influence the policies of sovereigns in their foreign economic relations. There was greater sophistication than in the previous age. Statesmen came to look to long-term stability of revenues, as well as the immediate raising of funds. In the previous age, any tax which produced money would be joyfully adopted even if, like tolls (or their sale), it dried up internal trade; or, like the sale of offices, corrupted administration; or, like export duties, hampered foreign trade. Now there was an increasing attempt to ensure that the needs of revenue were matched to the need to promote national economic efficiency. Policy in this respect had in most states become somewhat more rational.

Again, even if there was agreement on the doctrine of state-building, there could be differences on means to that end. The ruler might wish to embark on expensive foreign wars which his ministers believed to be imprudent. He might require revenues rapidly which the minister knew the state could not easily procure. The ministers were perhaps more disinterestedly and rationally concerned with state interests than were their masters. They might see that a particular royal extravagance would do little to promote long-term national interests. So Colbert, even while declaring himself the abject servant of his master, continually sought to persuade the king to reduce the huge sums he expended on Versailles, and to content himself with the Louvre alone. He had incessant brushes with Louvois, and sometimes with the king himself, over the costs of war with the Dutch, and almost resigned in 1673 when the king demanded another 60 million livres for the prosecution of the war[17] (though he himself was not averse to war for economic ends, and looked forward to the day when France would have defeated the United Provinces and acquired most of her commercial assets for herself). Where they agreed – and where there was no conflict of interest – was on the vital importance of the 'balance of trade' in building state power.

More often, the interest of rulers and ministers would coincide, but would conflict with that of other sections of the population. In the previous age, as we saw, rulers were always conscious of the interests of consumers: the policy of plenty, the securing of adequate supplies of food and other necessities, was nearly always paramount and usually prevailed over other economic ends, such as assisting domestic producers (as when exports were banned or heavily taxed, or special favours were shown to imports and to the foreign merchants who brought them). In this age, the priority was almost always the other way. The welfare of the mass of the population, a little less threatened by famine, now ranked lower. The need for cheap produce from abroad was usually regarded as of lesser importance than the need for a favourable trade balance, a flourishing shipping fleet or a flourishing local industry. As Charles Davenant, the English writer, put it, 'England could subsist, and the Poor perhaps would have fuller employment, if Foreign trade were quite laid aside; but this would ill-consist with our being great at Sea, upon which (under the present Posture of Affairs in Europe) all our Safety does certainly depend'.[18] In other words, the interests of the people sometimes had to be sacrificed to state interests, which included the need to be strong abroad. Similarly Josiah Child, admitted that 'if the present profit of the generality be barely and singularly considered' the Navigation Acts in England could have harmful effects; but, 'this Kingdom being an Island, the defence whereof has always been our Shipping and our Seamen, it seems to be absolutely necessary that Profit and Power ought jointly to be considered'.[19] Joint consideration of profit and power was precisely the policy that appealed to the great ministers of the day. For it was that policy, rather than the maximisation of economic welfare, which best furthered the principle of state-building which they had at heart.

The merchants now became a far more significant interest-group and a stronger influence on policy than they had been in the previous era. Ultimately, their most powerful influence was through their propaganda on commercial policy: the literature of the great mercantilist writers, many of them merchants, which now influenced the prevailing doctrine (see p. 11). But they also had more direct means of making their views heard at court. Their influence was most powerful in the United Provinces, a republic which, with no royal ruler (though the Stadtholder for much of the period had almost the same authority as a monarch), was virtually ruled by the merchant class, and whose state interests, even more than elsewhere, were wholly bound up with theirs. And the spectacular success of that country in promoting and extending its foreign trade meant that its trade-seeking policies were imitated in other states and in time brought almost equivalent attention to merchant interests there.

In England, too, the merchants were in a position to make their voice heard, especially through parliament. The merchants were closely consulted about the terms of the Navigation Acts, both in Cromwell's day and after the Restoration.[20] A Parliamentary Committee, heavily influenced by traders, was responsible for the introduction of the Staple Act of 1663, which compelled the colonies to buy through England virtually all the European goods they imported. The merchants were a powerful factor in bringing about the resumption of war against the Dutch in 1663–4: they succeeded in having passed in Parliament a Petition declaring that 'the wrongs, dishonours and indignities come to His Majesty by the subjects of the United Provinces, by invading of his rights in India, Africa and elsewhere, and the damages, affronts and injuries done by them to our merchants are the greatest obstruction of our foreign trade', and asked the king 'to take some speedy and effectual means for the redress thereof and for the prevention of the like in future'.[21] According to Clarendon, 'the merchants took much delight to discuss of the infinite benefit that would accrue from a barefaced war against the Dutch, how easily they might be subdued and the trade carried on by the English'.[22] And Bolingbroke, in negotiating the terms of the peace at the end of the War of Spanish Succession, was under constant pressure from merchant interests (for example to win for them a share in the lucrative Spanish trade to South America). It was on these grounds that Adam Smith attributed the development of the 'mercantile system', as he described it, to arguments 'addressed by merchants to Parliaments and the Councils of Princes'.[23] In France, though their voice counted for less, merchants were strongly represented in the Council of Commerce and even in the Conseil d'Etat, where the chartered companies, for example, were often represented. In other lands, though the influence of the merchants was usually more limited,[24] their views were usually at least taken into account in framing policy.

The interests of the merchants were by no means the same as those of the ministers. They were less concerned with state interests or power abroad and more concerned with commerce itself. In England, for instance, 'it was hardly to be expected ... that the merchants who wrote most of the mercantilist pamphlets would be chiefly interested in the power of the state. It was almost inevitable that their prime interests should be in commerce, and of course in the advantages they might expect from the various measures. For statesmen ... it was just as natural that considerations of power should take precedence over all others.'[25] Traders might be interested, for example, in doing business with some state not regarded with favour by their own government: such as the French trade with the Netherlands that Colbert suppressed. They could have an interest in imports from abroad, which the government frowned on for protectionist reasons: like the import of silk and other luxury goods from the Levant to France. They sometimes had an interest in importing exotic goods from a particular place, even though they exported little in return, and so caused a loss of bullion: such as the imports of calico, tea and other goods to England from India.[26] Finally, by bringing imports into the country, they could threaten employment at home: a consideration which, while never paramount, was also not forgotten at this time.[27]

To the great ministers, in other words, the profit of the individual traders, added together, did not necessarily equate with the profit of the state. Colbert begged his master to 'be on guard against the advice you will get from merchants, because you well know that they always consult only their individual interest without examining what would be for the public and the advantage of commerce in general'.[28] He frequently fumed at the French traders from Marseilles who special-ised in the Levant trade, because they bought more than they sold. For this reason, in France and other autocracies, the direct influence of the merchants was not very great. 'The administration normally kept the merchant interest at arm's length. Their petitions and counter-petitions were listened to and their advice was asked,' but 'the mer-chant did not as a rule penetrate far qua merchant into the arcana of government ... Colbert, a doctrinaire and an authoritarian himself, directed the organisation of trade and industry, dismissing the views of merchants as inevitably self-interested and myopic.'[29]

The merchants' interests were anyway by no means uniform. Those who were mainly interested in the export and re-export trade had quite a different interest from those who were importers; and those who exported raw materials or unfinished products had a different interest from those who were interested in manufactures, and from manufac-turers themselves. The exporters as in the previous age, were well aware of the dangers to their position abroad that could result from too blatant protectionism at home. The English Merchant Adventurers and their successors, who depended on reasonable conditions for selling wool cloth and other products abroad, were nervous about the effect of cutting back on imports, both because it reduced purchasing power among their customers and because it set an example to others elsewhere. 'English merchants engaged in the Hamburg trade in wool cloth never tired of explaining how the reduction of Irish linen exports to England caused a corresponding decline in wool exports',[30] and numerous petitions were presented to the House of Commons to demonstrate these dangers. Here, the exporters were in conflict with home producers who favoured protection. Conversely, the manufac-turers often protested at the activities of traders who exported raw materials to their rivals. Thus the wool cloth manufacturers in England succeeded in securing the passage of an Act in 1699 to prohibit the export of wool, woollen yarn, or woollen manufactures from the colonies to foreign countries, or to the colonies of other countries, while English iron-masters attempted to prohibit the manufacture in the colonies of iron, which could enter into competition with their own.

But the interests of merchants need not necessarily be in conflict with those of the state. Sometimes a kind of alliance was established that promoted the interests of merchants and state alike. The great chartered companies, for example, were generally expected to serve this purpose. Merchants were often the original stimulus to the foundation of the companies. 'Normally it was the merchants who agitated for the formation of the companies ... Everywhere merchants provided the bulk of the capital for overseas voyages, and it was they who carried the companies into the new lands.'[31] For such ventures, the merchants managed to secure the support and sponsorship of the state, often including protection by armed forces, though it was they themselves that drew most of the profit. They managed also to secure the participation of members of the aristocracy, and often of royal families and ministers, as well as financiers and bankers.[32] Such high-born backers would ensure that the interests of the companies were not forgotten in the councils of government. Occasionally, there were direct financial levers. Sometimes, the companies would give loans to ministers or monarchs in return for a monopoly or preferential duties or concessions in foreign lands, or the right to establish fortified posts in a foreign country.[33] And the state itself had an interest in the success of such ventures which was almost as great as that of the merchants: in access to valued materials, in strategic advantage, in winning trade, in forestalling rival states and in securing revenues from the sale of monopolies, honours and patents for the granting of the Charters. 'Both at home and abroad joint-stock companies were used for purposes of state such as the promotion of defence industries, for the planting of colonies, and for the prosecution of trade in competition with similar organized foreign groups in areas where the struggle for power was waged relentlessly, as in India. No small part of the favour accorded to the joint form of enterprise came as a result of its service in power politics.'[34] So a common interest was established between the merchants and the state to which they belonged and each could benefit from the success of the other. Once again profit and power were jointly considered.

Another important group with interests of its own were the bankers and financiers who backed much of the foreign trade. As the Italian states declined in political and economic power, the Italian bankers who had been based there had transferred their headquarters to other lands, especially the United Provinces, England and south Germany. In time, they were increasingly supplemented by native bankers, especially those of Amsterdam, by the goldsmiths who formed the first banks in England, and others elsewhere. Such people were not as powerful or influential as the Medicis and Fuggers in the previous age, for rulers and governments were less dependent on loans, or at least on personal loans of this kind: governments and rulers relied more on their normal fiscal machinery (including the sale of offices, which in France, Spain and other countries remained an essential source of finance). Finance was now less international than it had been, though there were some international finance houses, especially in Amsterdam, which were almost as cosmopolitan as were the Florentine bankers of the previous age. But whether national or international, bankers were still concerned with the security of their investments and the profitability of trade. Their interests now were, thus, closer to those of the merchant than to those of the state. Their loans were primarily to the private sector. Most of the trading ventures bringing expensive cargoes from distant quarters could hardly have been undertaken without the financial support of such backers (each buying, say, a 64th part of the cargo). The financiers thus shared the interest of both the merchants and the state in successful trading ventures abroad; and they used their influence, such as it was, to encourage the successful prosecution of the 'war of money'.

Finally, there existed the population as a whole. Though in most states they had little direct voice in the affairs of state, this does not mean that their interests were altogether ignored. The preoccupation of governments with promoting the power of the state had the effect that welfare in itself took a fairly low place in the policy consideration of governments. But it was not forgotten altogether: the need to maintain employment was asserted by writers such as Davenant, and there were indications that some governments too were concerned about those matters.[35] It would be wrong, however, to exaggerate the importance of such motives: in the economic policy of governments, in the setting of tariffs and the negotiation of trade agreements, it was the balance of trade that was constantly in mind, not the level of employment or the living standards of the people as a whole. Certainly, the working people themselves had little direct influence on the policies pursued.

The balance of influence between these various interest-groups varied considerably between one state and another. This depended partly on their numbers: where merchants were more numerous, as in the United Provinces and England, they were likely to be more influential. It varied also according to their constitutional system and social structure. Because parliament was powerful in England, and cared about commercial interests (even though there may not have been many merchants in parliament), because merchants had high status in the United Provinces and were closely involved in the machinery of state, those countries were more receptive to their views. But all over Europe the prevailing doctrine, with its emphasis on the balance of trade, brought a new attention to merchant interests, or at least to the trading interests of the state which in practice benefited the merchants. Nor was it by chance that where the merchants were most influential, commercial policy was most successful. It was partly, of course, that merchants were more likely to come to positions of prominence in successful trading nations; but it was also that, where a nation's merchants had secured a position of prominence, successful expansion of trade was more likely to be promoted.[36] But everywhere to some extent, in this age, merchants, and financiers with an interest in trade abroad, became a larger section of the population, more influential with public opinion or with that small part of it that mattered. More important was the fact that merchant *ideas* increasingly prevailed. 'The merchant's outlook as well as the merchant was counting for more. His business figures more frequently, not only in the House of Commons, but at Versailles, where his advice was more often sought, and honours were more often accorded to him.'[37] In a word, merchant interests were able increasingly to influence state action, whatever the social or political position of the merchant class.

Different interest-groups were often engaged in a struggle to make their views prevail among governments, and the policy finally adopted depended partly on the balance of forces in each state, partly on how far they could persuade others that their own interests coincided with those of the state. 'The waverings of state policy during the long period in which mercantilism held sway cannot be understood without realising the extent to which the state was a creature of warring commercial interests. The common aim was to have a strong state, providing that they could manipulate it to their exclusive advantage.'[38] Each interest, in other words, sought to make the state the instrument of its own ends; and all therefore wanted the state itself to be strong. The objective which most of the dominant interests shared was most clearly reflected in state policy – and in the doctine of the age: the promotion of a favourable trade balance. For the merchants, success in this effort meant more trade abroad and less competition at home. For the great ministers it meant an inflow of precious metals and so, it was believed, an increase in the wealth of the state.

So a kind of symbotic relationship developed. For many among the merchants, the state was a body whose duty it was to support them. 'For them the state was but the largest of the corporate bodies designed among other things for their benefit. By taxation, tariffs, subsidies, and the like, it could influence relations with competitors.'[39] Conversely, in the eyes of the state, the merchants and especially the trading corporations represented, in Colbert's words, the 'armies' with which they fought the great war for European trade. Thus the state was widely held to benefit from trade, and so from traders; while traders benefited from the support given them by the state to secure the increased trade. 'In England, throughout the period there was present in varying degree the idea of cooperation between government and governed, state and individual, between those who represented the intermediate interests of trading companies, sectional and local affairs, . . . and those who took (or claimed to take) the larger and longer view of the nation as a whole . . . Nothing is more typical of this quest than the government committees and boards of the trading companies of the Restoration, where princes and tradesmen sat side by side in conspiracy that was expected to be mutually advantageous.'[40]

In this as in subsequent ages, therefore, the economically potent forces had secured their end: they not only set their stamp on the doctrine which prevailed, but they also directly influenced policy. In this way, they made their own interests appear to be those of the state to which they belonged.

MERCHANTS AND MANUFACTURERS (1750–1870)

During the age that followed, there was a substantial change in social structure within states; this in turn affected the nature of the doctrines that prevailed and the type of economic relationships undertaken between states.

The most significant change within each society was the increasing importance, in both number and influence, of the rising manufacturing and commercial classes. They were still not (except possibly in the Netherlands) in control of the state anywhere. In a few countries, England and France, the Netherlands and Switzerland, the gradual extension of the franchise allowed their voice to be heard more clearly within parliament and the councils of state. Sometimes, they were scarcely represented in parliaments at all. They were distrusted, even despised, by the classes still ruling – aristocracy, land-owners and gentry – in many states (in describing England as a nation of shopkeepers, Napoleon did not intend flattery). But there was everywhere an increasing recognition of the importance of commercial success to the welfare and prosperity of the state; and there was greater willingness therefore to listen to those engaged in commercial activities.

The voice of these new classes was not always united. They certainly did not invariably favour freer trade. Many manufacturers, especially outside England, and at first in that country too, were more apprehensive of the effect of a reduction of tariff barriers on sales at home than hopeful of its assistance to sales abroad. The difficulty that the free traders, the economists and other thinkers had at this time in persuading the manufacturers of the benefits of free trade was the clearest possible evidence of the distaste with which many of the latter regarded the prospect. Where industry was weak, those exhortations usually fell on stony ground. However enthusiastic for free trade the French economists such as Chevalier and Say, they could not convince French industrialists that a reduction of tariffs could be anything but disastrous for them;[41] and it was for this reason that Napoleon III was obliged to conduct his early negotiations for tariff reductions in secret. Where industry was strong, as in England, such arguments found a more sympathetic hearing. But even here, producers took time to be convinced; and the speed and fervour of their conversion depended crucially on their degree of vulnerability to foreign competition. Only slowly did manufacturers, above all in the stronger states, begin to see that, provided reductions were reciprocal, tariff-cutting could help them by opening up new markets abroad, previously closed to them, which they might hope now to dominate.

The traders were usually quicker to see the benefit of freeing trade. In England particularly, to some extent elsewhere, many of the leaders of the free trade movement were themselves traders or had close connections with them.[42] Cobden had been a trader in muslins in his early years. Bright had commercial interests. The Anti-Corn Law League, the main pressure group acting in favour of freer trade in England, was centred in Manchester, the headquarters of the textile trade, and its members were predominantly from the commercial classes, above all those involved in textiles.[43]

Agricultural interests, especially the big land-owners, remained powerful in almost all countries. Their attitude to the new movement for freedom of trade varied according to local conditions. Where they could expect to benefit by higher sales of their produce abroad, they often favoured a reduction of barriers. They might expect from this a double benefit: cheaper industrial products imported more freely from abroad, and a larger market for their own products. The wine-producers of France were, on these grounds, one of the few interest-groups in that country which favoured a liberalising of tariffs.[44] The wool-growers took a similar viewpoint for the same reasons, while the manufacturers of woollens, like other manufacturers, remained protectionist. In Prussia, the land-owners and farmers, highly competitive themselves and with an interest in cheap manufactures from abroad, were a strong force for the lowering of tariffs. This was the main reason why Prussia was a pace-setter among European nations in this respect, having much lower tariffs than Britain (even after the reductions made by Pitt in the 1780s and Huskisson in the 1820s) until the comprehensive reductions made by Peel and Gladstone between 1845 and 1865. In Britain, however, the situation was reversed. British agriculture was not at this time sufficiently economic to be able to sell grain abroad; and it maintained its position in the home market only through the heavy protection afforded by the Corn Laws. Thus there the land-owners and farmers, far from supporting liberalisation, were the last bastions of protectionist sentiment. Even when, slowly, their views changed, it was mainly the land-owners, who might find alternative profit through higher land prices, rather than the tenant farmers, who were brought to alter their viewpoint.[45]

Thus interest-groups, even within the same country, often had sharply divergent interests in relation to foreign economic policy. The commercial and industrial classes in England resented the stubborn opposition of the land-owners to the liberalisation of trade in agricultural products; Bright was indignant that Lord Ashley, who led the movement for factory legislation (which the manufacturers intensely disliked), agitated against industrialists like himself who paid a respectable wage of 16 shillings a week, while he did nothing about his own farm labourers who earned less than half as much, and refused to bring down the price of food by repealing the Corn Laws. In Germany, the position was the reverse. The manufacturers of south Germany and the Rhineland resented the insistence of Prussian land-owners on low tariffs, which kept prices down in Prussia but exposed them to dangerous competition. This led to the paradox that the radical Cobden had in some ways more trust in Peel and the Tories and had 'not the same confidence in Lord John and the Whigs'.[46] Until 1850, nearly all liberalisation of trade in Britain was introduced by the Conservatives, who were responsible for the measures first attempted in 1713 and for those actually introduced in 1786, 1823 and the 1840s:[47] only after the mid-century, when the Liberals become more closely identified with trading interests than with land-owning, did they become responsible for the final spurt of liberalisation after 1860, while the Conservatives by the end of the century had become identified with 'fair trade', 'tariff reform' and the movement for protection.

In other cases, there was a conflict of interests between different *regions*. In Germany, the states of the north-east and the east, which were mainly dependent upon agriculture, and the cities of the north-west, such as Hamburg and Bremen which were dependent upon trade, were generally free trade in their views, while those areas dependent upon industry, such as the Rhineland (iron) and the south (textiles) were more protectionist in sentiment. Similarly, in the US, the manufacturing north-east was protectionist, while the south, depending upon imports of manufactures and exports of cotton, was more liberal. Nor was there necessarily always consistency in such attitudes. Regions would sometimes support protection for their own products and oppose it for those of other areas. In the US Congress after 1816, there were 'objections of northern members to a protecting duty on sugar and of southern members to giving protection to cotton manufactures. On the question of protection to iron, the north and the south united against the middle states.'[48]

Another group which normally supported the new doctrine was that of the financiers. Between 1815 and 1825, public loans were floated in London or through London for most countries in Europe and many in Latin America. Thirty-one public loans were floated between 1818 and 1825 in favour of seventeen different governments. Nathan Rothschild, in giving evidence before a parliamentary committee in 1832, declared that 'This country in general is the bank for the whole world ... All transactions in India, in China, in Germany, in the whole world, are guided here and settled through this country.'[49] No wonder that the Duc de Richelieu is reported to have said 'There are six Powers in Europe, Great Britain, France, Russia, Austria, Prussia and Baring Brothers'.[50] The bankers, at least in the stronger nations, used their weight in favour of the freeing of trade, from which they might be expected to benefit as much as others. Sometimes this influence was crucial. A petition protesting against 'every restrictive regulation of trade not essential to the revenues' presented to the House of Commons in 1820 was one of the first major expressions in parliament of free trade sentiment; but it won influential support only after Samuel Thornton, financier and merchant, and former governor of the Bank of England, agreed to sign, followed by half the directors of the Bank;[51] and the petition was actually laid before the House of Commons by Alexander Baring, head of the great banking house.

Government officials, too, came to be staunch supporters of the new doctrine, especially as time went on, and were highly influential. In England, the Board of Trade from the 1820s on became a powerful force for free trade policy and free trade views. J. D. Hume, who became joint secretary to the Board in 1828, 'was one of the most prominent free traders of his age',[52] and spoke repeatedly at meetings on the subject of free trade. His successor, John MacGregor, G. R. Porter, head of the statistical department, H. Labouchere, successively Vice-President and President of the Board, Sir J. Shaw-Lefevre, joint assistant-secretary, like Farrer and Mallet in a later day, were equally pronounced advocates of free trade, and equally outspoken in that cause. The Board of Trade thus became in Britain perhaps the most powerful and influential lobby for free trade.

So a variety of interest-groups gradually became convinced in favour of a freeing of trade. The essential task for those who favoured the change in policy was to win over others. The free trade movement in England organised a deliberate and highly articulate campaign for this purpose. On their side, they had such organs of radical opinion as the influential *Westminster Review*. They had certain well-known economic writers, Ricardo, Bentham, the Mills, McCulloch and others, over and above the revered Adam Smith. And they had vigorous champions in public life, Joseph Hume, Villiers, Clay and later Cobden and Bright. Finally, from 1838 they had an organised pressure-group, actively seeking to win over public opinion, the Anti-Corn Law League. This organised public meetings and lectures, published pamphlets and books, lobbied politicians, and even sought to have their own supporters elected to parliament. Whatever their own interest in trade, they were always able to proclaim that they favoured the free trade case not to promote their own advantage, but for the good of the public generally: to bring down the price of food and other necessities, to promote exports and create employment, to extend national power and national welfare, to promote peace.[53]

Parliaments too, where they existed and had power, were a major instrument for furthering the new doctrine. In England, there existed nearly always, from the end of the eighteenth century onwards, a significant proportion of the House of Commons who were influenced by free trade views. These were not at first seeking to promote the ends of particular interest-groups: such figures as Shelburne, Pitt, Eden and Tucker were rather the intellectual followers of Adam Smith and other writers. Later (though there were always some who were similarly influenced), many openly represented a particular interest. Joseph Hume, one of the most outspoken and effective proponents of free trade in parliament in the 1820s and 1830s, was himself an industrialist who had much to gain from the adoption of the views he upheld. Even Cobden and Bright, the ultimate leaders of the movement, though nobody could accuse them of plain self-interest, undoubtedly saw the matter from the point of view of those who had experience of business, as they both had. And there were many others, both in parliament and elsewhere, whose connections helped to make them feel that what was good for British manufacturing industry and commerce was also good for the country as a whole.

One of the most effective instruments for promoting such interests in parliament was the parliamentary committee. The British House of Commons had, for many years, a Committee on Trade and Plantations which examined commercial questions and to which commercial interests could express their grievances. When the West Indies lobby was seeking, after the American War of Independence, to persuade the British parliament to relax the restrictions on US trade with the West Indies, it was mainly to this committee that they appealed (without success). The General Chamber of the Manufacturers of Great Britain, for long the main pressure group of the manufacturers (until it was dissolved as a result of differences on the Eden Treaty of 1786), similarly sought to promote its interests in this Committee and in the corresponding committee of the Privy Council on Trade. Some committees of this kind were set up *ad hoc* for particular studies. Thus the petition of 1820 to the House of Commons, calling for a liberalisation of trade, led to the establishment of a Select Committee on the Means of Maintaining and Improving the Foreign Trade of the Country (a similar Committee was set up in the House of Lords). This had the effect its proposers had hoped. The Committee's report reflected the strong sentiment in favour of freer trade which the commercial interests had put to it: 'Your Committee are satisfied that the skill, enterprise and capital of British merchants and manufacturers require only an open and equal field for exertion ... They are convinced that every restriction of the freedom of commerce is in itself an evil, to be justified only by some adequate political expediency.' So, in the most powerful state of Europe, the new doctrine had won the official endorsement of parliament.

There were also, of course, bodies speaking for *particular* interests which could add their voices to the cause: 'the Manchester Manufacturers', 'the Merchants of London trading to Spain', the 'Committees of Commerce' of Exeter or Leeds, the Committees 'of the Norwich Merchants', or 'of Merchants trading to the West Indies', were among the bodies which British Governments expected to consult. These, too, mainly favoured a liberalisation of trade. During the negotiations on trade undertaken by Britain with a number of foreign governments in the 1780s, the Committee of Trade questioned such groups and other interested parties, including individual merchants and manufacturers, or individual chartered companies, such as the Russia Company, on the objectives they hoped the negotiations might procure. This was mainly before the negotiations began: 'they were not in the habit of consulting merchants or manufacturers once a negotiation was under way, except to ask for more factual information'.[54] This enabled government ministers and officials to negotiate more effectively on behalf of the principal interests affected. Some form of consultaton with bodies representative of interest-groups (where they existed) took place in most other states, though access to the decision-making authorities was often more difficult than in England. And often such consultation helped to inject free trade sentiments into official thinking.

So new interest-groups rose to prominence in this age, different in character from those of earlier ages, and stamped a new character on economic policy. Manufacturing and commercial interests were now more powerful and more vocal. In many countries, and above all in Britain, the dominant economic power of the age, they were able to exercise a significant influence on the prevalent thinking, and so eventually on policy. The interest of these classes, and of the governments of the dominant powers of the day, lay in a freeing of trade from the regulations and restrictions which had for so long surrounded it, and so securing better access to those markets abroad, both in Europe and overseas, which they had every hope of dominating. So, eventually, a new doctrine on foreign economic policy emerged: the new free trade policy which finally conquered almost everywhere.

BANKERS AND BONDHOLDERS (1870–1914)

In the age that followed, the social structure within states changed again. Developments within the capitalist economy brought new social groups to prominence and influence in many states.

As the scale of enterprise increased, the role of the individual proprietor owning and running his own business, and of the individual enterpriser matching money and opportunity, declined. New financial institutions and arrangements emerged which enabled new and larger organisations to finance their operations both at home and abroad. There was more – much more – money circulating within each economy, more people who held money, and more of these who wished to lend it to productive enterprise rather than expend it on land or consumption.

Thus the two archetypal figures of the age were the banker and the bondholder, the men of money prepared to lend it for interest. 'The London financial market derived its strength from great wealth, diversity, experience, world connections ... The great wealth had enlarged itself gradually through the pioneering organisation of machine industry, through the conduct of commerce throughout the world and the development of the resources of distant areas ... At the top of the pyramid of wealth there rested a substantial group whose great income and investing power was one of the revolutionary forces of the world ... These savings, available for capital expenditure of some kind, were mainly in the possession of those whose field of business and personal interests extended far beyond the British Isles.'[55]

The growth of these new financial resources affected the domestic and international economy alike. In each case, bondholder and banker had a vital role to play. At home, governments raised the finance they needed on an increasing scale by the issue of bonds and treasury bills, which were bought by both groups. Private companies likewise, the main agents of economic activity and industrial advance, were financed to an increasing extent by the issue of stock, which was also bought by both bankers and private shareholders. The same functions were performed internationally. The bondholders who invested their money by purchasing the bonds of their home governments subscribed equally enthusiastically to the issues of governments abroad. Since there were many governments and rulers of developing regions only too willing and anxious to raise money on the capital markets of European countries, whether to pay off old debts or to finance new activities, foreign issues now multiplied and flourished. And since there were, in addition, many private or semi-private undertakings to be financed in the same lands beyond the seas – whether the building of railways or the planting of rubber plantations, the construction of electricity stations or the mining of gold – these too could often be financed by investment from the ample savings of the monied classes in European states.

The most prominent and influential of the groups which provided finance in this way were the bankers who prospered and proliferated at this time. The banks of this age were of a number of different types. In Britain, apart from the big commercial banks, which were not usually involved in foreign investment, there were some banks specifically established to engage in business abroad: of this type were the Chartered Bank of India, Australia and China, the Hongkong and Shanghai Bank, the Anglo-Egyptian Bank, the London and Brazilian Bank, and so on. These were concerned especially with the financing of commerce and industry in the foreign areas concerned and thus had a direct interest in the establishment of favourable trading conditions in those countries. In addition, there were the specialised issue houses, of the type later known as merchant banks, such as Rothschilds, Barings, Brown Shipley, Glyn Mills and Curry, Schroders and so on, which specialised in the issue of bonds, whether on behalf of governments or for railways and other construction. There were smaller acceptance houses and issuing brokers, which handled much of the colonial borrowing, and smaller government and railway loans. Finally, there were financial, land and investment companies which undertook the promotion and underwriting of issues; that is, agreed to purchase a certain proportion of the bonds with a view to subsequent resale, and so enabled the more risky ventures to secure finance. It was to these various institutions, particularly the former group, that the impoverished and often debt-ridden governments of overseas lands usually turned to secure for themselves the finance that they needed.

In France, there existed a group of old and powerful banking houses, known as the Haute Banque, which were the bankers of sovereigns and foreign governments. From 1870, their place as issuing houses was increasingly taken over by newer banks, the industrial banks or banques d'affaires, and the banques de dépôts. The most successful among these were the Banque de Paris et Pays Bas, the Banque Française pour le Commerce et l'Industrie, and the Credit Mobilier, now revived after its crash in 1869–70. It was especially the industrial banks that in France were mainly responsible for floating the loans of foreign governments and, with the deposit banks, in selling the bonds among the French public through their branches throughout the country and through travelling security salesmen. Among the German banks, the most important were the four Ds: the Deutsche Bank, the Diskonto-Gesellschaft, the Dresdner Bank and the Darmstadter Bank. After these came another six or eight major deposit banks, based in other cities in Germany, and a number of major private banks centred especially in Frankfurt. Both types were responsible for launching the loans of foreign governments on the German markets as well as for financing German enterprise in different parts of the world: from the development of the Shantung area in China to the building of the Baghdad railway, from the launching of new shipping lines to the laying of cables, from the financing of trade in Latin America to the financing of oil production in Rumania. In many cases, these German banks held the bonds of foreign governments in their own vaults as security for their loans rather than selling them to the public. Different banks specialised in different areas of the world and different types of activity; and they would seek to avoid competing with each other in the same field.[56]

The bondholders, the other main source of investment, also became increasingly organised at this time. Since they were able to promote their own interests only through the activities of their governments in pressing their case with issuing governments abroad, it was important to them to have direct access through organisations which could put their case effectively. Thus, in most of the major European states there developed general organisations, such as the Corporation of Foreign Bondholders in Britain, which was established in 1859, and the Association Nationale des Porteurs Français des Valeurs Etrangères in France. In Britain there were interlocking directorships between the Corporation and the Bank of England: for years the vice-chairman of the Council of the Corporation of Foreign Bondholders was on the Board of Governors of the Bank. In most of the other capital-exporting countries there was a similar close relationship between the bondholders and governments or central banks. In addition, there were specialised organisations, concerned with the bonds issued by particular governments, such as the Committee of Peruvian Bondholders, the Committee of Portuguese Bondholders, and many similar organisations in Britain. These were powerful pressure-groups, representing important and influential sections of society. In dealing with the borrowing governments, they had important allies and important sanctions. The Corporation of Foreign Bondholders in Britain, 'besides its talent for persuasion and for the organisation of moral pressure, could muster to best advantage the aid of the banking community, the stock exchange, and the government. Defaulting governments found it impossible to secure new financial accommodation while their reckoning remained unsettled.'[57] So the sources of finance possessed powerful sanctions against those governments that made themselves dependent on them.

Traders also sought to bring their influence to bear on governments. They too were well organised to make their views felt; and governments increasingly listened to the views they put forward. Sometimes they did this through national organisations representing their interests: the various commercial or other business groups. In Britain, the big Chambers of Commerce of London, Manchester and Birmingham, for example, represented powerful voices, to which governments would listen with care. There were also more specialist groups: for example the China Society (later the China Association), extremely active in lobbying the British government on ways of easing the path for British traders in China, and the Imperial South Africa Association in Britain, or, in Germany, the German Commercial and Plantation Association of the Southern Seas, which did not merely lobby the German government, but was also given aid by it to increase its influence in the Pacific. In France, there were a number of Chambres and Sociétés which made representations to their government on such matters. When in 1882, for example, the French government was deliberating whether or not to send an expedition to conquer Tongking, the Chambre Syndicale des Négociants-Commissionnaires of Paris addressed the Ministry of Marine, supporting the proposal on the grounds that French penetration in that area could bring the 'opening of new markets for French production, exploitation of the mineral riches and products of the oil of Tongking'. The Chambre had therefore passed a resolution to the effect that 'the question of Tongking be promptly resolved by the occupation of the Red River and its customs houses in order to ensure the security of commerce and by the definite establishment of an effective protectorate.'[58] Only eleven days later, the Syndicat General des Unions du Commerce et de l'Industrie passed a similar resolution, declaring that 'the conquest of a new group of near to fifty million consumers markets where our manufactures will be easily exchanged for raw materials is a matter assuredly worth the trouble it entails.'[59] The Comité de l'Afrique Française, representing many broking, trading and industrial firms interested in African trade, similarly lobbied French governments for a more forward policy there; while the Comité de Maroc, representing similar firms interested in Morocco, campaigned for a French protectorate in that country and effectively mobilised parliamentary and public opinion in that cause.[60]

In Britain, chambers of commerce conducted similar campaigns. For example, in 1885, when the British government was hesitating whether or not to extend British power in Upper Burma, the London Chamber of Commerce delivered a memorial to the India Office specifically demanding the annexation of Upper Burma, an event shortly followed by the British expedition against Mandalay. The Liverpool Chamber of Commerce, which had an interest in trade in many parts of Africa, in 1892 bewailed the fact that, in the West Coast of Africa over the previous decade, British governments had been 'outstripped by Germany and France', and declared their firm opinion that 'wherever in the unappropriated territories of Africa preponderance of British trade existed, there British interests should have been secured by proclaiming such territories spheres of British influence'.[61] At about the same time, the London Chamber of Commerce was pressing for action in the Gold Coast to assert British interests there; and soon after, an attempt was made to open up the region north of Ashanti to link with the territory controlled by the Niger Company to the East.

Even more active, often, were the organisations concerned with trade in particular areas, including *local* organisations representing businessmen in cities or countries abroad. In France, for example, the Société du Haut Laos and the Société du Mekong were concerned with promoting commercial expansion in those areas. The former's 'stated objectives were to offset British commercial and political influence in Northern Laos and to attach this area to French Indo-China. It ... stands as an example of that kind of quasi-commercial organisation which flourished in the 1880s and 1890s as an expression of the patriotic fervour of colonial enthusiasts who saw in commerce a means to strengthen the political claims of their metropolis to overseas territories in dispute with other European powers.'[62] The attempts in London to push and prod the British government to a more forward policy in Burma were initiated and inspired by the Rangoon Chamber of Commerce, representing British traders in Burma: this sent several petitions to the government of India in Calcutta demanding that the kingdom of Burma should be annexed; and to promote this campaign it contacted Chambers of Commerce in Britain, inducing them 'to bombard the India Office with petitions for action'.[63] Even after an expedition to Mandalay had been despatched, the Rangoon Chamber of Commerce continued to make urgent representations that this should secure full-scale annexation, rather than simply a change of ruler, since only the former, it was thought, would afford security for British trade. Similarly, British business interests based in Singapore made successive representations to the British government for a more active intervention in Malaya in the 1880s.[64] And, in West Africa it was because of similar representations by merchants which claimed that he was obstructing freedom of trade that the king of Opobo was deported by the British acting Consul in 1887.

All these groups, therefore, had extensive influence with their own governments. These were not unwilling to be influenced. Government ministers themselves (often now upper-middle-class in background, rather than aristocratic as in the previous age) had in many cases close links of family or friendship with financial circles. Lord Rosebery, British prime minister at the end of the nineteenth century, was linked by marriage to the Rothschilds, who were closely involved in many overseas ventures. Lord Cromer, British representative in Egypt, was a member of the house of Baring, deeply engaged in financing commercial operations in Latin America and elsewhere. Goschen, Liberal minister and British emissary on behalf of the British bondholders in Egypt, was a partner in the finance house of Fruhling and Goschen.

Apart from family connections of this kind, the bankers and businessmen became closely involved in other ways with politics and politicians. Quite often they were able themselves to create the connection. Sometimes companies would make a point of appointing well-known political figures, especially an aristocrat, to the board of an undertaking, to give it both respectability and access to political circles: Goldie, in establishing the United African Company, was careful to appoint as president Lord Aberdare, a former Liberal politician who had served in Gladstone's first cabinet, as 'an influential and dignified figure-head',[65] in the hope of securing from Gladstone a charter and official protection for the company; while Rhodes invited the Duke of Abercorn and the Duke of Fife to become president and vice-president of his projected British South Africa Company, in an attempt to win influence with Salisbury whose support was crucial to him. 'Partners of the important issue houses sat in the House of Commons or among the Lords where they were in easy touch with the Ministry. In clubs, country weekends, shooting parties, Sir Ernest Cassel, Lord Rothschild or Lord Revelstoke could learn the official mind and reveal their own; there was ample opportunity to discuss the wisdom or needs of the moment.'[66]

The situation was similar in other countries. The Deutsche Bank was closely associated with German foreign policy in Turkey and the Near East. Disraeli held that 'in France finance, and even private finance, is politics'.[67] Salisbury believed that in Egypt 'France, Austria and Germany had all shaped their diplomatic action . . . purely to satisfy the interests of certain bankers who are able to put pressure on their foreign offices'.[68] Others held that British banks, in particular Rothschilds, which had lent to Disraeli to buy Suez Canal shares a few years earlier, had exerted significant influence on British policy in

Egypt (and Cromer, in his own book on Egypt, accepted that 'the origin of the Egyptian question in its present phase was financial').

The influence was not all in one direction. Governments also sought to influence the banks, and so indirectly the bondholders, for political reasons. They used this influence, for example, not infrequently to close capital markets altogether to foreign governments which they regarded as opponents: as the German market was closed to Russia from the late 1880s, as the French market was opened to her for the same reason from about that period, and as the London market was closed to her before 1906 but miraculously opened again from that year when political relations improved. Governments had all sorts of ways in which to bring their influence to bear on the bankers: for example, in favour of issues which they approved, and against those which they disapproved. 'In a variety of ways suggestions passed back and forth between the financial world and the government, subtle indications of each others' judgments. For the absence of any official formal requirement that the government be consulted before the emission of foreign loans did not mean that there was no interchange between the government and those who engaged in the loan business. The course of foreign investment was pointed in unofficial intercourse between those who shaped the country's political and financial behaviour. Without being compelled to do so, as Sir Edward Gray explained, financial groups contemplating an issue which might affect some official purpose often sought to inform themselves of official opinion ... Banking groups, alert as is their wont, were guided by some brief public intimation, a speech in the House of Commons or at a political dinner, or suggestions passed in the press.'[69] Often, there was no real conflict or difficulty in making influence effective since 'the feelings and decisions of the investors showed substantial identity with those of the government in power. Capital went primarily to those lands from the development of which the British people hoped for benefit – in the way of new sources of raw materials and foodstuffs, new markets ... From countries towards which antipathy existed it abstained.'[70]

Apart from these forms of collective influence, *individual* businessmen were often successful in winning governmental support for their enterprises. Adventurers – and there were many – whose aims were partly the exploration of new regions, partly the acquisition of commercial benefits, and partly to win glory for the national flag, often turned to their governments to give them official endorsement. Much of the impetus of German colonisation came from individual traders such as Adolf Woerman and Karl Peters. The former demanded government support for his firm's extensive operations in West Africa, sending a memorandum to the German Foreign Office in 1843 calling for German naval support for his operations, for a German base in Fernando Po, a full-time German Consul and resistance to the claims of Portugal and Britain in the area: an initiative which eventually had decisive influence on German policy in the region. Karl Peters was personally responsible for securing numerous 'treaties' with the chiefs of East Africa, for initiating German claims to large areas in that region, and eventually for getting the German government to establish the German protectorate of Tanganyika. Sir Harry Johnston, the explorer, having penetrated up the Niger river and secured 'treaties' with many of the local chiefs, was instrumental in bringing much of the upper Niger region under British control, first under the chartered Royal Niger Company and ultimately under the British government. George Goldie, seeking to extend the trade of the United Africa Company, was largely responsible for the expansion of British power in the Gold Coast and Southern Nigeria. The French adventurer Comte de Semelle, having founded a company concerned with exploiting equatorial Africa, succeeded in securing the authority of Gambetta to conclude 'treaties' with chiefs in the Niger valley and putting forward French claims to that area. Perhaps the classic adventurer of this type, successful in securing eventually the reluctant support of his own government, was Cecil Rhodes, who, having established, almost single-handed, the colony of Rhodesia and ensured the exploration of Bechuanaland and Matabeleland, ultimately induced the British government to establish protectorates or colonies throughout the region.[71] And apart from enterprising individuals of this kind, many private companies – Consolidated Goldfields, the German East Africa Society, the British India Steam Navigation Company, and many others having a strong interest in the extension of colonial power to protect their activities abroad – developed their own private lines to government, and so were able to amplify the representations of individual businessmen.

Governments, of course, did not blindly follow the urgings of the manifestly self-interested companies. Governments had interests of their own which were not identical with that of their businesses: strategic advantage, the desire not to offend foreign governments or local rulers unnecessarily, economy in government expenditure. The aim of promoting the interests of their own traders and businessmen was only one among a number of interests, though in this age a powerful one. Sometimes lobbying was resisted. British diplomats quite often rejected the demands of traders for more active support.[72] Often, however, especially where new claims were being staked out, there was no strong reason for not supporting local businessmen. In some cases, economic considerations were reinforced by other motives. For example, a main underlying motive for the British occupation of Egypt in 1882 was strategic, to safeguard the Canal route to India, as well as a desire to respond to the immediate disorder of the country. But there was undoubtedly 'strong support for military action in Egypt from British groups with economic interests – the Eastern shipping and trading companies and the British bondholders. Thus there was always an economic dimension to the Egyptian question.'[73] In other cases, lobbies were difficult to resist. The China lobby in the US – those concerned with the trade to the Far East – was a powerful influence in inducing the US to retain the Philippines after the war with Spain.[74] German firms trading to the Pacific were active in pressing Bismarck to pursue a forward policy in acquiring protectorates or colonies in that area; and though at first Bismarck resisted these pressures, he ultimately was prevailed upon to the extent of making successful claims to New Guinea and Samoa. British governments were pressed by British business groups interested in copra, sugar and other interests (as well as by the Australian and New Zealand governments) to make claims in the same area; and these pressures too eventually persuaded an originally unwilling British government to claim and secure Fiji, the Solomons, the Gilberts and other territories.

Besides organisations with a direct commercial interest, others existed whose aim was to promote the general cause of colonialism with their government and with public opinion generally. This development took place especially during the 1880s. A Colonial Association was formed in Germany in 1882. This was followed in the next year by the Society for German Colonisation: the Society and its economic committee 'took the line that existing colonies could be developed to provide important commercial and investment advantages; and if these possessions ultimately proved unsatisfactory or inadequate for German needs, then new territories should be acquired'.[75] During that decade, five separate bodies to promote colonisation were set up in Germany. Similarly, in Britain in 1884, the Primrose League was established by the Conservative party to promote the imperial cause. This was followed shortly afterwards by the

Imperial Federation League, associated mainly with the Liberals, designed to 'secure by federation the permanent unity of the empire'. These were followed by Chamberlain's Tariff Reform League which, since it wished to see the re-establishment of tariffs against rival nations, became in effect, like Chamberlain himself, dedicated to promoting the economic strength and cohesion of the British empire. Finally, in 1894 the Navy League was established in Britain (to be followed in 1898 by the German Flottenverein). In France, the Société de Géographie Commerciale was established, whose main function was to promote French commercial expansion. In addition, there were individual political parties, such as the National Liberal Party in Germany and the Chamberlain faction in Britain, which became ardent pressure-groups in favour of colonial expansion or consolidation.

Other sections of society – the lower-middle-class and working population as a whole – had comparatively little direct influence on governments. But the dominant groups were able, as in other ages, to win the support of other sectors of society in their own cause. They were able to do so in the traditional way, used by interested groups in other ages: by showing that their own interest was that of the state as a whole. They sought to show, for example, that the working people of the imperialist countries shared an interest in sheltered markets abroad because of the employment which they provided. So Joseph Chamberlain could argue in one of his speeches that 'if in any one of the places to which I have referred any change took place which deprived us of that control and influence of which I have been speaking, the first to suffer would be the working men of this country. Then indeed we should see a distress which should not be temporary but which would be chronic and we should find that England was entirely unable to support the enormous population which was now maintained by the aid of her foreign trade. If the working men of this country understand their own interests, they will never lend any countenance to the doctrines of those politicians who never lose an opportunity of pouring contempt and abuse upon the brave Englishmen who, even at this moment, in all parts of the world are carving out new dominions for Britain and are opening up markets for British commerce and laying out fresh fields for British labour.'[76] Even Gladstone, once unenthusiastic about imperial power and foreseeing the progressive independence of the colonies, suggested that 'the business of founding and of cherishing those colonies is one which had so distinctly been entrusted by Providence to the care of the people of this country that we should almost as soon think of renouncing the very name of Englishmen as of renouncing the very great duties imposed upon us with regard to the more distant but not less dear portions of this great British Empire'.[77] While working class organisations were often, in theory, anti-imperialist in sentiment, they rarely put this into effect by active opposition to colonial adventures abroad. European expansion in Africa, British intervention in Egypt and Burma, French action in Tunisia and Indo-China, aroused no angry denunciation among the labour movement in those two countries. Such opposition as there was came from middle-class radicals. Opposition to the French forward policy in Africa came from parliament and intellectuals, not from the workers; opposition in Britain to the Boer War came from Liberals in parliament and the press, not from the trades unions. Though without great enthusiasm for the new wave of imperialism, workers for the most part were sufficiently indoctrinated with the belief in the European mission as the vanguard of progress to feel little reason to dissent.

So the social structure of this age reflected the new character of the capitalist system. Reliance on borrowed money, whether for home industry or activities abroad, gave a new prominence and importance to the lenders of money, the individual rentier, investor or bondholder, and the bankers who could lend on behalf of their institutions. The manufacturers and traders too still enjoyed influence and could also be a force favouring expansion abroad and the winning of a dominant position in favourable markets (see p. 138). Because of their new importance, these forces were able to exercise a significant influence on governments. They were well represented in parliament, they could influence the press, they often had direct access to governments. They formed new organisations to represent their views and lobby the decision-makers. More important, they achieved, once more, a successful collectivisation of interests: so that their interests were conceived to be those of the nation as a whole and justified the huge cost and labour of maintaining an overseas empire. The rest of the population, including the industrial workers, were sufficiently under the influence of the prevailing beliefs to accept the leadership the newly dominant classes provided. So the state as a whole was brought under the influence of a new doctrine: that the expansion of European capital and enterprise – and so of European rule – to the remote parts of the globe served the interests not only of the capitalists but of the nations to which they belonged – and indeed of the world as a whole.

AUTOCRATS AND BUREAUCRATS (1914–50)

In the age that followed, the social structure of the dominant states changed again, and so transformed the attitude of governments to the international economic relationships in which they were engaged.

The most fundamental change was the dramatic increase in the power of governments, above all in the economic field. This was beginning, but only very slowly, before 1914. It was enormously intensified in the First World War, with the need of governments to assume total control of national economies for the prosecution of the war (see p. 36). It was maintained in the inter-war period when governments increasingly intervened in economic exchanges, to overcome imbalances in trade and payments in the 1920s, and to counteract depression in the 1930s. It was taken further than ever during the Second World War, when the requirements of total war required a mobilisation of each combatant state's total effort, involving direction of labour, capital, raw materials and production on a scale never seen before. And even after that war, the disruption created by the conflict and resulting shortages made necessary strict controls for a further decade. In one or two countries, such as the Soviet Union, the government took over the entire economy, in peace as much as in war. And in other states too, socialist parties, now increasingly powerful, demanded a greater degree of state control and, whether or not in a position to implement these policies themselves, influenced the thinking and conduct of governments everywhere.

One effect of the increasing role of governments was to give politicians a greater share in influencing economic policy, abroad as well as at home. The development of economic relationships, it came to be accepted, should not depend only on the blind forces of economic destiny, nor even on the individual decisions of businessmen and their customers. Statesmen could and should influence them by the decisions they took. Even in the main bastion of capitalism, the US, Roosevelt, within a few months of his inauguration, called for the reorganisation of industry and commerce under federal authority. Because politicians were concerned above all with the opinion and welfare of their own populations who had voted them to power, this change encouraged the trend towards autarchic economic policies. What mattered to statesmen was that the economic policies adopted should assure jobs for their people, that imports should not threaten the survival of domestic industries, that the maintenance of the gold standard should not create severe deflation and the destruction of jobs, that the principle of non-discrimination should not prevent bilateral arrangements to maintain production and exports. The needs of the international economy, the duty to maintain non-discrimination and the most favoured nation principle in trade, which had been important aims in the previous age, became increasingly marginal in relation to the short-term needs of national economies. As Roosevelt put it in his inaugural address in 1933: 'Our international trade relations, though vastly important, are in point of time and necessity secondary to the establishment of a sound national economy. I favour as a practical policy the putting of first things first. I shall spare no effort to restore world trade by international economic readjustments, but the emergency at home cannot wait on that accomplishment.'

It was the dictators who so widely came to power in this day (taking control of two-thirds of the countries of Europe) who most clearly manifested this trend. In acquiring a power that was virtually absolute, they secured full control of their national economies. And because the aim of dictators, even more than of democratic leaders, was to win and maintain popular support, they used their power over the economy to secure immediate and visible economic gains for their people. Since what their people most wanted was jobs, and since, on a superficial view, these could be created easily by blocking imports from abroad (that is, by destroying jobs elsewhere), they proceeded to insulate their own economies from those elsewhere. Their interest lay in the short-term performance of the national economy, not the long-term health of the international economy (on which it ultimately depended), and in arousing national sentiment for that end. They possessed both the power and the ambition to wield total control of their country's external economic relations: the volume of trade, direction of trade, use of foreign exchange, levels of inward and outward investment. So Stalin, Mussolini, Hitler, each in turn adopted their national plans, seeking economic salvation in self-sufficiency. And they were followed in time not only by the lesser dictators of eastern and southern Europe, but also by democratic leaders, equally concerned with immediate political survival. So the ambitions of autocrats and populist pressures everywhere destroyed the open international economy of the previous age.

But politicians were not the only group whose main concern was with the national economy. The rapid growth of governmental power brought an even greater dominance to another group, whose influence was more pervasive and more permanent. This was the bureaucracy, who advised, in some cases virtually controlled, the politicians. We have already seen (see p. 39) the huge growth in the numbers of civil servants in this period. More important, perhaps, was the growth in their influence and authority. This arose partly from the increasing complexity of government, especially in the economic field, which meant that the expertise of which the bureaucrats disposed was valued more highly than ever. It arose partly from the fragility of the political structure in many countries, with frequent changes of government, and even of political systems, leaving the bureaucracy as the only fairly stable and enduring element. But it arose above all from the increasing acceptance of the need for increased government intervention in many areas, conferring growing authority on those whose hands were closest to the levers of government power. With the rise of the bureaucrats went the rise in bureaucratic attitudes of mind: the sense that everything could be effectively controlled and that the mandarins were better able to foresee and judge what the economy required than was any other section of the population. This was particularly evident in the economic field where government intervention was most visible. And it was perhaps most particularly evident in international economic policy, where bureaucrats found it easiest and politically most acceptable to intervene: concerning the volume and type of imports, the direction of trade, the control of foreign exchange, and many other matters.

Typical of the powerful economic bureaucrats of this age in Britain were Sir Arthur Salter, who organised British and allied shipping during the First World War and occupied a senior post in the League before becoming an MP and minister in successive Conservative administrations; Lord Hankey, Secretary to the British Cabinet over many years; Sir John Anderson, a successful official in Africa, India and at home before becoming senior minister and eventually Chancellor; above all Maynard Keynes, a civil servant before becoming an adviser to governments. All of these were, in their day, powerful influences on economic policy, as no bureaucrat had been in earlier ages. These were the new elite. It is typical that two of them, Salter and Anderson, entered politics and so secured further influence for the bureaucratic minds by other means. In the US such figures as Moley, Tugwell, Berle and Johnson, advisers to the Roosevelt administration, wielded an equally important sway on economic policy. Central bankers were particularly powerful: Montague Norman, Governor of the Bank of England throughout the inter-war years, for example, wielded a huge influence on the conduct of international economic policy under a succession of governments. All these figures, like the politicians (and unlike the private traders and investors who dominated in the previous age), were essentially servants of the state, the employees of national governments, concerned with national objectives and subject to pressure from national interest-groups. If the policy they recommended threw millions of people abroad out of work, this was unfortunate but irrelevant: it was unemployment at home that they were employed to be concerned about. As Sir Arthur Salter, who had been able to see the process from both the bureaucratic and the political end, put it: 'Each official was the prisoner of his own national system, each item of which represented a protection to some home industry which was supported by those who had secured its adoption. He was responsible to ministers who were the prisoners of the groups who organised interests in their respective parliaments.'[78]

The power of the bureaucrats was, perhaps, greatest in the fully communist states such as the Soviet Union, and the East European client states which were associated with her just after the Second World War. Here the entire economy was run by bureaucrats of a kind, though the balance between the policy and view of party and bureaucracy was what finally counted (even party officials were essentially bureaucrats in mentality). In the dictatorships of West and Central Europe too, bureaucrats, with the growth and centralisation of state power, acquired increasing authority. Indeed, the dictators themselves can be seen in a sense as the arch-bureaucrats, able to manipulate and decree on a scale that the common-or-garden bureaucrat could never normally hope to emulate. But elsewhere too, in the 'democratic' states, the same trends, the extension of the power of government, the increasing disillusion with the free market as a satisfactory economic mechanism, the succession of crises – war, hesitant recovery, slump, war and its aftermath – brought about a consistent growth in the influence of government officials over economic events.

One of the effects of the growth of bureaucratic power was the gradual wresting of control from the bankers. Central banks and central bankers in many countries had previously been autonomous figures. Even though they controlled factors such as interest rates, and so indirectly investment, which were vital to the economy concerned, they had made their decisions largely independently of governments and their wishes. In some countries, as in Britain, they were largely controlled by private bankers. Now they were brought increasingly under government control. The change was visible in the inter-war decade: 'The 1920s were bankers' Europe. The 1930s saw the rise of government economic controllers. When Britain was forced off the gold standard in September 1931, laissez-faire in the international economy took a severe blow.'[79] The same change was visible at about the same time in the US: 'In the twenties the national monetary policy had been run to a great degree in New York by Benjamin Strong and the New York Federal Reserve Bank. Decisions basic to the nation's economic future were made not by government officials accountable to the people, but by bankers in Manhattan boardrooms. In 1933 ... this situation came to an end. The nation asserted its control over its monetary policy.'[80] In many countries, central banks were increasingly brought under the control, or at least the influence, of national finance ministries. In the US, under the Banking Act of 1935, the Federal Reserve Board was given stronger powers over the banking system and brought more directly under the control of the President who was given the power to appoint the board of govenors. Even in Britain, one of the last strongholds of the earlier system, the Bank of England was nationalised and brought under substantial government control in 1946.

The power of the private bankers was also reduced. In Britain, for example, the decline in the Bank of England's power brought also a decline in the power of the export-oriented merchant bankers who had directed it. In the US, bankers were widely detested and blamed for the disasters of the slump. Roosevelt saw himself as having won a momentous victory over the sinister financial circles which he believed had largely controlled the economy for a century before. 'The real proof of the matter,' he wrote to Colonel House, 'is, as you and I know, that a financial element in the largest centres has owned the government ever since the days of Andrew Jackson.'[81] And (though for a time he himself committed the folly of large scale gold-purchasing, and even made some concessions to the powerful silver lobby from the mountain states) he gradually asserted federal authority over the banking system and a more rational approach to monetary problems. As governments everywhere took more and more control of economic policy, including exchange rate and monetary policy, into their own hands, they reduced that previously exercised, both nationally and internationally, by bankers. In consequence, motives also changed: sound money and stable currencies, the primary concern of the bankers, increasingly gave way to the aim of securing full employment, the primary concern of the politicians. This affected international and domestic policy alike.

Against this growth in the power of bureaucrats, that of parliaments declined. There began during this period the growth in the power of the executive against that of the legislature which has proceeded implacably ever since. Governments were increasingly unwilling to submit the crucial decisions on economic policy which now fell into their hands to the unpredictable and untutored decisions of parliamentarians, who were even more subject than they were to political pressures, often irrational. Thus Roosevelt ensured that, under the Reciprocal Trade Agreements Act of 1933, the President was given the power to conclude commercial agreements without the approval of Congress (a proposal denounced by Senator Vandenberg as 'fascist in its philosophy, fascist in its objectives and palpably unconstitutional') and which was yet accepted by Congress. Elsewhere too, parliaments (even where they existed) were less and less regarded in the processes of international economic policy-making. Usually they merely heard and endorsed what their governments proposed to them. And since parliaments were at least as autarchically inclined as their governments, there was usually little reason for violent dissent.[82]

The influence of industry and 'business' too was probably less. In the eyes of many, the disasters of the depression discredited the businessmen who were held to have brought Western economies to disaster. Bureaucratic management and planning was now thought more efficient than the disconnected decisions of individual businessmen. So Senator Wagner, a supporter of the New Deal, declared 'I do not think we will ever have industry in order until we have a nationally planned economy';[83] and Senator La Follette ws an even more ardent advocate of planning. So were politicians of all parties in Europe; even within the Conservative party in Britain, for example, Harold Macmillan strongly advocated a rational planning of the economic machine. Thus parliaments, while they sometimes still represented the concerns and pressures of business groups, increasingly became concerned with a wider 'public interest', which was seen to require deliberate intervention by the government in the running of the economy and in controlling exchanges with other states.

Businessmen did not allow their voices to go unheard. But among industrial enterprises, it was increasingly the larger and more powerful that were able to make their views felt and most influenced policy. An example of the balance of influence within industry can be seen in Germany during the Nazi period. Hitler came to power on the votes of workers and small shopkeepers, pledged to curb the power of big business and to boost that of very small firms and producers in crafts, trade, agriculture, industry and culture. Centralised organisations representing these small producers were given the power to set prices and introduce regulations under the supervision of the government.

The Nazi party supported the strong-arm activities of small business-men, organised in the Combat League of Middle Class Trades-people, in instituting boycotts of big department stores and corporations. There was large-scale extortion of money from big business for the benefit of the party. With the increasing disruption of industry and the threat to employment which these activities brought, however, Hitler soon reversed this policy. He ordered a cessation of the harassment of department stores, and replaced the payments from industry by a fixed contribution from the Federation of German Industry and the German Employers Association. Increasingly, his government entered into an alliance with large-scale industry in Germany, including the large manufacturers of steel and armaments, in which each side collaborated with the other to pursue their respective purposes, abroad as well as at home.

Similarly in the US during the New Deal, Roosevelt, soon after coming to power, introduced his National Recovery Administration (NRA), compelling each industry to enter into codes of fair trading, covering collective bargaining, minimum wages, maximum hours, child labour and, at first, price-fixing. Here too, a kind of alliance was established. Big business at first welcomed the restraint on competi-tion which the new system provided, as well as the recovery of trade; and it was small businesses which increasingly rebelled. Big business also welcomed the administration's trade-creating measures, such as the Reciprocal Trade Agreements Act. But other New Deal measures, such as those to regulate the stock exchange, the communications industry, federal contracts, railway pensions, legislation on social insurance and housing, as well as the policy of deficit-financing, increasingly won the opposition of the business community, which organised against Roosevelt in such bodies as the American Liberty League. In this case, unlike in Germany, big business was not to be reconciled with the administration and eventually Roosevelt had to build an alternative coalition, based on labour, farmers and coloured voters, more sympathetic to managed trade, abroad as well as at home.

Whatever its attitude towards government, industry was now more and more organised to influence it. Lobbies of a highly organised kind emerged. Industrial and trade associations developed as never before and, in the difficult economic conditions of the day, were more and more anxious to make their influence felt. Sometimes, the desire to restrict, petition or share markets was a major motive for establishing associations.[84] In seeking to influence policy, these lobbies could operate both directly on governments and indirectly through parliaments. The development of democracy in many Western countries meant that governments were more responsive to such pressures than in earlier times. Politicians, concerned with their own re-election, brought pressure on governments for economic policies which would safeguard their constituents' interests, above all find them employment. Even Roosevelt was sometimes unwilling to defy strong organised pressures of this kind. 'Interest-group democracy had the tactical advantage of weakening opposition by incorporating potential opponents within the administration, but it also served to make the Roosevelt administration the prisoner of its own interest-groups. The President often shied away from decisions that might antagonise one or another of the elements in the coalition. Government sanction greatly enhanced the power of such groups as the Farm Bureau Federation and the Traders Association ... Roosevelt's predilection for balanced government often meant that the privileges granted by the New Deal were in precise proportion to the strength of the pressure groups which demanded them.'[85] The influence of such groups meant that governments were now highly susceptible to demands for protection from foreign competition. The health of the home economy, rather than of the worldwide economy, were what concerned them.

In most countries, governments consulted closely with the leaders of industry, sometimes themselves, with the development of oligopoly, a close-knit group. In the new age of bureaucratic planning, these were now sometimes willing to accept a considerable measure of government intervention. Even in the US, the cradle of free enterprise, businessmen were ready for a time, in the crisis of depression, to co-operate in the semi-corporatism of the NRA, and join in enforcing codes regulating their own activities, and even in production and price restraints. In West Europe, this new alliance between government and industry was even more highly developed: for example, in the compulsory cartels established in Germany and Japan in the 1930s, in the Van Zeeland 'new deal' in Belgium, the corporatist system of Italy and Portugal, and the Flandin economic decrees in France. Generally, industry accepted a degree of government regulation in return for restraints on competition.[86] This seemed a worthwhile deal.

It was above all over international economic policy that such groups demanded and secured action by governments. Hard hit by the depression and more influential than ever, they joined in calling for the state's assistance: in restraining imports, in assisting exports, in controlling the exchange rate, in organising bilateral and other governmental deals, and otherwise protecting them from the cold wind of an increasingly unwelcome free competition. In this way, the growing power of industrial organisations intensified the moves towards autarchy now everywhere adopted by governments.

Organised labour also became a more recognised influence on economic policy. They too used their influence in favour of protectionist policies. Not only in democratic Western states, but also in corporatist states, such as Italy, Japan and Germany, there was a new concern to pay at least lip-service to the aspirations of the trade union movement. In many countries, there were Labour parties linked in a close alliance with the unions, or other parties that claimed to represent the working population, which ensured that their viewpoint was expressed. Sometimes such parties for the first time formed governments or at least joined in them. In the US, organised labour helped to bring Roosevelt to power and he was consistently responsive to their views.[87] Such pressures made governments even more conscious of the special concerns of workers, especially about levels of employment and the protection of jobs. In international economic policy, it made governments more willing to abandon liberal trade policies and resort to protection and autarchy. Exchange controls, barter deals, restraints on imports, subsidies and all the other instruments devised by governments to distort the world economy in their favour benefited labour more than any other group.[88]

The most important change in this age, therefore, was the increasing power of governments, and so of those who determined government policy. Increasingly, this became the bureaucrats, who possessed the expertise which – because of the difficult economic circumstances and the increasing measure of government intervention this was held to demand – economic policy-making increasingly required. In theory, the bureaucrats were acting on behalf of the governmental masters of the time. But because they were both more knowledgable and more permanent than political leaders, their influence was probably more profound and more enduring. Politicians themselves were probably now (even in dictatorships) more conscious of and more concerned with popular feelings and desires. Both business and trade unions were more organised than in earlier times, and more skilled in making their views felt by governments. All these groups shared an interest in the doctrine of managed national economy. Against these increasingly potent nationalist groups, there were no significant international interests which could command attention and direct concern to the needs of the international economy. The interlocking nationalist groups were thus able to combine to pursue the only interest they shared in common: the maintenance of a reasonable level of economic activity at home, at whatever cost to economies abroad. So a whole series of separate national economies came into being, increasingly pursuing their own economic welfare, by their own endeavours, and with little regard for the wider international economy outside.

CORPORATIONS AND CONGRESSMEN (1950–80)

In the age that followed, there were new changes in the character of the dominant elites and their influence on the world economy.

Throughout the Western world, rich states were now more 'democratic' than ever before. In most rich countries, and some poor ones, parliamentary systems prevailed. At least in theory, there was greater opportunity for parliaments, parliamentary committees, political parties, employers, trades union and other elements in society to exercise an influence on government economic policy. In practice, the inexorable increase in executive power in all states, together with the close bonds existing between the administration and the majority in parliament in most, meant that governments had little to fear from parliamentary power and took little account of it in framing their policies. Still less need they take account of most other representative bodies. Though there was frequently a show of 'consultation' with such forces, in practice such procedures were used rather as a means by which governments could influence other groups than those groups could influence governments. As a result, on their general economic policies governments were rarely deflected from their chosen course by constitutional procedures of this kind.

More significant was direct representation by pressure groups to governments, designed to bring about changes of policy on specific issues. Pressure groups were now more organised than at any earlier time. They were often accorded a recognised place within the political system. The most important were national bodies representing employers and unions – congresses and confederations – with whom institutionalised consultation took place. But strong pressure was also often brought by employers and unions within individual industries. With the internationalisation of the economy, it was often on international economic policy that they were most concerned to exercise influence. Employers and employed alike in threatened industries were anxious at the effects of trade policy on production and employment; and they organised themselves into powerful lobbies to protect home industries against undue increases in imports: calling for quotas, anti-dumping duties, import surcharges, voluntary restraints and other types of safeguard action. In successful industries, the most powerful enterprises sought government assistance in winning access to markets abroad, in guaranteeing loans and investment, in resisting nationalisation.

The success of these lobbies varied. Farmers, in general, partly because of skilful organisation and persistent pressure, but mainly because of their large numbers (in most countries), were the most uniformly successful in protecting their position, even against the interests of consumers generally who were yet more numerous: as we have seen, in practice agriculture was the only area where the internationalisation of markets was never seriously attempted. A few other industries were successful in securing government action against imports, especially where employment was high and the technology old; as in the case of textiles, footwear, shipbuilding, steel and a few other industries. Against this, the high technology, high growth industries, especially in the most powerful countries, used their influence in favour of an integrated world economy in which they could compete on equal terms. And protectionism was counteracted, more significantly, by the commitment of the prevailing doctrine to liberalisation which most powerful governments had endorsed.

Thus, the main influence on policy was that of governments exercising a closer control of national economies than ever before. The performance of national economies was now widely believed to depend not on the performance of individuals or even of companies, but on the performance of governments in directing their national economies. In this belief, governments intervened to control rates of interest and the level of credit, and so of business activity generally; the size of the budget surplus or deficit; trade and tariff policy; regional policy; sometimes even the level of prices and incomes, and the direction of investment. These techniques, it was believed, made it possible for governments to maintain their economies in something like a stable equilibrium: simultaneously achieving steady growth, high employment and a reasonable balance of international payments. And the most successful economies – those of Japan, West Germany, Switzerland and a few 'newly industrialising countries' – did succeed for a time in combining these objectives to an extent never seen before. But though many of the concerns of governments were domestic – especially levels of employment, the rate of economic growth and the control of inflation – few now believed their economies could be totally insulated. The internationalisation of the world economy had gone too far. Not only must they, as before, worry about the balance of trade and payments, the rate of exchange, levels of inward and outward investment, and so on. What really mattered to the health of their economies was the level of world activity. And this depended on decisions elsewhere – about rates of growth in other countries, US interest rates or IMF credit policy. So individual governments found that, in seeking to achieve their ends, both domestic and external, they were increasingly confronted with international economic forces, over which they had little influence, let alone control.

For the growth in the power of governments over their economies was constrained by the growing internationalisation of all economic life. The growth in governmental power which occurred was matched by an even greater increase in the power of international economic forces. Among these were the large corporations operating in a large number of different countries. Though in many industries there remained many small firms, sometimes extremely successful, more typical was the rise, in most major industries, of very large firms, whose employees were numbered in tens or even hundreds of thousands, and who controlled an increasingly large share of the market within each industry, not only within their own country, but in many others as well. A new situation of worldwide oligopoly became the natural condition in many industries: for example in computers, chemicals, oil, pharmaceuticals, aerospace, automobiles, and many others. The decisions of firms such as IBM, General Motors, Exxon, Alcan, ITT, and others, could have a significant impact, not only on the economies of their own countries, but also on those of many others. With or without overt collusion, they were able to share out markets between them and to avoid excessive disruption through unhelpful pricing policies. Thus the number of centres of significant decision-making became far smaller than ever before. Power in the international economy was now concentrated as in no earlier period.

These great corporations were able to exercise three types of influence. Firstly, they exercised a significant *direct* impact on the world economy: by their own autonomous decisions on investment; on the distribution of manufacture and sales among their own subsidiaries; on the procurement of components and raw materials; on the import and export of production to and from particular areas in which they operated. Secondly, the companies were able, because of their economic importance, to exert influence on governments in their own countries, an influence which they could use to further their own interests. So in the US, for example, such companies established large offices in Washington, whose purpose it was to influence legislatures, administration and individual departments of state to take those actions that would best promote their interests (often identified as the 'national interest').[89] So in Japan, similarly, large Japanese corporations acted in close co-operation with government agencies such as MITI, to the mutual benefit of both.[90] There was a tacit assumption that what benefited these major undertakings in their operations abroad benefited the state as well: that what was good, for example, for General Motors (or Exxon, Lockhead or IBM) was also good for the US.[91] As Henry Ford put it: 'there is a widespread misconception that it is somehow wrong for corporations ... to attempt to influence legislation affecting their interests. Nothing could be further from the truth ... Things for which business may fight in self-interest may also be very much in the national interest.' While at home the relationship between government and administration could sometimes be antagonistic, abroad a common interest was usually shared. A growth in sales for the transnational would mean greater exports for the home country; an increase in investment abroad might ultimately improve the balance of payments at home. One of the tasks of a country's diplomacy and foreign policy was increasingly to promote the interests of its main companies abroad.

Thirdly, there was the influence that such giant organisations acquired within the economies of the third world states where they operated. Their decisions concerning investment, re-investment, marketing, employment policies and other questions could have a crucial effect; and their capacity to switch production, trade, profits and prices between the different states in which they manufactured or traded, or merely to switch large volumes of funds, gave them a power with which it was increasingly difficult for individual governments to contend. Yet these decisions could be vital to the individual countries in which they operated.[92] Because the companies undertook worldwide operations, whose ends were quite independent of those of each individual economy, they might be willing to shut down production in one state, shift sales from one subsidiary to another, and make decisions on imports and exports, which took little account of the interests of each individual country.[93]

This power was not only economic, but could be political as well. This was shown, for example, in the role of the United Fruit Company in helping to secure intervention against the Arbenz government in

Guatemala in 1954; in the role of the Belgian firm, Union Miniere, in helping to bring about the secession of Katanga in the Congo in 1960; in the support given by Safrap, the French oil company, to the decessionist regime in Biafra during the Nigerian Civil War in 1969–70; in the activities of Lonrho in helping to secure the restoration of Numeiri in Sudan in 1971 and other political activities in Africa; in the role of ITT in securing the overthrow of Allende in Chile; and in many other cases. Interventions of this kind (unlike the similar clandestine operations of governments) were dictated not by political preferences but by economic interests. The effect was to bring power or keep in power regimes that would conform with the interests of these large corporations. Their interest was the prosperity of world commerce; and they were increasingly able to act independently to achieve it.

At least as important was the development of transnational banking. In the previous era, with the exception of a small number of specialised institutions, most banks had operated mainly within a single state. Now this changed dramatically. The growth of the Euro-dollar and Euro-bond markets gave an entirely new scope to international banking. Especially in the 1960s and 1970s, there was a sudden proliferation of overseas banks, with headquarters in the US or Europe but operating throughout the world. Money could now be transmitted across international boundaries more easily than in any earlier time. The value of such transactions multiplied many times. Even more than the transnational manufacturing companies, therefore, these banks acquired huge power. While the Euromarkets undoubtedly performed an important economic function, in making possible a far greater international mobility of capital (and particularly in recycling the huge surpluses of oil-producing states), they also accorded an unprecedented economic power to the major international banks involved, predominantly US banks. These were enabled to insulate themselves to a considerable extent from their home economies, and indeed from any individual economy, and to switch funds to where the highest returns could be secured. But by their willingness to lend (or stop lending), and in particular their willingness to reschedule debts, they could determine the fate of many small economies. This system enabled many poor countries (about 50 per cent of their funds were lent to developing countries) to secure credit when in serious balance of payments difficulties; but in exchange it made them crucially dependent on the goodwill of the institutions that provided the funds. Just as, in the late nineteenth century, large numbers of small and poor states mortgaged themselves to the governments of rich states, now small and poor states, shattered by the rise in oil and other prices, were mortgaged to the large private banks, on which they became increasingly dependent.

No other international economic forces acquired comparable power. Trades unions, for example, though they began to be organised, like other factors of production, on an international basis, acquired little effective international solidarity across national boundaries. The trades union movements of different countries joined in federations that were supposed to promote co-operation. But they were divided, for political or religious reasons, between three separate federations (Communist, non-Communist and Catholic), a division that seriously reduced their influence. In practice, in any case, the federations had no say over the essential decisions. More significant in their effect were the trade secretariats that were set up to link the workers in *individual* industries. Of these, the largest and best organised was the International Metal-Workers' Federation. This established a 'programme of action' on multinational companies (1977). But, in practice, it rarely negotiated as a body with such companies.[94] And even these secretariats exercised little influence on their members, and rarely organised effective action across frontiers. While, therefore, organised labour was powerful within states, internationally it remained weak. International strikes, organised by workers in different countries on behalf of those elsewhere, or of the group as a whole, though occurring occasionally – for example, among seamen and dockers – were uncommon and usually unsuccessful. International labour organisations were rarely consulted in the major decision-making bodies on economic matters, such as the UN agencies, the economic summits among Western states, or in the North–South dialogue. And there was little serious effort among trades unions or their members to protect their interests by organisation and action at the international level.

Employers were even more poorly organised at the international level. There existed an International Chamber of Commerce. There were international federations of employers in most major industries. And there were particular organisations for particular fora, such as the employers' group operating within the International Labour Organisation (ILO) and a similar body representing employers in the EEC. But these were little regarded, and the chief influence of companies was exerted by individual corporations rather than by federations of this type.

In this new transnational economy, therefore, governments acting individually were increasingly powerless. Among private groups neither international labour employers' organisations were able to exercise much influence. Only the great transnational corporations and banks appeared effective forces. Effective countervailing power should have been wielded by another transnational force, that of the international organisations.

The power of these organisations, however, was generally weak. Even over governments, their power was limited. They were, especially at the beginning of the period, heavily under the influence of the major developed states, which, following liberal policies, had least interest in imposing effective international authority. Such countries, despite endemic and acute balance of payments problems, usually avoided becoming dependent on the IMF for help. It was almost exclusively poor countries which had to rely, for shorter or longer periods, on the Fund, which acquired at least a short-term influence over their policies that was often unwelcome but usually difficult to withstand. The World Bank, on which an even larger number of poor governments relied for investment funds (of which it became by far the largest source), was also able to exercise some influence over such countries, at least on development strategies. GATT was able, through its negotiating machinery, to influence some commercial policies; but it was based on principles which mainly benefited the more developed states. UNCTAD, where poor countries had more power, had minimal authority. The influence of these international bodies on private economic forces was insignificant. The Euro-dollar market and the activities of the international banks generally were unregulated. Attempts were made to establish guidelines to govern the conduct of the 'multinational' corporations; and a UN Commission on Transnational Corporations was established to examine their activities. But these were largely toothless. No international institutions were created that had the capacity to control the activities of private forces within the world economy. Even regional organisations – of which the EEC was by far the strongest – made little attempt to control the companies.

Within international organisations, however, new interest-groups emerged to promote the interests of particular types of state. For the first time, there existed associations of *governments* designed to promote the economic interests of their members. The largest was the Group of 77 (whose membership grew to about 125), the alliance of developing countries which emerged from the mid-1960s to promote the interests of those countries in international fora. Though standards of living and interests among its members varied widely, it was able to maintain a remarkable degree of cohesion and so maximised the bargaining power available to poor and weak states. Other *ad hoc* groups were formed for particular purposes – among the least developed (the 31 poorest of all), the most seriously affected (those especially affected by oil price rises), the 'landlocked and geographically disadvantaged' – but these did not significantly weaken the unity of the Group of 77 on the main questions arising between rich and poor states. Nonetheless, however united, the poor states were unable to bring about any significant change in the prevailing international system. For the wealthier states likewise organised themselves, in a variety of ways, to promote their own interests. From 1945 on, they had secured for themselves a privileged position in many of the main institutions: not only in the World Bank and the IMF, through the special voting arrangements laid down which based votes on economic strength, but also in other specialised agencies through special representation for the 'chief industrial states' (in ILO), states 'of chief importance' in aviation (in the International Civil Aviation Organisation), principal ship-owning and ship-using states (in the International Maritime Organisation), and so on. *Ad hoc* groups were established for particular purposes such as the Group of Ten, and afterwards the Group of Five within the IMF. And later there were exclusive economic 'summits' among the six or seven most advanced states of all, whose decisions were far more important for the future of the international economy than those of any of the wider institutions.

More significant in securing a shift in economic power was the creation of associations of states producing particular commodities to promote their interests: above all, the creation of OPEC, the organisation linking some of the main oil-producing states. By its influence on pricing and production policy, OPEC was able to maximise the strength of the producing countries in relation to the oil companies which produced and marketed their oil (though far more important was the change in economic realities, that is, the growing demand for oil in Western countries and the decline in their own production). In this way, the organisation transformed the world economy. It brought about a direct transfer of resources from industrialised to oil-producing countries. But, in doing so, it created severe balance of payments problems and consequent recession for many importing states, both rich and poor. And it raised price levels and the rate of inflation generally in all parts of the world. The effect was therefore only to benefit a small number of previously poor states, and to make others far worse off than before. But the first oil-price rise in 1973 had, for poor countries, considerable symbolic importance: for it represented the first occasion on which the economic power of richer states had been challenged by developing countries. In this respect, it was seen by all, rich and poor alike, as a significant precedent for the future. A new type of interest-group had been established; and a new way found to promote the interests of poor states.

In the world economy that emerged after 1950, therefore, a new set of dominant actors emerged. The most important of these were the huge new industrial and banking organisations, which increasingly operated on an international rather than a national basis. These began to acquire an independent economic power that it was increasingly difficult for individual governments, within either their home states or the host states, to master effectively. Their control of investment, production, trade, prices and sales enabled them to switch transactions from one economy to another to secure the maximum economic advantage for themselves; and, as a result, their total share of world sales and world investment increased inexorably. International banks, acquiring vast new resources (especially because of the continuing US trade dificits and the surpluses of the oil-producing countries), secured for themselves an economic power which increased all the time. The goals these organisations shared – i.e. an open, free-trading world economy, with the minimum of constraints on their own activities, whether from host country governments or their own governments at home, and the maximum freedom for them to switch investment and trade to maximise their own profits – became in time the goals of their own governments and part and parcel of the economic thinking of the day. Governments and companies alike in richer states shared an interest in the free flow of trade and investment, in the maximisation of market forces and the minimum of control by public authorities, national or international. Though many new international economic organisations appeared, their power remained weak. A wholly new type of international economy had developed, with a new balance of forces among those who exercised economic power, leading to new economic doctrines and a new set of policies by governments.

3 Motives

A society is characterised partly by the motivations that animate its members. Whether they are concerned with competition or co-operation, financial advantage or spiritual satisfaction, success or salvation, will determine the whole character of social existence.

It is partly society itself which instils the characteristic motivations. To a limited extent, motives may be *deliberately* instilled by governing authorities seeking to indoctrinate their subjects, for example into more socially co-operative attitudes, or more heroic and warlike sentiments; or seeking to create a 'new man' according to their own conceptions of the ideal society and the ideal citizen. Far more often, however, they result from the socialisation process within society, to which all members are subjected: social pressures exerted from a very early age, the customs, traditions and expectations of society generally. These, together, teach people how to feel and what to want, teach them to acquire particular conceptions of success, a particular set of ends and desires that influence behaviour. So one society may teach people to seek high incomes and large cars, another social respect and many sons, another success in war and an early death, another dignified labour and spiritual satisfaction.

Within international society, the motives that matter are those of the nations which are the society's members. We have noted elsewhere how widely the motives of states have varied in different societies or ages of international history; and we saw how changes in the motives led to changes in the nature of international society generally.[1] So, for example, the dynastic motives governing the rulers of states in the late Middle Ages created a particular type of relationship among states and so a particular type of society. When they were replaced by the religious motivations of the following period – between 1559 and 1648 – a different type of international society again came into being, characterised by a different type of behaviour among states. When these in turn gave way to different aspirations and ambitions, first in the age of sovereignty to 1789 then in the age of nationalism to 1914,

114

new types of international system again, with their own social structure and relationships, emerged. So, in international society too, the changing demands and desires of the members of society – in this case the states themselves – are reflected in a significant change in the entire character of the society.

Economic motivations play their own part in determining the character of a particular society. A domestic society where the profit-motive is the prime incentive, where the universal desire is to get rich quick, at the expense of others if necessary, is a wholly different society from one where the governing economic motive is self-sufficiency, or work-satisfaction, or co-operation in a common task. So too among societies of states: an international society where the main goal of states is to conquer trade abroad is quite different from one where their goal is self-reliance. As new conceptions arise among states of their external economic aims, new types of economic relationship, and so new types of economic society, emerge.

One of the principal distinctions, in the economic as in the political field, is how far states conceive of their economic relations in coercive or in co-operative terms. At certain periods, states have felt it normal that they should acquire economic rights elsewhere – say trading or investment rights – by the exercise of power against other states, even by acts of war. So, in the late Middle Ages, states such as Venice and Pisa sought to acquire trading rights around the seas they bordered by warlike actions, through which other states were compelled to trade with them on terms advantageous to themselves; and in the nineteenth century European powers regarded it as normal (for example in China, south-east Asia and parts of Africa) to secure for themselves by force or threat of force trading rights, even to acquire whole areas, as colonies or leased territories, where they could trade on terms favourable to themselves. In other societies, the assumption has been that nations should negotiate together on such questions to maximise their mutual benefit: so today, for example, though war remains relatively frequent, it is not made from economic motives and trading rights are not acquired by force. Yet economic aims are as important as ever. So richer states today may seek to liberalise opportunities for trade and investment everywhere; while poorer states may seek a more protective system, with greater authority for international organisations over economic affairs.

When discussing motivations in this context we are concerned with two kinds of motives: those of governments, and those of citizens and commercial organisations under their jurisdiction. In many cases the motives coincide. Because the successful commercial operations of individual citizens and enterprises to some extent benefit the whole nation, the aim of the private citizen or firm – to acquire a market abroad, to find new investment opportunities or new sources of raw materials – also becomes the aim of the state. Because increased influence for the state in a particular area may mean increased commercial opportunities for companies, the latter share an interest in the state's expansion of influence. Yet motives are not identical. The government will have aims of its own which are independent of those of its citizens. For example, it may wish to raise revenue; and do so at the cost of its companies trading abroad. It may wish, on foreign policy grounds, to promote good relations with one country, or to damage the interests of another; and will modify economic relations with each accordingly – offering aid, concessional trade terms to one, refusing most-favoured-nation treatment to another, even to the disadvantage of its own citizens. Finally, the government will be concerned with the entire framework of international relationships in which it operates, in a way that private interests will not, and in a way that may even conflict with the wishes of some of those private interests: governments of developed countries today, for example, may wish, for the sake of North–South relations, to make concessions to poor countries – say over the sea-bed or over commodity agreements – which bring few benefits, and even positive disadvantages, to their own population.

In the last chapter, in considering the pressures brought to bear on governments, we were concerned mainly with the interests of individual groups and organisations in relation to foreign states. Here, we are concerned mainly with the motives of the state as a whole. The motives of states will take account of those of private individuals and organisations, and will, indeed, normally reflect them. But because states have interests and purposes of their own, their motivations contain other elements too. And the particular form which economic relations take in individual ages and societies will depend on the motivations acquired by states as a whole in each of those periods and societies.

THE BALANCE OF TREASURE (1300–1600)

During the later Middle Ages, when the monarchs themselves largely controlled policy, the primary economic objectives of states were those of interest to the rulers themselves.

One of the main concerns of rulers in controlling foreign economic relations was the balance of treasure: to ensure that more gold and silver entered the country than left it. Every effort was made by rulers to conserve what bullion they already had. One of the complaints widely made against the Italian merchants who spread across Europe was that they took gold out of the country, and brought in exchange only useless fripperies (such as silk, spices and oriental finery). And one of the main reasons behind the sumptuary laws so widely enforced was to prevent the wasteful expense of precious bullion on useless adornment. Many prohibited any export of gold and silver.[2] Merchants were required to bring back bullion to the full value of the goods they had sold. Richard II laid it down that merchants of the wool staple should bring to the Mint an ounce of gold for every sack of wool which they sold abroad. And later, when the English kings established a mint at Calais, they forced the merchants of the Staple to sell a proportion of the coins they acquired from sales abroad to the Mint in return for English nobles for the same reason. Similarly, they prohibited the sale of wool on credit since this deprived the Mint of gold. Foreign merchants were attracted partly to win their gold: it was 'to replenish the realm with money and plate of gold and silver' that the English home staple was established.[3] Even these measures were not always enough to satisfy the rulers in their demands to safeguard their stocks of gold: Edward II turned to the alchemists to replenish his supply, while Louis XI searched for new sources of gold in the remotest parts of Africa.

But the rulers had another motive that was partly conflicting: the desire to secure supplies for their subjects at reasonable prices. This involved welcoming foreign merchants even though they took out treasure. And it meant that food supplies must be hoarded at home though they could earn precious metals abroad. In this age, unlike almost all others, imports were generally preferred to exports.[4] The export of grain and other food was frequently prohibited. Conversely, special facilities were offered to foreign merchants bringing needed imports. These desired imports were not only strategic goods, such as so-called Baltic products (timber, hemp, pitch and so on), but also essentials required for the people's livelihood, such as food and textiles.

Of course, any of these aims might have to be modified for the sake of foreign policy goals. Where conflicts developed with particular states, for example, economic measures might be taken against them, even if they damaged the interests of domestic producers, traders or consumers. Bans were imposed on exports of particular goods to particular countries, goods of foreign merchants were confiscated, their ships were seized or sunk, even though from a strictly economic viewpoint those measures did as much harm to the ruler's own country as to his enemies. Conversely, the need to conciliate another power, or to win an ally, might cause economic concessions to be made to another state. So the trade of England with Flanders, or of France with Italy, reflected the ups and downs of their political relations. The English kings varied the treatment of foreign merchants, Lombards or Hansards, partly according to the state of their relations with the home country. And they even decided the location of the wool staple partly on diplomatic grounds.[5]

But each of these contradictory aims had to be balanced with another that conflicted with both. This was the ruler's desire for revenue. Traditional sources of revenue were declining (see p. 5) and a new tax base was required. Some revenues could be got from the sale of offices, titles, tolls, charters and markets, but not enough. Thus an obvious way to raise money was to tax the trade from which so many of their subjects profited. So, even though this could reduce the inflow of treasure by making exports dearer, or reduce provision by deterring imports, both imports and exports were widely taxed. So the English kings for 200 years won large revenues by taxing the country's main export, wool. Other kings, such as the French, relied more on taxes on imports, especially those regarded as luxuries, such as wines, silks, spices, beverages and other non-essentials. This concern for revenues, over and above the concern for gold reserves, caused kings to be increasingly concerned with questions of foreign trade.[6] And the acquisition of new markets abroad, or the establishment of fairs or staples at home, became an interest of the rulers as much as of the traders.

The rulers had another important motive in their economic policy, their concern to protect their strategic interests, especially their supplies of essential materials: the so-called policy of power (see p. 6). This led them to prohibit trade that could weaken the kingdom. For example, the export of horses, at this time an important instrument of war, was widely prohibited. The emigration of skilled artisans was forbidden. The import of strategic materials – pitch, timber, hemp, cordage, and others – was encouraged and facilitated, while their export was prohibited. Saltpetre production (from the excrement of men, horses and doves) was encouraged and supported, as the basis for the manufacture of gunpowder. The export of copper was prohibited:

as by Henry VIII in England on the grounds that 'all other realms and countries be full of artilleries and munitions and this realm is likely to lack'.[7] The export of strategic materials was forbidden and trade secrets protected by edict: as by Lucca towards the end of the fourteenth century and by Florence in a series of measures. Sometimes only native sailors were to be used in native ships, to ensure a good supply of seafarers in times of war, and ships were to be built in home shipyards: such regulations were introduced by Aragon in the thirteenth century, by England in the fourteenth, by the Hansards in the fifteenth.[8] Thus, in innumerable ways, the normal pattern of trade was distorted by the arbitrary acts of the rulers, in order to promote the power of their realms.

Another aim of rulers that emerged at this time was to make their own states more self-sufficient, especially in manufacture. 'Both the Spanish monarchs and the Italian princes cherished the conviction that the establishment within their states of all kinds of manufactures greatly added to their power and prestige. Such was the dawn of mercantilist aspirations: in every case there were aspirations to autarky, which naturally led to protectionist measures.'[9] This 'state-building' motive was, as this quotation suggests, more typical of the age to follow, but already at this time the desire had begun to make itself felt. Indeed, it was even easier in this age of autocratic regulation than later to impose measures of this sort. This could be done by immediate edict: and it took the form not of attempts to restrain particular types of imports by quotas, tariffs or other restrictions, as in most subsequent ages, but by simple abolition of such imports.[10] Such bans were especially imposed on luxury goods. These were of no value in maintaining the standard of living of the masses, yet could drain from the country precious bullion. Thus the import of silk from abroad was often prohibited (in England in 1463 and 1484, in Genoa and Milan at about the same time, and in France several times in the fifteenth and sixteenth centuries). For the same reason, acts were introduced in England in the latter half of the fifteenth century, prohibiting the import of tennis balls, dice, lace, caps, chafing dishes, painted images, holy water stoups and sacring bells.[11]

Finally, governments began to be concerned with purely protective purposes: to defend local industries. Town governments, in which producers often held a dominant place, were especially active in restricting imports which represented unwelcome foreign competition. In many towns in the fifteenth century, the import of cloth or clothes from neighbouring towns was forbidden.[12] During the early fourteenth century, Pisa banned first the importation of semi-finished woollen goods and later of all foreign woollen cloth. In Flanders, the import of woollen cloth was prohibited from time to time to protect the native industry. In the fifteenth century, these prohibitions became much more common. Increasingly, as local producers became able to satisfy local needs, rulers and cities became governed by the desire to keep goods out rather than bring them in to satisfy their people's needs.

So, with shifts in the balance of influence in different societies, the balance of motivations began to change.

THE BALANCE OF TRADE (1600–1750)

In the age of state-building that emerged in the early seventeenth century, a new type of international society emerged, in which the interests of states were conceived in a new way. The essential difference was that there was now a much more self-conscious concern with the interests of the *state*, as opposed to those of the rulers themselves, whose interests had earlier been usually the decisive factor.

This change derived in part directly from the growth of state power and the national sentiments that went with this. All men, but especially rulers and their ministers, now came to identify their own interests with those of the state. (Louis XIV, in identifying his state with himself, only articulated more openly what other rulers felt.) The main motive of the ruler was therefore now to increase the power and prosperity of his own state.

Some of the motives of the previous age now counted for less. The so-called policy of plenty played a smaller part, if only because it was less needed: there was less risk of famine at home, less need, therefore, to welcome and favour imports and the foreign merchants who brought them. This was demonstrated in the way the Hansards, for example, so favoured by kings, aristocracy and ordinary people in England, Norway and Flanders in the preceding rea, were now sent away: they were ejected from London in 1598 at the moment our age began, and had lost most of their privileges there 40 years earlier. If special measures were required at all to help the consumer in this age, they were found rather in preventing native goods from being exported than in welcoming imports. The English government continued to ban grain exports, at intervals, for this reason. Even the trading city of Hamburg did not permit the free export of corn until 1748. And until the end of this period most governments placed some restraint on food exports to assure supplies at home. But, in general, apart from this declining restriction, the needs of provision now played little part in the considerations of governments.

Governments also had less need to weigh the needs of revenue against those of state-building. This was not because their needs for revenue were less. On the contrary, they were greater. But they had now far larger alternative sources of domestic revenue. They were also more conscious than their predecessors of the implications of taxes for alternative economic ends.[13] They were thus willing to forgo revenue from duties on exports for the sake of assisting the export trade and would even spend money to provide bounties for exports. They were conversely more willing to tax imports, so combining the raising of revenue with support for local industry. Almost everywhere the burden of taxation was shifted from exports to imports.

The main concern of all states was now the 'glory' of which Louis XIV spoke so incessantly. Other states differed not in that aim but only in their capacity to achieve it. The objective was still sought partly through the policy of power in the crudest and most military sense. Every government sought to reduce its dependence on foreign sources of strategic goods and to build up domestic supplies. In England, at a number of different times, the export of saltpetre, copper, timber and other materials was forbidden: under the Statute of Monopolies of 1622–4, the production of saltpetre and gunpowder was exempted from the general prohibition of monopoly. And one of the reasons for the special interest of England and the United Provinces in the colonisation of New England was that it was hoped it might become an alternative source of supply for naval supplies, timber, tar and other essential goods to replace those from the Baltic which were now increasingly threatened, above all by the power of the Danes and the Swedes.

A wider aim was to win *trade* generally. If necessary, wars were fought for that purpose (in this as in almost no other age of history, national wars were sometimes fought mainly for commercial motives.) Thus one of the main aims of the French in their war against the Dutch in 1672–8 was to damage their commercial pre-eminence and to secure some of their assets for France: Colbert explicitly held out the latter prize to his master. Conversely, the Dutch, after their surpising success in that war, demanded the abolition of the tariffs raised against them by Colbert in 1664 and 1667; while in 1697, after the Nine Years War, they extracted a new commercial treaty with the French which again included a return to the old tariff of 1664. Other peace terms provide evidence of the importance of this motivation. At the end of the War of Spanish Succession, the English demanded and secured the conclusion of a Treaty of Commerce and a reduction of French tariffs (subsequently turned down by the English parliament because the reductions did not cover English woollens, still the major English export). In the same treaty, England obtained for herself the valuable asiento (which France had previously secured from Spain); that is, the contract to trade slaves to South America and the right to send an annual trading voyage to that area. On the same occasion, United Provinces and England each obtained, as part of the peace terms, commercial treaties with metropolitan Spain. Finally, governments sought and won in such settlements the transfer of colonies, also essentially for economic reasons: as, for example, in the struggle between England and France for Newfoundland and its fishing potential, for Hudson Bay and its fur trade, for the Caribbean islands with their sugar plantations, for West Africa and the slaving trade, for the trading posts of India and the East Indies. Everywhere, war was at this time widely used as a means for winning trade (see p. 167). More than in any other age, one of the main spoils of war was commercial rights: the surest possible sign of the importance of commercial objectives among the motives of states.

To win trade for one's own nation was not enough, however. In an age when other states were seen essentially as rivals, an equally important motive was to *damage* the commerce of neighbours. Jealousy was a widespread and openly avowed motive among states in this day. It was felt, above all, against the Dutch, whose successes were too much for their neighbours to bear. Pepys records how he was told by the King's brewer that all the court were 'mad for a Dutch War', and how one of the biggest English merchants had said that 'the trade of the world is too little for us two, therefore one must down'.[14] Colbert declared the Dutch to be 'mortal enemies' and ceaselessly indicated his satisfaction at any French action that did them harm. During the war against the Dutch of 1672, he dreamed rosy dreams of a Holland incorporated into the monarchy of Louis XIV so that its trade and business would gradually be transferred into the hands of the French.[15] William Beckford, an English merchant trading to the West Indies, was equally determined to do down the French, declaring that 'our trade will improve with the extinction of theirs'. The desire to do harm to the interests of others was thus an important influence on policy. So in the seventeenth century, France and the United Provinces altogether banned the import to each of the products of the other, regardless of the damage this did to themselves, as a means of spiting their enemy. And in the eighteenth century, England forbade the import of French colonial products even in peace-time, damaging herself, by cutting off imports for which there was demand, as much as she damaged France.

Thus trade was seen everywhere as a weapon of the state. A success in commerce was seen as an accretion of national power. The Dutch, according to Colbert, believed 'that if they had the mastery of trade, their powers will continually wax on land and sea and will make them so mighty that they will be able to set up as arbiters of peace and war in Europe and set terms at their pleasure to the justice and all the plans of princes'.[16] In the same way Shaftesbury declared that 'it is Trade and Commerce alone that draweth store of wealth along with it and Potency at sea by shipping, which is not otherwise to be had'.[17] The general view was not so much the crude one that economic success was needed to buy power, nor that power was needed to conquer economic assets, but that the two were somehow closely related: an increase in one was likely to be furthered by an increase in the other. As Josiah Child put it, 'Foreign trade produces riches, riches power, power preserves our trade and religion'[18]; or, in the words of Lord Boling-broke: 'By trade and commerce we grow a rich and powerful nation and by their decay we are growing poor and impotent. As trade and commerce enrich, so they fortify our country.'[19] And this view led to Colbert's famous dictum that 'trade is the source of finance, and finance is the vital sinew of war'.[20]

But while a major aim was to win trade, perhaps the most important single aim was to secure a favourable *balance of trade*. The goal of nations was the aim of the salesman; to win and develop trade and make a profit. The need of a nation ultimately to secure an overall balance was an economic necessity felt in every age. The peculiarity now was threefold. Firstly, there was little acceptance that a legitimate object would be a balance over the *long term*: that is might be alright for a state to incur a deficit for a year or two so long as it restored the position in the future. The aim was to be in balance all the time. Secondly, the aim was not a mere balance but a surplus, so that more and more treasure could be brought in. Thirdly, even more oddly, the aim was not merely to win an overall balance but, as we have seen, a balance in each individual trade. Thus Colbert resented and chided the deficit in the trade of Marseilles with the Levant – without considering whether it might be made up for by the surpluses won at other ports (or even by the Marseilles trade with other areas). So too the Commissioners of Trade and Plantation in England, reporting on the state of the national economy in 1701–2, listed the deficits in trade with Sweden, the Baltic, Denmark, the East Indies and France, and mourned each of them equally.[21] The trade with each country was seen as a separate 'bargain' and the object was to get the better in all of them.[22]

This, the most widely held economic motive, must by its very nature lead to conflict. The aim of all nations to increase their exports and restrict their imports was mutually contradictory, in a way that was not always perceived. Every nation wished to attain self-sufficiency for itself, but to continue to enjoy a surplus with others. There was no willingness to recognise that other nations might need to export in order to import, and that actions that reduced their trade therefore might also reduce one's own (Josiah Child was almost the only writer in this age to acknowledge this point): the conception was always of cut-throat competition among all states to acquire a larger share in the limited total quantity of trade available.

One effect of this aim to maintain a continuing surplus, and the bigger the better, was a desire to *restrict consumption* at home. The consumption of foreign goods, especially luxuries, was harmful to the economic welfare of the nation. So Locke, for example, declared: 'We have seen how Riches and Money are got, kept or lost in any Country; and that is by consuming less of Foreign Commodities than what by Commodities or Labour is paid for'.[23] And Mun, similarly, warned that, 'if England were to consume more than it earned it will fare in England in short time as it doth with a man of great yearly living, that spendeth more yearly than his own revenue and spendeth of the stock besides'. There was little feeling that the whole object of economic activity might be to aid the consumption of individual citizens: still less that all trade must bring benefit to both sides. It was state interests rather than the interests of the individual that were uppermost in people's minds. And it was believed that the interest of the state in securing a surplus might require a sacrifice on the part of all individual citizens.

A widespread aim, therefore, was *import-saving*. Some imports were, of course, always necessary. There were a number of materials, including strategic materials, that most European countries must acquire from overseas: hemp, saltpetre, sugar, tobacco, spices, cotton and sometimes salt and fish. Other imports were tolerated because they were immediately re-exported: about a quarter of all English exports at the end of the seventeenth century were re-exports, especially tobacco, ginger and oriental textiles. But luxury imports were frowned on and often subjected to duties. The complementary aim was to promote exports. The Dutch were much envied because they possessed the capacity to process the materials they imported and so to export the finished product: sugar refineries, factories for cutting and twisting tobacco, tanneries for curing and tanning skins, cardboard factories, and above all mills for finishing textiles. The aim to emulate this led the English to consider the so-called 'Cockayne project' to establish a finishing industry in England for the grey cloth normally sent to the Dutch to finish. The Spanish government, following the French, set up factories for textiles, tapestry, glassware, porcelain and cabinetwork, for purposes of export as well as import-saving. Frederick the Great spent large sums in seeking to build up manufacturing industry in Prussia, especially silk and other textiles, iron, porcelain and sugar refinery, and he prevented the export of raw materials and the import of manufactures to that end; the aim of a state, he said, should be 'to consume all its own new materials in home manufactures, to found other skilled industries for working over imported materials and to make production cheap in order to obtain control of foreign markets'.[24] The object was to secure as large a share as possible in manufacture, and so of the total available exports. Like commerce, manufacturing could be increased only at the expense of other nations. Like commerce, it was a great aid in increasing the stock of money in the country. So, increasingly, the building up of manufacturing capacity came to be one of the important motives of states: an aim that in this age was not conceived to be purely domestic in effect, since it was designed to expand domestic capacity at the expense of that of other nations.

The desire to improve the balance of trade – and to promote self-sufficiency – created a consequential aim; to *build up native shipping fleets*. The French, for example, until 1660 were almost totally dependent on foreign ships and foreign merchants for the carriage of their imports and exports. Most trade from north Europe came in Dutch and English ships and that from Spain and South America in Spanish and later Dutch ships. Colbert, therefore, introduced measures to squeeze out the Dutch traders and carriers: subsidies for building and buying ships, favourable offers to attract English and Dutch shipwrights to France. England introduced the Navigation and Staple Acts at about the same time, to promote English shipping and reduce dependence on the Dutch. Here too, self-sufficiency (as well as the need for adequate shipping in time of war) was the aim. As Henry

Robinson wrote in 1649, 'What Nation so ever can attain to and continue the greatest trade and number of shipping will get and keep the sovereignty of the seas, and consequently the greatest Dominion of the World.'

Another objective, which flowed from the desire for a good balance of trade, was to secure *monopolies* in particular areas abroad or in particular types of product. The object was to secure access to particularly needed materials, or more often simply to dominate a particular trade. Governments often had a big hand in these ventures.[25] It was easy enough to give the chartered company a monopoly in relation to fellow-nationals of the *same* state: this was normally a condition of the original charter. But usually the aim was to secure monopoly in the area concerned against other states. For this, it was necessary to supply some kind of political backing. So, often, to stake out a claim the navy was sent in support. And eventually, in many cases, the areas where the companies settled to trade were sooner or later taken over as colonies by the state.

Thus, the establishment of colonies was not, at this period, an aim in itself. On the contrary, it was often forced on semi-reluctant governments by the chartered company or other traders, who settled under crown patronage or subsequently called for colonial protection. But governments became increasingly aware of the trading and other benefits they could acquire from colonies, so they were fitted into the conceptions of sovereignty then being developed in Europe. The trade, the production, the saving in precious bullion which it was hoped the colonies would secure were seen not as those of the colonies, but as those of the metropolitan nation.[26]

One very direct benefit a colony could provide was a source of important and especially *strategic materials*. Thus Hakluyt held that the discoveries in America could 'afford unto us, for little or nothing ... either all or a great part of the commodities previously bought more dearly or more dangerously elsewhere'. But almost equally advantageous, and more frequent, was the aim to provide a source of materials that could be profitably traded elsewhere. So the United Provinces, England and Portugal vied for the East Indies for the sake of the spice trade, and for West African territories for the sake of the slave trade; England and France contested the Caribbean islands for the sake of the sugar trade, and North America for the fur and fish trade. These products were not seen so much as valuable imports for the home country – imports, by definition in this age, could not be valuable – but as items of trade that could be profitably exported elsewhere.

Once established colonies could also represent *markets* for home manufactures, since they were largely dependent on imports for many of their needs and could easily be prohibited from buying these elsewhere: Hakluyt declared that if the Western discoveries were properly exploited, 'in short time we shall vent as great a mass of cloth in those parts as ever we did in the Netherlands'.[27] Colonies could even sometimes create *employment*. Net emigration to them was usually regarded as a loss in itself, but, so long as they could trade only with the mother country, they might, as Child argued,[28] through their demand for imports, create employment at home as well: an Englishman with ten native workers under him could produce far more in the colonies than he could working alone at home, and the combined demand of the eleven would keep at least four workers in England employed. This whole philosophy, of course, implied that the economy of the colonies must be regulated and controlled largely to suit the interests of the mother country. It should provide essential materials, but be prevented from providing inconvenient competition: thus the English prevented Ireland (essentially a colony) from developing wool manufactures which might compete with English products, but developed the linen industry there for its import-saving and foreign trade value.[29]

Motives were thus different from those of the previous age, in a number of ways. They were now those of the state rather than those of the ruler. They concerned commercial advantage rather than revenues. They looked far more to future, and not only to present needs; to the building of a strong and self-sufficient economy and a continuing export surplus, rather than to the immediate requirements of the exchequer. Economic motives became, moreover, a more important factor within the whole range of foreign policy aims. As we saw, they often dictated the terms imposed in peace treaties, as happened in almost no other age. Economic rivalry even outweighed ideological rivalry, the religious antagonisms which only a few decades before had played such an important role in political relationships. Thus the English, during the Commonwealth, and the Dutch, though both were protestant and republican, were soon at war with each other, mainly for commercial reasons; while Cromwell had no hesitation in allying himself with Catholic France and monarchist Sweden against the Dutch, since the latter, though protestants and anti-monarchists like the English, were his main economic rivals. Intense commercial rivalry thus influenced not only economic relationships among states but political relations as well.

These new motives of states, of course, reflected partly the new class structure: the different balance of interests within states which we considered in the last chapter. But they reflected also a more indirect change. States themselves, and many within states who were not merchants, including the rulers and above all the great ministers, had become increasingly concerned with commercial advantage. They had become persuaded (as Adam Smith later lamented) that the merchant interest, the interest in preserving trade at home and acquiring it abroad, must be a dominant motive of the state as a whole.

MARKETS FOR MANUFACTURERS (1740–1870)

During the age that followed the objectives of governments in their foreign economic policies changed again.

Concern with the trade *balance*, and especially the balance of individual trades, declined. Anxiety over strategic supplies and the policy of power generally was also less. Increasingly, the aim of governments was to develop markets abroad for emerging manufacturing industry. So the aim of successive British trade negotiations in the 1780s was 'to protect the revenue' but also 'to open markets more freely to the flow of British goods, by whatever methods seemed appropriate to the case ... The object was in general to preserve or seek as favourable an exchange of goods as the national circumstances allowed, particularly through the medium of increased exports.'[30] The same description of governmental motives could have been applied to some extent to most European nations of the time. Though the industrial strength of nations varied considerably, all had exportable produce, including some developing manufactures. And even when they still sought to protect these in the home markets, they now wanted to acquire markets for them abroad as well. The trade desired was no longer simply carrying trade, or the re-export of goods acquired from the colonies: it was the export of goods produced at home.

One of the objects of foreign policy generally, therefore, was to promote the commercial, as well as the political and military, advantage of the state. One of the main motives of Britain, for example, in recognising the newly independent states of Latin America after the Napoleonic wars (even overcoming her marked aversion to the republican systems of government they had adopted), was to enable British traders to continue the successful penetration of those markets which had already begun during the wars:[31] thus she refused to support in the Concert of Europe Spain's demands to recover her territories, was the first European government to recognise the principal independent states, Mexico, Gran Colombia and what became Argentina, and quickly concluded commercial treaties with them to establish her trading position there. Similarly, the main objective of all Britain's dealings with the Chinese Empire, from the Macartney mission of 1793 until the two wars of 1839–41 and 1856–60, was to create more favourable conditions for British traders in that country, conditions which the Chinese Empire for long contemptuously refused but which Britain finally secured for herself by force. Again Britain's policies towards the Dutch overseas possessions during the Napoleonic wars, the occupation of Java, Cape Town and Ceylon (as well as the private enterprise occupation of Singapore), were designed to promote Britain's commercial as much as her strategic interest. And later Britain's extensive diplomacy among the lesser states of Germany, designed to weaken the Zollverein and prevent its extension, was motivated by the same aim. France's activities, political and military, in North Africa and the Near East, Germany's in Greece, Turkey and South America, were equally influenced by the desire to secure markets abroad. And the motives of the United States in declaring the Monroe doctrine, in securing huge territories from Mexico and in opening up Japan to the outside world, were at least in part commercial.

Statesmen explicitly recognised this major aim of foreign policy. Thus Pitt declared in so many words that 'British policy is British trade'.[32] In the next century, this was even more taken for granted: Palmerston told the Commons in 1834 that to accuse a British Foreign Secretary of indifference to the country's commercial interest was 'to accuse him of being deficient in common sense'. And Lord Granville, who replaced Palmerston, as Foreign Secretary in 1851, in a memorandum prepared for Queen Victoria shortly afterwards on the main aims of British foreign policy, said that one of the first duties of a British government abroad must always be 'to obtain for our foreign trade that security which is essential to its success'. It was this idea, that successful trade required an element of security, that inspired many of the presuppositions of foreign policy at this time. It meant that, very often, the conclusion of a commercial treaty, laying down the conditions of trade and the protection to be provided for merchants living abroad, was necessary to protect national interests; while in remoter parts only the establishment of some military presence, or even the acquisition of full sovereignty, could, it was felt, assure and protect the trade that was so widely desired.

It was widely believed that political influence and commercial influence often went together. This was not in general an age of imperialism, in the sense of a widespread search for territorial possessions abroad. Few believed much in further expansion. Disraeli regarded colonies as a millstone around the necks of the imperial power, which would have to pay far more in defence and administration than it could conceivably get in commercial advantage. There were even calls on governments, such as that of Bentham, to 'emancipate your colonies'. There was some colonisation: for example, that of the French in North Africa and of the British in Hong Kong, Singapore and Penang. Equally often, commercial expansion was pursued through an extension of influence short of full-scale occupation. So France, for reasons that were commercial as well as political, extended her influence in the Levant. So Britain, mainly to safeguard the Indian Empire, but certainly not without regard for possible commercial benefits established her influence in Persia and the Persian Gulf. And in East and West Africa, Britain, France and other powers were beginning to establish footholds, even to penetrate to the interior, largely to promote the commercial potentialities of those regions.

An equally important motive was the desire to *counter* the commercial or colonial pretensions of others. In the previous era, most governments, at least in their public acts, if not always privately, recognised the commercial monopoly of other European powers in their own colonies, and their right to impose restrictions even in spheres of influence. Now this became less and less the case. Britain (which even earlier had connived at smuggling between the West Indies and Spanish America) now, in the Free Ports Acts of 1765, 1787 and 1805, deliberately sought to promote trade, even illegal trade, from that area to Spanish- and Portuguese-controlled Latin America. Britain sought to prevent too great an extension of French commercial and political influence in south-east Asia and the East Indies (in the latter case by allowing the Dutch to resume control there), just as she sought to counter it in the Levant. Britain and France competed with each other for influence, commercial and political, in Muscat and the Indian Ocean. Russia, mediating between China and the British and French in 1859–60, was careful not only to extract huge territorial concessions from China in return but also to win for herself commercial treatment in China equivalent to that accorded to the Western European powers. The door, though not yet open, was beginning to be pushed ajar.

In Europe, too, the main economic object of governments was to expand trade, here usually through diplomatic means. Large numbers of commercial treaties were negotiated; and the ability to conclude these depended very much on political circumstances (see p. 178). But there was a difference in the objectives of states according to their economic circumstances. The main motive of those that were most industrially advanced, above all Britain, was a general *lowering of restrictions*: liberalisation favoured them since they were well able to compete on more than equal terms. British statesmen at this time, just as much as English economic writers, expressed their confidence that Britain could benefit from any free competition for trade, both in Europe and elsewhere. Thus Castlereagh, in 1815, explicitly rejected an offer from Spain of special trading privileges in return for assistance in recovering her Latin American colonies, on the grounds that 'the views of both nations ought to be liberal to South America and not invidious to other nations ... The Prince Regent has never sought for any exclusive advantages. He has always recommended the commerce of South America to be opened to all nations upon moderate duties, with reasonable preference to Spain herself.'[33] The House of Commons Select Committee on Foreign Trade, set up in 1820, concluded that 'the skill, enterprise and capital of British merchants and manufacturers require only an open and equal field for exertion'. Canning declared, in 1824, that Britain sought 'no exclusive privileges of trade, no invidious preference but equal freedom of commerce for all'. And Lord Malmesbury, in 1858, declared that the British Government 'looked for no commercial advantages in any quarter which they would not be prepared to share with every other nation in the world'. These were not mere words. In concluding treaties with Turkey, China, Persia, Japan and other countries, Britain did indeed seek no special privileges but a reduction in the general outer tariff barrier, confident that she could compete effectively with all in such conditions.

The economically weaker nations had an interest in resisting this attempt to establish a free trading system. They wished still to protect their own industries and only slowly changed their views. But the ideology of free trade had been so powerfully instilled that it eventually carried the day almost everywhere. So the new Latin American states, though they might from time to time complain, submitted to treaties that committed them, to their own disadvantage, to tariff policies more liberal than many in Europe. Britain consistently resisted demands by Venezuela that the commercial treaty first signed with her in 1825 should be revised, on the grounds that it was an international agreement and could be changed only by mutual consent. And China, which was totally without manufacturing industry of her own, was induced to accept a maximum tariff of 5 per cent, well below what almost any country in Europe, with far stronger industries, was prepared to concede; and Turkey, in a similar condition, one of 3 per cent.[34] Even among European nations, whether they were industrially weak or strong, the free trade ideology gradually prevailed. So Napoleon III, despite the intense reluctance of many of his industrialists, committed his country to the Cobden Treaty with Britain of 1860, and proceeded thereafter to negotiate comparable agreements with Belgium, Italy, Austria and many other states. By that decade, 1860–70, almost all the governments of Europe had become inspired by the new zeal for reducing duties and other trading barriers.

For the same reason, the economically powerful states would normally favour *reciprocity* in any arrangements made, while the weaker states resisted this. When Britain was negotiating with Spain for a commercial treaty in 1786, Pitt, in his instructions to the British negotiator, explicitly underlined the fact that the demand for most-favoured-nation treatment in respect to the coastal trade would be to Britain's advantage, since she had the shipping to undertake this off Spain's coast, while Spain would not be able to reciprocate. Similarly in her series of commercial treaties with Latin American countries after 1825 the negotiation of exactly reciprocal rights was bound to benefit Britain, since she had a capacity to sell goods in those countries which they could in no way match in Britain (until Argentina developed meat exports at the end of the century). Britain had the same interest in negotiating commercial treaties with China, Turkey, Morocco and other states. Thus the concept of non-discrimination and reciprocity, and the increasing use of the most-favoured-nation clause, were devices which suited the economically powerful states, but were less advantageous to others. Even the abandonment by Britain of colonial preferences and of her own monopoly position in the colonies in the late 1840s could benefit her, since she would anyway remain the dominant supplier in those markets but could acquire a strong position in the colonies of other states, if they were to follow her example.

Another new aim pursued by some governments for promoting trade was the establishment of limited *customs unions*, in which tariffs were lowered amongst the members while they maintained a common outer tariff barrier. Here the aim was often as much political as commercial. Thus Prussia from the 1820s sought, for partly political reasons, to persuade the other states of Germany to join with her in a union under which their mutual tariffs would be abolished: that union, first formed in 1838, gradually extended until it became the nucleus of a united Germany. So France established a customs union with Belgium, which it was equally hoped would form the cement for a political union. While, however, the main objective of governments in such projects was often political, they received strong support from manufacturing and commercial interests likely to derive substantial benefit from them: by creating larger markets, they served to help the expansion of manufacturing industry, while the common outer tariff maintained a defence against competitors from further afield. In this way, political and economic motives, those of the state and those of private interests, coincided.

Little less powerful was the desire of rival powers to *frustrate* the creation of such unions: again for political as much as for economic reasons. Britain, for example, alarmed by Prussia's efforts to create the Zollverein, used all her influence to dissuade German states from joining it. She formed a rival union (the Central League) as a counterweight, and signed treaties with a number of individual states to induce them to stay out. She used her considerable political leverage in Hanover (from where her royal family derived) to this end, and negotiated a commercial treaty of her own with her in 1833. She also sought to influence the policy of the Zollverein itself, joining with Bavaria to try to secure a reduction in its outer tariffs.[35] Nor was she alone in such efforts. All countries that might be adversely affected by a customs union would seek to influence it. In 1850, Belgium and Switzerland used all their efforts behind the scenes to ensure that the conference of the Zollverein at Cassel would not agree to the increase in duties which the south German states were demanding; whilst Austria, conversely, wished to support the south German states, yet hoped the duties would not be raised, partly for the strictly non-economic motive that the south German states would remain dissatisfied with Prussia as a result.

The willingness to abandon imposts on foreign trade was made easier by the lesser importance of revenue-raising as a motive. Duties on trade had for centuries been the most important single source of government revenue. Even in 1840, they remained 40 per cent of the revenue of Britain. But the introduction of income tax in Britain in 1842 (and its retention as a permanent feature in 1860) followed by France in 1851, together with the development of other forms of taxation, meant that this constraint now counted for less. In the US revenue considerations had been the main reason for introducing tariffs in the 1780s. But with the increase in land sales in the next century, which now became more and more the main source of federal funds, this motive diminished. Everywhere it came to be recognised that it was ridiculous that commercial policy abroad should be determined by domestic revenue needs. Duties were explicitly categorised as either for revenue or for protective purposes. There began to be in Europe a commitment to free trade as an end of policy, only limited by the needs of protection where necessary.

While foreign policy was often influenced by commercial motives, commercial actions could also be affected by political considerations. In signing a commercial treaty with Portugal in 1783, France sought not only trade but a loosening of the historical alliance between Portugal and England. Britain, seeking a commercial treaty with Spain at about the same time, sought to wean Spain away from France. A few years later, Britain and France were competing to secure a commercial treaty with Russia, for diplomatic as much as for commercial reasons. Conversely, poor political relations could lead to a damaging of economic contacts: thus Spain's poor relationship with Holland in the 1780s led to a loosening of commercial links as well.

Sometimes, strategic motives affected economic policy. England approached Poland and Prussia in the late 1780s to secure an alternative source of supply to Russia for Baltic goods. During the Napoleonic wars, strategic motives were overriding, leading to mutual trade embargoes. In peacetime, political factors were more important. Britain's reason for entering into a commercial treaty with Austria in 1838 was largely political and she even allowed Austria to bend the rules (in counting some foreign ports as part of Austria's territory for the purposes of the Navigation Act) for that reason.[36] Austria's motives for joining the Zollverein later were more political than economic. And the reasons for the Anglo–French Treaty of 1860 were also partly political, on both sides (Louis Napoleon wanted to ease his political isolation after his Italian adventure while British leaders wanted to restore damaged relations): so Gladstone justified the treaty by declaring that 'the commercial relations of England with France have always borne a political character'. Conversely, the south German states refused, for political reasons, to join in the economic treaty which Prussia signed with France in 1862, unless a similar agreement was reached with Austria.

As the influence and ideas of the commercial classes increased, however, these traditional motives – strategic and political – declined in proportion to the general desire to open up trade. One motive for tariff-cutting was simply the desire to keep prices down. For the first time since the Middle Ages, there began to be almost as much concern for the consumer as for the producer. Arguments about the need to keep down the cost of living and reduce food prices were influential in promoting free trade setiment in Britain; and helped to make her ready even to make unilateral reductions in tariffs without securing corresponding reductions from others in return. This willingness to take unilateral action, criticised by Disraeli and others, was a phenomenon which had not been seen in international economic affairs for a century or so (and was not even now to last for long). The aim of reducing prices often encouraged such moves: as when Britain abolished the Corn Laws; or when she removed the preference for colonial sugar and accepted instead the bounty-assisted sugar produc- tion of European countries; or when France moved towards free trade in the 1850s. And it was partly on the same grounds that the wide- spread restrictions on colonial trade had been widely attacked (for example by McCulloch and James Mill in Britain) as economically irrational, and were gradually reduced.

A final motive influencing policy, certainly much spoken of in these days (though it may have been almost as much a rationalisation as a genuine reason for action), was the aim to promote a more peaceful and integrated world. Freer trade, it was widely held, would be the bond that would link nations more closely together and make war between them increasingly unthinkable. So J. S. Mill wrote, in his *Principles of Political Economy*, that 'it is commerce which is rapidly rendering war obsolete, by strengthening and multiplying the personal interests which are in natural opposition to it. And it may be said without exaggeration that the great extent and rapid increase of international trade, in being the principal guarantee of the peace of the world, is the great permanent security for the uninterrupted progress of the ideas, the institutions and the character of the human race.' Cobden, equally, in campaigning for free trade, frequently extolled it as the means of preserving world peace.[37] When appointed to negotiate the treaty with France in 1860, he wrote to Chevalier, an enthusiastic French advocate of a treaty: 'The people of the two nations must be brought into mutual dependence by supplying each other's wants. There is no other way of counteracting the antagonism of language and race. It is God's own method of producing an entente cordiale and no other plan is worth a farthing.'[38] And Gladstone, looking back on the treaty with France years later, commended it as having perhaps been instrumental in preventing war against France.[39] The extension of commerce, it was widely believed, was necessary as the means of spreading peace, as well as progress throughout the world.

The collective motives of states in this age, therefore, more than in previous ages, varied from nation to nation according to their economic circumstances. Within the more advanced countries, the free trade ideology spread slowly, though traditional attitudes in favour of protection and controls were still firmly held in some quarters. During the half-century between 1820 and 1870, however, and especially in the last decade or two of that period, the new ideas were adopted by many governments. Almost everywhere therefore, the main aim came to be to expand trade and trading contacts, in the belief that this was of benefit to all alike.

Only when trade flagged in the 1870s, when export markets became harder to win, and when home markets began to be threatned, above all when the huge new flow of grain from the plains of North America began to flood to Europe in the cheaper shipping of that day, did the new motives begin to falter. Except in the traditional trading nations, Britain and the Netherlands, the preservation of the home market rather than penetration of the foreign, the defence of growing industries rather than their stimulation through the bracing winds of competition, increasingly became the main objective. And, for some at least, a new opportunity began to emerge: investment in foreign countries, in developing ports and railways, in tea, rubber and coffee plantations, in public utilities, and other enterprises which, without the exertion of trading activity, might yet bring large and growing returns to those who possessed the capital to undertake it.

LOANS FOR LENDERS (1870–1914)

In the age that followed, therefore, a new set of motives emerged, reflecting a different economic and social structure.

The rise of a substantial rentier class created new attitudes to the international economy. The new rich, both those who had inherited wealth and those who had made it themselves, possessed a larger volume of investible funds than had ever existed before. At home, the opportunities for investing these were limited. There was thus an increasing disposition to look for alternative openings in new lands across the waters, where there were more opportunities and higher returns. In France, for example, 'much of the savings sought the liquidity, the presumed safety, of investment in securities. French industry did not call for it all, and could not then offer as high returns as did foreign petitioners – even when judgement was passed on relative risk ... The rate of return on the bonds of the French governmental bodies and of the stronger French industrial enterprises fell continually till the middle of the nineties ... From the outer world better paying offers and proposals came and French savers accepted them.'[40] Similar opportunities tempted the substantial rentier class in other developed countries.

As a result, the motives of governments also began to change. In part, this merely reflected the new interests and desires among their own nationals. The bondholding class, which was fairly widespread (in France it is said to have numbered two or three million), were influential with governments. So were the financial institutions that specialised in foreign lending. As we saw (p. 90), there were sometimes ties of friendship and family between governments and financial institutions, and always frequent contacts. Moreover, an increase in opportunities for investment and trade abroad benefited the state as well as the individual. Of course, governments were concerned with other national interests, political and strategic. But these were not usually in conflict with financial ends: more commonly, the two reinforced each other. A state might have an economic as well as a political interest in winning financial domination of semi-colonial states, such as Egypt, Turkey or China; or in acquiring a new protectorate or colony (or preventing a rival from acquiring it). Though not always the dominant consideration for governments, therefore, the economic interests were rarely forgotten.

The search for opportunities to lend and invest in foreign lands was a new development. In previous ages, the search had been for trade, not for investment. Now, because of the prolonged depression in Europe from the early 1870s onwards, there was less opportunity for trade, but growing funds to invest. Opportunities to invest had to be found abroad.[41] Beyond the oceans, there were impoverished governments which desperately required investment funds, either for the direct support of over-strained budgets, or for the development of railways, ports or other facilities. Higher rates of interest could normally be secured on such loans than on similar loans in Europe: interest rates of 12 per cent were offered on Egyptian bonds, for example, about double what was offered in Europe, and the banks obtained handsome commissions in addition.[42] Wage rates were infinitely lower and hours of work longer.[43] The total income to be acquired from foreign investment was huge. In Britain, it more than quadrupled in thirty years between the early 1880s and 1913–14, and by the end of that time equalled about 10 per cent of national income.

It is not surprising, therefore, that for the more developed countries an almost universal motive was to find new opportunities *to lend abroad*. French banking and estate companies saw vast profits to be made in loans to Tunis and Eastern Europe, as British banks did in loans to Latin America and Australia, and Germans in loans to Turkey and South Africa. Even American bankers had ambitions of this kind: as the President of the American Bankers' Association said at Denver in 1898: 'We have long been the granary of the world; we now aspire to be its workshop; then we want to be its clearing house'.[44] Such objectives inevitably affected the actions of governments. The young Clemenceau, perceiving such motives behind the occupation of Tunis by the French government in 1881, declared: 'In all these enterprises ... I see only persons in Paris who wish to do business and make money on the stock exchange ... In short, it is to satisfy such interests that you have made war, violated the constitution and have placed parliament face to face with an accomplished fact.'

A particular form of this motive was the desire for *investment in railways* in other lands. For investors this could bring a relatively safe return: the economic profitability of such enterprises had already been proved in Europe and North America and was unlikely to be different elsewhere. For industry, it could bring orders and employment. As a British committee reported a little later: 'The development of foreign and colonial railway systems abroad out of British capital, when British materials, British savings and British engineering enterprise were opening up the world for the supply of food and raw materials, was greatly in the interest of this country as well as of the world'.[45] For governments, it could have strategic and political advantages, as well as economic ones for their nationals. For these various reasons, governments battled with each other to win railway contracts: in Tunisia as in Burma, in Turkey as in Morocco, in Argentina as in China. And such battles could, as in the case of the Berlin–Baghdad railway, or the various proposals for railways in Persia and in the Balkans, go on for years, and have political as much as economic implications. Sometimes the motive was strategic. Britain's decision to build a railway from Mombasa to Uganda in 1886 was based on strategic, not economic motives, while Rhodes' dream of a Cape to Cairo railway had clear political objectives.[46] Conversely, railways built for commercial reasons often had political consequences. When the French proposed building a railway in Indo-China to the Yangtze, though the main motivation was commercial, it paved the way for a dominant French influence in southern China. The French government's desire to build a trans-Saharan railway became an important reason for France to extend her influence in Senegal and Sudan.[47] Control of the North–South railway in Manchuria gave political dominance there to Russia and Japan in turn.[48]

This aim, to lend at interest, gave rise to yet another new motivation: the desire to *protect foreign investment* already undertaken, especially that of the bondholders who had lent to governments. This could be justified as designed to protect legality, the rule of law and the sanctity of contracts. Even Gladstone could claim as justification of the use of force in Egypt that 'we seek the maintenance of all established rights ... whether they be those of the Sultan, those of the Khedive, those of the people of England or those of the foreign bondholders'. Palmerston had laid down in the previous age that British governments would intervene for this purpose only when the question of 'international right' was involved, which he interpreted broadly to include 'any well-founded complaint which any of its subjects may prefer against the government of another country, or any wrong which from such foreign government the subjects may have sustained'.[49] Neither Palmerston nor his diplomats were always enthusiastic about all such claims. But from the 1870s onwards the willingness of British governments to intervene on behalf of their bondholders increased. Representations were frequently made by ambassadors on their behalf in Latin America. British consuls were in some cases even instructed to act as agents for the bondholders.[50] France, too, took strong action on behalf of her own bondholders: for example, with the governments of Greece in 1898, of Bulgaria in 1902 and of Serbia in 1905.[51] She offered dire threats against Turkey on such grounds in 1901 and against Morocco in 1907–8. Germany threatened force against Honduras in the same cause in 1901, and she joined in international measures against Portugal in the 1890s, Greece in 1894, Venezuela in 1902, and Bulgaria in 1908.[52]

Another major economic motive was to win *'concessions'* within less developed countries. In this age, it was not enough for individual companies or financiers to bid for each contract in equal competition. Governments sought more general assurances: the right for their own nationals to build all railways within a particular area, or for a monopoly on the provision of electric power, gas or harbour installations. And it was governments rather than individual constructors or financiers who could secure such concessions. Thus 'diplomacy discovered that its end might be realised by alliance with private capital and enterprise. ... To aid private capital and enterprise in a world in which such ambitions were active, and such conditions prevailed, became an important activity of government, whatever the nature of the country's aims.'[53] In Britain, for example, 'the demand increased that the government use the power of the state to aid British industry, secure openings and contracts abroad; and, in response to the demand, the government yielded'.[54] Many of the most favourable opportunities arose in the weaker states of the world, where pressures were most likely to be effective. 'It was in the under-developed, disorganized Chinese empire, in the lands on the road to India, Turkey, Persia and Egypt, and in the continent of Africa that the government stepped to the fore, strove with, by and for British private groups. Sometimes this effort had no other object than helping an English group to secure equitable consideration. Sometimes it was bent on having a field of opportunity set aside for British capital and enterprise. ... That judgement was shaped by a recognition that the initiative of these groups was building up Great Britain's power in disputed regions; and these groups themselves, through their influence in Parliament and outside, had much weight in deciding the course pursued.'[55]

The disparity in power, both military and economic, between the lending and borrowing countries, inevitably helped to make these pressures effective. For governments, there were often political as well as economic reasons for seeking success in the battle for concessions. That success, apart from its commercial value, could also symbolise political dominance.[56] Conversely, political power might bring economic dominance. The Paris Chamber of Commerce was not going beyond the demands normally made of European governments when it passed a resolution declaring that 'whenever a foreign loan is admitted to official listing, admission should be made conditional upon the concession of advantages for French commerce and industry'.[57] French ministers prided themselves on their assiduity in winning contracts and orders for French business. Pichon, the Secretary for Foreign Affairs, told the Chamber of Deputies in 1911 that 'it is generally thanks to the intervention of our Minister of Foreign Affairs, in accord with the Ministers of Finance and Commerce, that we have been able to secure important orders'. The German government was particularly active in seeking concessions for German industry: for railways in Turkey, Persia, South Africa and elsewhere, for mining and other activities in China, for public utilities and construction in North Africa and South America. It assisted German cable companies, intervened on behalf of German banks, assisted and promoted the German merchant marine: so much so that 'the Government was felt to be the driving power in much of German foreign investment'.[58]

Political and economic motives became fused. 'All felt that their future growth depended upon the acquisition, under their direction and influence, of markets, of raw material supplies, of lucrative opportunities in foreign regions. . . . In thought and plan these desires for commercial and financial expansion became fused with dreams of an extension of German political dominion . . . Germany, thus moved and thus led, entered the competition with Great Britain and France for foreign commerce, concessions, financial advantages, colonies, control.'[59]

The desire to *win trade* in foreign lands was not, of course, a novel one. But it took now a slightly new form. With the decline in activity in Europe and the raising of tariff barriers there,[60] there was a special attraction in winning access to markets in distant lands, especially if these could be brought under the full control of the European country concerned. Thus the desire to win access to trade provided a motive for the expansion of political power too. It was quite explicitly the search for trade (or better conditions for trade) which impelled Britain and France to expand and enlarge their presence in Siam, Burma and Indo-China in the 1860s and 1870s.[61] It was largely the same desire which caused the main European powers to seek leases and treaty ports in China in the last decade of the century (though strategic motives and the desire to keep up with rivals also played a part). Finally, the desire for trade was a major motive too (together with strategic competition) behind the scramble for Africa in the 1870s and 1880s, and the partition of the Pacific in the same period (see p. 93).

There was, of course, a special value in *seeking colonies.* For there most trade, through preferences or other restrictions, could be reserved totally for the home country's merchants. Colonies were indeed seen in large part as a means to trade (see pp. 32–3). It was generally taken for granted that trade would follow the flag. (In many places it had preceded the flag, but the flag consolidated and multiplied it.) Sir H. Johnston, who had considered the increase in British trade in West Africa as 'sufficient justification' for continued British rule, declared in an article in the *Times* in 1888 that it had become 'a necessity for us to protect ourselves and forestall other European nations in localities we desired to honestly exploit'.[62] Similarly, the Syndicat Générale de Commerce et de l'Industrie in France declared that 'the conquest of a new group of near to fifty million consumers in the area around Tongking, which will open to our commerce markets where our manufactures will be easily exchanged for raw materials is a matter assuredly worth the trouble it entails'.[63]

The developed countries did not always demand exclusive rights or even preferences. In some cases, a Western power would claim only that it sought the 'open door': as the US demanded in China, and as Britain had demanded not only in that case but in many others. But that demand was made mainly by those powers which expected to win in trade competition with rival states anyway, and usually in cases where it was feared that the market otherwise would be reserved to a rival. Thus the US demanded the open door in China in the late 1890s, at the moment when European powers were threatening to carve that market up and reserve it for themselves (and that demand did not prevent the US awarding herself preferences in the Philippines in the same period). Similarly, Theodore Roosevelt demanded the open door in Morocco in 1905, because he saw that otherwise France might establish there a privileged position for herself. And Britain at first welcomed Germany as a colonial power because she would keep markets more open than rival powers were likely to do. So Lord Granville told Bismarck in June 1884 that 'it cannot be otherwise than alright with us if Germany pursues a colonial policy and opens barbarous lands to civilisation and trade; we would certainly be glad of it. It is quite different with France for, wherever they colonise, the French introduce high tariffs, up to 50%, and thereby injure us severely.'

But whether or not a privileged position was in mind, the desire for access to such markets was a powerful one. For this reason, another important motive was established *trade routes* that would favour home businessmen and traders. An important aim in French expansion in the interior of Senegal (besides the strategic desire to create a route to Sudan) was to ensure that trade links were established from there with French ports on the coast rather than with British rivals. In the Niger region, in the same way, France wanted to secure a route from the coast to the inland areas she already controlled.[64] Britain also was concerned to establish trade routes to ports on the West African coast, if only to maximise the customs revenues there.[65] Similarly, she attempted to secure the area north of Ashanti in 1892 as a means of securing access to trade in the Niger region. Russia expended huge sums on the trans-Siberian railway in a drive to secure a trade route to the Far East, and planned branches south from the railway to China to win trade there. France was concerned to establish a trade route from Tongking to southern China; and the French parliament, which in the early 1880s was reluctant to sanction French action to colonise the Red River area, was ready to tolerate action designed to open up trade from there to the Eldorado believed to exist in southern China. Britain planned a railway from Burma to Yunnan for the same reason. The treaty Britain imposed on Burma after the second Burma war allowed British ships and merchants to operate along the whole of the Irrawaddy to Mandalay, while generously offering freedom of navigation to Burmese ships on the lower reaches of the river. The construction of channels of communication, such as the Suez and Panama Canal, and their control thereafter (even in the territory of other countries), became important for the major powers, partly for strategic reasons, but above all as a means of promoting and expanding their own trade. All over the world, therefore, the desire of the powerful Western states for trade made it necessary to demand also facilities that would guarantee access to it.

For the same reasons, *ports* and *entrepôts* were often an important objective. A principal aim in the French occupation of Cochin-China in 1858–62 was the desire to secure Saigon as an entrepôt for trade with China, comparable to that provided for Britain by Hong Kong. France sought for a time to acquire an island in the Philippines, and considered securing a part of the Malay peninsula, for similar reasons. Britain acquired Rangoon and strengthened Singapore and Penang essentially as trading stations. In Asia, such stations were particularly necessary. 'European traders operating at such vast distances from home and at the mercy of local governments needed both commercial bases and also, as the use of sea vessels increased, coaling stations along the trading routes. The result during the half century before 1880 was a string of small entrepôts in addition to existing Dutch and Portuguese bases in the archipelago and at Macao: Rangoon, Singapore, Labuan, Saigon and Hong Kong.'[66]

Another concern in this age, and a commonly avowed one, was for access to valued *raw materials*. As Sir Frederick Lugard, one of the foremost empire-builders of the day, put it: 'the tropics produce in abundance a class of raw materials and foodstuffs which cannot be grown in the temperate zone and are so united to the needs of civilised man that they have in very truth become essential to civilisation. It was the realisation of this fact ... which led the nations of Europe to compete for control of the African tropics.'[67] One of the reasons that the Chambre Syndicale des Negociants-Commissionaires of Paris gave for demanding the annexation of the Red River area (see p. 88) was the 'exploitation of the mineral riches and products of the soil of Tongking' and the 'direct importation of raw materials for which France is presently dependent on other nations'. There was a desire among all the imperial powers to make themselves more self-sufficient, less reliant on sources of supply that were under foreign control. Cotton, rubber, tea, cocoa, coffee, cane sugar, were all materials which could not be obtained in Europe, but which every European nation required. None, even with their colonies, attained self-sufficiency – France had to import nine-tenths of her raw materials even at the end of this period.[68] But the motive was undoubtedly present. The desire to acquire access to the believed mineral wealth of southern China, and to supplies of raw silk for the Lyons silk industry, was a significant reason for the extension of French power from Indo-China to the north in 1883–5; just as the wish to secure control of the ground-nut producing areas of the interior was the main reason for her expanding the boundaries of Senegal to the east a decade or two earlier. When they competed for power in the interior and in the Niger basin in the 1880s, Britain and France were each eager to win access to African areas producing palm-oil. The rising price of cotton and vegetable oil in Europe was one of the motives leading to the increased interest of European powers in securing alternative supplies in the Pacific islands from the 1860s onwards; as was also the desire to secure copra, coffee, cocoa and, later, phosphates. The US engineered the accession of Hawaii to the US in 1892 largely because this would secure assured supplies of sugar which the US sugar interests badly needed and demanded. Finally, one of the motives for the interest of British business, and eventually the British government, in extending British power in South Africa was access to the gold and diamonds of the area.[69]

A more general motive was simply the desire to secure *economic influence* in territories abroad, rather than specific economic objectives. One of the main reasons for French intervention in Tunis in 1881 was to ensure that its government became more sympathetic to French economic aspirations in that country and less inclined to show favour – in granting concessions for railways, ports and telegraphs, for example – to Italy. One of the reasons for the heavy indemnity imposed on China after her war with Japan in 1895 was to increase her dependence on foreign powers and therefore the economic influence they could wield with her.[70] There was obvious advantage in winning influence over, or better control of, the tariff policies of dependent states and so ensuring that no excessive barriers were placed in the way of European exports. So in China, Turkey, Morocco and other places, the European powers imposed maximum duties, at very low levels; and even, as in China, placed the whole system of customs collection under Western officials. For similar motives, and to ensure debt repayment, the US later secured direct control of the customs of the Dominican Republic in 1905–7, in Nicaragua (after its forcible occupation) in 1915, and in Haiti in the same year.[71] And an important general aim was simply to keep out rival influences, for political as well as economic reasons: so the powers competed with each other – to win concessions in Tunis, to build railways in Turkey, to secure spheres of influence in China and so on – as much to reduce the influence of rivals at to win it for themselves.

In some cases, finally, economic actions were taken to promote *political objectives*. Financial domination was increasingly seen as a political asset: 'The official circles of lending countries gradually came to envisage the foreign investments of their citizens, not as private financial transactions, but as one of the instruments through which national destiny was achieved. Financial force was often used to buy or build political friendship or alliance, was often lent or withheld in accordance with political calculations.'[72] Borrowing would be permitted to friendly powers and allies, to strengthen them, but refused to rivals or enemies. So France gave Russia, her ally, every facility in raising money in the Paris market, while closing the market to potential enemies, and even to Russia's potential enemies. Similarly, Britain opened her market to Japan from about 1902, the date of her alliance with Japan, and to Russia in 1906 just before her understanding with Russia, but firmly closed it to them before those dates. Bismarck pressed German banks to lend money to Italy in the 1880s when he was seeking her alliance; just as German bankers were pressed to lend to Morocco in the early years of the next century as a means of winning influence there.[73] There was competition to lend to those countries where influence was sought. So all the main European powers competed to lend money to Turkey; Britain and Russia competed to lend to Persia; Britain, France and Germany to China, for political as much as economic reasons.[74]

In the same way, bankers were expected to take careful account of their country's political interests, as well as their own economic advantage, in the selection of the governments they would assist. So the Board of Directors of the Comptoire Nationale d'Escompte in France declared in 1910: 'In the selection of securities which we offer to our clientele, we undertake, as a rule, not only to seek security of investment, but also to take into account the views of our government and the economic and political advantages that may be obtained for France by loans contracted by other countries'.[75] Conversely, the politicians regarded the bankers as allies and instruments in the promotion of national power: Poincaré, the French prime minister, announced in 1912 that his aim was to 'combine with French military and naval power, as converging and connecting forces, the financial power which is so great an aid to France'. The French finance minister in the following year stated that during his six years in control of the public finances, he had 'admitted to quotation only those foreign loans which assured France political and economic advantages'. And it was on similar grounds of national interest that all states provided special borrowing facilities for their own colonies but not for those of other states.

Motives therefore now changed again from those of the previous age. The desire for investment opportunities was even more important than that for trade. Such opportunities were now sought abroad rather than at home; in more distant lands rather than among immediate neighbours. Governments, through diplomacy, influence, occasionally through force or the threat of force, played a major role in securing these opportunities and in protecting the investments already made. But trade, too, remained important, and the desire for access to favourable markets, and for secure routes to get there, became a major concern for governments and traders alike. The need to win valued raw materials – rubber, sugar, coffee, gold, diamonds and others – became a significant consideration. Above all, the domination of other states was often seen as an important condition for securing these objectives, so that to win a predominant influence or outright control became a motive in itself.

So the new balance of social forces in this age, and a new conception of collective economic interests, brought into being a different set of collective motives, and so a different type of economic society, from those of earlier times.

AUTARKY FOR AUTOCRATS (1914–50)

In the age that followed, motives changed yet again.

The first, and by far the most important change, was that external economic objectives declined in importance in relation to domestic economic ones. There was less concern about finding new investment opportunities, markets or colonies abroad; much more about the levels of activity and of employment at home. Governments were overwhelmingly preoccupied with the effort to revive economic activity, at whatever cost to the levels of international exchange, even to the previously accepted rules of the international economy. We have already seen (p. 47) Roosevelt's determination to put 'first things first': the revival of the national economy above the needs of international trade. Moley, one of his lieutenants and a main architect of the New Deal, was even more dismissive of any attempt at international economic action, declaring that any attempt to reduce tariffs was incompatible 'with the idea of a managed national economy'; and roundly denouncing the 'still more ominous policy of internationalism which is threatening the integrity and unity of the New Deal on every side'.[76] So too Ramsay Macdonald, when his government introduced major tariffs for the first time in Britain for nearly a century in 1931, felt that the first aim must be to restore national solvency and national credit: he, Snowdon and Chamberlain all justified the raising of tariffs and of taxation on the grounds that the first task was to restore confidence and a stable currency at home, and this must take priority over seeking to promote international trade. As Macdonald put it, 'the present state of world trade is, in all goodness, small enough and limited enough in its compass, but to that would have been added chaos of currency, and not only would the streams have been thin and shallow but they would have been stirred by uncertainty' if Britain had sought recovery through the revival of international trade.[77] This philosophy of putting the national economy first was expressed most forcefully in Nazi Germany after Hitler's assumption of power in 1933. In the Memorandum which Hitler personally wrote in 1936 about the tasks of the Four Year Plan, he wrote: 'The nation does not live for the economy, for economic leaders, or for economic or financial theories; on the contrary it is finance and the economy, economic leaders and theories, which all owe unqualified service in this struggle for the self-assertion of our nation'.[78] Everywhere the feeling was that in a critical situation the first need was to restore national economic strength: only when this had been secured would the restoration of international economic relationships follow.

A widespread motive, which reflected this concept, was the concern for *national self-sufficiency*. This was partly for purely economic reasons. There was a wish to isolate each state from the uncertainty of dependence on the economic decisions of others. As depression developed, trade abroad declined; and there was the more need to stimulate activity at home to replace it. Thus Keynes wrote an article in the *Yale Review* in June 1933, extolling such 'self-sufficiency': 'We all need to be as free as possible of interference from economic changes elsewhere in order to make our own favourite experiments towards the ideal social republic of the future.' In an age of intense national rivalries, there were strategic reasons for promoting self-sufficiency: a renewal, in other words, of the age-old policy of power which had induced attempts at economic independence from the Middle Ages onwards. Again, Nazi Germany demonstrates the most striking example. In the same memorandum, Hitler wrote that 'it is essential to ensure all the food supplies required in peace-time and above all those means for the conduct of a war which can be secured by human energy and activity ... Foreign exchange must be saved in all those areas where our needs can be satisfied by German production ... Accordingly German fuel production must now be stepped up with the utmost speed ... The mass production of synthetic rubber must also be organised and achieved with the same urgency.' All this should be done without any consideration of costs. When this memorandum was read out at a Cabinet meeting on 4 September 1936, Goering stated that 'we must strive with the greatest energy for autarky in all those spheres in which it is technically possible'.[79] While most other governments did not carry the pursuit of self-sufficiency to this extreme, there was a general demand to reduce reliance on imports; and the consumption of home-produced goods ('buy British', 'French', 'Italian') was increasingly demanded. Everywhere the demand for autarky became an increasingly important motive for governments.

Another universal motivation contributing to the concern for the national as opposed to the international economy, was the desire to secure a *revival of employment.* This new concern arose not only because unemployment was now higher – though certainly at the height of the depression unemployment was far higher, in the US and most of West Europe, than at most times in recent decades: it was also that people were more *conscious* of unemployment and its effects. Barefoot children, persistent dole queues, angry hunger marches, hit the headlines in a way that the even greater penury and far more extensive concealed unemployment of earlier times had never been able to do. Populations themselves were less willing now to tolerate enforced idleness and the poverty that accompanied it. Marches, demonstrations, disturbances, even incipient revolution, manifested their discontent. Whether because they knew their own survival might depend on it or because of genuine concern, governments became preoccupied by the problem as never before. So they were tempted to seek the easy way out by exporting the problem to others. The sufferings of their own populations as a result of worklessness were constantly before them: those they might inflict on populations abroad were less obvious. They were therefore willing to block off traditional commercial exchanges if by so doing they could preserve activity at home. So Neville Chamberlain, Chancellor of the Exchequer in the National government in 1931, could justify the introduction of protection with the barefaced argument that it would transmit unemployment from Britain to workers elsewhere: 'We propose, by a system of modest protection ... to transfer to our own factories and our own fields work which is now done elsewhere, and thereby decrease unemployment in the only satisfactory way in which it can be diminished.'[80] Such a statement could not have been made in the preceding age: if only because, in that age, concern about employment levels played little part in determining international economic policy. It could not have been made in the following age: because that concern, though still felt, would never have been expressed with such crude disregard for the problems of others elsewhere. The combination of determination to protect employment at home with indifference to unemployment elsewhere was an attitude peculiar to this age.

Another important objective was to *restore balance of payments equilibrium*. This also required government intervention, if necessary by manipulating trading patterns or the movement of foreign exchange. There was no longer any willingness to await the slow and uncertain adjustment of the gold standard; nor to trust to free market mechanisms generally. The balance of payments position of many countries was, at this time, especially precarious. During the First World War, all normal trading patterns were disrupted and trade largely controlled by governments. After that war, the economies of many countries remained in disorder for many years; new states which were barely economically viable had come into existence, many new trading barriers had been erected, and the gold exchange mechanism, revived only briefly from the mid-1920s to the early 1930s, quickly collapsed. Arbitrarily adopted parities allowed some countries to buy surpluses with the deficits of others. The depression brought a still greater contraction of trade; to be followed by another world war and a new suspension of normal trade patterns. So a normal trade system, with equilibrium maintained by appropriate parities, scarcely came into existence throughout this period. The required balance of payments had to be secured by other means. All governments everywhere, above all those in deficit, introduced special measures to ensure sufficient foreign exchange supplies at least to meet their essential import requirements: through tariffs, quotas, barter arrangements, exchange controls, export subsidies, dumping, banning of inessential imports, import-saving, investment in synthetic materials, and many others.

An unusual aim in this period, perhaps unique to the age, was the desire to *raise prices*. A feature of the depression years was a widespread fall in price levels, above all in prices of agricultural commodities. So instead of seeking desperately to hold down prices, as in the years of inflation to follow, governments sometimes sought deliberately to raise them, so as to bring about an increase in agricultural incomes and so in the demand for other goods. In his message to the World Economic Conference of June 1933, Roosevelt placed among the three main objectives for restoring economic order 'international action to raise prices'. His main object in providing for price-fixing under the NRA codes for individual industries was to ensure minimum, rather than maximum prices. The objective of his agricultural price-support system, based on a 'parity' to maintain the purchasing power resulting to farmers from each agricultural sale, was equally to keep prices up. Similarly, the motive behind the many attempts at this period to negotiate commodity agreements, through quotas of production, minimum prices or other devices, was to raise the price level of such commodities. That aim was extended to industrial goods. Some statesmen even wanted to see industrial production limited in order to maintain price levels. So Neville Chamberlain, speaking in the British House of Commons on 2 June 1933, at the opening of the World Economic Conference, denied that the cause of world economic conditions was a deficiency of demand, declaring that 'the reality is that there is over-production ... and that the restriction that is required is a restriction of over-production ... To allow production to go unchecked, unregulated and unplanned in these modern conditions ... seems to me to be absolute folly ... By this regulation and planning of international production through agreement among producers themselves, I believe that we can do perhaps more than in any other individual direction to raise prices as we desire to do.'[81] So, too, Roosevelt had instructed Moley, his representative at the International Economic Conference of 1933, that 'the essential thing is that you impress on the delegation and the others that my primary international objective is to raise the world price level'.[82]

Related to this desire for inflation, to replace deflation, was the general concern to secure *stabilisation* generally, at home and abroad alike: a restoration of normality. This was seen in the attempt, pursued for fifteen years after the end of the First World War, to secure a return to the gold standard. It was seen in the demand for balanced budgets, which were almost everywhere regarded as the only respectable objective.[83] There was a general hankering for the safety and the comfort of the secure pre-war years. So, it was felt, the need was not to expand credit, still less to liberalise and encourage foreign trade: it was to control credit and limit, in the narrow national interest, foreign exchanges that could threaten the balance of payments and imperil economic stability and employment at home. Retrenchment was the cry: a retrenchment designed to restore the stability of a bygone age.

These primary aims – to increase self-sufficiency, to restore unemployment, to maintain the balance of payments, to maintain prices, to re-establish stability – led to another, more general aim: to increase the degree of *control* which governments could exercise on the economy as a whole, both domestically and externally. To maintain fuller employment, many types of control were needed, affecting foreign economic relations as much as domestic. As Keynes declared, 'the controls necessary to ensure full employment will of course involve a large extension of the traditional function of government'.[84] Controls were equally necessary to conserve foreign exchange and to secure a trading balance. As many economic commentators of the time observed, this required a wide range of economic planning and a considerable measure of direct control, through fiscal, monetary and even more direct means. In the long run, to make good the dearth of private investment which depression has caused, direct control even of investment might be required. So Keynes declared that he conceived that 'a somewhat comprehensive socialization of investment would prove the only means of securing an approximation to full employment'.[85] Thus emerged the new, and eventually universal motive: the attempt to secure 'demand management', the use of fiscal and monetary measures to bring a deliberate, government-created balance between demand and supply at a level that would secure full employment.

All this affected foreign economic policy, and indeed the whole international economy, since demand-management in one country could directly affect the level of demand in others. But for each government it was demand at home alone that counted. Foreign trade, and foreign economic activity generally, became increasingly marginal in the calculations of each government in relation to economic activity at home. And, while the need to regulate each national economy was widely accepted, the idea of regulating the world economy had not even begun to dawn.

For, finally, a still more widespread influence on economic policy generally was nationalism in the broadest sense. It was taken for granted, as in the seventeenth century, that economic policies should assist in the *promotion of national power.* This was seen most clearly in the policies of those nations – such as Germany, Italy and Japan – which, under the most blatantly nationalistic governments, planned the promotion of their own power at the expense of others. So, in the memorandum which he wrote on economic policy in 1936, Hitler laid down unequivocally that 'parallel with the military and political rearmament and mobilization of our nation must go its economic rearmament and mobilization, and this must be affected in the same tempo, with the same determination, and if need be with the same ruthlessness as well . . . There is only one interest, the interest of a nation; only one view, the bringing of Germany to the point of political and economic self-sufficiency'.[86] The Japanese and Italian governments equally sought to submit the economy to the nation's military goals. Other governments more reluctantly accepted the need to mobilise economic power for national ends. Nationalistic motives especially influenced trade policy. Germany, for example, had political aims in seeking through bilateral agreements and clearing arrangements to dominate the trade of south-east Europe, thereby bringing about a greater degree of dependence among those countries and disrupting France's alliances with Yugoslavia and Czechoslovakia.[87] It was partly for the same reason that she sought to develop trading contacts in the Middle East and Latin America and developed a Mark zone in East Europe. There was also a political motivation behind France's attempt to develop a Franc zone in southern Europe, and Britain's promotion of closer trading links with the countries of the British Commonwealth.[88] Trading arrangements were adopted or avoided because of their possible strategic implications.[89] Imports were restrained and exports promoted partly on these grounds. A new mercantilism emerged. In the words of the German general, Georg Thomas: 'Without exports there can be no foreign exchange, without foreign exchange there can be no armament production' – almost exactly echoing Colbert's famous words about trade as the source of finance and finance as the vital sinew of war.

In this age, therefore, a totally new set of motives emerged amongst governments and businessmen alike. The desire for economic expansion – in the form of new investment abroad, new markets or new colonial territories – declined. In an age when trade and activity was threatened, the concern was to preserve existing markets, especially at home, not to seek new ones abroad. Instead, states sought to insulate themselves from the threat posed to them by economies elsewhere.

They sought above all to preserve, or to revive, levels of employment which were everywhere threatened. They believed that stability and 'retrenchment', balanced budgets and payments surpluses, rather than expansion and deficits, might be the means to achieving economic recovery once more. They devised new ways of cutting off imports, new ways of protecting home industries, especially strategically sensitive ones. Intensive exchange controls were introduced to prevent the leakage of investment funds or speculation damaging to the currency. More than ever before trade policy was influenced by political goals. But they were now *domestic* political goals, the goals of governments deeply uninterested in the economic fate of those elsewhere and ethnocentric enough to believe they could recreate prosperity in isolation: capitalism in one country increasingly became the aim.

TURNOVER FOR TRANSNATIONALS (1950–80)

In the age that followed, a new set of motivations emerged. There was a general desire to abandon the autarchic policies of the previous era. A widespread goal was the progressive removal of barriers to trade and investment between states: in other words, '*liberalisation*'. This goal reflected the interests of the most powerful economic forces within the most advanced states. It was shared within such states by governments and business interests alike. Indeed, the motives of the two increasingly coalesced. This was not because governments were taken over by business and became its puppets: on the contrary, governments had purposes that were quite distinct from those of the major business groups, especially in their management of the domestic economy, and acted frequently in ways which placed constraints on their freedom. But in their attitude to the international economy, motives were similar. The expansion of trade and investment abroad usually benefited each equally. And both therefore assisted each other in this aim.

Of course, not all governments of developed countries, nor all companies in those countries, had an equal interest in liberalisation. As in the ealy nineteenth century, it was the nations that were commercially strongest – at first the US above all – which had the strongest interest in breaking down the previous trade barriers. In the US, 'it became abundantly evident to most industrial, labour and agricultural organisations that the competitive ability of American producers in foreign markets was very high. What was needed to take advantage of vast market expansions was the removal of import quotas and the easing of tariff and other non-tariff barriers in other countries.

In short the opportunities for market expansion abroad far exceeded the dangers of domestic market penetration by foreign producers, and a policy of freer multilateral trade appeared to be in the economic interests of most major economic groups'.[90] Many reasons were found to demonstrate the benefits of liberalisation: in the words of a State Department memorandom of that day, 'a great expansion in the volume of international trade after the war will be essential to the attainment of full and effective employment in the US and elsewhere, to the preservation of private enterprise, and to the success of an international security system to prevent future wars'.[91] Once more, as a century before, free trade was presented as the only sure road to peace.

The motives of the main interest groups in the US were thus similar to those of British commercial groups at the time of their dominance in the early nineteenth century. Other industrialised countries, highly conscious of the economic power which the US had developed during the Second World War, and of their own weakness as a result of that war, were at first cautious in accepting the new goal. That eventually the aim came to be widely shared was partly a result of the widespread reaction against the restrictive policies of the previous age; and partly because of the dominant influence of the US in the years immediately after the war. Motives, however, varied in strength according to trading fortunes. As US predominance declined and her balance of payments weakened, she became less committed to the cause of liberalisation, herself introducing restrictions on foreign investment, an 'equalisation tax' for foreign loans, restraints on imports, and for a time an import surcharge. Conversely, as their situation improved, the stronger trading nations, such as West Germany, Japan and the 'newly industrialised countries', became more committed to the goal and its loudest advocates. But to some extent most states, at least most developed ones, came to accept that prosperity was to be secured by an expansion of trade rather than its protection: by a mutual opening of markets rather than a competitive closing of them.

Thus one motive for all states was the desire to *increase their share* of an expanding world trade. The fact that each country agreed to make itself more vulnerable to imports meant that exports needed to be increased to match. The contest was one in which, by definition, there must be victors and defeated: the surpluses of the winners created the deficits of the losers. All therefore sought new means to promote their capacity to win exports. 'Export or Die' replaced 'Buy British' or 'Buy American', as the prescription for prosperity. Governments provided for their companies all the incentives which the rules permitted (and sometimes a few more) to seek markets abroad (see p. 200). Poor countries shared in this aim as much as the rich. They had even stronger motives to increase their exports, though far greater constraints against doing so. Requiring to import all capital and many consumer goods, most energy and much food, they felt the need to increase substantially their sales to rich countries. But they found the prices of their chief exports – primary products – unstable or declining or both; and access for their few manufactures, and for many of their agricultural exports, carefully restricted. In other words, the demand to export, that was so widely felt, did not always bring about any corresponding willingness to import in return.

This motive – to liberalise trade – had always to be balanced against another motive which was often in conflict: the *protection of employment*. The huge levels of unemployment seen in the inter-war years promoted a determination to prevent such events recurring. In the years after 1945, 'full employment' became the universal watchword. In Britain, a White Paper committing the government to that aim in the post-war years was issued even while the war was still on. In 1946, the US government introduced an 'Employment Act' pledging it to the same end. Other industrial countries shared the aim of avoiding the high unemployment of the inter-war years. That goal was adopted even by the international community. The IMF, a body generally held to favour deflationary remedies, paid lip-service to the aim: under its Articles of Agreement, it was 'to facilitate the expansion and balanced growth of international trade and to contribute thereby to the promotion and maintenance of high levels of employment'. In the early 1950s, the UN commissioned a report on 'International Measures for Full Employment', which recommended the policies both governments and international organisations would need to pursue to achieve that end. In theory, everybody supported the thesis that high employment should be promoted through trade expansion. In practice, as time went on, governments were increasingly tempted sometimes to save employment by restricting trade. When threatened with imports from elsewhere they began to devise new forms of protection to save jobs. While at first, therefore, it was developing countries in particular which found it necessary, for balance of payments rather than employment reasons, to place special controls on imports,[92] as the manufacturing capacity of poor states increased, it was the rich countries which increasingly resorted to these measures. These conflicting motives – liberalisation in principle, but protection in particular cases – led in time to the use of a whole battery of new measures for selective protection, less crude than the simple barriers of the previous era, but little less effective (see p. 199).

Another major aim affecting foreign economic policy at this time was the desire to *contain inflation*. Logically, this should have caused governments in their international policies to *lower* barriers and welcome imports, especially from low cost countries, so as to reduce the cost of living for consumers at home. But since this could have threatened the equally important aim of maintaining employment, the aim was expressed internationally above all in concern about the inflation of *others*. More deflationary policies by other governments, especially those with balance of payments deficits, were generally demanded: both by organisations such as the IMF and by the creditor states who exercised equally powerful influence. Measures to promote growth abroad – more liberal lending policies by the IMF, increased aid, debt re-scheduling, above all the allocation of special drawing rights to poor countries – were resisted on the grounds that such measures could have inflationary effects on the world economy. The effect was that the price of containing international inflation was laid principally at the door of the poor countries of the world (and of deficit countries generally), though the poor countries argued in turn (for example in the writings of their prophet, Raoul Prebisch) that world inflation often resulted from the more highly organised labour forces of the rich states, which caused manufactured prices to rise more than those of primary products. In practice, whatever its causes might be, inflation continued apace in rich countries and poor alike. And this intensified the demand for those policies thought most likely to contain it.

These four aims, therefore, trade liberalisation, the promotion of exports, job protection and the control of inflation, were the main objectives of governments in developed countries. But the motives of *governments* became increasingly irrelevant in relation to the motives of the major private companies in those states. Here the most important change was that such companies, instead of manufacturing in the home state and exporting abroad, became concerned to expand production abroad for sale there or at home: in other words, instead of transmitting goods themselves, they transmitted the capacity to produce goods. Foreign investment now, therefore, was no longer investment in government bonds, as in the age of bankers and bondholders, nor in the shares of foreign companies abroad, as between the wars: the new aim was *direct investment*, the creation or acquisition of manufacturing and other assets abroad by domestic companies. This provided a number of advantages. Production was often far cheaper, with lower labour and construction costs than at home. It was closer to the final markets. It took place inside the tariff barriers of the producing country. It secured the benefits of local knowledge of markets and distribution. It could take advantage of tax concessions and development grants offered by foreign governments to attract such investment. It could be financed by locally acquired trading profits which could not always be remitted. And it expanded the return which could be secured for large research and investment costs already made at home. For all these reasons, it expanded very fast. In 1950, at the beginning of this period, the total value of direct foreign investment by US companies was only about 11.8 billion dollars* (against 7.2 billion in 1935 and 3.9 billion in 1914). By 1967, this had risen to 59 billion dollars.[93] Ten years later, it was 350 billion dollars. By 1970, 75 per cent of the capital outflow of the leading industrial nations was in direct investment of this kind.[94] By that time, international investment was rising twice as fast as world trade, and the value of the sales of US manufacturing subsidiaries abroad was more than five times the exports of manufactures from the US itself.[95] The sales of US subsidiaries abroad were now increasing twice as fast as the sales of US firms at home. It is scarcely surprising that the expansion of such activities became a major aim.

An associated motive, for both governments and companies, was to provide *protection for investment* abroad. For this purpose, governments of the rich countries sought to negotiate bilateral agreements with poor countries, providing guarantees that the investment would be safeguarded and that the facilities would not be nationalised without adequate compensation. Attempts were made to internationalise these arrangements. The OECD in 1967 drew up a draft convention on protection for foreign property to which all states could adhere. The World Bank drafted a Convention on the Settlement of Investment Disputes, which would commit governments so willing to seek measures of arbitration or conciliation over such questions, and established an International Centre for the Settlement of Investment Disputes to hear such cases (though it was, in practice, little used). The Bank also proposed a set of draft articles of agreement for an international investment insurance agency. And other types of sanction for the protection of investment were used: the US Congress, for example, passed legislation under which any state nationalising a US company without compensation would forfeit all future US aid.

The motives of poor states in the international economy were often in direct conflict with those of the rich states and their companies. Their aims were set out in the demands they put forward over the years

* Billion = thousand million.

in various international negotiations. And they were eventually (in the mid-1970s) formulated comprehensively in their proposals for a 'new international economic order', which was to tip the balance of the existing international economic system in their favour.

They wished, firstly, to break away from the principle of universal non-discrimination, favoured by the rich states, demanding instead a form of *deliberate* discrimination, related not to political preferences but to the economic circumstances of each state. For this purpose, they wanted a system of generalised tariff preferences for all developing countries, to replace the selective preferences given previously by particular rich states, mainly to their own ex-colonies. Eventually, this change was largely accepted by the rich countries, though preferences to particular chosen areas were still given and nearly all the rich states hedged around their offers of preferences with many exceptions. Secondly, poor countries, seeking like rich states to promote their own exports, were concerned to win access to the markets of the rich countries where the most trade was to be had. In particular, they sought access for their agricultural products, for their simple manufac- tures, above all textiles (almost the only manufactured goods in which they could compete), and for goods processed from their own raw materials. These aims immediately conflicted with the desire of rich states to protect their markets and employment; with the effect that they refused, in each of these three cases, to apply the principles of liberalisation which they had themselves demanded elsewhere. Simi- larly, the poor countries sought industrial 'adjustment' by rich states, the phasing out of declining industries to leave room for imports from poor countries where comparative costs were lower; but again they found that rich countries, given their high levels of unemployment, were unwilling to allow such displacement, especially for labour- intensive industries of the kind in which the poor states specialised. Thirdly, the poor countries wanted better prices for their exports of primary products, which they believed to have fallen relatively to the prices of the manufactured goods they bought; or at least to win greater stability for those prices. On these grounds, they called for commodity agreements to hold up the prices of particular com- modities, with a 'common fund' to help finance such a programme. But here, too, there was a conflict of motives. Though, in theory, producers and consumers alike shared an interest in price-stability, the gap between their ideas concerning reasonable prices and above all on what represented 'long-term market trends' (as well as differences between the producers themselves on the system to be used) made it impossible to conclude more than a handful of such agreements.

Other motives of poor countries conflicted equally with those of rich. They were concerned not only with trade but also with industrialisation, which might reduce their dependence on the sale of raw materials and extend their economic opportunities generally. For this purpose, they required above all a remedying of the most fundamental inequality of all, that in technology. They proposed binding agreements under which individual companies from the rich states would have to make available the know-how making it possible for them to compete effectively. But this aim conflicted with the obvious interest of the companies in retaining the advantage they had acquired (and paid for in costly research), and was therefore refused by the rich countries. Similarly, poor countries, badly needing development funds, wanted large-scale inter-governmental aid, on soft terms, which would not add too greatly to their indebtedness. They wanted relief for the debts which they had already accumulated over the years. And they needed increased access to special drawing rights or other forms of liquidity to reduce their payments problems. All of these could be obtained only by concessions from the rich; concessions they were mainly unwilling to make.

The poor countries had other more general objectives which also conflicted with the aims of the rich. They wished to acquire for themselves a greater share in the management of the entire international economy. Until that time, it seemed to them, all the economic decisions that mattered were made thousands of miles from their shores within the rich countries: either in the boardrooms of the major international companies deciding on investment or marketing; or by the governments of rich states deciding their policies on international trade or monetary questions; or in international organisations, such as the IMF and the World Bank, where the rich controlled decision-making. The poor countries sought by various means to redress the balance. They sought to channel discussion of economic questions to the UN itself, where they enjoyed a majority position. They set up new institutions where their voice would be stronger (UNCTAD, UNIDO, and the 'Committee of the Whole' of the UN). They called for changes in the voting system within the World Bank and the IMF to give a larger voice to poor countries. And they demanded 'global negotiations' to discuss these demands. But since the rich countries were by no means disposed to abandon the dominance they already enjoyed, little was done to make such changes. So the principles applied within those organisations, the conditions on which credit was granted, and on which the world economy therefore operated, in general remained those approved by the rich countries and the dominant interests there.

Finally, the poor states were concerned to win greater control over the activities of large foreign corporations operating in their territory. These, they felt, placed their small and weak economies under the power, or at least the dominant influence, of entities which had no long-term interest in their welfare.[96] Yet because they depended, for capital, technology and managerial expertise on the companies, their ability to control them was limited. They sought to determine the remission of profits abroad, the proportion of profits reinvested, the proportion of labour and materials that were obtained locally. And in time they began to make more ambitious demands; for 'participation' by their own nationals in the ownership and management of the undertaking; even in a few cases for divestment or 'fade-out' under which within a few years the company was to be made over altogether to local interests. Once again this objective, to reduce the influence and control of foreign companies, inevitably conflicted with the aim of such companies in maintaining their operations. And since the latter could always threaten total withdrawal, with the loss of capital, technology, management and marketing skills the companies provided, their will usually prevailed. In most cases, therefore, the activities of these mammoth organisations were little affected. The only 'guidelines' on their operation they were prepared to accept (see p. 203) placed few constraints on them. And their direct investments, as we saw, continued to grow and mutliply.

In many ways, therefore, the motives of rich states and poor states in this age were in conflict. Each wanted to trade in the markets of the other; but each restricted in different ways the exports of the other to their own markets. Each wanted investment from rich countries to poor; but they wanted it on entirely different terms. While poor countries wanted commodity agreements that would enhance the prices of raw materials, rich countries wanted them only if they did not. While poor countries wanted technology transferred on an obligatory basis, rich countries wanted it only at the discretion of the companies who owned it (which meant very little transfer). While poor countries wanted more aid and monetary support on soft terms, rich countries in general wanted less, and on rigorous terms. Above all, while the poor countries wanted to acquire a greater say in the decisions that counted within the international economy as a whole, the rich countries were unwilling to concede them the means of securing this: that is, greater power for international organisations to regulate the world economy and greater power for poor states within them. Over all the major issues of the day, therefore, motives remained in conflict. And it was, almost invariably, the aims of the rich states which finally prevailed.

4 Means

Societies are distinguished not only by the type of motivation that is widespread within them, but also by the means that are commonly employed to fulfil those motives. Aspirations for power or prestige, for example, may be pursued in totally different ways in different types of society. Power may be sought by military exploits in one and commercial acumen in another. Prestige may be gained by conspicuous consumption in one society, and by good works and gifts to charity in another. Thus, in analysing the differing characters of different societies, it is necessary to consider not only the changing motivations which drive their members, but also the changing means regarded as suitable to fulfil those motivations in each.

Within international society too, means, as well as motives, may change from one age to another. In one society, for example, national expansion may be promoted by dynastic marriage, in another by aggressive war, and in another by economic penetration. The desire to gain influence may be pursued in one age by diplomacy, in another by alliance policy, and in another by economic domination.

A variety of means is available to states even within the economic field. Thus economic expansion may be pursued by trade, by colonialism or by foreign investment. Moreover, each individual aim may be pursued by different means: the expansion of trade may be won by compelling foreign merchants to come to particular markets or towns (as during the Middle Ages in Europe); by the enterprise of individual merchants all over the world (as in the following centuries); or by trade negotiations and trade promotion by governments (as more recently).

At first sight the means that are widespread must follow inevitably from the motives that prevail. If foreign conquest is a widely held aim, foreign war will be a widely used means. If peaceful relations with neighbours is the aim, then conciliatory diplomacy will be the favoured means. In the economic sphere too, some means follow, almost automatically, from ends. If an increase in foreign trade is the aim, then the promotion of exports and assistance to exporters will be a widely-used means; if industrialisation is the aim, protection will be commonly adopted. In practice, as we shall see in the sections that follow, there nearly always exist alternative means for achieving any given goal. Those that are, in fact, adopted depend partly on what means are available to each state at any one time and partly on the character of the society as a whole.

In the age of princes, for example, when power was concentrated in a single individual, it was natural that a favoured means to economic ends was the use of dictatorial decrees by the sovereign. So the loss of bullion, for example, which, as we saw, was so widely feared at this time, could be prevented with a simple prohibition of its export; enemies could be deprived of strategic goods or skilled manpower by the simple process of banning them from leaving the country. In the age of free trade, conversely, a different set of means was adopted, sometimes for the same ends: the balance of trade was preserved by promoting exports rather than preventing imports, economic stability by the gold exchange mechanism rather than protection or other interferences in trade exchanges. The choice of means will depend partly on the national interest, even more on the prevailing doctrine.

Let us, therefore, look briefly at the differing sets of means that have been employed by governments at different times to promote their chosen ends within the world economy; and see how these have varied from age to age according to the prevailing social relationships and economic doctrine of the time.

BANS AND BOYCOTTS (1300–1600)

During the later Middle Ages, when the princes controlled state power, the means employed to promote their economic ends were simple and direct.

The simplest of all was *war*. War might be the means of conquering prosperous cities or states which could bring riches to the conqueror: so, for a century, Milan was a tempting prize for French kings to conquer, while France itself was coveted by the English kings, partly because of the riches it could bring the conquerors. War could be the means of acquiring plunder and ransom, an attraction not only for the rulers but also for nobles, knights and even common soldiers who all shared the incentive of economic gain.[1] War could provide, even without permanent conquest, the ability to demand concessions or indemnities: the large ransom Edward III obtained for returning the

French king in 1360 was an example of such gains, and Edward IV's attack on France in 1474 can be seen as a form of highwayman's stick-up, abandoned as soon as France agreed to pay the necessary price to buy him off. More frequently, wars were a means of securing trading advantage. Venice and Genoa were in constant conflict for the control of trade in the eastern Mediterranean, from the twelfth century onwards. To the west, Genoa and Pisa were involved in similar warfare to control the trade between Italy and the French and Spanish coasts. In northern Europe between 1367 and 1474, the Hanseatic League fought successive wars with Holland, Denmark and England for the control of trade in that area. The League of the Rhine went to war to defend its trading position against encroachments by the local nobles.

Sometimes *limited force* was used to capture trade. When a town was strong enough, it could compel its neighbours to bring their trade to its own market and to no others.[2] In many cases, foreign merchants were obliged to dispose of all their goods at a certain port and not allowed to travel further to trade. Vienna made south German merchants wishing to trade to East Europe sell in Vienna so that Viennese merchants could trade the goods further. Cologne in the thirteenth century made itself the enforced terminus for trade from every direction. Danzig and Riga captured for themselves the rich trade between east and west Europe, which was compelled to pass through the hands of their merchants. Thus cities would contest with each other to secure control of a trade route so that they could monopolise it.

A little less drastic was to cut off all trade: the *boycott*. This was used above all by those in a dominant trading position, such as the Hanse, on whom some countries totally depended for essential imports.[3] It was used by the Hanse against Novgorod (1288, 1388 and 1416), Bruges (1280 and 1305), Norway (1284), Flanders (1358, 1388, 1436 and 1451–7), England (1388 and 1469) and Bremen (1427); and in virtually every case it succeeded in winning extensive trading privileges. The Hanse were in a specially powerful position to employ this weapon because in general the goods they supplied, such as corn, timber and wax, were more essential than those they bought, such as wool or cloth: the threat to withhold supplies was therefore usually sufficient to secure concessions from the importing countries. Other countries normally had to content themselves with lesser sanctions. A simple sanction, always available, was to remove trading privileges. When England and the Hanse began their periodic disputes on trading questions, from the end of the fourteenth century onwards, they each pursued this method against the other: so England, as she became better able to dispense with Hanse goods, successively removed the exemptions previously enjoyed by the merchants from the customs, subsidy, poundage and tonnage, confiscated goods, cut off all trade, and progressed ultimately to the imprisonment of the Hanse traders, in her effort to secure better rights for her own traders in East Europe.

Less drastic again was the *prohibition of particular exports.* This was done for foreign policy as much as for purely economic reasons: as when Louis XI imposed restrictions on the export of grain abroad, or when Edward III cut off the export of wool to Flanders in 1336. But restrictions were sometimes imposed for economic reasons too. In 1326 the London cloth merchants secured a ban on the export of fuller's earth to the Low Countries to damage their rivals there. In other cases the motive was provision. In the fourteenth century in England, frequent proclamations were issued, forbidding the export of particular kinds of food (except occasionally under license) to preserve supplies in England. In Sweden during the sixteenth century, during a short period of 40 years, there were nearly a hundred export prohibitions limiting the export of oxen, hides, horses, copper and so on.[4] There were similar compulsions placed on imports. Towns would occasionally ensure that in every shipment of freight brought to them a certain proportion of wheat was included. They would force private traders to bring whatever the town needed. And they would even undertake state trading – that is, communal trading in communal ships – to ensure that essential food supplies and other goods were available.

Another widely used method was to create *monopolies* for local merchants. In the cities, the main purpose of the gilds had been to establish a monopoly for their members in each craft. It is not surprising that there were similar efforts to create monopolies for entire cities and eventually for entire states. Once a state had acquired dominance over another, it could use its position to enforce a monopoly for its own traders. 'A wholly successful policy meant complete monopoly of the trade in some commodities, unchallenged command over some vital route or sole access to some market, together with freedom from fiscal and other interference in the trade so monopolised ... Even where absolute monopoly was not within reach it was possible to win most favoured nation treatment, especially in the matter of custom and even, like the Germans in England and Venetians in Byzantium, to gain terms more favourable than those allowed to native merchants themselves. Below such triumphs was every grade of partial success in attaching advantage to oneself and denying it to others.'[5]

Where foreign goods were needed, however, the simplest form of protectionism, in an age of autocratic regulations, was *direct control* of the activities of foreign merchants. Though desired and attracted for some of the products they could provide, they had to be prevented from competing too effectively with local traders. A wide variety of regulations were introduced to this end. They were restricted in where they could live within a town (a particular quarter or street); in where they could trade (particular markets); in when they could trade (particular days or seasons); and in what they could buy and sell (being, for example, forbidden to buy food or raw materials or to sell certain finished goods). Often they were not permitted to engage in retail trade; or to deal with other foreigners; or to buy on local markets until the local merchants had finished purchasing. A whole range of special regulations were in this way devised to ensure that foreign trade was adjusted to the needs of the local community, consumers and traders alike.

Another form of trade regulation, though used largely for securing revenue from trade, was the imposition of *duties*, on both exports and imports. Again this mirrored a system used domestically. Duties represented the equivalent at the national level of the tolls so widely used at the gates of the cities. But there was no rationality about their use. Export duties reduced the volume of exports of the ruler's own state, while import duties, applied for revenue rather than protection, raised the price of imports, especially of those imported across many lands. Where duties were protective, the desire was usually to promote strategic interest or reduce the loss of bullion. Protective measures were not taken only against foreigners: King Martin of Aragon ordered the destruction of cloth factories in one part of his kingdom to prevent them competing with those operating in another part. Similarly, the Dukes of Milan prevented the import to Milan of woollen and silk cloth, even from other parts of his own dukedom, in order to protect the markets of local producers.

Again, direct *state assistance* was used to establish local industries. In 1350, King Ferdinand of Naples granted a master craftsman from Venice a loan of a thousand escudos free of interest on condition that he set up a factory in Naples for making silk cloth. In Bologna in 1288, the import of silk spindles was encouraged by special assistance, and their export forbidden. Louis XI of France gave special help to establish a silk industry in Lyons and Tours. Certain exports were banned to preserve and encourage home industry and to prevent it being established elsewhere. The English kings prohibited the export of unfinished cloth on these grounds; while the export of sheep from

Spain was prohibited several times for similar reasons. Imports of raw materials were encouraged. 'Measures ... were taken ... to improve the supply of raw materials: imports were actually facilitated by abolishing or reducing import duties, while exports were discouraged by imposing export duties or even by absolute prohibition. Measures of this kind were adopted in respect of the raw materials of the textile industry especially ... In addition to their efforts to increase the supply of the production-factors, governments readily granted exemptions or reliefs from taxation, or even loans or credit facilities, in favour of those manufactures they wanted to develop.'[6]

So in this age, drastic means were found to implement the rulers' economic objectives. Exports of particular goods were banned. Foreign merchants were rigidly controlled in what, where and when they could buy and sell. Monopolies were established. Taxes were abruptly imposed and as abruptly removed, on imports and exports alike. Trade to another country was suddenly halted altogether. In the final resort, force could be used, whether to compel foreign traders to the local market or to capture trading rights in particular localities abroad. In a word, the means were autocratic means, appropriate to an age where autocrats were the dominant economic actors, to procure the ends that were important to rulers: revenues for themselves and provision for their populations.

BOUNTIES AND BARRIERS (1600–1750)

In the age of state-building that followed, a new set of strategies were adopted, reflecting the differing motives of that age. The aim was no longer to raise revenue, preserve bullion or feed the population. It was to promote the power of the state.

As we saw, the doctrine of the day declared that there existed among states no natural harmony of interests, but a natural conflict. The general belief was that there existed only finite quantities both of power and of trade; and nations must compete with each other to secure a balance of each which was favourable to themselves: the 'balance of trade' meant (as the 'balance of power' often meant) not an equilibrium, but a favourable balance. It was thus taken for granted that, to secure benefit for one's own state, it was necessary to damage others. So Josiah Child declared that 'all trade is a kind of warfare'. And Colbert, in speaking of the 'war' for trade and money, merely reflected the approach to international economic policy that was prevalent in this age.[7]

A favourable balance of trade was, as we saw, the most widely coveted objective. The means required for this was to win a dominant control over sources of materials, over trade routes, over trade itself and, to a lesser extent, over markets. Since the sharing of any of these was unacceptable, the aim was often to achieve a monopoly, or at least a substantial domination over all. The sources of materials could be reserved through the establishment of colonies, or at least an exclusive position, in the areas from which they came. The domination of trade routes could be won by the establishment of trading and naval posts, such as those of the Dutch on the route to the East, or of the English in West Africa, the Caribbean and North America. The monopoly of trade could be won by seeking to be first in the field in newly discovered areas and by reserving colonial exports to the home market. The control of markets could be secured by political alliances and trade agreements, by a more systematic use of tariffs to the disadvantage of opponents, and by seeking to establish a manufacturing capacity in advance of others; and in colonies by reserving all imports to home producers (as under the English Staple Acts).

In almost all of these fields, *armed power* could be of major importance. It was not by chance that it was as Dutch military power diminished in the eighteenth century that Dutch commercial fortune declined likewise, while growing English commercial success accompanied the growing success of the English at arms in the same period. Everywhere, military power and commercial success were closely linked together in men's minds. As Colbert recognised, 'trade causes perpetual strife, both in time of war and in time of peace, between all the nations of Europe to decide which of them shall have the greatest share'. None of the statesmen of the age and few of the merchants doubted the close relationship that existed, as Josiah Child had asserted, between power and profit. 'The idea of international conflict was inherent in balance-of-trade dogma. Economic warfare led imperceptibly to warfare proper. For when the pace of peaceful progress proved too slow to satisfy the more impatient spirits (as it invariably did), the temptation to take a military short-cut was strong.'[8]

The simplest means available in the struggle for trade, therefore, continued to be *war* in the most literal sense. This is almost the only age in recent history when it could be said that some wars occurred in considerable part from commercial motives (though the general competition for prestige and power was still usually a more important cause).[9] In the early seventeenth century, for example, the Dutch succeeded in dispossessing the Portuguese of the favourable trading positions they occupied in parts of Latin America, West Africa, Ceylon and the East Indies, and did so (temporarily or permanently) by force. They ejected the English from Amboyna in the Spice Islands by the same means. The three wars between the Dutch and the English, and the two between the French and the Dutch, in the middle of the seventeenth century, were fought mainly for reasons of trade rivalry.[10] The French made no secret of their desire to wrest from the Dutch their dominant trading position by whatever means possible: Colbert painted to Louis XIV a seductive picture of the absorption by France of many of the economic assets enjoyed by the Dutch if they could defeat them in war. In the following century, England went to war with Spain in 1739 far more because of their conflicting commercial ambitions in America and the West Indies (especially the inconvenient Spanish propensity to interfere with British smugglers operating between the West Indies and Spanish America) than because of Jenkin's famous ear. Moreover, wars fought for other reasons could be made the instrument of economic gains. Though the War of Austrian Succession and the Seven Years War were not fought mainly for economic reasons, both the English and the French saw them as opportunities to wrest from each other trading advantages in the Caribbean, North America and elsewhere.[11] Thus, during the Seven Years War, Britain took the opportunity to conquer the most prosperous French sugar-producing islands, Guadeloupe and Martinique (though competing British growers compelled their return at the end of the war), Senegal in Africa (which she also kept only until 1783), and made more permanent gains in North America and India which were economically advantageous. And, as we saw, in many other cases governments secured for themselves commercial benefit as a *result* of victory in war (see p. 122), even though it may not have been the chief motive for which war was fought.

Violent means short of all-out war could also be adopted for commercial ends. The English challenged the Dutch trading position in West Africa by military means, though without declaration of war, just as the Dutch had displaced the Portuguese there earlier by similar means. The French and the English began harrying each other for positions in North America in 1754, two years before the nations were formally at war in 1756. Privateering, essentially legalised piracy, continued to be employed by the main maritime powers, especially the English and the Dutch, during much of this period: in the West Indies, off the Americas, and off West Africa. During their period of conflict in the middle of the seventeenth century, both the English and Dutch accused each other (with good reason) of allowing or encouraging piracy against the other: the English claimed that Flemish pirates from Dutch harbours preyed on their ships in the narrow seas, and that in the East Indies English ships were continually being seized illegally by the Dutch; while the Dutch in turn accused the English of permitting privateering even after this had been officially renounced in the Anglo–Dutch Treaty of 1654. English privateers were used against French shipping in the middle of that century, and operated continually against Spanish shipping to the Americas at times when the countries were not at war. It was taken for granted, in other words, both by merchants and governments, that trade might need to be seized, or protected, by armed force, even by nations that were at peace.

Even where no violence at all was used, governments had little hesitation in using arbitrary and dictatorial means to damage the trade of other states with which they were in conflict. Though not quite so unpredictable as the princely rulers of the age before, the great ministers and their masters could still act with ruthlessness against rivals. *Trade boycotts* were widely used. States would prohibit trade with their opponents altogether. When Portugal was under Spanish rule between 1580 and 1640, Portuguese ports, which previously had a flourishing trade with the Dutch, were totally closed to Dutch ships by the Spanish as a measure against the Dutch, though this damaged Portugal (and, therefore, Spain) far more than it did the Dutch. In the mid-seventeenth century, the English prohibited the export to the Dutch of wool, woollen yarn, fuller's earth, piped clay and other goods well before the Anglo–Dutch wars broke out, in order to damage the Dutch textile industry. They even planned for a time (in 1651 and 1662) to buy up the wool of Spain, the only other obvious alternative source for the Dutch, not because England needed it, but to deprive their opponents who depended so heavily on that raw material. The Dutch prohibited all exports to France before the outbreak of war with that country in 1672, while France reciprocated with a similar boycott as a means of weakening their enemy. After 1678, when France had become the chief threat to her, both commercially and politically, and long before war broke out in 1689, England prohibited all trade with France. Even without a boycott, very high tariffs could be maintained against rivals. After peace was finally made with France in 1713, the English parliament rejected Bolingbroke's proposed trade treaty so as to maintain high tariffs on French goods and virtually exclude them from the English market, while French colonial products were prohibited altogether, regardless of the interests of English consumers.

Another means now more and more employed for commercial ends was traditional *diplomacy*. An alliance could buy trade, or trade purchase an alliance. England renewed her alliance with Portugal partly to give English merchants the opportunity to trade with the Portuguese possessions in South America, Africa and Asia. The Methuem Treaty of 1703, between the same two countries, though motivated partly by political factors, afforded mutual trading privileges of a kind which each did not allow to others. In trade negotiations, a state's 'ambassadors could with gifts win the favour of the Grand Turk or the Tsar and secure discrimination against rivals. Down to the time of Wedgwood it was expected that an Ambassador's duty would include those of acting as commercial traveller for his nation's industries abroad.'[12] Even diplomatic marriages could have important commercial consequences. Charles II's marriage to Catherine of Braganza in 1661, and the resulting treaty, brought England access to the commercially valuable ports of Bombay and Tangier. Conversely, trade was used as a means of promoting an alliance or peace. Clarendon hoped that commercial treaties between England on the one hand and Portugal and the Dutch on the other, with corresponding treaties between France and the same countries, might link together the principal trading nations of Europe in political bonds which would secure peace between them. But this was a somewhat unusual ambition for the time. More usually, the role of the diplomat was to win not a general peace, but a partial alliance; and in doing so to promote the commercial, as well as the strategic, interest of his country.

Other new means were devised. States began to set up *state institutions* to assist in the promotion of trade. In England, the Board of Trade and Plantations was established by Parliament in 1696, with the main role of promoting English trading interest abroad. In France a few years later, Louis XIV set up the Conseil de Commerce for the same purpose. The English parliament established select committees to examine whether enough was being done by government to promote trade in particular areas. For the first time, officials were sent out to different parts of the world specifically to assist merchants abroad. From the seventeenth century onwards, a number of European states had consuls in the Levant to deal with the Ottoman administration there and generally assist their merchants in a number of ways. Towards the end of that century, France took the lead in despatching consuls to other parts of the world to perform similar functions, an example subsequently followed by other countries.

Tariff policy was also used to promote home trade and to damage that of other nations. There was less concern with revenue and more with increasing a country's trading capacity and economic strength, and duties therefore now performed a different function from their role in the previous age.[13] Duties on exports, which had been, as we saw, an important source of revenue, were now, with the widespread concern with trade balance, increasingly abandoned. On the contrary, not only were exports freed from duties, but in many cases they were granted bounties, or subsidies, in addition. In England, duties on exports were progressively removed from the middle of the seventeenth century (especially in 1699 and 1722), while bounties were increasingly introduced, especially during the eighteenth century. Duties on imports, however, were higher than ever, for revenue as much as protective reasons: but even then drawbacks, or rebates, were granted on re-exports. Because this was an age of rivalry, when measures were introduced as much to damage others as to help oneself, such aid was given especially to counter the successful exports of another country. Far from welcoming the cheap imports from another state, as would have been rational (but for the seller mentality that everywhere prevailed), the feeling was that a rival should not be allowed to corner any lucrative trade, and home producers should be offered attractive inducements to keep such imports out. The English government, troubled at the flourishing import of linen from Germany and the United Provinces, gave special assistance to Scottish and Irish producers in order to dispense with them. The governments of France, Sweden and Germany supported local woollen industries to reduce dependence on imports from England. The Dutch, alarmed at the possibility that England might take over the finishing of cloth in which the Dutch had long specialised, prohibited for a time the import or sale of cloth finished in England. Duties were thus sometimes as much designed to damage opponents as to assist the home industry. The French tariffs of 1664–7 were explicitly directed at damaging the Dutch (though France was obliged to abandon them in the Treaty of Nymegen), while English tariffs were often aimed against the French. Tariff schedules, such as those of Colbert in 1664–7 and those of Walpole in 1720–3, were carefully calculated, not only to protect domestic producers, but also to damage foreign industry. In each case, political motives were almost as powerful as commercial ones (indeed, in this age it is often difficult to separate the two considerations).

Thus tariffs were now increasingly used not only to promote revenue, but for the express purpose of *protection*. Many governments supported luxury industries such as silk, tapestries and glassware. There was a belief that, while every country would need to import part of its raw materials, in the manufacturing sector every country should, so far as was possible, provide for all its own needs and so keep out foreign competitors. For this purpose, very high duties were imposed, and some imports prohibited altogether. Corresponding drawbacks or exemptions were given to promote exports or re-exports. Import-saving was equally important. Part of the reason for draining and cultivating the fens in England was to grow native flax, oats and hemp, and so dispense with imports. To compete with the flourishing Dutch fishing industry, England tried to develop the technique of salting and barrelling herring, as well as prohibiting imports of Dutch fish. The mining of precious metals was everywhere encouraged, to reduce the loss of treasure and to pay for imports. In general the aim was to admit raw materials and skilled workpeople but to keep out rival manufactures. Colbert in France, concerned to develop the porcelain, glass, tapestry, linen and metal industries, subsidised the import of Flemish and Dutch artisans for this purpose, hoping to win a leading role for France in industries formerly dominated by Italy and the Low Countries. For Gobelin tapestries and Van Robais woollens, he even set up state workshops, in a type of early socialism; while for other industries he maintained an elaborate system of state inspection to maintain the quality and reputation of French products. The whole business of commerce, Colbert declared, consists in 'facilitating the import of those goods which serve a country's manufactures, and placing embargoes on those which enter in a manufactured state'.

Protection was used most widely in relation to *shipping*. Besides its obvious strategic importance, this had a role in the competition for money. Governments increasingly resented seeing so much of the trade of their own country, both imports and exports, carried in foreign ships, annoyingly often Dutch. Support for native shipping thus helped in achieving another important objective of the age, saving the specie paid out in freight charges and insurance. Governments commonly laid down that all trade coming from their own colonies should be carried exclusively in native ships. The English tried to carry this further, extending it to all trade from outside Europe. Under the Navigation Act of 1651, no goods from Asia, Africa or America were to be imported in foreign ships. From Europe, goods must be carried either in English ships or in ships of the country of origin, while the coasting trade was to be reserved for vessels entirely owned by Englishmen. These measures were aimed directly against the entrepôt trade of the Dutch, who traded between the country of origin and third countries.[14] The French, too, introduced measures to reduce the dominance of the Dutch, who had formerly exported much of the produce of the French Caribbean colonies, in such trade. Colbert introduced regulations confining trade from French possessions to French ships. Everywhere nations were concerned to increase not only their own share of the goods traded but also their share of the shipping which carried that trade.

Another means widely used by the chief trading nations to win and increase their share in trade was the establishment of state-sponsored, or at least state-licensed, *chartered companies* to trade with particular areas. the first of such companies went back to the first half of the sixteenth century, but it was in the present period that they reached their peak. The East India Company, the largest and most important of English companies, was founded in 1601 as the period began, while the Dutch East India Company, for long its main rival, was created in the following year. (The corresponding French company was established by Colbert to break into the oriental trade in 1664.) The companies expanded rapidly, especially between 1650 and 1720: in England in the seventy years before the boom burst at the time of the South Sea Bubble, the capital of the East India Company doubled, that of the Hudson Bay company trebled and that of the Royal Africa Company quadrupled. Such companies 'were not created simply for economic reasons; many had as their main purpose the securing of monopolies, trading privileges of state support that would not be given to individuals'.[15] Some of them, such as the Merchant Adventurers in England, were regulated companies which were supposed to be open to all who wanted to join. Others were associations limited to their original members. But increasingly from the seventeenth century, the joint stock company emerged: instead of capital for a single voyage, or a limited term of years, shares of a fixed amount were issued, which could be bought and sold. Whatever the formal structure, they were often granted monopolies in the trade to large areas of the world. As a result, in this period about the only countries to which private English merchants could trade freely were France, Spain and Portugal.[16]

The establishment of such companies was, like other measures, often directed against a specific rival. The main purpose of the Royal Africa Company and the Corporation of the Royal Fishery in England was to drive the Dutch from their previously dominant position in

West Africa and North Sea fishing (the virulently anti-Dutch Duke of York, later James II, was governor of both). The Dutch East India Company was largely founded to conquer the trade previously controlled by Spain and Portugal, then united, with which the Dutch were at war.[17] But from the end of the seventeenth century, the monopolies began to be withdrawn. In England the Merchant Adventurers, the Eastland Company and the Royal Africa Company all lost their monopolies in the last quarter of the seventeenth century. In 1699, the trade to Newfoundland and Russia was thrown open. The monopoly of the Levant Company was ended in 1773. Only the East India Company and the Hudson Bay Company maintained their monopolies a little longer, despite constant attacks on them in the English parliament. The national interest in trade now seemed better forwarded by opening it to wider participation by the growing merchant class.

Another means of securing a favourable trading position was the planting of *colonies*. In many cases the original purpose of the Europeans in settling in remote foreign parts was to win access to particular products which could be traded in Europe: gold and silver in South America, spices in the East, sugar and tobacco in the Caribbean, silk and other textiles in India. Only in New England was the object settlement for its own sake. Colonisation was thus an effect of the search for trade rather than an object in itself. Only later, after settlement had taken place, did governments, wishing to reserve the trade for themselves, or seeking better protection for their settlers, acquiesce, often without enthusiasm, in the formal foundation of colonies. This made it possible to reserve the trade of an entire area to the mother country. For this reason, as the period progressed, the desire for colonies became keener. But at this time the object was still the trade that resulted, not the pride in possession. It was for commercial reasons that England demanded and acquired Jamaica from Spain in 1665, Newfoundland, Hudson Bay and Arcadia (Nova Scotia) from France in 1713; it was for trading purposes that France acquired Hispaniola from Spain in 1697; and for the same reasons too that France and England fought each other so bitterly in the Caribbean, Canada and India during the mid-eighteenth century. Such possessions, of course, had a strategic value as well, but often the main strategic concern was to be able to protect the commercial benefits. There was a continuous interaction between commercial and strategic interests. A fortified post or naval station might be acquired originally to protect trade, but later became an asset to be defended in its own right. The traders needed some degree of armed power to protect themselves, even if the government would not provide it. For this reason, the chartered companies would often build their own forts: so the Royal Africa Company and its successors, the Company of Merchants Trading to Africa, had itself to maintain the nine British forts in the Gold Coast, Gambia and Whydah to protect the British traders operating there (just as the old wool staple had once had to take responsibility for maintaining the fortification of Calais). Whoever provided it, military power was often the only sure means of maintaining economic power.

Thus the new economic ambitions of this age, with the changed social structure of states, promoted the use of new means to fulfil them. The most widely desired economic objective of states was a favourable balance of trade, and to a lesser extent a flourishing trade generally. To this end, trade was captured by war if necessary, or by other violent means, through state-sponsored companies, by colonialism, by diplomacy, by appropriate tariff and other policies. Exports were promoted by bounties and subsidies, for a time by monopolies. Imports were deterred by duties and other inhibitions, by Navigation Acts restricting certain trade to native shipping, and other means. These means were marginally less dictatorial, less abrupt and unpredictable in their incidence, than those of the monarchs in the previous age. But they were, at root, more nationalistic in intention, concerned with the ambitions of states rather than of rulers. They were somewhat more deliberate and carefully considered than earlier strategies, but they took equally little account of the effects on other nations. And they were now means that were likely to benefit not only the ruling monarchs themselves, but also the lesser nobility and wealthier classes generally, including the growing merchant community who wielded increasing influence within every state.

TARIFF-CUTS AND TREATIES (1750–1870)

The growing influence of this merchant class meant that a different set of means was used, to secure a different set of economic objectives, in the age that followed. The dominant motive was no longer to protect the balance of trade, national revenues and particular national industries. Increasingly it was, for nations as for individuals, to win markets abroad. This called for new strategies.

Some of the means that had been characteristic of the age before were now no longer used. The cruder measures began to be abandoned. Wars were now rarely fought, like those of England and France against the Dutch, mainly for economic reasons. Trade boycotts against other states were not used in peacetime, such as those formerly imposed by Spain and France against the Dutch. Colonies were not now mainly acquired for economic reasons (and not much acquired at all). Chartered companies were not created for winning trade (though both these methods were to be revived in the age that followed). Bounties, drawbacks and subsidies were widely abandoned. Colonial monopolies began to be given up.

The influence of the growing commercial classes and of commercial motives, together with the new doctrine associated with Adam Smith that reflected their concerns, altered the strategies adopted. There was less emphasis on restrictions and other state interventions, the universally favoured instruments of the previous age. The state's economic interests abroad, it was increasingly claimed, could be best promoted by its individual citizens doing business there; and the state's basic role was to assist them in that business, not to place impositions on them.

Since the main aim was to increase trade, the simplest means for governments was negotiation with other states to expand trading opportunities. All states, even those that were not economically powerful, were anxious to negotiate trade treaties for mutual advantage: creating market opportunites for the main exports of the other state – especially if they were not produced at home – in return for corresponding opportunities for home exports in the other state. This strategy of course, was specially advantageous to those states that were economically powerful – which meant mainly Britain. The imbalance of economic power had the effect that a mutual reduction of tariff and other barriers, even a general freeing of trade, would win more trade for these advanced states than they could lose at home. Mutual reductions could be won by negotiation (as in the Eden Treaty of 1786 and the Cobden Treaty of 1860, both between Britain and France). But such states might also introduce unilateral reductions, in the belief that not only would this benefit consumers at home but would also encourage corresponding reductions abroad in the future. So Britain opened India and other possessions to foreign trade in 1833, and all British colonies in 1849–52; while France abandoned its Navigation Act excluding foreign traders from its colonies in 1864.

Thus diplomacy was seen as an essential weapon for winning trade abroad. Governments continually entered into negotiations with other states to conclude new commercial treaties. In the years from 1785 to

1793, Britain undertook prolonged and intensive commercial negotiations with France, Portugal, Spain, Russia, Poland, Prussia, the Two Sicilies and Holland, sending special missions for that purpose, as well as undertaking lesser negotiations with Sweden, Turkey and the Austrian Netherlands. Lord Macartney was sent as far as China to talk about the opening up of trade. In the next century, negotiations were almost as intensive. For ambassadors, it was an important task to seek openings for commerce, to protect trade and other interests abroad, including redressing the claims of individual citizens.[18] Diplomacy was not normally used to seek to win trade for individual firms (a matter which sometimes caused resentment among the latter). But it was frequently and forcefully employed, especially with weaker states, to secure concessions in particular areas or better trading conditions generally.

New machinery was developed for this purpose. Colbert's example in the previous age in appointing consuls whose main function was to expand trading opportunities was now widely copied by other governments. Britain increasingly appointed, in major cities throughout Europe and in some other areas, consuls and consul-generals whose job was largely to protect local British traders. Other nations, especially Prussia, Austria and the Netherlands, followed suit. The machinery for this purpose in capitals was also improved. Parliamentary or other committees were established to consider problems surrounding a particular trade, or trade in particular areas. Boards of Trade and Departments of Commerce grew rapidly. A commercial department was created in the British Foreign Office in 1866. Commercial attachés began to be appointed to British embassies abroad in the next 20 years.

A new diplomatic instrument for expanding trade was devised in the Treaty of Navigation and Commerce. This normally set out the conditions of trade between two states, laying down the treatment that would be accorded to traders, conditions of residence, travel, the level of duties, port dues and customs facilities. Often these explicitly provided for full 'national treatment' – in other words the right to buy or rent property, trade, employ labour, and so on, on the same terms as local nationals. Some treaties provided simply for reciprocal concessions between two governments. But, in this age, they increasingly included a most-favoured-nation clause, extending to the country concerned the most favourable concessions granted to any other state. A few were 'open door' treaties, declaring that all states would automatically enjoy equal treatment.

In such negotiations, nations naturally sought to strike bargains on the basis most favourable to themselves. So Britain sought mainly the reduction of tariffs on industrial goods elsewhere. Prussia, and other states strong in grain production, demanded above all reductions in agricultural restrictions (such as Britain's own Corn Laws). Sometimes, diplomacy was used, equally aggressively, to counter the commercial arrangements of other states, as when Britain sought to hinder the Zollverein (see p. 133). Sometimes, a country would take action against another as a lever to bring about concessions: as when Portugal in the early 1780s (knowing that Britain specially valued the Portuguese trade which yielded a favourable balance) unilaterally stopped British exports of Irish goods and raised duties on other products, so as to bargain from a position of strength for better conditions for her wine exports.

As in other ages, a means open to the economically powerful states was to proclaim or extend new trading principles – the reduction of protection, and the principles of reciprocity and non-discrimination – which they knew were likely to benefit mainly themselves. In 1815, Britain was able to induce the US to accept a treaty in which both governments pledged themselves not to introduce discriminatory duties. In Turkey, Persia and China, she helped persuade the governments there to adopt low tariffs which applied equally to all outside powers, on the general grounds that low tariffs were always good. Twice, in 1776 and 1860, she negotiated with France treaties which brought about a huge expansion of trade, mainly to her own advantage.[19] When Argentina began to raise her tariffs in 1837, Palmerston instructed the British Minister to 'try to convince the Argentines of the merit of Free Trade and of the disaster that would inevitably follow from a policy of high tariffs';[20] and in 1851, a circular was sent to British envoys abroad instructing them to bring the advantages of free trade to the notice of foreign governments. Gladstone, proposing that Britain should hold New Granada to the most-favoured-nation treaty it had negotiated, argued that otherwise 'unsophisticated Latin American governments might use the opportunity to adopt unrestrained protection, under the misguided impression, derived from European experience, that it would provide the key to national wealth':[21] ignoring the possibility that there could be differences in the economic situation of different states, or that protection might have been a perfectly valid policy for Britain herself at an earlier time.

More brutal means than negotiations were still sometimes used, especially with non-European states. All-out warfare was, from time to time, employed. Britain made war on China in 1839 – or at least caused a trivial incident to be made into a war – in order to secure better access to markets that had previously been jealously guarded; and she joined with France in a similar war for similar purposes, against the same country, 20 years later. The French occupation of Algiers and its hinterland, if not undertaken primarily for commercial reasons, became the means for providing new outlets for the commerce and capital of Marseilles and the settlement of large numbers of French population from the southern coast-lands. France's war against Mexico, though undertaken primarily to win national prestige was expected to bring economic benefits, as was her occupation of Senegal. In other cases, the result of a war could be *used* as the opportunity to secure commercial benefits: as when, after Britain's defeat in the War of American Independence, France and Spain demanded and secured new and more favourable commercial agreements as part of the peace terms. Armed force short of war was used to protect economic interests: as where Britain employed force in Latin America to ensure that her bondholders received payments due to them (according to one calculation between 1820 and 1914 Britain used or threatened armed force against Latin American states at least 40 times, including 14 times to enforce the claims of British subjects, 12 to 'restore order' or protect property, and 10 to avenge offences against national honour or dignity).[22] British naval power was used to protect or promote British commercial interests in Argentina in 1845, in Greece in 1850 and in Mexico in 1861. French naval power was used against Cochin China in 1847 and 1858 before its annexation in 1862. And Britain and France combined in occupying the Piraeus in 1859 to ensure repayment of a loan.

Sometimes, trade was promoted, or the trade of others damaged, by economic sanctions. Since Britain had the most powerful navy, this method was used especially by her: against neutrals in wartime and against any small state which failed to pay its debts in peacetime. But since Britain was believed to be particularly dependent on trade, the measure was also used especially *against* her. Soon after war broke out between Britain and France in 1793, France banned the entry of all commodities made and manufactured in Britain or the British colonies (or even of goods 'reputed' to be made there). In the Berlin Decrees of 1806, Napoleon went further, prohibiting all commercial relations between any of the countries under his control and Britain, declaring that any vessels that had touched Britain's ports were lawful prize; at the same time he raised France's duties against all foreign countries (an action which caused far greater damage to France than any other state because of the shortage of goods and the rise in prices which it brought about). This kind of economic warfare aroused intense resentment among neutrals and there was an attempt to negotiate special provisions to guard against it. So in 1778 the US concluded a treaty with France under which she reserved the right to trade with an enemy of France without interference: an undertaking at first observed by France when war broke out with Britain in 1793, but abandoned in the Berlin Decrees of 1806 which allowed no exception for US ships. A more comprehensive effort to change the rules was made by Sweden, which in the 1770s sought an international Congress to establish a code of neutrality; and, when this attempt failed, by Russia, Sweden and Denmark which joined in 1780 in affirming the principle of 'armed neutrality', under which neutral goods in enemy ships and enemy goods in neutral ships were declared immune from seizure and only fully effective blockades recognised as legitimate: principles that were eventually generally confirmed (even by Britain) in the Convention on Maritime Warfare of 1856.

So, once more the means adopted were largely conditioned by the character of the elites in power and the motives that inspired them. With the merchant class and merchant interests increasingly to the fore, new aims and new methods prevailed. The road to economic power, which had formerly been found in the rigid protection and supervision by each government of its own industry, was now sought in the abolition of such restraints and the establishment of a competitive commercial struggle, similar to that taking place *within* most states: each nation for itself and let the devil take the hindmost. Such measures often created great difficulties for the more backward states of Europe, still seeking to build up their own industries; and still more for the underdeveloped countries of Asia, the Near East and Latin America with little control of their own destinies and no industries of their own. They suited the interests of the dominant groups in the dominant states of the system: the industrial and commercial classes of Britain and, later, of the other industrial powers of Western Europe that followed in her path.

CONCESSIONS AND COLONIES (1870–1914)

In the age that followed, a new set of strategies was adopted, again reflecting the economic aspirations of the newly dominant interest-groups in that era.

The dominant groups in this age were holders of capital, the bondholders and bankers who sought new opportunities to invest beyond the seas. In this aim, they were aided and abetted by their governments, which increasingly assisted them in securing the opportunities they sought.

The most widely adopted means was the use of *diplomatic pressures* on other governments. While it was the banks which floated the loans, governments would often pave the way for this through diplomatic negotiations. Both would make sure that the other was fully aware of what it was doing. There was, as we saw, often a close relationship between governments and their own financial institutions (see p. 90). In Germany, for example, it was 'by private, direct, unofficial but steady communication with the directing heads of the important banks that the Kaiser and the foreign office assured themselves of the adjustment of capital movements to their judgements and policies ... With the drawing together within the same circles of the ambition of the monarchy, the naval and military advocates, and the commercial and financial interests ... it became customary on the part of the banks to consult the foreign office in regard to foreign loans to which a political interest might attach, or to which serious objection might be entertained.'[23] Conversely, 'the government ... often sought to induce the banks and investors to finance projects deemed essential to the advancement of imperial aims, to sway judgements and action in favour of lands where a prospect of increased German trade and power was seen'.[24] Similarly in France, 'the government was to be found in the lead in the negotiation of foreign loans which it wished to see in the possession of Frenchmen ... Often it induced the banks to accept business of which they were in doubt, cooperated with them in the public sale of loans by creating a popular understanding that patriotism demanded their purchase.'[25] The British government likewise, though somewhat less inclined to intervene actively on behalf of British business, gave support where necessary. As Sir Edward Grey put it in the House of Commons shortly before the opening of the First World War: 'I regard it as our duty, wherever bona fide British capital is forthcoming in any part of the world, and is applying for concessions for which there are no valid political objections, that we should give it the utmost support we can and endeavour to convince the foreign governments concerned that it is to its interests as well as to our own to give the concessions for railways and so forth to British firms who carry them out at reasonable prices and in the best possible way.'[26]

A particular means of expanding a country's economic power was by winning *'concessions' and contracts.*[27] Diplomatic representatives abroad competed with each other to win such rights. In Tunis, the French, Italian and British consuls engaged in bitter competition to win railway, telegraph and other contracts; as did British and Russian representatives in Persia, British and French in Egypt and Siam, and all the major powers in Turkey, China, and Latin America. New means of winning such contracts was devised. From the 1880s, in face of increasing foreign pressures, British governments began to overcome their traditional reluctance to give diplomatic assistance to individual financial and commercial concerns (previously they had not normally needed it). The Brice Memorandum on Diplomatic and Consular Assistance to British Trade Abroad, of July 1886, set out the kind of assistance which a British representative ought to be prepared to give to British business. This included introducing or recommending British traders and businessmen to foreign officials, securing 'fair hearing and full consideration' for them in any matter of concessions and contracts and 'where exceptional pressure is being used by these [foreign] Envoys, ... to exert similar pressure'.[28] Sir Edward Grey endorsed the need for such pressure if necessary, stating that 'where diplomatic pressure was the rule, commercial interest could not succeed without it'.[29] So the British minister in Peking believed that 'to be efficient and render the best service within their power to British commerce, [consuls] ought not only to report commercial matters to the Foreign Office and Her Majesty's Legation, but also to be on the lookout to show British merchants and traders when and how to take advantage of commercial openings, and if necessary to introduce British agents willingly, yet with just discrimination, to the local authorities'.[30]

Railway concessions were particularly sought after: they could bring the chance to make not only loans to the government or railway authorities concerned, but also subsidiary contracts for construction and purchase of equipment. All over the world, governments and financial institutions, and sometimes industry, combined to secure railway concessions for their own country, often for reasons that were as much political as economic. Lord Lansdowne assured the House of Lords in 1903 that 'the associations which represent British interests in the matter of railway construction in China will certainly receive from His Majesty's government backing which I hope will bear comparison with that received by the representatives of other countries'.[31] The French government shared the same concern: 'To secure the cession to French interests of the right to build in [Tunis and Morocco] roads, railroads and portworks, to exploit mineral deposits, and to found banks, the French representatives used all the art of pleading. When proof of mutual benefit and other forms of inducement failed, and a rival government secured rights that might be turned to political claims, financial pressure or forceful menaces were applied to prevent these regions from escaping French hegemony. By these means a monopoly of railroad and port construction was obtained.'[32] So, all over the world, in the Near East as in the Far East, in Turkey as in Persia, in Latin America as in Africa, the European powers competed with each other for railway concessions. In Abyssinia, Italy, France and Britain even negotiated with each other for rail contracts, partitioning the country between them for this purpose, with little regard for the views of the Abyssinian government. In China, the powers claimed and acquired the right to build railways in different areas, leaving the country with half a dozen different rail systems and three different gauges. Moreover, in many cases a considerable degree of control was maintained for the foreigners even after the lines were built. European managers were frequently appointed to run as well as to build them. The financing groups were given a share in the control of the operation of the railways in China and in the British colonies; and in Turkey, India, Mexico, Argentina and Brazil the railway concessions awarded gave the financing group full control of operations.[33]

A new means that began to be employed in this age was the *tying* of loans: making them conditional on orders for domestic industry. Many governments conformed with the demand contained in a resolution passed by the Paris Chamber of Commerce that 'whenever a foreign loan is admitted to official listing, this should be made conditional upon the concession of advantages to French commerce and industry'.[34] The French and German governments, in their negotiations with Latin American governments about loans, consistently demanded that the proceeds should be spent on orders for their industry, or even that their own nationals should be placed in the management of the enterprise.[35] When French banks were negotiating loans to Russia and Japan in 1908, the French government, pressed by the steel and iron industry, asked for orders for French industry as a condition. In 1912, the French government asked the city of Prague in return for the granting of a loan to the city, to undertake to place orders in France.[36] In Turkey and the Balkans, particularly, the French government 'endeavoured to ensure that these needy and belligerent borrowers placed their orders where they found the favour of a loan'.[37] These were frequently orders for war materials, and the chief French manufacturer of war materials at this time, Creusot, sometimes itself took part in the negotiation of loans. German loans were particularly often tied, because of the close connection between the banks, which made the loans, and domestic industry. The British at first were less inclined to demand tying of this kind, because of their traditional belief in free competition (and, no doubt, their faith in their ability to win contracts without tying), but they too adopted the system occasionally: the Canton–Kowloon railway loan agreement of 1907, for example, provided that 'at equal rates and qualities goods of British manufacture shall be given preference over other goods of foreign origin'. And one of the reasons why governments did so much to assist investment in their own colonies, giving them, for example, special facilities in their capital markets (the British government for example granted them 'trusteeship' status), was the confident knowledge that most would be spent in home markets: 95 per cent of the borrowed funds of the government of India are said to have been spent in Britain. And the French Chamber of Deputies, in granting authorisation for loans to colonies, often inserted a provision that materials for public works not found in the borrowing colony should be of French origin and be carried in French ships.[38]

Government officials increasingly helped industry to win trade abroad. From about 1880, Britain appointed commercial attachés abroad and, for a time at the end of the century, 'commercial agents'. More significant, perhaps, consuls and other official representatives gave a considerable amount of 'commercial intelligence' to their own traders. The whole business of obtaining and spreading this intelligence was highly organised in Britain and other countries. A departmental committee on commercial intelligence was set up in Britain in 1898, and as a result of its report an Advisory Committee on Commercial Intelligence was established, while an intelligence branch was set up in the Board of Trade in addition. Ambassadors and other representatives were expected to secure introductions for visiting businessmen.[39] In some cases, the consuls even held agencies for home firms and acted on their behalf in seeking business: for example, British consuls in Latin America, besides acting as agents on behalf of bondholders, held agencies for the Royal Mail Line and English insurance companies; one acted as chairman of the committee of a railway company, and another as chief cashier of a bank.[40] Finally, from about this time also began the custom of sending visiting commercial missions, groups of businessmen, often officially supported, seeking to examine the market and establish contacts with local importers and retailers, to promising markets abroad.

But as common as the use of political means for financial ends was the use of financial instruments for political ends. For example as we saw earlier, the *control of capital markets* was used to make sure that the available financial resources went to allies only and not to potential enemies (see p. 145). Subtle ways were found of making the financial institutions aware of governments' views on such matters. In Britain, for example, meetings of the Bank of England Board of Governors 'brought together representatives of large investment houses; through them a government policy could easily be conveyed. Financial institutions outside this group were in business relations with the Bank of England, and could hear echoes of official desires. Often the Bank's approval of contemplated issues was definitely asked, especially when the state of the money market made it possibly inadvisable to issue foreign loans.'[41] The French government were even more concerned to ensure that loans went only to friends.[42] The German government too was concerned to influence the lending of its banks. Bismarck intervened to stop the Reischsbank from accepting Russian bonds as collateral security in 1886–7, and his successors intervened to stop borrowing by Serbia in 1893 and 1906. Conversely, the German government sometimes sought to stimulate lending by German banks in politically favourable areas; it 'addressed the banks not so much to restrain them as to induce them to accept new responsibilities, to undertake loans and enterprises deemed of service to the German state and German economy'.[43] Everywhere, the banks were seen in part as instruments of government policy which should back up and reinforce the efforts which governments made by political means.

Sometimes *banks* were used even more directly as the instruments of the governments' political aims. Banks were deliberately founded to secure influence in a particular country. The British government set up the Imperial Bank of Persia in 1889, through a royal charter, in order to promote national interests in that country;[44] a move countered by the establishment of the Banque des Prets de Perse, set up by the Russian government to compete in lending to the Shah with the same motives. The French government helped to promote the establishment of the Banque Industrielle de Chine in 1902–3; while Britain in turn used the Hong Kong and Shanghai Bank as 'the chosen instrument' of British financial diplomacy in China.[45] The German government stimulated German banks to enter into the development of Morocco, using the whole weight of German diplomacy on their behalf; and it promoted and assisted the Deutsche Asiatische Bank in its effort to win a share in the financing of the Chinese government. In Turkey, the National Bank of Turkey 'was the direct brainchild of the

[British] foreign office' and 'was intended to restore the British position, creating – in emulation of the French-dominated Imperial Ottoman Bank and the Deutsche Bank – a single centre of British financial enterprise and influence at Constantinople'.[46]

Various political means were open to governments for extending or defending their economic interests. One of the instruments of diplomacy in less advanced parts of the world was the offer of *'treaties'*, according certain kinds of benefit in return for commercial rights. In Africa, European explorers, traders and adventurers, with or without authorisation from their own governments, freely offered 'treaties' to local chieftains, who would gladly bargain away their rights in return for monetary payments or the promise of valued goods, such as firearms and alcohol. So the British businessman, Taubman, founder of the United African Company, is said to have drawn up more than 400 treaties to be signed by native chieftains in West Africa. Explorers in Africa would simply carry around with them blank treaty forms which could be used to secure signatures from unsuspecting chiefs encountered on their journey; these might subsequently discover they had pledged a dominant control, or even full sovereignty, to some foreign monarch of whom they had previously never even heard, or at least granted commercial pre-eminence to the European state concerned.[47] Commercial rights could also be acquired through the conclusion of treaties with more advanced states. Britain virtually imposed a treaty on Morocco in 1856, which opened up Morocco to British trade, allowed Britons to trade in any part of the country, and exempted British subjects from all taxation except customs duties. The European powers secured a succession of treaties with China, Turkey, Siam, Persia and Latin American countries, providing for themselves commercial opportunities, often on very favourable terms. In many cases, the object of such treaties was to provide for their own nationals a more favourable trading position than that of the merchants of other states.

A surer means of securing commercial domination in particular areas was to make arrangements not with local rulers but with other European powers themselves: for example, through establishing *'spheres of interest'*. Most of the eastern part of China, for example, the only part of interest to foreigners, was divided between the chief European powers into such 'spheres', in each of which one of them had dominant, although not usually exclusive rights. It would then have a prior claim to concessions and contracts granted in that area, a general commercial pre-eminence, and sometimes leased territory, bases or other special facilities. So Britain claimed the prosperous Yangtze Valley, France southern China (close to her Indo-China possessions), Germany the Shantung coast, while Russia and Japan at different times held dominance in Manchuria. In East Africa Britain and Germany quite explicitly (in 1885–7 and 1890) divided the area into 'spheres' of economic and political influence, quite regardless of the views of the inhabitants of the area. Similarly in 1899, Britain and France divided most of North Africa into spheres of influence where each would be pre-eminent, and in 1904 agreed a similar partition in south-east Asia, Newfoundland, the Pacific and elsewhere, again without consulting the views of the local inhabitants. Sometimes, indeed, European powers would agree amongst themselves such a division of interest without consulting the responsible European power, still less the local peoples: Britain, in 1885, acknowledged a German sphere of interest in the Congo (although that territory was controlled by the king of the Belgians); in 1898, Germany and Britain accorded economic spheres of influence to each other in the Portuguese African colonies; and in 1914, Britain, Germany and France made secret agreements which would have divided up the whole of the Near East between them if the war had not supervened.

A still greater degree of economic dominance could be secured by the establishment of '*protectorates*'. This was another new device, almost exclusive to this age. A protectorate looked more respectable, and less provocative to others, than full-scale annexation or creation of a 'colony'. Yet it gave all the essential attributes of control for economic (and strategic) purposes without the inconvenient burden of direct administration. The degree of economic control acquired was scarcely distinguishable from that in colonies. French economic control in Tunis and Morocco, which were ostensibly protectorates, was little less complete than in Algiers, which was alleged to be part of France itself. Nearly all the British acquisitions of this period – Nigeria, Nyasaland, Uganda, British East Africa (later Kenya), Zanzibar, Bechuanaland, Swaziland, Basutoland, the northern territories of the Gold Coast, the Aden hinterland, the Malay States, the Maldives, the Solomons, Brunei, Tonga and other Pacific territories – were called protectorates or (in the case of the more organised and advanced) 'protected states', but in administration were little different from full-scale colonies. Similarly the German acquisitions of the period – South-West Africa, Ruanda, Burundi, Togo, Cameroon, and New Guinea – were named protectorates, though colonies in all but name.[48]

Whether the territories controlled were named protectorates or colonies, the economic power wielded by the metropolitan states was complete. Tariffs were imposed to suit their own interests (this was one of their main motives – Rhodes declared that 'the future government of the world is a question of tariffs'). Preferences were given to their own traders that were not granted to others. In some cases, the rights were exclusive: in King Leopold's Congo, a total monopoly was maintained either for the state (as for rubber and ivory production) or for Belgian firms: concessions covering entire provinces were given which granted companies almost sovereign powers to raise taxes and impose forced labour, under appalling conditions and on threat of execution, while the king enjoyed an equally privileged position in his own royal domain.[49] In other words, a wide variety of means were used to ensure that the colonies controlled brought as handsome a return as possible to the businesses of the metropolitan powers. It is not surprising that the London Chamber of Commerce, in a report of April 1893, said in relation to Uganda: 'The uniform experience of the country from 1568 down to the present reign is that colonies amply repay the first expenditure in blood and money, and that they pay both by the extension of trade and shipping and in the growth of national power and status ... It should be sufficient for us to know that investments of this class are invariably good in the long run.' How far the investment was profitable to the government, after all the extensive costs of administration are taken into account, may be debated. That it was very profitable to some of their nation's businessmen and companies is beyond dispute.

There were other ways of extending economic power, by more indirect means. One was the revival of *trading companies*, which became, in effect, administrative agencies. This gave most of the financial responsibility to commercial organisations, yet at the same time effectively established a national presence in each area. So Germany, having acquired in 1884–5 three protectorates in Southwest Africa, East Africa and New Guinea, set up three chartered companies, all established in 1885, which in effect administered each region while also pursuing their own economic interests there. Britain, having acquired its sphere of influence in the lower Niger region in 1886, chartered the Royal Niger Company to perform a similar function there: in return for undertaking all administration, including the administration of justice, the company could impose customs duties (a right it exercised to keep out inconvenient foreign rivals) and pocket the proceeds. The British South Africa Company, a company run by Rhodes from South Africa, was given a royal charter and became responsible for the colonisation and administration of Rhodesia until 1923, when Rhodesia became self-governing; the African Lakes Company (later the British Central Africa Company) performed a similar function in Nyasaland; as did the Imperial British East Africa Company in Kenya and Uganda. The North Borneo Company was given a charter in 1881 which entitled it to administer that area. Sometimes, a chartered company even effectively administered part of the colonies of *other* states: in Mozambique, for example, three British companies holding charters from the Portuguese government not only operated the water works, telegraphs and tramways, controlled mining operation and constructed railways, but in effect carried out the administration of large parts of the country. Most extraordinary of all, perhaps, among these arrangements was the so-called 'Congo Free State', which was technically not a colony at all, since it claimed an independent sovereignty distinct from that of Belgium, yet was to a large extent the personal property of the king of the Belgians, who administered the territory exclusively for his own interest and that of Belgium, and to a lesser extent of other European financiers: there the companies holding concessions were in effect given freedom to run their own territories largely independently, which they did, not surprisingly, very much to their own profit and at very heavy cost, human and economic, to the local inhabitants.

Another means used by European powers to win economic advantages in their dealings with less powerful states was the *control of tariffs*. So Britain secured from the Bey of Tunis an undertaking to limit import duties on British goods to 8 per cent (a concession later extended to imports from other states). Similarly, the ruler of Morocco was persuaded to accept a maximum tariff of 10 per cent from 1886, while the Sultan of Zanzibar and the Burmese government had to accept maximum levels of 5 per cent. The tariff of the Ottoman Empire had been limited to a maximum of 3 per cent after the Crimean War, but authority to raise it was graciously granted in 1907. France secured from the impotent Chinese emperor, after his defeat by Japan in 1895, reductions of 30–40 per cent in the tariffs imposed on goods from Indo-China. In other cases, a more far-reaching control was established: the entire administration of customs was taken over by European powers. The Liberian customs were controlled by Britain in the period when her loans were usually raised in London, and taken over by the US in 1912, when an American receiver-general and financial adviser were appointed. Britain managed to ensure that the Chinese customs system continued to be run throughout this period by a Briton, even though there were attempts by other European powers, especially the French, to take over that privilege. In other cases, a form of collective control of the revenues of the dependent state was instituted by two or more powers acting together, to safeguard the payment of interest charges (see p. 229). Still more easily could the advanced powers control the level of tariffs in their own colonial territories. And, naturally, such tariffs were normally regulated not to aid the development of infant industries in the territory concerned, but to suit the commercial and industrial interests of the metropolitan power concerned.

Another means that was widely used was the use of *financial sanctions* to enforce concessions of one kind or another. The countries which were the main source of loans were, of course, particularly well equipped to use such pressure. Thus the Congo Free State was permitted to borrow money in Paris only in return for a territorial concession to France. A Danish bank was refused access to the French capital market in 1902 unless Denmark revoked increases in duties on French wines which were then planned. In 1889, France warned Spain that the French capital market would be closed to her if she reduced the rate of interest on past loans as she had planned. In Britain, 'even before the formation of the Corporation [of Foreign Bondholders], the stock exchange had used its retaliatory powers against governments which had violated the conditions of their loan contracts ... With the creation of the Corporation the Stock Exchange, concerting its action with that of the protective association, joined to block or reduce the credit in London of the defaulter.'[50] There was no shame in a creditor seeking to ensure its debts were paid. But the resulting relationship was scarcely one of equality.

In more extreme cases, the *threat of force* could be used for economic ends by the more powerful states. So, for example, when it looked as if the Portuguese government might fail to satisfy the claims of the foreign bondholders, the French Minister of Foreign Affairs, M. Delcasse, declared in the French Senate, with scarcely veiled menace: 'I would hope, gentlemen, that the Portuguese government will recognise that it is in the interest of Portugal to give to the foreign bondholders that satisfaction which they have so long awaited. The government is aware that we do not lack the means of supporting the just claims of our countrymen, and it cannot doubt that in case of need we are fully resolved to employ them.'[51] France threatened naval action against the Bey of Tunis in 1879 to force him to recognise the claim of a French Count in dispute with his government over property (just as, in 1851, Britain had threatened a naval blockade against Morocco to induce the Sultan to sign a commercial treaty). France sent a battleship to support a French-owned bank against the Dominican Republic in 1892; and in 1901 she sent a naval force to Mytilene and seized the customs station there to settle a claim against the Turkish government, declaring 'that we wish to show that, to long and persistent denials of justice, to systematic detractions of our rights and interests, France, after exemplary patience, has something besides protests to put forward' (the claim was settled the day after the fleet arrived). Britain sent a warship to Guatemala in 1913 to ensure the repayment of a loan partly held by British investors; sent an ultimatum to Haiti to enforce the payment of compensation to a British subject for damage caused during a revolution; and between 1910 and 1914 bullied Mexico and Honduras into meeting the claims of British bondholders.[52] In 1901, Germany undertook a show of force against Honduras to deter that country from settling US but not other claims. And when Germany and Britain together sent naval forces against Venezuela in 1902, they sank two of her gunboats, captured others and imposed a blockade, to enforce the repayment of loans to their bondholders and reparation on other matters in dispute. In other words, in this age gunboat diplomacy was widely employed, not only to secure political objectives but for economic ends as well.

In the final resort, *force* might be used on a larger scale. So, for example, in 1881 France occupied Tunis for reasons that were largely economic. So, in the next year, Britain occupied Egypt by force, again for reasons that were at least partly economic (to protect the interest of the British bondholders), though also to restore law and order, and to protect Britain's strategic interests in the Suez Canal. Germany sent a naval squadron, under Prince Henry, to China in 1897 to help to secure the 'lease' of Kaiochow as a commercial and naval base. Russia gave armed assistance to a counter-coup designed to restore the deposed Shah of Persia in 1911–12 (and subsequently coolly asked Persia to pay the cost of sending Russian troops), and later helped organise a coup d'état to establish a government acceptable to her: again for reasons which, though primarily political, had economic overtones as well. Britain sent a naval force to assert British supremacy in the Persian Gulf in 1903. Force was used most frequently to acquire colonies: so France acquired Tongking and Annam, Britain annexed Upper Burma in 1885, Germany in effect conquered Tanganyika in 1890, Italy tried to conquer Abyssinia in 1894–6 and did conquer Libya in 1911–14, the US, after the conquest of Spain in 1897, annexed Puerto Rico and retained control of the Philippines for fifty years. In all these cases, economic considerations played at least a significant role among the motivations. In other words, in an age when force was tolerated, if not approved, as a means of settling differences, and when economic factors increasingly influenced other relationships, economic ends were sometimes secured by brute force.

So a considerable range of alternative means was used in this age to secure economic ends. More than at almost any other time there existed huge inequalities in power among states; especially between the European states on the one hand, and the extremely weak nations and territories of other parts of the world. The means adopted by states to secure economic ends reflected this imbalance of power. The more powerful states were often able to dictate the tariff policies of the weaker states. They could acquire control of their tax and customs systems, especially if they experienced any difficulty in repaying their debts (a difficulty the dominant states and their banks themselves helped create by lending far beyond the capacity to repay). They won trade preferences, trade routes and control of raw materials. They even found new constitutional devices to maintain this domination: the sphere of interest, the protectorate, the financial control. These means protected the interests of dominant forces in their own states. Nor did they feel any undue guilt about exercising economic power over other states in these ways. The unequal partnership that resulted was, in their eyes, merely the price, the reasonable price, that 'backward' economies had to pay as the cost of sharing the untold blessings of economic progress that the dominant powers benevolently bestowed.

PROTECTION AND PARITIES (1914–50)

In the age that followed, the strategies employed by governments changed again. The dominant force in society, not only in highly centralised dictatorships such as the Soviet Union, Germany, Japan and Italy but in democratic states too, was now the governmental machine itself, increasingly concerned to secure control of the domestic economy. And the means now used thus involved a far greater degree of active governmental intervention in international economic exchanges than had been seen in the previous two centuries.

New forms of intervention were developed, first, to secure the balance of payments. International payments were now derived less from the balance of trade alone. Increasingly, they included payments of interest on past debts, payments for shipping, insurance and other services, and capital flows. The old system for regulating the balance of international payments by means of the gold standard had broken down in 1914. Despite a brief attempt to revive it in the 1920s, it was never properly restored. Its slow-moving adjustment process, working gradually on prices and so eventually on employment in the deficit country, was now regarded by many governments as damagingly slow-moving and deflationary in its effects. Yet, because of major differences in economic strength, the varying burden of war debts and reparations, and finally world slump with the resulting collapse of commodity prices, imbalances were greater than ever. There was also now a new concern to safeguard employment and promote self-sufficiency. In an age of intervention, the simplest way to secure trading and monetary balance seemed to be by direct government action or bureaucratic regulation.

Some of the measures were revivals of those used for centuries for similar purposes. The *tariff*, the commonest of all the familiar instruments of protection, was now used on a scale never seen before. The Smoot-Hawley tariff, introduced in the US in 1930, was the highest of all the very high tariffs introduced over the years in that country of strong protectionist lobbies. Even Britain, for a century the apostle of free trade and its most consistent and full-hearted practitioner, now reimposed tariffs, only relieved – or, in the eyes of some, aggravated – by discrimination in favour of the British Commonwealth and Empire. The new countries of central and east Europe, with weak and fragmented economies, practised protection on a scale rarely seen before, with maximum government control of trade.[53]

To the traditional tariff – a tax to raise the price of the imported product – were now added quantitative controls in the form of *import quotas*. Controls of this kind could regulate even more precisely the volumes of a particular product which could be imported and the amount of foreign exchange which would be used for this. Fascist Germany, Italy and Spain all sought their economic salvation through direct control of the volume of imports. In other cases, licences were required to import, and were allocated or sold on the basis of need as assessed by the bureaucratic controllers. This system was used in France after 1933 and in Germany after 1934. Occasionally, the total prohibition of particular kinds of imports was introduced: a measure widely used in east Europe. Conversely, subsidies were often given for exports. Germany gave special inducements to industry to export, and even the US subsidised agricultural exports after 1938.

Another new set of measures was introduced to protect the balance

of payments. Strict and detailed *foreign exchange controls* were introduced in many countries. Available foreign exchange was sometimes
auctioned to the highest bidder. More often, it was allocated by
officials. In Germany, for example, under Schacht's New Plan of 1934,
importers were obliged to obtain foreign currency permits from the
supervisory offices which controlled foreign trade; and these permits
were at first restricted to importers wishing to purchase vital foodstuffs, raw materials or semi-manufactured goods. East and central
European governments instituted equally rigorous controls. Many
other governments elsewhere adopted similar methods for rationing
the use of foreign exchange. Such methods transferred the responsibility for deciding what should be imported from the merchant, acting on
the basis of market indicators, to the government, acting on the basis of
its own conception of national interest: 'This system enabled the
government to plan ahead for imports and to allocate foreign exchange
according to its own priority rather than leaving the decision to the
individual importers. It also enabled the government to determine not
only *what* goods and raw materials should be imported, but also *where*
the goods should come from ... This gave the government power to
regulate trade in accordance with political objectives, discriminating
between one country and another on diplomatic or strategic
grounds.'[54]

Competitive devaluation was another method much followed to
restore the balance of payments. Parities were altered far more
frequently than in earlier times to minimise the national interest.
France won an advantage for herself by devaluation in 1927, Britain
retaliated by devaluing in turn in 1931, the US responded in 1933,
while France turned the tables again in 1936. The parities set did not
necessarily correspond with the purchasing power of currencies. The
effect was to subject international exchanges to deliberate distortions
designed to serve the purposes of individual states. There was no
longer a conception, as under the gold standard, of the impartial
disciplines of an international economy. Each nation sought to promote its own economic purposes through unilateral measures.

A particular form which governmental intervention of this kind took
was the conclusion of *bilateral agreements* for the exchange of trade,
often on special terms. Such agreements could help in maintaining the
balance of payments and safeguarding levels of employment. These
too substituted the judgement of governments and officials for that of
merchants in deciding which trade was necessary. State trading nations, such as the Soviet Union, of course undertook all trade in this

way. But much of the trade of other nations was in this age carried out by those means. A great deal of trade in Germany, Japan and other countries was undertaken bilaterally, sometimes on a barter basis, often to serve their diplomatic as well as their economic policies. Most of the trade of the central and east European countries was directly controlled. In Germany's case, 'bilateral trade had to be regulated by trade agreements between governments. This gave the government power to regulate trade in accordance with political objectives, discriminating between one country and another on diplomatic or strategic grounds ... It became the main aim of German foreign trade policy to reorientate German trade to Europe and to those parts of the world which were not subject to colonial trade preference agreements, in particular Latin America.'[55] Even fully capitalist countries adopted similar methods. The US, for example, entered into trade agreements with 30 or 40 other countries. Indeed, many in the US during the New Deal, including Roosevelt's Foreign Trade Adviser, George Peek, believed that such a system of managed trade was the answer to the problems of this age: 'I believe,' he wrote, 'this situation represents a permanent change in the character of international trade ... The whole problem is one of finding methods whereby mutually advantageous exchanges of goods may take place.'[56] The Reciprocal Trade Agreements Act, which Roosevelt put through Congress in 1934, was designed to allow the US government to bring about a recovery of business in the US through a series of such agreements. Sometimes, bilateral agreements were for straight barter deals: Germany arranged to purchase wheat and other foodstuffs from east Europe in return for exports of manufactures, and she obtained oil from Russia through a similar arrangement. The German Foreign Office Memorandum of June 1934 concerning foreign trade policy specifically spoke of the value of 'the concept of barter in German commercial policy' and advocated 'making producers and suppliers of ... raw materials and consuming goods aware of the necessity of accepting increased imports of German industrial products in return.'[57]

These bilateral arrangements, of course, involved *discrimination* and the abandonment of principles which had been accepted (more or less) for more than a century. Bureaucratic intervention in economic exchanges made it easy to manipulate trade flows for political reasons. As the circular issued by the German Foreign Office in June 1934 put it (and similar sentiments would have been expressed by many other governments): 'the "most favoured nation" principle which, under normal economic conditions, ... had proved to be the best method of commercial policy, could not be maintained in its original form under the pressure of the crisis situation . . . The following measures have best served this purpose in German commercial policy during the past year: monopoly management of a number of the most important products, the introduction of embargoes on imports with simultaneously setting of quotas, and the increased application of tariff quotas. Import and tariff quotas have sometimes been introduced unilaterally and sometimes by means of treaties . . . Tariff rates . . . have, however, nowadays lost a great deal of their significance for trade as compared with restriction on imports and foreign exchange.'[58]

A particular form of discrimination in trade (which again often had a political motivation) was the creation of *trading blocks* of various kinds. The desire to establish or reinforce political relationships with economic links was shown in Germany's effort to establish a Mark zone and special trading arrangements with south-east Europe; and in the establishment of the imperial preference system with other British Commonwealth countries by Britain. The customs unions proposed between Germany and Austria in 1931 and between the Benelux countries in 1932, as well as the Benelux system which finally came into being after the Second World War, all had a political as well as an economic motivation (which was why the first two were prevented from coming about). Sometimes, discrimination in such a group took the form of offering goods at lower prices than were available to others, or through the use of special exchange rates or export subsidies (as in the case of the German arrangements with south-east Europe). Particular goods might be made available which were not available to others, through bilateral agreements or clearing arrangements (as in the same case and Soviet bilateral treaties). Or they could involve giving a special preference to reduce the effect of tariffs (as in the case of British imperial preference arrangements). In other cases, expecially close trading arrangements were established between the countries of a particular region; as occurred in Scandinavia, the Balkans and Latin America.[59]

Another form of intervention used by governments was the *control of foreign investment* in accordance with their own conceptions of national interest. Sometimes the total volume of foreign lending was limited for balance of payments or other reasons. The West European countries, and especially Britain, which in the pre-war period had been the main foreign lenders, no longer had the foreign exchange, or in some cases even the capital resources, to remain the world's bankers (though Britain remained the largest exporter of long-term capital in Europe).[60] Their place was taken during the first decade after the war by the US (a net importer of capital before it): she now became a major lender to Europe, especially to Germany whose economy, crippled by reparations and severe inflation, badly required external investment funds. Investment in this period was increasingly private investment, for industry, or short-term lending to governments, rather than investment in government bonds as in the age before, and was often influenced by relative rates of interest or possible capital gains.[61] From 1928–9, because of the stock exchange crisis in the US, much of this US capital was repatriated. From 1930, with industrial depression and increasing chaos in the world monetary system, governments began to control more closely the volume and direction of investment. Germany encouraged investment by her nationals in such areas as eastern Europe, where she sought a dominant influence (just as France had in the same countries in the 1920s), in Latin America where she still hoped for some, and in the Middle East with its crucial strategic importance. France sought to concentrate her lending in her own colonies and to 'actual or potential allied countries'.[62] And Britain, in creating the 'sterling area', gave the right to politically reliable sterling area countries – Commonwealth and other friendly states – to raise money in the London market.

Against these nationalist interventions, governments would only occasionally seek recourse to a different kind of measure, designed to break out of the self-perpetuating cycle of restrictions and discrimination: attempts at *international co-operation*. New international institutions were set up with a view to establishing such co-operation: in the International Labour Organisation (1919), the economic organs of the League (1919), the Bank for International Settlements (1930). But these international authorities were never able to match the effectiveness of the *national* economic regulation which developed everywhere in this age. A succession of international conferences – especially in the immediate post-war years, in 1927 and in 1933 – regularly called for a reduction of tariffs and other restrictions. But these were little heeded. There was agreement on a moratorium on tariff increases in 1930. But few governments signed it, and it was quickly overtaken by events. The ILO proposed, in 1931, a programme of simultaneous public works in all countries to raise levels of employment, a measure that could have had substantial effect in counteracting the slump. But again there was no response (though Germany introduced public works measures even before Hitler came to power, the US from 1933 and France from 1936). Roosevelt and Ramsay Macdonald, after a meeting in Washington in 1933, agreed that 'governments can contribute [to economic recovery] by the development of appropriate programmes of capital expenditure'; and the US delegate to the World Economic Conference of 1933 (apparently inspired by an idea put forward by Keynes in a pamphlet the previous year) proposed a 'synchronised programme of governmental expenditure in the different countries along parallel lines'. But this had equally little impact. There were attempts to negotiate commodity agreements to restrict production of commodities in surplus (notably rubber, tin, sugar, tea and, briefly, wheat). But most of these proved ineffective. In many cases, there were unilateral policies, of an unorthodox and enlightened kind, such as the expansionary policies, often including deficit financing, used in Sweden and Germany in 1932 and 1933, the US in 1934, and France in 1936; the cheap money policies followed in Britain and Sweden during the 1930s; or the policies for minimum prices introduced in the US in 1933 and France in 1936. But these too were introduced primarily for national purposes, and had little effect on the world economy as a whole. Governments were more concerned to seek economic salvation by individual measures affecting their own economies alone, rather than through *common* action designed to affect the international economy generally.

Thus a new set of strategies began to be employed in this age, reflecting the new motives of governments, the new balance of social and political power, and the new policy instruments which the now dominant forces – the bureaucrats and autocrats – had at their disposal. Motives were nationalistic and autarchic. The instruments were those which the increased capacity (and willingness) of governments to interfere in economic life now made available. So, to the familiar tariff, the most widely used economic weapon for several centuries, a whole host of more direct measures were now added, controlling imports and exports, the use of currencies, the level of parities, interest rates, prices, and many other factors formerly determined by market forces. Discrimination, from being an aberration, became the norm. New economic groupings of states were established, for political as well as economic purposes, within which various types of discrimination were practised. The strategy of bureaucratic intervention for narrow nationalist ends everywhere ruled supreme.

TECHNOLOGY AND TRANSFER PRICES (1950–80)

In the age that followed, the strategies used by states to promote their economic interests abroad changed once more. New methods were found, corresponding to the interests of new groups.

The prevailing doctrine rejected the autarchic policies of the previous age. Thus the cruder types of restrictions on trade were widely discarded. Import quotas were largely given up. Exchange controls were gradually dismantled. Bilateral arrangements were abandoned. Tariffs were reduced.

Yet the aim of protection was not abandoned. Rich countries felt themselves justified, for example in limiting the exports of poor countries competing with traditional industries of their own. Poor countries felt that they could not afford to open their markets to the rich. Both wished to limit imports from more successful countries of their own kind. New and more sophisticated ways were now devised to keep out unwanted imports. Excise taxes were widely used against products of interest to developing countries, especially coffee, tea and cocoa. Quantitative restrictions (quotas) were applied against their products: textiles, shoes, gloves and similar simple manufactures. 'Voluntary' agreements were used by which the exporters themselves were induced to restrict their exports on pain of more severe measures. Import surcharges were used to restrain imports. Non-tariff barriers – customs valuations, health regulations, pollution controls, safety standards and other devices – were used as a means of excluding unwanted imports. 'Countervailing duties' and 'safeguards' were imposed against unwanted imports of particular kinds from particular countries.

Conversely, special measures were introduced to assist home industries: just as much a distortion of trade, though less discouraged in this age. Special assistance was given to industries in difficulty – such as shipbuilding, airlines, motor cars, steel, shipping, fishing, and many others. Aid was given to regions in difficulty. Agriculture was almost universally subsidised on a huge scale. Generous export credits, guarantees of the credit given by private institutions, and sometimes export subsidies were granted. Flag discrimination was used to encourage the use of national shipping lines. Government procurement and other contracts favoured local firms. Tax holidays, accelerated depreciation and other inducements were given to promote investment. Finally, monetary measures, such as multiple exchange rates or 'dirty floating' (government intervention in exchange markets) were used by governments as a means of cheapening their own exports or deterring imports.

Governments also gave special assistance to their companies in investing abroad. The exchange controls that had once deterred them were now relaxed or abandoned altogether. In some cases, governments themselves gave guarantees or partial guarantees against the political risks of investment. In other cases, similar guarantees were negotiated with the host government. In addition to the World Bank Convention on the settlement of disputes concerning investment (see p. 157) and the Bank's international centre for the settlement of investment disputes, the OECD prepared a Draft Convention on the Protection of Foreign Property. Sanctions of various kinds were imposed against governments which might seek to expropriate such investment: in the US, for example, the Hickenlooper Amendment compelled the US government to withdraw aid from any government which nationalised without adequate compensation. In other cases, the governments of industrialised countries combined to frustrate attempts at nationalisation: as when the oil companies of the Western world combined in refusing to distribute oil from Iran after the expropriation of the Anglo–Iranian Oil Company in 1951. All these measures served to protect and so to stimulate the high rate of foreign investment that took place during this period.

Governments gave other kinds of assistance to their companies operating abroad. They organised export promotion campaigns, arranged trade missions and trade fairs, and devoted a considerable part of the efforts of their foreign embassies to the promotion of exports. When companies bid for contracts abroad, governments would give strong diplomatic support. The winning of contracts and the promotion of exports came to be a large part of the business of an ambassador, and his career prospects were largely determined by his success in it. In such efforts, political as well as purely economic considerations were appealed to: political goodwill was often suggested as being dependent on commercial favours; or political favours were directly offered in return for a commercial concessions (as when the US suggested to Japan that the return of Okinawa would be more likely if Japanese exports of textiles to the US were reduced).[63]

At the same time, governments sought to counter the economic aims of their rivals, and especially of their political enemies. Where trade with opponents was concerned, exceptions to the rule of non-discrimination were made. The US prohibited any trade at all with China for twenty years, and with Cuba for almost as long. Most-favoured-nation treatment was refused by the US to the Soviet Union. Exports of goods which could be defined as 'strategic' were particularly rigorously banned: Western countries maintained an elaborate procedure for scrutinising all proposals for the export of goods to communist countries, and increasingly limited the export of any high technology products that could benefit their opponents. Policy in international organisations was influenced to the same end: so when Chile briefly elected a Marxist government between 1969 and 1973, she was denied not only aid and credits from the US, but also loans from the World Bank and Inter-American Development Bank. Sugar quotas were used by the US government to reward countries which followed policies it approved and to punish those it disliked: Peru's quota was doubled after she broke relations with Cuba in the early 1960s and reduced again a decade later when she confiscated assets owned by US companies.

Overseas aid was even more widely used as a means of political influence. US bilateral aid was overwhelmingly directed towards allies whose economic and military well-being was regarded as vital to US interests: such countries as South Korea, Taiwan and Jordan received aid per head many times greater than India, for example, whose economic need was far greater. Countries associated with former colonial powers did much better than those that were not. Even countries which professed to be concerned only with economic factors (such as the Scandinavian countries) in fact gave aid partly on political criteria.[64] Sudden changes in aid policy would therefore result from changes in political circumstances. Thus in Central America and the Caribbean, for example, in the late 1970s, the availability of foreign aid depended crucially on the political policies pursued: US banks refused to provide finance for the government of Jamaica when it was believed to be becoming too receptive to Cuban influence, but flocked to invest when the government changed; food aid was cut off from Nicaragua when a left-wing government took control. The political use of economic sanctions was not confined to developed countries. It was used also by developing states, as when the Arab countries stopped oil exports to the US and Netherlands in 1973, and cut off aid to Egypt after her settlement with Israel in 1978. And the aid given by the communist states (such as it was) was dictated almost entirely by political considerations, going only to left-wing governments – approved by the donors – such as those in Cuba, Vietnam, Ethiopia, Mozambique, for example.

But it was not only the strategies of governments which determined the shape of the world economy during this age. The efforts of governments to promote trade and investment abroad were reinforced by the strategies of the companies that undertook it. The large companies involved, as was seen in the last chapter, were impelled by a powerful drive for growth, and increasingly saw the best opportunities for growth abroad, within rich and poor states alike. The companies undertook various activities to maintain or extend their position. They undertook large expenditure for advertising and public relations to demonstrate the benefits, in terms of employment, managerial skills and transfer of technology, which they could bring to the host country.[65] They established close political links with governmental authorities in the host states to build up constituencies of support there. In some cases, at least, they were not averse to engaging in corrupt practices to maintain their positions within such countries, or to secure particular contracts.[66] Yet they maintained a high degree of centralisation of their activities, so that control was less subject to influence by host governments.[67] Finally, they maintained a tight hold on the technology which they possessed, often taking out patents in large numbers of countries that were not used at all, to prevent the development of similar technology by others.

Against these strategies of the richer nations, the developing countries devised others of their own to counter them. Their governments began to use new methods to control the activities of large corporations in their territories. From an early stage, many of them took steps to limit remittances abroad, or to demand a particular level of re-investment. They sought the employment of a higher proportion of their own nationals within the companies. In time, they came to demand more. They bagan to call for, or to enforce, 'participation'; that is, the sharing of ownership of the resources concerned with shareholders from the host country, or with the government of that country.[68] They demanded 'joint ventures', in which the transnational corporation went into partnership with a local enterprise. They called for a gradual divestiture or 'fade-out' by the companies, leading to a situation in which the majority holding, or even total ownership, was in the hands of local people.[69] Sometimes, entire industries were banned to foreign investment.[70] And in a few cases, especially in the case of mining and extraction industries, they undertook full-scale nationalisation, with or without compensation.

The ultimate aim of most poor countries was to bring about the transfer of technology itself, to make them less dependent on the nationals of foreign countries for essential economic development. But they found that the Western companies were willing to share this technology, if at all, only at very high cost. Poor countries found that they remained dependent on the payment of royalties, leases and licences for the use of technology developed in the rich countries. And they had to pay high prices for consultants, for management contracts, or for 'turn-key' contracts involving the construction of whole plants.

Or technology was transferred only on condition that the finished product could not be exported. In a number of cases, developing countries began to establish national registries of technology or similar agencies, whose purpose was to supervise all such agreements to ensure that they operated to the advantage of the licensees and of the host state generally.[71] Ultimately, however, they were often left with the agonising choice between paying a very high price for the technology they required or remaining content with more backward techniques and a lower level of development.

As time went on, poor countries became rather more skilled in their dealings with the transnationals. Sometimes, they were able to call in alternative competition to improve their bargaining power: as when Iran turned to the Italian Oil Corporation (ENI) when boycotted by British and US firms in 1951, when Saudi Arabia began dealing with Japanese marketing organisations as an alternative to Aramco, when Chile sought alternative copper producers to Anaconda, and Guyana alternative aluminium smelters to Alcan. Sometimes, they were able to ensure that raw materials were processed within their own territories, rather than exported for processing elsewhere. They increasingly demanded assurances concerning the local procurement of materials and the use of local sub-contractors. Contracts were re-negotiated to establish that minerals extracted were sold to an indigenous company, at agreed or concessionary prices. In many cases they asked for the right to renegotiate previously existing arrangements to obtain better terms than had been granted in less favourable circumstances in the past. Above all, they sought the establishment of international guidelines or codes of conduct to regulate the behaviour of the companies: on restrictive business practices (negotiated in UNCTAD); corrupt practices (in the UN Economic and Social Council); transfer of technology (in UNCTAD); employment and social policy (in ILO); and on the general conduct of the multinationals (UN Commission on Transnational Corporations).[72]

These various measures no doubt slightly strengthened the hands of host countries. But it is doubtful if they more than marginally altered the balance. Poor countries remained dependent on the companies for capital, technology, management and marketing skills, and indeed often competed among themselves to secure these. The companies themselves, on the other hand, could always move elsewhere (so Alcan, when Guyana and Jamaica proposed participation in its operations in their countries, simply moved to Australia and Brazil). Participation, even when put into effect locally, often did not alter the basis of control, since the board of directors in the parent company, and even its management, almost always remained in the hands of foreigners. Service and management contracts often provided the foreign companies with as large profits, and as extensive domination of the market, as they had enjoyed before.[73] And the power of the home management to switch production, to adjust prices to suit their own convenience, to undertake intra-firm transactions at prices of their own choice, to control marketing, to restrict exports or promote imports, to advance or retard payments on exchange risk grounds, more than counterbalanced the increased powers which the host government now took.

But the strategy most widely used by poor countries, in this age, to promote their economic aims was through *collective action.* Already in the 1940s, some of them had demanded, and obtained, a small UN programme for providing technical assistance. In the 1950s, they demanded (but did not obtain) a Special UN Fund for Economic Development, financed through compulsory contributions. In the 1960s, they secured the establishment of a new organisation primarily concerned with their own problems, UNCTAD, in which both development and trade matters were discussed. In the 1970s, they initiated special meetings of the General Assembly, devoted to the problems of poor countries, a long conference in Paris in the middle of the decade, as well as innumerable meetings of other international bodies. By 1980, they were calling for a new set of 'global negotiations' to examine in different fora the principal issues that concerned them. If they could have secured an increase in the authority over the world's economy of international organisations, committed to the principles they, as the majority, advocated, they might have been able to promote their own interests more effectively. But in such discussions their only weapons were their number and the loudness of their voices. The economic power they wielded was minimal. In consequence, though a few marginal modifications were made to the way the world's economy operated (see p. 59), these collective negotiations secured for them no significant improvement in their overall economic situation. Only collective action by states controlling some important raw material, like that of OPEC (see p. 112), could procure advantages for a few developing countries; but that was obtained only at the expense of the majority of poor countries who were less fortunate.

Thus the means employed in this age varied greatly according to the economic circumstances of states. Among the rich countries which dominated the world economy, trade was sought through high-powered export promotion and a willingness to open markets at home in return for their opening abroad. But this was accompanied by new forms of protection, mainly against the exports of poor countries. They promoted foreign investment, not only within other rich states, but in poor states as well, where foreign companies won dominant positions. And the great transnational companies which were the main agents of economic expansion, through increased exports and expanding investment, thus acquired an increasingly powerful place, both in the world economy as a whole and in individual states. Among poor countries, too, there was an effort to promote exports or, when barriers were erected against them in the markets of rich countries, to expand their trade with each other. They, too, employed protection on a large scale in the effort to build up local industries. While welcoming foreign investment on the right terms, they sought to acquire increasing control of the activities of the great transnational companies in their territory, especially those exploiting their own raw materials. But their main instruments for promoting their economic interests were the same as those long employed by the underprivileged workers within states: combination, collective action, and negotiation on behalf of the group as a whole. They won few benefits with that strategy. In this age, as never before, the economic interests of states were pursued not by each one individually, but by groups negotiating with each other on the distribution of benefits among them. It is not surprising that the most effective instruments were in the hands of the group whose economic power was greatest.

5 Economic Dominance and Dependence

So far we have been concerned with the ideas about economic relations among states that have prevailed in different periods; the way they have reflected the interests of particular states and particular groups within states; the economic motives most widely held among nations in different ages; and the means they have used to promote them. We now come to the outcome of these various factors: the economic relationships that have resulted among states.

In all societies, there exist differences in resouces, capacities and wealth. These allow some to secure greater power or influence, while others sink into relative dependence. In international societies, the same process takes place: some states acquire a position of increasing domination; while others become dependent on the strong. At its simplest, this stratification among states has taken the form of straightforward military domination and military dependence. But there exist a considerable number of other types of authority or prestige that can be gained by states, and corresponding forms of subordination or weakness which result among the rest.[1]

Economic dominance and dependence are merely special forms of this phenomenon. Economic dominance may derive independently of political dominance, though often they go together. It may result from the actions of individuals rather than governments, and benefit them as much as their states; though usually the actions of both are required. While economic dominance has not perhaps been as widely or as ardently pursued by governments as military or political dominance, it has often been one of their goals. And in recent times, it has probably become the preferred form of pre-eminence among states, a goal which has influenced a larger and larger share of their actions.

Even within the same period of history, there have usually been a number of alternative types of economic advantage to be acquired. In recent times, for example, it has been possible for states to secure a dominant position within the money markets of the world (as secured by Britain for a period); a dominant trading position and a very strong balance of payments (as acquired for long by West Germany or Japan); widespread activity by large numbers of big corporations in many parts of the world (as acquired by the US); or the control of one or more particularly valued commodities exploited on a monopoly basis (as acquired by the oil-producing states).

But perhaps more visible and more significant are changes in the types of economic domination over time. The type of domination acquired obviously depends partly on what are the main economic goals. When trade was the chief objective, it was a dominant trading position that was sought. When it was the search for secure overseas markets, it was dominance in those areas. When it was economic growth, it was dominance in production worldwide.

In recent times, economic dominance has been associated especially with financial power. One of the major changes in the last century was that brought about through the increasing mobility of capital. Even in the Middle Ages, capital moved to some extent: the big Italian banking families, such as the Medicis, in lending their funds to other states, could acquire there a powerful position, especially through their loans to foreign kings. But the number of individuals involved in such transactions was small: and it was individual royal families or governments rather than the entire economy of other lands that came under the control of such foreign financiers. As time has gone on, however, and especially from the nineteenth century onwards, capital has been moved freely around the world. In some cases, a considerable proportion of a country's resources has in this way come under the control of foreign owners. In the nineteenth century, this control occurred particularly in the case of raw materials – rubber, timber, copper or oil – or of infrastructure such as railways and other public facilities – which were largely financed by foreign interests and for the benefit mainly of foreign economies. In the present century, this process has been extended further. Large parts of manufacturing industry and many kinds of financial institution have, in some countries, fallen into the hands of foreign owners.

In these cases, states become dependent on the *private* interests of other countries. But in other cases, a country may become more directly dependent on foreign *states*. For example, they may obtain loans from these, become liable to large interest payments, and sometimes then require further help in order to repay them. Eventually, those goverments which have provided the funds may acquire a position of dominance over the entire economy. China, Turkey and Egypt became depedent in this sense during the nineteenth century; as did the countries of east Europe during the period between the wars. A similar indebtedness has erected a similar depedence in large numbers of poorer countries since 1945. This is the direct dependence of the debtor on the creditor.

Or there may be an imbalance of advantage based on the trading situation. One state, for example, by having access to particularly valued commodities, may acquire superior bargaining power (like the control of the Hanseatic merchants over Baltic goods in the Middle Ages, the control of the United Provinces over the trade in salt, herrings and naval products in the seventeenth century, the control of Britain over trade in coal, iron and textiles in the nineteenth century, or the control of a few states over oil, uranium, chemicals, jet aircraft or micro-processors today: in this situation there ceases to be an equality of negotiating position. There may be monopoly control of particularly valuable minerals, such as Spain's control of the gold and silver of South America or south German control over copper supplies in the Middle Ages, or of certain states over oil or gold today. Or advantage may be enjoyed by control of a specially favoured area or trade route (like the Levant once or the Suez Canal today) which again can be used to obtain special advantages. Probably more important than these, however, today is control of markets: thus, in modern times, rich countries bargain on trade questions from a position of advantage because they can offer access to larger and richer markets, where purchasing power is far greater than in developing countries with which they bargain.

We may thus already distinguish four or five main types of economic domination which we shall trace, in different forms in different ages, in the pages that follow. Firstly, there is direct domination of the economies of other states through military coercion or political control as undertaken sometimes in the Middle Ages and in the colonial period. Next, there is control of raw materials and the sources from which they come: designed usually in the first place to ensure security of supply, but often leading to dominance of the entire market in particular products. Next, there is manufacturing and commercial dominance, by which countries in a strong trading position make use of their advantage to extract further gains from those less well placed. Next, there is financial dominance, by which those nations having greater control over available financial resources ration assistance to less well placed countries in such a way as to leave them in a position of dependence (as used by the European powers in rationing credit to such countries as Turkey, Greece, Egypt, Tunis, Persia and China, at the end of the nineteenth century or by aid donors and the IMF today). Finally, there is investment domination (or depedence) under which nations with greater control over investible resources acquire through them an increasing share in control over the economic assets of other states.

These are some of the ways in which particular nations can acquire commercial and economic advantage over others. Much of the activities of states in the international economy can be analysed as a struggle between economically dominant and dependent countries. It is to an analysis of the different forms which this struggle has taken in different periods and in different types of international society that we must now turn.

THE CONTROL OF COMMERCE (1300–1600)

During the late Middle Ages, when princely power was the dominant force, the types of domination established reflected the ambitions of those who controlled each state.

Usually, it was control over trade that was most desired. In the extreme case, a conquering ruler or state might acquire a position of total economic *control* over another state: a position in which the trading policies of the subdued state would be directly and permanently dominated by the victorious power. Venice, in conquering her neighbours, secured a position that was virtually one of colonialism. She ensured, for example, that Ragusa traded with nobody but herself; and that even then the merchants of Ragusa should not compete in a way dangerous to her own merchants. Subject Ravenna was allowed to send corn and salt only to Venice herself. Genoa imposed a treaty on St Gilles under which all sea trade to the latter was to be conducted by Genoa and by Genoa alone; and later secured a treaty with Aragon under which her great rival, Pisa, was excluded from all trade throughout the area. Over Savona, Genoa established a still more humiliating ascendency: all Savona's ships trading to Barcelona must first sail to Genoa, must there take on board a number of Genoese merchants, and must return from the voyage first to Genoese ports before going back to their home base.[2] The Hanse towns acquired, often through armed force, a similarly dominant, and often monopolistic, trading position in the towns they controlled in Scandinavia and the Baltic. In all these cases, by use of a considerable measure of coercion, substantial control was obtained over the external economic policies of other states.

Even without overt military compulsion, however, a powerful state might acquire a dominant economic influence among its neighbours, or throughout a region. In some cases, a form of trade *penetration* was established. Stronger nations were able to impose conditions which enabled their own merchants to trade on favourable conditions in the territory of weaker states, or secured an adequate supply of goods and trade for themselves through the establishment of a staple. 'Strong towns dealing with the weak could use a thorough-going and compulsory staple system to achieve their ends, and could turn supply regions into private reserves. Thirteenth century Venice demonstrated the use of such overriding powers.'[3] Besides securing a treaty which made her the only city at which Ravenna merchants could sell corn and salt, she demanded a monopoly of the export of corn in the lower Po valley and the Mark of Treviso and a virtual monopoly further south. Trade was to be captured: by force if necessary. The Hanseatic cities, apart from the total domination which they attained in Scandinavia, acquired often by war a dominant trading position in Flanders, England and eastern Europe, in almost every case gaining for themselves privileges more favourable than those they gave to merchants of the other country within their own lands, and in some cases (as in England) more favourable than those enjoyed by local merchants.[4] This was perhaps the classic form of dominant relationship of the commercially strong over the commercially weak in this age.[5]

Conversely, a weak but prosperous state was sometimes especially vulnerable to poor but powerful neighbours. The wealth of Flanders, for example, made it a frequent object of economic demands by nearby states. Flanders depended on France for supplies of food, and on England for supplies of wool. Both neighbours frequently sought to use this leverage to secure Flanders' alliance or economic co-operation. Already in the twelfth century, Henry II brought economic presssure to bear to induce Flanders to leave a coalition formed against him. Richard I and John prohibited the export of grain and wool to Flanders, and confiscated the goods of Flemish merchants in London, to force her to join their coalition against Philip Augustus. Nearly a century later, when Flanders again moved closer to France (her feudal overlord), Edward I withdraw protection from the Flemish merchants in England and granted commercial privileges to their rivals from Holland, Brabant and Germany. But when Flanders, as a result of this pressure, reverted to her English alliance, her merchants in France were arrested in turn. When, a few years later, England and France were at peace again, Edward I, in return for a promise by France to ban trade with Scotland, excluded the Flemish from trading in England. And in the 1330s, Edward III, by banning the export of wool to Flanders, yet again used economic pressure against the Count to secure his alliance. So, in a constantly inferior military position, Flanders found herself, despite her wealth, an economic vassal, her interests continually vulnerable to the twists and turns of policy of her powerful neighbours.

Norway is another example of an economically dependent state. In the fourteenth century, the Hanseatics won control of the grain trade to that country, and later of the fish trade, each of which was essential to Norway. They established a great trading factory in Bergan, through which virtually all trade passed, so making Norway almost a colony. They became the dominant suppliers of wool, cloth, wax, wine and Baltic goods. They virtually monopolised the export of Norwegian fish which they sold throughout west Europe. As a result of this stranglehold, the Norwegians no longer exercised full control of their own economy.

While economic dominance was sometimes acquired by political or military means, political gains were sometimes acquired by economic measures. For example, alliances could sometimes be purchased. During the early stages of the Hundred Years War, Edward III, to all intents and purposes, purchased (with the help of Florentine bankers) the alliance of Brabant, of the Counts of Guelders, Cleves and Juliers, even of the Emperor Louis of Bavaria (though the uncertainty of this method was shown when the latter soon deserted the English cause without any thought of repaying the sums he had received). These were not the only expenditures for the sake of alliances. Money might also sometimes have to be spent to persuade foreign rulers *not* to ally themselves with an enemy. 'Closely related to military costs were expenditures for diplomacy – the making of allies or the endeavour to subvert or neutralise potential enemies. The amounts spent for such purposes cannot be detailed, but there is no doubt that they were substantial and recurrent. Money flowed from England to Flanders, to Holland and to Bavaria at various times during the course of the Hundred Years war; it passed from France to the kingdom of Castile, to Savoy, and, during the final phase of the war to Burgundy.'[6] The military power a state could monopolise thus depended partly on financial assets (or at least available credit). And the relative wealth of states could, of course, have an even more direct effect on their power, by determining their ability to pay for arms and for mercenary forces.

The converse of this financial power was the *dependence* of the debtor monarchs. Edward III, after only four or five years of war against France, found himself and his state virtually bankrupt and desperate for assistance. Though he overcame the immediate crisis by the simple device of repudiating his debts and ruining his creditors (as well as taking a share in the English wool trade), this did not reduce his long-term dependence but increased it, since bankers became less willing to lend to him. Smaller and poorer states were still more dependent. With less to offer as security (since this usually took the form of a share in the customs revenues, they required a reasonably flourishing trade and an effective collection system to satisfy the creditors), they often had difficulty in raising a loan. A state such as Portugal, for example, involved in frequent conflicts in the Iberian peninsula, had to rely largely on local revenues which were quite inadequate. Similarly, the poorer cities of Italy, especially those of the south and the west, had far greater difficulty in raising funds to finance war than did the prosperous cities, such as Florence and Milan, and their relative poverty was therefore compounded. So strong states became wealthy and wealthy states strong. Conversely, the poor states (with a few exceptions), without credit to rely on, fell into a state of even greater dependence.

Political dominance could also be sought by the use of *trade sanctions*. Louis XI, in seeking to restore Margaret of Anjou to the English throne after the victory of Edward IV, cut off exports to England, while Edward IV in return forbade the importation of Gascon wine from France. Trade incentives could be used to influence the policies of third parties. Charles VII of France in 1442 agreed to offer trading privileges to the Hanseatic merchants, on condition that the latter broke off all their ties with England. And Louis XI a few years later gave a comprehensive charter to the Hansards, granting them the right to trade throughout France so long as they did not trade with the English or charter English ships.

Since this was a dynastic age, economic domination was sometimes the effect of dynastic factors. When Queen Margaret of Denmark managed to unite the three kingdoms of Denmark, Norway and Sweden, she was able to use the economic resources of Sweden and Norway to strengthen the Danish crown and promote Danish dominance. When her successor, Christian, was driven out of Sweden nearly a century later, he was able to replace Sweden's resources with those of

Schleswig and Holstein which he inherited from his uncle, and which became virtually Danish colonies. Charles V acquired economic as well as political strength in merging the wealth of the Netherlands, Burgundy and Milan with that of Spain. Dynastic claims were thus often the means of bringing economic gains that were sometimes more enduring than political ones. The English kings' titles in France, bringing English rule in Gascony for over 250 years, created the basis for the economic links between Gascony and England which were to prove so flourishing for many years.

One form of economic power was control of shipping. While the Hansards traded their own goods and those they bought in their own ships, the French found most of their trade in the hands of foreigners – the Lombards, Flemings and Hansards. Most of England's trade was in the hands of foreigners until the end of the fourteenth century (mainly Hansards, Lombards and Gascons), but the share in English hands grew to 60 per cent by the middle of the fifteenth century. Conversely, that of Flanders, which had been in native hands in the fourteenth century, progressively fell into those of foreigners, and this was one of the reasons for her decline.

Another form of economic power was financial: the transnational power of the big banking houses rather than that of nations. In the middle of the fourteenth century, the Alberti company had banks in Venice, Rouen, London, Barcelona, Paris, Genoa, Avignon, Naples, Perugia and Spoleto,[7] while the Medicis at the beginning of the next century had branches in Rome, London, Rouen, Pisa, Milan, Avignon, Venice, Lyons, Naples and Basel, as well as Florence. The Fuggers had substantial influence over a number of rulers of Europe who were financed by them. They used this for their own advantage, and so indirectly for that of their state. Because copper, exported by the Hanseatics from Sweden to west Europe, was a dangerous competitor to the exports of Hungarian copper which the Fuggers financed, they gave financial support to the kings of Denmark in their conflict with Sweden: in return for being given protection and the right to build a copper mill by Christian II of Denmark, they equipped six ships for him for his war against Gustavus Vasa.

Private groups also sometimes dominated, singly or collectively, the supply of particular raw materials. Thus the Genoese merchants, in controlling the alum mines of Phocaea, controlled the supply of materials essential for textile industries all over Europe. The supply of sugar was largely controlled by the Venetian merchants trading with Cyprus and the Far East. The Italians, buying cloth, tin or iron in west

Europe and selling it in the Levant or Egypt for sugar, pepper or silk, dominated the trade in luxury goods: as a result, 'because of the extension of their interests and the sophistication of their methods, Italian merchant communities scattered about Europe and the Mediterranean constituted a commercial network which to a large extent dominated European trade'.[8]

In this, as in later ages, therefore, differences in economic power affected the political as well as the economic relations of states. Those relations were determined by the activities of private interests as much as those of governments. Powerful states were able to secure domination over the trade of poor states; and this in turn benefited private interests as much as public.

PROFIT AND POWER (1600–50)

In the age of state-building that began around 1600, economic domination began to take a rather different form.

As we have seen, the chief concern of the great ministers and their royal masters was with the 'balance of trade'. Success in international commerce was required to win a favourable balance in trade and specie. But it was demanded even more as a measure of national greatness and power. There was everywhere widespread admiration for the accomplishments of the Dutch in this field (an admiration heavily tinged with jealousy). The object of other states was to secure for themselves the pre-eminence in international trade which the Dutch then enjoyed. Colbert complained to Louis XIV that the Dutch thought 'to acquire the trade of the world into their own hands . . . and to rob other nations of the same'; and stated that they did this with political as much as economic motives, 'knowing full well that if they but have the mastery of trade, their powers will continually wax on land and sea and make them so mighty that they will be able to set up as arbiters of peace and war in Europe and set bounds at their pleasure to the justice and all the plans of princes'. And Colbert did not conceal that his own ambitions were almost identical. He wrote two years later to the French Ambassador in the Hague: 'It is certain that their whole power has hitherto consisted in trade. If we could manage their trade, they might find it more difficult in future to carry out their preparations for war than they have hitherto done'. And in 1670 he urged on his royal master the importance of a French victory in this war for trade, asserting that 'this war, in which the most powerful republic since the Roman Empire is the price of victory, must engage your Majesty's chief attention during the whole of your life'.[9]

Trade was thus identified with power almost everywhere. This meant that the state itself must be concerned with the attempt to win trade from other states. As Lord Shaftesbury wrote: 'That which makes Consideration of Trade of far greater import now than ever is that the interest of Commerce, though formerly neglected, is of late years become an express Affair of State, as well with the French as with the Hollander and Swede ... It is Trade and Commerce alone that draweth store of Wealth along with it and Potency at sea by shipping which is not otherwise to be had'.[10] But since it was generally believed that there existed only a limited quantity of international trade, any attempt to win a larger share could only be at the expense of others. Nations must therefore be prepared if necessary to fight wars for this purpose (or to find provocations for wars which might have that effect). Envy of the commercial power of the Dutch was the main dynamic generating the four wars fought by the English and the French against them between 1650 and 1680; and there was a widespread hope that victory in such a war could lead to the transfer of some of the Hollanders' exorbitant share of trade to the victorious power.

Ambition for commercial domination was sometimes a demand for domination in particular areas. One of the complaints of the English was that the Dutch sought to declare themselves 'Lords of the South Seas'. Downing, the English emissary at the Hague, complained, with some reason, of the Dutch that 'these people doe arrogate to them-selves St Peter's Powers upon the seas. It is mare liberum in the British Seas but mare clausum on ye coast of Africa and in ye East Indies.'[11] The Spanish sought to control the entire trade to Spanish America (all of which had, in theory to pass from the port of Seville), and even in the seas which approached it. The French sought to win control of all trade to the Levant, displacing the Dutch there in the eighteenth century, as the Dutch had replaced the Venetians a century earlier. The English sought similarly to win dominance in the trade to Russia.

The conception that the merchants of two nations could easily trade side by side in different parts of the world was rarely entertained. Because rights were regarded as exclusive, they were fought for bitterly. So the Dutch felt it necessary to eject the English from Amboyna rather than have to compete with them there; just as the English sought to eject the Dutch from Pula Run for the same reason. So the same two powers sought to turn each other out in turn from New

Amsterdam and West Africa. And so the English and the French thought to displace the other from the Caribbean islands and North America, and later fought more bitter and extensive struggles for control of India and Canada. The sharing of economic rights had no place in the economic philosophy of this age. Just as foreign merchants, who had been so widely welcomed in mediaeval times, had been increasingly squeezed out of trade in the domestic market, so too when new trading positions were acquired abroad, it was taken for granted that foreigners should be kept out if possible. The capture of trade continued, but it was now carried out not in the staple towns and other trading centres of Europe, but in all the outlying areas of the world.

Together with these aspirations for the capture and control of trade went a competition for dominance in shipping. For long the Dutch enjoyed such a mastery. In this way she secured further revenue over and above that from trade itself. The state with a large shipping fleet might, moreover, undertake a large entrepôt trade, carrying in its ships goods traded between third states at great profit: another advantage the Dutch mainly enjoyed in this period. Other states resented this domination, and sought to reduce their own dependence. This was partly for strategic reasons. A country with a large merchant shipping fleet would be better able to preserve its trade in wartime and to provide the necessary naval vessels and crews in time of war. Downing, the same English representative in the Hague, asked his masters whether 'it was not better to have ships of our owne, though without guns, and your owne seamen employed, your owne Victualls spent in the Victualling of them, the money paid for freight and cargoes kept at home, than to have foreign ships and seamen employed, their Victualls spent, and so much money carried out out of the kingdome as is yearly used for freight and wages'.[12] It was, anyway, humiliating for a country which might have a fairly large total volume of trade to find that most of it was carried in foreign ships. This was the case for France in the early part of the seventeenth century. In the famous passage when Colbert recited the estimated numbers of ships belonging to different nations (see p. 10), he exhibited the jealousy of the ship-using country against the ship-owning one, a jealousy common at this time (and felt once more among emerging nations more recently).

So all sought to increase their fleets, for commercial as well as for strategic reasons. The English Navigation Acts of 1651 and 1660, and the Staple Act of 1663, not only reserved for English ships, and predominantly English crews, the trade to and from English colonies, where the English had been granted a monopoly, and other places outside Europe, but also explicity banned entrepôt trade; and the measures Colbert introduced a few years later reflected this same ambition to carry native trade in native ships. Governments were naturally concerned when a large proportion of their strategic imports were carried in foreign ships. The English, for example, particularly resented the fact that more than half of their imports of naval goods from the Baltic were carried in Dutch ships.[13] So strategic interests combined with commercial ambition to lead governments to seek a larger share of the total shipping business.

Another form of economic advantage that was increasingly coveted at this time was manufacturing capacity. This was a new form of economic power. It was, in this age, highly concentrated. Most countries specialised only in one or two particular industries suited to their own agricultural or other products: thus England specialised in wool and woollen cloth, Italy and the United Provinces in textiles of various kinds, France in silks, tapestries and various other luxury products, Sweden in metals. But a country that could acquire a more broad-based manufacturing capacity could assure itself of huge advantages. It could save in imports and profit from exports. It could import the necessary raw materials or unfinished goods from elsewhere, process or manufacture them and might then enjoy a substantial monopoly in the trade of finished products throughout Europe. Once again, it was the Dutch who had advanced furthest on this road, and who most aroused the envy and resentment of other nations. Their capacity in the refining of sugar, the curing of fish, the finishing of cloth, the milling of oil-seeds, the brewing of beer, enabled them to win the far higher profits to be derived from trade in finished products than from that in raw materials. The English, who in the following age were envied for much the same advantage, now resented the fact that the Dutch bought from them only raw materials and semi-manufactures, but sold expensive manufactures.[14] Similarly, French observers were concerned at the profits the Dutch managed to make at their expense: one of the main objects of the duties imposed by Colbert in 1665 (on sugar, for example) and in 1667 was to build up comparable French capacity in sugar refinery, woollen textiles, metal industries and glass production. Such countries felt (as developing countries were to do in the twentieth century) at a severe disadvantage in being unable to compete in processing and manufacture. So the advances made by the dominant powers led soon (as in later years) to imitation by the others seeking to reduce the technology gap and to remedy their dependence.

Another advantage, inevitably highly valued, was control of particular materials. The Spanish had perhaps the most enviable position of all in controlling the main source of European gold and silver and so of 'wealth'. The Dutch too, by acquiring control of the East Indies, possessed a virtual monopoly in the supply of highly prized commodities – nutmeg, cinnamon, cloves, spices and pepper – which were much valued in Europe and sold there at something like a hundred times their cost of production. The control of the sugar trade had been largely in Portuguese hands in the second half of the sixteenth century, when Brazil and Madeira were the principal sources. It passed temporarily to the Dutch when they controlled parts of Brazil and the Caribbean; to the English in the latter part of the seventeenth century, when they acquired Jamaica and other Caribbean islands (and techniques of cultivation from the Dutch); and finally in the eighteenth century it came to be dominated by the French, with production from St Domingue and Guadeloupe. Even within Europe, domination of particular trades could develop. Thus the Dutch controlled not only the greater part of the Baltic trade, which included vital strategic commodities but also of the trade in the vital commodity of salt, and in fish. Domination of this kind (like that of oil-producers in the twentieth century) inevitably provoked a reaction designed to reduce it among those made dependent. So the French sought to reduce the Dutch hold on the salt trade, and to develop her own fisheries in the west Atlantic; while England sought to develop her own fisheries, challenged the right of the Dutch to the herring close to the English coast and finally banned the import of fish from the United Provinces altogether.

Equally important could be the control of particular trade routes. By acquiring footholds in West Africa, the Cape, Ceylon and the Malabar coast of India, the Dutch managed to secure the vital trade route to the East Indies. The English acquisitions of Bermuda, the Leeward Islands, New Amsterdam and Arcadia were more important in maintaining communications and trade between the Caribbean and the North American colonies than they were as a source of commodities. Even in Europe, trade routes were of considerable importance. Spanish control of the route from north Italy to her possessions in the Low Countries had an economic as well as a strategic importance for Spain; and French expansion into Alsace, by threatening that route, had economic as well as strategic consequences. Venice, by its position in the eastern Mediterranean, had been able to exercise a stranglehold (though not a monopoly) on the trade from the Levant, which was broken only when the Dutch, during the seventeenth century, began to trade direct to west Europe from that area, followed by the English trading through Leghorn and the French from Marseilles. Control of the Baltic, and especially of the Sound at its entry (like the control of the Hormuz Straits or the Suez Canal in a later age) was vital because of the importance of the strategic materials which were traded from that area. So the Danes, in controlling the Sound, possessed a valuable bargaining counter, which they could use with special effect with the Dutch who carried much of the trade: to ensure that their imports came through the Sound duty-free was vitally important to the Dutch, and alliance with the Danes could be a price worth paying for it.[15] Conversely, the threat that such a Dutch-Danish alliance could represent to these supplies caused the English to look for alternative supplies of naval goods in North America.

It is not surprising that this competition for dominant control of valued materials and trade routes eventually stimulated a competition for colonies, which could secure both at once. At first, the occupation of trading posts abroad did not necessarily entail a claim to sovereignty. But the posts required protection, and to maintain exclusive rights in the area governments were increasingly obliged to provide some degree of military support – forts and garisons – for their traders; and eventually to claim full sovereignty. While at first effective control was only maintained in limited areas close to the ports, this eventually made necessary the extension of administrative control into the interior. Governments began to be more conscious of the material advantages, commercial as well as strategic, of acquiring control of substantial territories under the national flag. There was especially intense competition for territory whose economic value was most prized: between the Dutch and the Portuguese for Brazil with its sugar and the East Indies with its spices, between the English and the Dutch for West Africa and its slave trade, between the French and the English for the furs of Hudson Bay, the fish of Newfoundland, the calicoes of India, and the sugar and tobacco of the Caribbean. Once acquired, the colonies were reserved exclusively for home traders; and could even, as was hoped in the case of the North American colonies, be a useful source of government revenues.

Colonies could thus procure a whole range of advantages over other states. They could be a source of valued materials, which could, at the same time, be denied to others. They could provide a monopoly of some types of trade, sometimes especially valuable. They could (as Josiah Child pointed out) be a source of 'more economical production', since the cost of labour was lower in such areas. They could provide a valuable market for home manufactures (a particularly reliable one since they would normally not be permitted to purchase elsewhere). They could provide strategic positions and naval stations, which were assets in themselves. They might provide supplies of naval produce. They might even provide outlets for employment for parts of the home population, at a time when unemployment and under-employment were universal. Thus it is not altogether surprising that competition for trade developed into competition for territorial control in large parts of the wider world. Economic benefits were not the only ones at stake. But unless there had been economic advantages to be acquired in the first place, it is doubtful if the competition for colonies would even have begun. This competition brought in its wake, unintended, a new form of economic domination. Alien peoples suddenly found control of their economies, their trade and their raw materials taken wholly out of their hands and exercised by strange masters sprung from distant lands which they had never seen. Economic dependence of the most total kind was in this way created.

So the types of economic dominance over other states that were sought in this age reflected the nature of the elites in power and the goals that inspired them. Control of trade and a healthy trade balance were now the major aims of the ruling ministers and monarchs. The type of dominance sought was that which helped attain these goals (or resulted from their attainment). It included control of raw materials, of trade routes, of trading areas, of shipping fleets and, increasingly, of colonial territories abroad. The dependence of weaker states meant the obverse of this: reliance on manufactures sold by others, dependence on the shipping of others, lack of control over trade routes or raw materials, failure to find trading areas or colonies abroad. Above all, it was the dependence of the newly-found overseas lands themselves which now became merely the passive instruments of far more powerful states from across the seas which controlled all their territories and all their resources.

THE TRIUMPH OF TRADE (1750–1870)

In the age that followed, some of the earlier forms of economic domination declined. There was less concern to win favourable balances of trade over other states and to interfere with normal commercial flows for that purpose. There was less concern to win and defend monopolies, whether in the trade of particular areas, such as the East Indies or Latin America, or of particular products, such as spices or slaves. There was less concern to ensure that all native trade was carried in native ships. With the rapid increase in international trade, it was less possible to monopolise or even dominate particular trade routes. And the desire to win trade through the acquisition of colonies abroad also abated for a period.

The most significant form of domination that developed in this age was that which resulted from industrial superiority. It was Britain, above all, that now enjoyed this superiority, as a result of her technological advance. One way of maintaining that superiority was to try to ensure that the advances did not spread to other countries (just as patent laws were used to halt the transfer of technology in a later age). The British government was thus reluctant to relax the rules about the export of technical secrets and skilled workers. Even in 1824, when Huskisson, among other measures of liberalisation, at last modified these rules, he maintained a licensing system to ensure that England's industrial supremacy was not seriously endangered. And if some knowledge was finally allowed to spread, it was in the hope that Britain had such an advance over other countries that they would now find it difficult or impossible to catch up.

Thus for most of this period, Britain retained her lead. Many British writers of this age, as we saw (p. 83), were confident that the superiority of British manufacture was such that she could expect under equal competition to dominate international commerce. Already in the eighteenth century, Josiah Tucker declared that, even if the American colonies became free, 'the superiority of British Capitals over those of every other country in the Universe' would allow Britain to retain dominance in the trade to America.[16] He later recommended that the best policy for Britain was 'to have trusted solely to the goodness and cheapness of our manufactures and to the long credit we can give, for procuring them a Vent', and to rely on 'the Strength of our Capitals' to command the goods of the world.[17] Similarly, when Pitt was recommending the liberalisation of trade with Ireland in 1785, he declared that this would benefit England because English manufactures were 'so superior' that 'there can be no danger in admitting the Irish articles to our markets': because of its backward state, 'there were great obstacles to the planting of any manufacture in Ireland', so the House should not fear that 'a poor country, merely because she enjoyed some comparative exemption from taxes, was so able to cope with a rich and powerful country'.[18] Again, in justifying the Eden

Treaty with France two years later, Pitt said that, because Britain had made 'exclusively her own important parts of manufacture, she had so completely the advantage of her neighbours as to put competition at defiance'.

The idea that countries that were industrially stronger than others would win many other advantages, especially with freer competition, was promoted still further in the next century. Henry Brougham, in his 'Enquiry into Colonial Policy' declared that British commodities were 'better and cheaper' because of 'the greater extent of manufacturing capital', and the 'superior skill and industry of its workmen'. There was a direct connection between 'capital', 'industry' and 'marine' (that is shipping), and by her pre-eminence in the first, Britain had gained a 'general superiority in all three circumstances'. Ricardo thought that so long as England developed her manufacturing capacity to enable her to import food and raw materials from abroad, it was difficult to say where the limit is at which you would cease to accumulate wealth and to derive profit from its employment'.[19] So too, in 1846, Peel declared that England, besides enjoying 'a maritime strength and superiority', had much iron and coal 'which gave her advantages over every rival in the great competition for industry' and 'capital which far exceeds what they can command'. Because of these advantages, England (like Japan in a later age) was 'at the head of those nations which profit in the free interchange of their products'. The advantage provided by free trade to countries of greater industrial strength was here openly proclaimed.

On the basis of this industrial superiority, stronger nations could expect to win commercial superiority. A country like Britain, because of its superior technology, could out-sell any of its rivals, so long as it could secure access to their markets. So the English writer, Robert Torrens, quite explicitly saw trade as the means to 'power' and 'empire', pointing to the examples of Sidon, Tyre, Carthage, Venice, Genoa, the Hanse towns and Holland in the past, whose trade had given them a 'degree of political power and consideration ... far beyond their own resources': Britain likewise could 'by the wonders of her commerce create the means for taking an ascendancy in Europe'.[20] A Whig member of parliament in the House of Commons went further in declaring in 1846 that the growth of British trade could have the effect that 'foreign nations will become valuable colonies to us without imposing on us the responsibility of governing them'. And another MP in the same year declared that foreign commerce was 'the acknow-ledged source of Great Britain's wealth, power and greatness' and expressed the view that through it Britain had made 'every corner of the globe a tributary to her wants'.[21]

Britain, in fact, did succeed at this time in securing such an ascendancy in trade. Already at the beginning of the century, she had over a third of world trade.[22] After Peel's reduction of tariffs in the 1840s, British exports expanded rapidly: their value in 1851 was already 51 per cent above that of 1842, considerably more (despite the repeal of the Corn Laws and reductions in her own tariffs) than the increase (34 per cent) in the value of her imports.[23] By 1873, at the end of this period, exports had increased by 355 per cent, an average rate of growth of 11 per cent a year.[24] Export *values* increased even more: by 439 per cent, or 14 per cent a year.[25] Though this was not entirely the result of liberalisation (the relative strength of British industry would anyway have made possible considerable export growth at this period), it was certainly considerably helped through that process. This is shown by the fact that the annual growth of exports in the 25 years before 1842 had been only $1\frac{1}{2}$ per cent in value and only 17 per cent in volume. Though imports also increased (Britain had, after all, lowered her tariffs more than anybody), the increase was not so great (the rise in import value was 364 per cent, or 12 per cent a year). Thus the effect of liberalisation at first was that the trade balance improved for the industrially stronger country.[26]

The powers in that situation could win an increase in trade but not always a balance of payments surplus. For much of this period, Britain normally had a deficit in its trade balance. It was, however, able to offset this by its earnings on investments and services, such as shipping and insurance. The 'balance of trade' was thus now of less importance: it was the balance of payments that counted. But the real benefit in the eyes of the dominant groups was the increased economic activity and the industrial growth that followed. It was the *growth* of trade rather than the balance of trade which was now valued. For this brought prosperity and profits for individual manufacturers and traders, and so to some extent to the nation generally.

So the dominant countries, especially Britain, sought treaties that would make possible this growth of trade. The ideal was not selective liberalisation, but a genuinely free trade treaty, providing for a general reduction in or abolition of tariffs on a universal basis.[27] Many British statesmen and writers regarded a full free trade treaty as being the only true objective; and Gladstone, looking back at the 1860 treaty with France, regretted that it had not implemented his ideals in this respect.[28]

But it was the commercial treaties with non-European powers which most clearly reflected the interest of the most advanced states. These were mainly so-called 'open-door treaties', a type which emphasised their most defensible aspect: the fact that they were designed not to discriminate among European powers. Typical examples of these are the treaties concluded between Britain and Venezuela, China, Persia, Turkey, Morocco and Japan. They included most-favoured-nation clauses which, in theory, allowed all European nations similar privileges (though, with less industrial and commercial strength, many were not likely to be able to benefit on an equal scale). They certainly benefited the European powers as a whole, since they prevented the non-European parties from practising the same form of protectionism which the Europeans themselves had adopted at an earlier stage. In many cases, their tariffs were held down to very low levels: levels far lower than the comparable duties currently levied by European states at the time. The first Turkish treaty with Britain provided for import duties of 3 per cent, the Chinese treaty concluded at the end of the first Chinese war for a maximum duty of 5 per cent, and so on. Similarly, monopolies which had been granted within such states restricting foreign trade (though not unlike some which still existed in Europe at the time) were to be abolished: the Balta Liman convention concluded with Turkey in 1838 put an end to Turkish and Egyptian monopolies which restricted British trading opportunities.

There were differences of interest between the European nations themselves on these questions. The stronger nations were more insistent on strict equality of treatment and the most-favoured-nation principle, whilst the weaker sought to negotiate for themselves special treatment. Thus while France managed to negotiate preferential treatment for French merchants in certain areas of China under the treaties of Saigon and Tientsin, Britain, later supported by the United States, demanded a strict 'open-door' policy allowing equal access to all foreign merchants everywhere (she was assisted in this admirable posture in having already established for herself a dominant position in the most prosperous and commercially active part of China, the Yangtze valley).

There was another form of dominance which the industrially stronger nations were able to secure for themselves at this time (and again it foreshadowed the type of advantage that still more developed nations were to seek in future ages): investment in foreign countries. The country that was industrially strong was likely to dispose of investment resources that could be used abroad as well as at home. London was not only the capital of the strongest industrial power in Europe and indeed the world; it was also the principal money market and financial centre of the world. Even in the previous century, Lord

Mornington, praising British manufacturers, spoke of the 'substantial foundation of capital on which they had placed our trade – a capital which had . . . been well described as predominant and tyrant over the trade of the whole world'.[29] Pitt, speaking in the same debate, claimed that 'the powers of capital were irresistible in trade; it domineered, it ruled, it even tyrannised in the market, it enticed the strong and controlled the weak'.[30] Early in the next century, Brougham held that the development of industry in Britain had produced 'such a pitch of wealth as to give rise to an overflowing capital' which required new outlets abroad, above all in the colonies.[31] Throughout this period, Britain was investing abroad on a large scale. The total is estimated to have increased from about £10 million in 1815 to £1000 million in 1875: between 1842 and 1850 alone, the British stock of capital abroad is estimated to have increased by a third.[32] The net income from foreign interest and dividends gained by Britain rose from under £1 million a year in 1816 to about £10 million a year in 1850 and over £50 million a year in 1873.[33] Though this was still nowhere near so great as in the following period, Britain was building up a position for herself as investor to the world.

Highly industrialised countries could also obtain advantages from their superiority in shipping. By the beginning of the nineteenth century, Britain had a large shipping fleet, but its opportunities were limited by restrictive policies elsewhere. Once more the open door would enable the country with the strongest and most efficient fleet to win advantages. So in this field too the strong countries sought liberalisation. Navigation Acts and other forms of discrimination were abandoned or relaxed: as by Britain in 1849–52. Reciprocity agreements were negotiated, from which normally the stronger state benefited most: Britain's shipping activity after 1824 grew twice as fast on 'unprotected routes' after such agreements were negotiated.[34] During the following decades, with increased liberalisation, British shipping continued to grow; its percentage of world steam and motor shipping increased from 15 per cent in 1820 to nearly 40 per cent in 1870 (and 60 per cent in 1890).[35] Again, there were very substantial revenues: rising from under £10 million a year in 1816, for Britain, to over £50 million in 1873 (and nearly £70 million at the end of the century). Insurance and brokerage was another field in which one or two states dominated: British takings increased from £3 million in 1816 to £17 million sixty years later. Finally, Britain's net profit on trade between third countries and other services rose from £5 million in 1816 to £35 million in 1873.[36]

In the final resort, the stronger states could, by more ruthless means, win still greater commercial advantages: substantial control of the economic policies of other states. Through Britain's military victory over China in 1839–40, she was able to impose a maximum tariff and to open up five ports for foreign commerce; and through her subsequent victory in 1859–60, she was able to open further treaty ports, impose a low tariff, acquire control of Chinese customs, and secure the right to diplomatic representation. In 1844–6, Britain took armed action against the Argentine ruler of Uruguay to secure the independence of the latter, and so the safeguarding of British trade there. In 1861–2, France, Britain and Spain joined in a military expedition against Mexico to secure the payment of compensation for damage to European property in the Mexican civil war (and Britain and Spain withdrew only when it became clear that France had political as well as economic objectives – believing, apparently, that military action was legitimate only for the pursuit of economic ends). In Persia, both Britain and Russia used their military dominance in different parts of the country to seek for themselves commercial privileges.

Force could be used, finally, to establish new colonies which, whether or not acquired mainly for commercial reasons (usually not), once acquired, became sources of commerical advantage. Though this was not, in general, an age of colonial expansion – it was, in this sense, an interlude between the preceding and succeeding ages – there were many at the time who recognised the economic benefits which colonies could bring, and indirectly this had some influence on governments. Henry Brougham, the English writer, noted in the early 1800s that colonies provided precisely the type of market which a rapidly expanding British industry needed, a market which 'certainly and rapidly increases'; and declared that 'the settlement of a new country opens new sources of profit' and creates 'an issue for capital which was ill-employed':[37] in other words, an outlet for the 'super-abundant' capital that could not be accommodated in Britain itself. Twenty or thirty years later Edward Wakefield, believing that 'the quantity of capital which can be employed in agriculture is limited ... by the quantity of land to which capital can be applied', saw colonial expansion as a way of providing an outlet for that capital and securing food supplies which could be exchanged for British manufactures. Even Gladstone, though scarcely an imperialist, in his Chester address of November 1855, claimed that colonies were a means of promoting (in addition to the moral advancement of their inhabitants) both trade and employment. On these grounds, when the opportunities for colonial expansion occurred in this age – as for Britain at the end of the Napoleonic Wars or for France in Algiers and South East Asia – the chance was not discarded; and the economic motive was rarely entirely absent from the minds of the statesmen in such situations.

Thus in this age, with new elites exerting influence in the more powerful states, a new type of economic dominance emerged. Governments no longer sought to increase their country's economic strength through state action to nurture, subsidise and protect industry or shipping, as in the previous age. Now they relied rather on the enterprise and industrial skills of their own traders and businessmen; and aided them mainly through diplomatic, and occasionally military, efforts to open markets abroad where they could trade profitably. This might be done by encouraging other states to lower their tariff barriers, by negotiation, or by unilateral example to that end; or it could be done by opening up markets in less developed areas, whether colonies, as in the Caribbean and southern Asia, or semi-colonies, such as the backward and dependent states of Latin America, North Africa and the Far East. Either way, it provided a more painless method of winning pre-eminence than in earlier times. The strong could feel that all they sought was to develop trade; knowing that in free competition, they themselves would prevail. Dominance now was the dominance of industrial and trading strength which an advanced technology provided. Dependence, on the other hand was the dependence of the technically weak, without the capacity to trade on equal terms with more advantaged states, except through a level of protection which they were normally not allowed to undertake.

THE CONQUEST OF CAPITAL (1870–1914)

The characteristic feature of the age that followed was the development of international lending and borrowing which, for the first time now, became as important in economic relations among states as international trade. New forms of domination and dependence emerged from that relationship.

The main form of dependence in this age was the dependence of debtor states on their creditors. International lending, as we have seen, was partly for industrial and agricultural undertakings, especially mines and plantations; much more for railways and public utilities of various kinds; but it was, above all, lending direct to governments.

Many governments, especially in North Africa, Asia and Latin America, found themselves dependent on loans from other states not only to undertake the modernisation which Western contacts inspired, but also to meet their everyday needs and to repay old debts. Even European states were often in a position of dependence on their wealthier neighbours. Portugal and Spain, for example, in continual financial difficulties, Turkey and Greece, even more constrained, above all the smaller Balkan countries, relied continually on foreign borrowing, especially from France, Germany and Britain. Even Russia, though somewhat more advanced, was a chronic debtor and found herself far more dependent in consequence than her financially stronger rivals.[38]

The dependence of still less developed states was far greater. The semi-colonial countries – Tunis, Persia, Egypt, China – whose dependence was partly bound by treaty – and the semi-colonial Latin American states, whose dependence was economic, were even more obliged to take account of the opinions and attitudes that prevailed among their creditors. In many cases, their finances were either totally or partially under the control of the creditor states or of the individual creditors (the bondholders). They were obliged to reduce their tariffs to the level the creditors demanded. They were persuaded to grant 'concessions' – the right to build railways and other undertakings – on favourable terms. They were compelled in time – as the debts that were thrust on them built up – to permit their customs services, their railways, even their financial administration, to be largely or totally run by foreign nationals. They found large parts of their national income used to finance repayments at high rates of interest (in the mid-1870s, Egypt was sending two-thirds of all government income abroad to service its debt). Almost always politically as well as financially dependent – the two were closely related, though it would not always be easy to say which was cause and which effect – they had no option but to heed carefully the advice or injunctions given them by the more powerful states which dominated the world economy.

Most dependent of all were the fully colonial territories. With the new wave of colonialism which now took place in the Pacific, in Asia, above all in Africa, there were now more colonies than ever. These – even if formally termed protectorates rather than colonies, as most of them were – found that their financial and economic affairs were totally controlled by foreign rulers situated many thousands of miles away. Only if the local community had white faces, that is were of the same race as the colonisers – as in Canada, Australia, New Zealand

and South Africa – were such territories allowed in time the privilege of self-government and so of running their own financial affairs (and, as in all those cases, secured thereby rapid economic development). For the most part, the inhabitants of each territory found themselves in the position of children, whose financial situation was entirely dependent on the wishes and whims of their current guardians.

Against this, was the dominance of the creditors. Sometimes, this dominance was exercised by collective means. In a number of areas, the creditor-states acted together to protect their interests. Thus in Turkey they established an elaborate system, originally designed to ensure that repayments of debts were made when due, but which in effect secured for them a tight control of that country's financial and fiscal system. In Tunis, an international commission representing the French, Italian and British bondholders was set up, which secured ultimate responsibility for the country's revenues and debts during the following years. In Egypt, there existed, for a time after 1876, a four-power control, the Caisse de la Dette, through which representatives of Britain, France, Austria and Italy were able to supervise the revenues of the country as a whole. In Morocco from 1906, the customs were placed under international control, while at the same time French, German and Spanish 'censors' were appointed to supervise the government's finances and the state banks. In China, in addition to foreign control of the customs, the consortium of foreign banks which undertook loans to the government acquired a wide degree of control over the country's tax revenues. Somewhat similar systems of creditor control – which were almost unique to this age – were established elsewhere: in Serbia in 1895; in Greece in 1898; and in Bulgaria in 1902. A similar system was proposed for Portugal by Germany and France in 1899, but was prevented by Britain, which was not anxious to see too much intervention in Portugal's affairs by those countries.

In other cases, control was more concentrated: only two powers ran the financial system. This was the situation in Egypt immediately before 1882, under the system of Dual Control organised by Britain and France (with British and French 'Controllers of Receipts and Expenditure'). This was, in effect, the position in Morocco after 1909, when Germany was admitted by France to share in the economic control of the country in return for acknowledging French political supremacy. And it was the *de facto* situation in Persia, where Russia and Britain each controlled their own zones of the country, economically as well as politically.

In other cases again, domination was enjoyed by a single power which in practice exercised almost unlimited control. This was the position in all colonies, where the finances were run by the metropolitan power. Though there was not usually a direct financial tribute from colony to mother country (and sometimes some significant cost to the latter), the way the country's economy was run was usually influenced more by the interests of the mother country than those of the colony itself. No real effort was made to industrialise these territories, and in a few cases this was actually deterred.[39] In the semi-colonial states, European powers often acquired an almost equal degree of economic domination. In Tunis, France was virtually in control of the economy from the time the Franco–Tunisian financial commission was set up in 1869, and still more so after the setting up of the protectorate in 1881. In Egypt after 1882, Britain had full and unlimited control of Egypt's finances (even though she verbally acknowledged the ultimate authority of the Ottoman sultan). In Cuba after 1900, in the Dominican Republic after 1904, in Nicaragua after 1911, in Liberia after 1912, in Haiti and El Salvador after 1916, the US wholly or partly controlled the financial systems.

But even when there was no such tangible presence within the dependent country, ultimate economic control was often no less clearly exercised by the dominant economic powers. The ultimate leverage was financial. The concentration of investible funds in the major developed countries gave them a unique form of influence. Though the funds were, in this age, lent largely by private individuals rather than by governments, the latter could still control the flows. Access to their capital markets became a privilege which they jealously guarded, and was one which accentuated the dependence of the less privileged states. This type of control could be used, as we saw, against other European powers as much as against those overseas, sometimes for purely political reasons (see p. 145). But poorer countries, whether in Europe or overseas, faced greater difficulties, if only because their need was greater.

Thus Serbia, Rumania, Bulgaria, and Greece met constant difficulties in seeking to raise loans in Paris, Berlin or Hamburg. These difficulties could sometimes be overcome only in return for political concessions. For example, in 1913–14, France was willing to lend to Bulgaria only in return for a change in the Bulgarian cabinet (in order to make it less pro-German).[40] More often, the conditions imposed involved an extension of economic influence. For example, a German banking syndicate was willing to make a loan to Bulgaria at the same period, only in return for concessions for railway construction, harbour development, coal mines and other privileges. Rumania obtained loans from Germany in the 1880s and 1890s only in return for pledging the revenues of the Oriental railways, customs, prospecting rights and harbour fees. The French Minister of Foreign Affairs, Poincaré, admitted quite frankly in the French Chamber in 1912 that 'when a request is addressed to the government it is examined with an appreciation of the financial interest and French political interest. . . . In all requests the French interest should take precedence over the financial interest.' Sometimes, the price of a loan was pitched high. In 1893, France offered a loan to Portugal that was to be guaranteed by a mortgage on the revenues of certain colonies: a condition that would have given France a substantial say in the future of those colonies. In 1898, Britain demanded, in return for making a loan to Portugal, economic control of the Delgado bay region in Mozambique. In 1908, the new Moroccan sultan was obliged to accept a loan to repay the debts of his predecessor, in return for which he had not only to accept still closer scrutiny of his own finances, but also to pay the cost of the French military action which had helped bring him to power. In 1913, France demanded, as the price of a loan to Rumania, that the latter should buy her imports only from France for the next two years.[41] Similarly, a price could be asked for loans for industrial or other undertakings. As Pichon, the French Minister of Foreign Affairs, put it in 1912: 'we ask ordinarily that France be represented in the Board of Directors that may be set up as a result of the operation, so that our commerce and industry are able to profit as much as possible from the use of the borrowed funds'.[42]

Thus economic power in this age was, above all, financial power. Those countries that were financially, politically and militarily weak found themselves in a position of continual dependence. A classic example is that of Persia, whose weak ruler from the early 1870s became more and more dependent on Britain and Russia, who were at the time engaged in a bitter struggle with each other for influence there. In 1872–3, in return for a loan, the Persian government granted a concession to a British subject, strongly supported by the British government, Baron Reuter, granting him an almost complete control of the economic life of Persia. Though this was never finally put into effect, because of the outrage that it aroused, in 1889–90 the Baron, again with the support of the British government, set up the Imperial Bank of Persia, which was given the exclusive right of issue (an extraordinary privilege for a foreign bank, even for those days).

Britain and Russia both proceeded to seek economic concessions in Persia in return for loans. Britain was granted the monopoly of all tobacco sales, navigation rights on the Karoon River, and a part of the customs revenues; while Russia was granted concessions for fisheries in the Caspian Sea, navigation rights in that sea, and grants for the exploitation of mines, forest-lands, and telegraphs. Later, in return for further loans, Russia secured further tariff concessions, and the right to build a railway from Teheran to the Russian border, while Britain obtained the revenues of the posts and telegraphs, of the Caspian fisheries and further customs revenues. The British government pressed on the Shah proposals for British road-building in south Persia, an extension of the Indo–European Telegraph Company's network, new provincial agencies of the Imperial Bank, and, above all, the D'Arcy oil concession from which the Anglo–Persian Oil Company emerged. After 1907, when Britain and Russia came to an understanding on spheres of influence, pressure on Persia became no less. Indeed, interference in her affairs increased. Though the agreement purported to pledge respect for the 'integrity and independence' of Persia, in fact it divided economic and political control of most of the country between the two states. Each obtained control over the customs revenues in its own sphere of influence, and in effect the right to virtually all concessions that were offered there. The two worked together to prevent any economic rights being accorded to Germany or other powers. In March 1910, they demanded, as a condition of further financial aid, a programme which included the granting of yet more concessions and the organisation of the police force under foreign officers (a programme which even the weak Persian government was not willing to accept). Finally, they succeeded in securing the removal of a US official who had been engaged in bringing about reforms of the entire Persian fiscal system, apparently successfully, because those reforms, by increasing the independence of the Persian government, would have threatened the leverage available to the two powers. In other words, they combined successfully to keep the country economically, as well as politically, firmly under their own control.[43]

There was a somewhat similar story in China. After the Japanese victory over China in the war of 1895, France and Russia intervened to compel Japan to renounce part of her territorial gains. They then used the influence so acquired with the Chinese government to secure both political and economic advantages for themselves. Among the latter, was the right to lend the money needed by China to pay off the indemnity Japan had demanded, and to rebuff British and German bids to undertake these loans. Russia, at the same time, secured a pledge that she would share in any right of financial control which China might grant to any foreign government, while France secured promises of railway and mining concessions and the participation of French nationals in the Chinese customs service, hitherto dominated by Britain. British and German interests, concerned at this threatened Franco–Russian dominance, retaliated. British and German banks, with their governments' support, became still more active in seeking to lend to the Chinese government, and agreed among themselves to co-operate for this purpose. In 1897, when China had to pay a further instalment on her indemnity, the French sought, in return for a further loan, full control of the customs administration, together with special privileges in three Chinese provinces. Britain and Germany, alarmed at this threat, offered a loan on slightly less onerous terms; and were thus granted the privilege of making it. In the following year, Russia demanded, in return for a further loan, the right to finance, build, and control railways throughout north China and Manchuria, and the appointment of a Russian as Inspector-General of Customs. Britain, to whom China in desperation turned, then demanded further rights to build railways in the Yangtze Valley, together with an assurance that territory in that region would not be alienated to any other power and an undertaking that the Inspector-General of Customs would remain a Briton. China eventually secured the loan she needed from an Anglo–German group, in return for guarantees of customs, salt tax and certain other revenues, which were to be supervised by the foreign-controlled maritime customs administration. Thus, while China was sometimes able to play off one Western country against another, gradually, with each new loan, she had to make new concessions forfeiting her economic independence.[44]

The various forms of control established by the creditor countries understandably aroused considerable resentment among the populations of the weaker states. Often they were the cause of powerful political movements in those countries. The governments of such states, though themselves resentful of dependence, were above all concerned to secure the further loans they needed (on which their own survival might depend). On the other hand, their populations were conscious only of the national humiliation which foreign supervision of their country's finances represented. In Greece the supervision of domestic revenues by the bondholders which was imposed after 1898 was intensely unpopular; and on one occasion the Greek parliament overturned a government that was willing to give foreign interests a place in the national bank. In Bulgaria in 1902, the parliament twice rejected proposals providing for foreign creditors' financial control in return for a loan, and the king was obliged to dissolve parliament and secure the re-election of another more compliant with that arrangement. In Persia at the beginning of the century, the main nationalist party, which controlled the Majlis, resisted further foreign loans and the foreign control of Persian affairs which resulted; and, in 1906–7, this led to a major constitutional crisis, and efforts by Russia to eliminate altogether the influence of the inconvenient Majlis. In China in 1912, foreign loans and the consequent degree of external control were equally unpopular, and Yuan Shih-kai secured a new loan only by failing to refer it to parliament (which rightly feared the use to which he might put it). Thus the dominance of the financially powerful states increasingly evoked the resentment of the dependent states and their peoples: a resentment even more powerful than the similar sentiment felt against the IMF, performing a precisely similar role, a century later, since dependence on identifiable and arbitrary foreign governments was even more intolerable than dependence on an international body purporting to apply consistent principles.

The dominance enjoyed by the more developed countries was not only financial. They had, for example, a preponderant share in the world's trade. They exported most of the world's manufactures, and imported a large proportion of the raw materials that were traded. Among the developed countries, Britain still enjoyed a huge share of these. In 1872–3, at the beginning of the period, British trade was 23 per cent of all world trade (if re-exports are included), and the proportion was still one sixth in 1913.[45] Britain's share of imports was even greater: her imports were over a quarter of the rest of the world's exports (26 per cent) in 1872–3; at the turn of the century they remained 20 per cent; and they were still 17 per cent in 1913.[46] Britain was followed by Germany, the US and France; these between them had 29 per cent of world trade in 1874, and 31 per cent in 1913. The four nations together, therefore, controlled almost half of world trade just before the First World War. Among the rest, there were some which secured a rapid increase in exports. These were mainly agricultural producers – Australia, Argentina, Japan and Canada – and, as in later years, these exporting countries were usually the nations which secured the highest rates of growth generally. Other countries could secure any worthwhile share in total world trade only if they had some particular product which was in demand elsewhere: rice (Burma, Thailand, Indo-China), rubber (Ceylon and Malaya), cocoa (Gold

Coast), coffee (Brazil), or palm oil (West Africa). Most countries, without such crops, or with declining crops such as sugar, suffered considerable difficulties in winning any significant share of world trade. During the long depression of 1873–95, the terms of trade turned against the agricultural producers: and even though there was an up-turn in their favour after 1900, this did not fully redress the decline in their relative position.

Another type of domination resulted from the control of investment. Again there was a concentration among a small number of the most developed countries. Britain remained by far the largest investing country. Her foreign investment grew rapidly during this period (at the expense of domestic investment, which was proportionately much lower than that of the US and Germany). It quadrupled from 1875 to 1914, to about four billion pounds or 18 billion dollars. By that time, that of France was 9 billion dollars; that of Germany 5.8 billion; that of the US 3.5 billion.[47] Most countries were net importers of capital, and many had debt problems. The largest importer was Russia. But others who borrowed heavily were Turkey, Egypt, China and most of the Latin American countries. Many of these found very serious difficulties, especially during the long depression, with its low agricultural prices, in maintaining payments on their debts. There were already requests for rescheduling during the 1870s from Turkey, Egypt, Spain, Uruguay, Peru, Bolivia and other countries. And some states, especially in Latin America, finding increasing difficulty in maintaining export earnings, defaulted altogether.

In this age, therefore, there emerged new types of economic domination and dependence among states. The most important development was the rise in international lending. Many governments in the less developed parts of the world became more and more dependent for the funds they urgently needed on the financial institutions, and ultimately on the governments, of more developed states. The latter did not hesitate to secure for themselves, as the price of such funds, concessions, leases, above all financial control. Mainly, lending was undertaken direct to governments for general government needs, repayment of earlier debts, and for infrastructure. Very little went for manufacturing industry. Trade and trade services were also dominated by the most advanced states, especially, though to a declining extent, by Britain. The most blatant form of domination, and therefore of corresponding dependence, was that which the colonial powers exercised within their own colonies. The economic development of such territories was never at this time an overriding concern; and the metropolitan powers were often more concerned with the value of the territories for their own home economies than with local purposes. Though governments extracted little from the colonies for themselves (there was less *direct* 'exploitation' than was often alleged), they likewise put little into them: most were expected to be financially self-sufficient. As the main source of investment funds and the main generators of trade, the advanced countries were the main active force within the world economy, to which others responded only passively. The world economy was based mainly on the exchange of manufactured goods from their own countries for raw materials and food from elsewhere: this helped to promote industrial development within their own states, but little elsewhere. If, despite large borrowing, states and territories in other parts of the world, on the basis of this division of labour, remained mainly unindustrialised and underdeveloped, this was not normally a matter of great concern to the financial interests that increasingly dominated the international economy.

ECONOMIC ASCENDANCY THROUGH POLITICAL INFLUENCE (1914–50)

In the age that followed, new types of dominance and dependence emerged. These reflected the new social structure within states, the new doctrines concerning economic life that resulted, and the changed motives of states in their economic relations with each other.

The most important change in social structure was the increasing influence of political leaders and of the bureaucrats that worked for them, resulting from the growing power of governments generally. The increasing disposition of governments to intervene in the working of the economy changed the nature of international economic relationships. National economies became more and more divorced from each other, partitioned by the barriers which each government erected. While direct control of one economy by another became less, the disparities between the separate national economies became greater than ever. And while the expansion of private interests into dependent economies diminished for a time, the dominance of the most powerful states (rather than of private interests within states) was now greater than ever before.

The most important source of these differences in economic power was the increasing difference in industrial strength. In earlier periods, this had not always been decisive in international exchanges. In the seventeenth century, the Netherlands was dominant in international economy because of her commercial rather than industrial strength. In the years before 1914, Britain likewise retained a dominant position as much because of her trading as industrial power, which relatively declined. In the new age, trade declined as a proportion of national income and economic activity as a whole. More and more it was industrial strength (and the financial strength that accompanied it) that determined economic power and influence in general. And in this age, unquestionably the world's leading industrial power was the United States (which had a relatively small foreign trade).

Already the world's largest industrial power at the opening of the First World War, she increased this advantage in the following fifteen years. After a severe set-back during the depression, which affected her economy more seriously than that of any other nation, she again increased her industrial strength, both absolutely and relatively, during and immediately after the Second World War. The share of the US in world production, which was already 36 per cent in 1913, rose to 42 per cent in 1926–9 fell to 32 per cent in the late 1930s whilst she remained in depression, but rose to nearly 50 per cent, a staggering proportion, after the Second World War. Germany had already overtaken Britain as an industrial power by 1913. Her share of world industrial production was then 16 per cent against Britain's 14 per cent.[48] Her continued growth was interrupted only by severe disruption through defeat in two world wars. Russia and Japan also advanced significantly during the latter part of this period. Britain and France declined relatively, though remaining substantial industrial powers: Britain's share of world industrial production fell from 14 per cent in 1913 to 9 per cent in 1936–8, and France's from nearly 7 per cent to 4.5 per cent.[49] Japan doubled her production in the decade after 1913, and trebled it again by 1940, but the total remained small as a proportion of world production until after the Second World War.

These changes had immediate consequences for the role of each country in the international economy. Because the US was the dominant industrial power, and after the First World War was less constrained by balance of payments and debt problems than most of the west European countries, she became overwhelmingly the most important capital-exporter. During the 1920s, she lent heavily to Europe, especially to Germany, both in the form of private investment and in loans to governments.[50] Thus, during the 1920s the US replaced European countries as the major foreign investor. Between 1919 and

1929, her longterm investments abroad rose by nearly $9 billion: this accounted for two-thirds of the world's total increase, and raised her stake to nearly one-third of the world total.[51] This flow of investment funds was reversed from 1929, and was scarcely resumed during the 1930s; beginning again on a larger scale only after the Second World War.

Britain continued to be a net lender abroad, but the scale was now far less than before 1914. France, too, invested much less abroad (mainly to her own possessions), but did not recoup the losses in her holdings that took place during the war.[52] The role of the west European countries as lenders was reduced still further as a result of the Second World War, when they again lost a large part of their foreign holdings. Countries such as Britain and France, which had continued to secure a substantial income on their investments, now lost most of this source of income.[53]

Most of the investment that did occur was in other developed countries. The industrialised countries of the West, their economies run by governments pursuing autarchic policies, now strictly control-led the flow of foreign exchange abroad. The main borrowers were Germany in the 1920s, and to a lesser extent the countries of temperate climate, Canada, Australia, Argentina, and so on. The genuinely poor countries and territories, still largely under colonial rule, received little. The US, though easily the largest foreign lender, did not lend abroad on anything like the scale that Britain had done in the years before the First World War. In general, all economies were now inward-turned; and in this sense, both dominance and dependence – the dominance of lenders and the dependence of borrowers – were probably less than they had been during the preceding period.

Dominance began now to take new forms. It was now the creation of governments rather than of financial forces. A new development was the attempt by leading powers to establish trading blocks and similar economic associations. In 1932 Britain, having for the first time for a century raised protective barriers, established under the Ottawa agreements a preferential system with her partners and dependencies in the British Commonwealth and Empire (within which, as the only fully developed industrial power, she was assured of playing a domin-ant part). A few years later, Germany, while raising still more stringent controls against imports from most of her trading partners and rivals, entered into arrangements with the smaller countries of central and eastern Europe for mutual trade, including barter: a block which Germany, as almost the only developed industrial power, was equally certain to dominate. France in 1933, alone of the major powers in not devaluing at that time, formed a gold block with weaker countries, such as Italy, the Netherlands, Belgium, Switzerland and Poland, in which she too was able to play the leading role. Finally, the US, while she led no recognised trade grouping, by entering into a series of bilateral agreements with smaller states in Latin America from 1934 onwards, created a trading area in which she played an equally dominant part. While all of the three former blocks disintegrated or weakened after 1939, the dominance the US enjoyed in Latin America was greatly strengthened by the war. After the war, it was extended for a time to the whole of the Western world, where she alone survived the war economically strong and dominated the new world economy that emerged. By that time, in the other half of Europe the Soviet Union, the other major victorious power, established for herself a role which was even more supreme among the economies of eastern Europe.

In the field of trade too, a new pattern emerged. Britain, far and away the most important trading nation of the pre-1914 period, now declined drastically; her relative position had weakened somewhat even before the First World War, but her trade declined between the wars even in absolute terms.[54] The share of other west European countries such as France and Germany, though it increased slightly between the wars, was again sharply reduced after 1945. Against this, the US share of world trade, after a severe slump in the 1930s, rose dramatically; and although her trade remained a fairly small proportion of her national income, the US became, after the end of the Second World War, the world's major trading nation, on which many other states became increasingly dependent for their needs in many areas, especially for capital goods, some raw materials and grain. Japan's rise as a commercial nation was possibly even more dramatic, though her share of world trade by the late 1930s remained fairly small, and was again cut back sharply after her defeat in war. Non-European nations, such as Canada, Australia and Argentina, after a set-back when relative prices of primary products declined sharply during the 1920s and 1930s, regained a larger share of world trade in and after the Second World War. Russia, beginning with a tiny share of world trade in 1914, had, with the autarchic policies pursued by the Soviet government, only marginally increased that share by the early 1950s.

Commercial power brought with it another type of economic advantage which was important in this period. In an age of erratic trade policies and shifting balance of payments, the strength of central bank reserves became a crucial factor affecting the economic independence of states. Here, once more, the US was in a uniquely favourable position. After the First World War, she continued to win gold and foreign exchange both from trade and above all from vast war debts and reparations payments. In this way, she attracted into her coffers a considerable proportion of the world's stock of monetary gold. Thus she never at any time during this period, not even during the depression, had, like other states, to be concerned with pressures on her reserves, since these covered her foreign trade many times over. Russia, though in other ways an infinitely weaker economy, was also immune from such problems, because of limited foreign trade, the use of barter and large-scale production of gold at home. No other nation found itself in this happy position. Britain, for example, though she continued to enjoy a balance of payments surplus for much of this period, partly because of earnings on invisibles – interest on remaining investments as well as profits on shipping and insurance – nonetheless suffered serious foreign exchange constraints because her gold reserves in London were quite inadequate in relation to the potential claims on them, especially those of central banks (which, in a major crisis such as that of 1931, found it necessary hurriedly to withdraw their deposits). Other countries, beset by sudden payments problems because of the contraction of trade in the period of the decline in commodity prices, also found their reserves inadequate to sustain a liberal trading policy, and were thus forced into protection. And after the Second World War, almost all countries other than the US, their industry destroyed or weakened during that conflict and requiring to import many of their essential needs, were without the reserves of gold or foreign exchange to finance these imports: they thus had to enter into special clearing arrangements, or to secure aid or credits from US, to enable their economies to expand once more. This balance of payments weakness (as in the subsequent age) brought a situation of dependence in all economic negotiations. It was one of the main reasons why Britain, immediately after the Second World War, was compelled to negotiate with the US for a long-term loan as well as arrangements concerning a future world monetary system, in circumstances very unfavourable to herself (committing herself, for example, to introduce convertibility of sterling long before she was economically in a position to do this). Now, once more as in the previous age, it was the creditors that called the tune.

The dominance which the most advanced states were able to secure, in production, trade, foreign investment and other fields, produced for them a leverage that could be used for political purposes. Perhaps the most blatant example was the penetration of central and eastern Europe by Germany during the 1930s. The countries of that area were already in a situation of acute dependence, with large debts to the outside world, depleted or non-existent reserves, small export receipts and considerable import requirements. Germany was willing to exploit this situation for both economic and political ends. 'By offering a ready market for primary products in exchange for imports of equipment Germany came to exercise increasing dominance over the trade and development of eastern Europe ... Germany was able to dictate the prices to be paid for the region's primary products and at the same time she piled up huge import surpluses with the countries in question which were not matched by German exports ... And though the eastern countries did secure some capital equipment from Germany it was too little and too late to do much in the way of transforming the structure of their economies. Finally, economic penetration paved the way for ultimate military and political conquest of Germany's eastern neighbours'.[55] In east Asia, Japan's effort to establish a 'co-prosperity sphere' with the far weaker states of the region, most finally conquered and under her military control, provided an equally dominant position for her own economy, and acute dependence for their partners.

In other cases, the relationship was more subtle. The imperial preference scheme established within the British Commonwealth secured reciprocal advantages for the overseas dominions, able to find better markets for primary produce, and for Britain, assured of preferential markets for her industrial products abroad; but the relationship established was one which helped to maintain Britain in the position of the dominant manufacturing partner, while her fellow-members were encouraged to remain primarily agricultural producers. Similarly, agreements made by the US with Britain and other west European countries at the end of the Second World War, committing the latter to rapid liberalisation of their trade at a time when their own manufacturing industries were weak, assured the US of easy access to markets in which she should expect to occupy a dominant position: just as her attempts to secure liberalisation in aviation (at this time the US owned more than half the Western world's commercial aircraft) were likely to bring US domination in that field too. The estalishment of a free market in western Europe not only brought better opportunities for US industry but also re-established the type of economic system to which the US was politically committed, and perhaps even made that area more subject to US political influence. In other words, as in all other ages, economic power produced its political spin-off.

Against the economic and political advantages acquired by the more powerful states, was the dependence of the weaker countries. Even in Europe, there were many states that found themselves permanently in a dependent situation. The new, small and underdeveloped countries of eastern and central Europe, many of them fragments of the old Austro-Hungarian Empire, were among the poorest in Europe. They found themselves, with the partial exception of Czechoslovakia, with little industry, backward agriculture, poor communications and the additional problems posed by innumerable new national frontiers and the economic barriers which accompanied them. They won little investment or credit from elsewhere, and suffered difficulties which successive inflations, devaluations and protection could not alleviate. Almost all were seriously in debt and became more so (despite small-scale assistance from the League) as time went on. It was this vulnerability that made them so easily subject to German domination during the 1930s and made easier Soviet control in the 1940s.

The underdeveloped countries outside Europe, even when they were independent, as in Latin America, were even more backward (again with rare exceptions, such as Argentina) in relation to the advanced countries of the Western world. They, too, were crippled by large government debts and (until they defaulted) had to spend much of their export earnings in paying them off. They were beset by unfavourable terms of trade and subject to all the special difficulties of primary-producing countries in this age. All were thus dependent for their economic welfare on the more powerful states, a dependence which the collapse of primary prices in the depression only accentuated. Latin American states became more than ever dependent on the US market and on US economic policy, while the subject countries of Asia and Africa were made even more dependent on their colonial masters.

Primary-producing countries suffered special difficulties in this age. Prices were always unstable. They were also, from 1928, abysmally low. Primary prices sank more than those of manufactured goods and, until the Second World War, revived less. Primary producers were peculiarly dependent on other countries: 74 per cent of all primary produce was imported by twelve advanced industrial countries.[56] The decline in world activity during the depression resulted in a far more than proportionate decline in the prices of primary products.[57] The volume of trade also fell sharply. Many of the primary producers were anyway in debt, and were forced into further debts and devaluation.[58]

Even the slow revival of the 1930s had little effect on them.[59] Colonial territories – covering almost half the world – were usually (though not always) still worse off. They were backward in the first place; they attracted little outside investment; and their economies were controlled by the metropolitan countries, distracted by their own severe problems, not themselves.

Many countries were in a weak position because of the burden of debt. In order to pay the interest on their loans, they needed to export substantially more than they imported. This was especially difficult to do in a period of contracting trade. Countries that had received substantial investment in earlier years, therefore – Argentina, Australia, New Zealand, South Africa – or those that had recently been receiving it – Germany and Austria, for example – had to make huge efforts to increase their exports. But many debtors were poor countries. Of these, most were primary producers, and so suffered double difficulties.[60] With the catastrophic fall in the prices of primary produce, it became especially difficult, if not impossible, for them to secure the increase in export earnings required. At the same time, creditor countries were not prepared to postpone repayments or maintain lending to make it possible.[61] Defaulting became frequent, especially in the 1930s: many of the countries of Latin America, and some other poor countries too, were forced into this situation. By 1932, many countries had been forced to devalue, to repudiate debts, to suspend interest payments, or to impose rigid exchange controls.[62]

Another group which suffered special problems were those defeated in the two world conflicts. Whether or not it was poetic justice, it was a fact that these countries suffered severe economic difficulties in the aftermath of war. This was particularly so after the First World War, when the problems anyway associated with defeat were compounded, first by a food blockade and shortages which amounted to famine,[63] by lack of raw materials, above all by the huge burdens placed by the victorious powers in the form of reparations. Germany was originally required to pay reparations to the tune of £6600 million. Although the sum was gradually scaled down to £125 million a year in 1924 – of which only a small fraction was eventually paid – it nonetheless represented a considerable burden on an economy that was anyway greatly weakened by war and subsequent inflation. The burden of the payments (accompanied by an occupation of the main industrial areas when reparations faltered) contributed to hyper-inflation in the early 1920s, and perhaps to the high level of unemployment ten years later.[64] Other defeated countries, such as the component parts of the

Austro–Hungarian empire and Turkey, were less severely penalised for their defeat though, like Germany, they were obliged to seek substantial loans to help with reconstruction. Their economies were shattered far more than those of most of the victorious countries and, with the establishment of new states, had to be started again from scratch. In many cases, new currencies were established. All suffered economic problems of one kind or another. Russia, racked by civil war as well as by defeat in the main conflict, and subsequently isolated by the rest of the international community, perhaps suffered a more severe decline than any.

After the Second World War, economic retribution on the defeated was also severe at first: again, reparations were demanded from Germany and, to a small extent, from Japan. But this time both benefited from the fact that their support soon came to be required by one side in the emerging cold war between East and West. Thus relatively quickly the disabilities were removed and revival fostered; and, in practice, newly re-equipped, these two countries showed the most spectacular economic advance of any in the period that was to follow. Only the defeated countries of eastern Europe this time suffered the full rigours of reparations payments, before they too were eventually seen as allies rather than victims by the conquering power. They remained, however, far more than those defeated in the West, totally in the control of the state that had occupied them, which to a considerable extent merely absorbed them within its own economic system. Dependency in their case was greater than ever.

In this age, then, a new pattern of dominance and dependence emerged. Because bureaucratic intervention in all states had the effect of cutting off one country from another, economic relations generally were less close than in most other ages. But in many cases, whether from motives of political expansion or of economic penetration, powerful states established a commanding position in relation to the economies of weaker countries. So Germany acquired dominance among the economies of central and south-eastern Europe between the wars, just as Japan did in much of east Asia; Britain established a looser economic relationship with the states of the British Commonwealth and Empire, as did the US with Latin America. In all these cases, the link was between a dominant manufacturing and a dependent primary producing area. After the Second World War, the US was the strongest economy of the world. Through generous aid programmes and the promotion of selective liberalisation, she gave substantial help to other states; but in doing so she reinforced the power and influence of her own economy. In eastern Europe, the Soviet Union, by cruder means, acquired an even greater dominance over the economies of the countries of the region. In each case, the most significant element in this new domination was that each super-power established not only its own economic preponderance amongst the dependent countries all around, but also the victory of the entire economic system in which it believed within its own part of the world. In much of the rest of the world, colonial dependency persisted. And because the differences in economic strength between states were greater than at any earlier time in history, the degree of domination that occurred, as well as the degree of subordination of those countries less fortunate, became perhaps greater now than at any other time.

TECHNOLOGICAL ASCENDANCY AND FINANCIAL POWER (1950–80)

In the age that followed, the characteristic pattern of domination and dependence changed again.

The dominant powers were now more than ever a small number of Western industrialised states. These controlled between them well over half of world production, two-thirds of world trade, and almost all foreign investment. It was the economic decisions which they reached which, to a large extent, determined the course of the international economy.

All these countries enjoyed, for more than two decades, a period of rapid and sustained growth, punctuated only by brief and mild recessions. By far the strongest of them was the US, at first even more pre-eminent than she had been in the age before. While almost every other nation had been weakened in the Second World War, the US economy had grown vastly stronger. Most other nations for a time, therefore, became dependent for most of their needs on imports of US goods, especially capital goods. At the same time, the US was in a position to shape many of the international economic institutions of the post-war world. From the early 1960s, with increasing balance of payments problems, with an ever weakening dollar, and with worldwide over-commitment, economically as much as politically and militarily, the US lost some of this relative superiority. Her economy, though remaining strong domestically, became increasingly weak internationally. There was an even more dramatic decline in the fortunes of Britain. Shattered by war, and weakened by social and industrial problems, she was now overtaken by many of her neighbours in western Europe. Against the decline of these two countries, there was a dramatic growth in economic strength among other industrial countries: notably Japan, which in thirty odd years raised herself from defeat to becoming the world's third economic power; western Germany; and some smaller states such as Sweden and Switzerland.

But, despite these variations, all the developed Western countries shared for a time in an era of substantial prosperity. The relative position of the group as a whole improved against the other main groups: the Eastern bloc countries, weakened by excessive centralisation, market deficiencies, lack of incentives, and a sluggish agriculture, and the third world, suffering from past underdevelopment, low investment, lack of trading opportunities and excessive population growth.

The richer countries were able to strengthen this substantial advantage further by imposing a new structure on the international economy after 1945. Because of the almost total domination they held, they were able to lay down the rules that were to operate, both in the trading and in the monetary fields. They were able to establish a system that was highly favourable to their own interests and would improve their position still further in the years to come. For example the system was, as we saw, relatively liberal with respect to manufactures, especially advanced industrial products; but allowed continued protection for agriculture, for processed goods and for simple manufactures, especially textiles. In other words, the Ricardian principle of comparative advantage was applied to the products they themselves produced most efficiently, but it was not applied to those where the advantage lay with poorer countries. In consequence, the domination of world trade enjoyed by the developed Western countries grew still further as the period progressed. By 1970 exports of the advanced Western countries had become 72 per cent of world trade (against 63 per cent in 1953), while those of poor countries were only 17.7 per cent (against 27 per cent).[65] The declining share of poor countries resulted partly from differential protection, and partly from the declining proportion of trade in primary products. Trade in manufactured goods, on the other hand, especially the sophisticated goods in which Western states specialised, grew fastest.

The domination of a small number of richer countries was also seen in the new monetary system established. As in earlier ages, creditor

countries acquired a substantial degree of control over those compelled to borrow. But this was now exercised in collective form: through
institutional rather than bilateral pressures. The new international
body established to provide such help was formed in such a way that
developed countries, though under a quarter of the membership,
wielded 60–70 per cent of the votes. They used this to demand stern,
usually restrictive conditions for loans. The countries obliged to seek
help were condemned to policies – reductions in public spending,
credit and parities – which not only caused considerable social problems, but which many believed inappropriate to countries whose
payments problems derived mainly from external sources. Most of the
rich states, on the other hand, though they suffered from frequent and
serious balance of payments problems, only on rare occasions submitted themselves to the discipline of the new organisation. They obtained
the necessary credit instead by private arrangements, outside the
framework of the IMF: through currency swaps, central bank support,
bilateral loans, and undertakings to reduce pressure on the debtor
state (for example, undertakings not to exchange dollars for gold). In
this way the more serious constraints imposed by the IMF were
usually avoided. The US, which for long suffered the worst balance of
payments and currency problems of any country, never went to the
IMF for support, but secured support from elsewhere by other means:
above all the willingness of central banks to hold dollars of declining
value. Many poor countries therefore claimed that the rich countries,
by avoiding the deflationary disciplines of the IMF, were enabled to
export inflation to them, in the form of higher prices for manufactured
goods, while their own exports (with the exception of oil) were not able
to attain equivalent purchasing power. The allocation of quotas and
SDRs, being based largely on shares of world trade, made much more
new credit available to rich countries than the poor countries which
needed it most. Finally, the structure of the system was subsequently
adjusted to suit the convenience of Western countries: for example,
floating rates were, except in exceptional circumstances, severely
disapproved by the Fund in its first two decades of life, but evoked little
complaint when they were widely adopted by the rich countries
themselves in the early 1970s.

Other new institutions of the day both reflected and intensified the
economic domination of the wealthier states. In the World Bank, too,
the voting system provided that the chief industrial powers enjoyed a
clear majority of the votes, though they represented far less than a
quarter of the membership. A privileged position was given to them

under various formulae (see p. 112) in the main specialised agencies. To some extent this merely reflected reality: the major states would not have accorded significant powers to these organisations unless they were assured of majority power within them (and on many matters, anyway, these bodies operated by consensus). But even if few votes were taken, the formal voting system undoubtedly strengthened the influence the rich states could secure. In addition, they created influential bodies of their own, the OECD and the IEA, the BIS and the Group of Ten, which discussed many matters of importance to the world economy, and in which the poor were not represented at all. The seven most powerful economic states of all met periodically in economic 'summits' that were more significant in determining what actually happened in the world economy than any more representative and broadly-based body.

Apart from their domination of institutions, the rich countries enjoyed a powerful financial hold over poor states. The latter were dependent on the rich states for most of their financial needs. Private investment, export credits, inter-governmental lending, bank loans, aid, all of these came overwhelmingly from a handful of developed countries. Though much was subject only to commercial conditions, politics often played at least a part in influencing availability or terms. Left-wing governments (such as those of Allende's Chile, or Cuba or Vietnam) found it much harder to obtain loans than those that were reliably pro-Western. Even where credit was granted, it created a form of financial dependence which accorded considerable power to the institutions that provided it. In many cases, loans came from private banks. These too, therefore, could, through their lending policies, especially their willingness to renew or reschedule loans, determine the economic fortunes of a large number of states, the value of imports they could finance, the scale of their development plans, whether or not a new steel mill could be built or a new airline established. And, in this way, they acquired imperceptibly a control over poor countries' economic development that was perhaps greater than that of the Western governments themselves.

The advantages enjoyed by the rich states were thus supplemented by the domination of their private institutions. Apart from the international banks, these were the major transnational corporations involved in manufacturing. Though their operations in poor states were far less than those in other rich states, they represented a far higher proportion of all economic activities there. Because of the scale of their operations and their worldwide character, the corporations acquired an economic power that it was difficult for individual governments to counter. Because their head offices remained far away, in alien territory and under foreign jurisdiction, it was impossible for any host government to bring them under control, or even to influence effectively their decisions or activities. By engaging in differential pricing, they could secure the maximum revenues where the tax burden was least, or even avoid taxation altogether on parts of their earnings. They could switch imports and exports, adjust their purchasing and sub-contracting, in order to promote their own benefit. And international efforts to control their activities – for example, the formulation of guidelines to influence their conduct (see p. 203) – remained feeble and without effective sanctions.

These corporations enjoyed a degree of commercial dominance never previously seen. Not only did their overall sales grow faster than rates of growth generally; with the acquisition of increasing shares of industry elsewhere, their sales abroad grew faster still. During the 1970s, while their total sales grew at an annual compound rate of 6.2 per cent, the sales of their foreign affiliates grew at a compound rate of 11.1 per cent a year.[66] The latter were then growing 40 per cent faster than world exports.[67] Since they were concentrated in technically advanced sectors, which were the fastest growing, this increase in their share was likely to be maintained. According to some estimates, by the year 2000 something like half the world production could be in the hands of two or three hundred such corporations.[68] Most had invested large sums in research and development, which could be recovered only through growth in the future. In some industries, one or two firms had already acquired an overwhelmingly dominant position. In computers, one firm enjoyed 65 per cent of the market (while most of its main competitors were also US firms). In oil, seven firms enjoyed by far the greater part of world sales. In pharmaceuticals, aerospace, motor manufacture and a number of others, a small and declining number of firms shared the market between them. While at the beginning of the period there were five or ten major firms in each European state in these industries, by the end there were only one or two, and even these were not always large enough to compete effectively against their US and Japanese rivals (with which they therefore increasingly sought to make co-operative arrangements). For small developing countries, the dominance of the major transnational corporations was even greater. And such firms, while they performed undoubted services which could not otherwise have been performed, extracted large revenues: the flow of profits, dividends, royalties and fees, which represented a considerable balance of payments drain, in most cases exceeded the inflow of new investments.[69]

These advantages on the side of the rich states were mirrored by a corresponding dependency on the side of the developing countries. These were, first, obliged to accept the trading and monetary systems which they found when they came to independence, mainly after the period began. In the field of trade, they found a system committed to liberalisation of a kind that the rich states had rejected for themselves at an earlier stage of their development. They were dependent on imports from the advanced countries for most manufactures, for all capital goods, and sometimes for food or materials as well. Yet they themselves faced considerable obstacles in securing access to those countries for their own exports (except for raw materials, which not all of them possessed). The products which they exported, primary produce and simple manufactures, in which they possessed a comparative advantage, represented declining shares of world trade, and the former were highly unstable in price. There was no genuine reciprocity in their situation. While poor countries were unable to dispense with imports of capital equipment, some consumer goods and even food from rich countries, the latter could dispense, at little cost, with many of the exports of poorer countries, most of which they produced themselves, even if at higher cost. Thus, having a smaller share in trade, and smaller markets to offer, their bargaining position in the periodic trade negotiations which took place was fatally weak.[70]

In the monetary field, likewise, poor countries found that the system established appeared weighted against them. It outlawed some of the practices which they found most attractive (and which again had often been used by richer states in the past): exchange controls, multiple rates of exchange, high protection and expansionary monetary policies. The organisation on which they depended for credit demanded the abandonment of such policies as the price of its credit. And in order to obtain assistance from that organisation when in balance of payments difficulties, they found themselves compelled to adopt trade liberalisation, a relaxation of exchange controls, high interest rates, credit squeezes, and other remedies which they found unsuitable to their situation.

Thirdly, poor countries were dependent on Western countries for the investment funds which they so badly lacked. Traditionally, most foreign investment in developing countries had been for the production of raw materials and other primary produce. But in the post-war world, an increasing proportion of food and raw materials was produced in the rich countries themselves. In any case, primary produce represented a declining element in economic exchanges and so in world trade. Most investment was now, therefore, for manufactures. Much of this was more profitably undertaken in rich countries, close to the main markets. An increasing proportion was in highly sophisticated products, where production was concentrated in the rich countries themselves. Even the small amount of investment in the so-called 'foot-loose' industries – mainly textiles, shoes, electrical goods and other simple manufactures – designed to secure the benefits of low labour costs in poor countries, became less profitable with the increasing protection placed against such goods in the rich states. Thus, by the 1970s, foreign investment in developing countries was only about a quarter of all overseas investment,[71] a proportion which declined (despite substantial investment in minerals) as the period continued. Even this amount was mainly invested in a relatively small number of newly industrialising countries of high income per head, especially in Latin America. And the majority of poor states attracted virtually no private foreign investment at all: they therefore suffered the still more humiliating dependence on government aid on concessional terms.

Finally, the dependence that was perhaps most profound in its effect was the dependence in the field of technology. More than in any earlier age, economic growth depended on securing technological development. But this was increasingly difficult and expensive to obtain. In Western countries, huge sums were spent on research and development. Since poor states could not hope to match this, the technological gap, already wide, tended to increase all the time. The gap condemned poor countries to rely on exports of relatively unsophisticated products which occupied a declining share of world trade. The fast-growing advanced sector – computers, aerospace, electronics, chemicals, scientific instruments and pharmaceuticals, for example – remained overwhelmingly based in rich countries. To a large extent, poor countries were dependent on the activities of transnational corporations for acquiring the new technology. They therefore had the unpleasant choice between welcoming the activities of such corporations, or condemning themselves to technical backwardness. Nor was the dependence confined to the industrial field. Poor countries were equally dependent on companies of Western states for essential economic services such as banking, insurance, and in many cases shipping. Since they usually possessed few major undertakings in these fields, they were obliged to rely on services provided at very high cost by foreign companies whose concern was primarily elsewhere.

Whether in services or in manufacturing, the foreign subsidiary was dependent ultimately on decisions reached within another state. In many cases, restrictions were placed on the subsidiary's use of local components and personnel, its pricing and production policies. The processing of raw materials was usually undertaken in the home country or in some other developed economy rather than where the materials were produced.[72] In many cases, the poor country concerned was seen mainly as a source of cheap labour for manufacturing products which would be mainly sold elsewhere. Even in so-called joint ventures, ultimate control was usually kept tightly in the home country.[73] And any threat to that control could provoke a total walkout, which would be even more damaging to the host country.

As a result of these various problems, the living standards in most poor countries, already far lower than those in rich states, also improved, for most of this period, more slowly. Only a few poor countries escaped this trend: six or eight 'newly industrialising' countries, a similar number of substantial oil-producers. But they were the exception. While the total growth rate and income a head in *all* developing countries (including the oil-producers) was faster than that in rich countries, in low-income countries, containing a large part of their population, they grew more slowly. The thirty or forty 'least developed' were worst off of all. Often small, landlocked, or afflicted by deserts or other unfavourable geographical circumstances, these in some cases suffered an absolute decline in living standards. They emerged as the new poor within an increasingly stratified international community: totally dependent on the rich for aid, technology, skilled manpower and training.

So new types of economic domination and dependence emerged in this age. The overall gap, whether measured in absolute national income or income a head, was far greater than in any earlier time. The richest states enjoyed a degree of economic independence that was denied to the poor. Their share in world production, trade and investment, already high when the period began, increased still further as time went on. While they suffered significant problems of their own – inflation, unemployment and declining resources – their economies continued to expand; and their companies acquired an increasingly dominant place within the economies of the poor states. There they obtained a growing share of production, domestic sales and exports. Above all, it was their decisions that determined the course of the world economy: whether it grew or stagnated. Against this, most of the poor states remained dependent on the rich for many of their most basic needs. They were dependent on them for capital funds for developing their own resources. They were dependent on them for many advanced products which they were unable to manufacture for themselves. They were dependent on sales in their markets to acquire the means of purchasing these. They were dependent on them for managerial and other skills. They were dependent on them for the technology which was essential if they were eventually to be able to secure anything like a comparable level of economic development or standard of living. They were dependent on them for balance of payments support. Above all, they depended on their decisions about the world economy as a whole: rates of interest, rescheduling, reflation.

As economic transactions increased, these various forms of dependence grew rather than declined. The recessions of the rich states affected poor countries still more. So did their inflation. Decisions made within a single state, the US – on interest rates and budget deficits – affected economic development throughout the world. Poor states grew richer, and relatively fast; but in absolute terms, poor countries became more indebted to the rich, more reliant on their markets, more affected by their prices, more damaged by their low demand for commodities. And the dependence of those with least advantage became more pronounced, more visible and, above all, more unacceptable.

6 Conclusions: Private Interests and Public Welfare in International Society

PRIVATE INTERESTS IN INTERNATIONAL SOCIETY

We have now surveyed five periods of international economic history over the last five centuries, and seen the variations over that time in the prevailing ideas concerning economic relationships between states; in the dominant interest-groups affecting those relations; in the motives inspiring these groups and the governments they influence; in the means used by governments to achieve their ends; and therefore, finally, in the type of economic domination and dependence that resulted.

The survey suggests that of those various factors, the decisive part is played by the nature of the dominant interest-groups. As we saw in Chapter 2, the character of the prevailing doctrines is usually closely related to the demands of these groups. While not necessarily produced with the aims of justifying their demands, the doctrines tend to reflect their attitudes and aspirations. When, in the later Middle Ages, the kings and their advisers had undisputed control of economic decisions, prevailing theories – the policy of provision and the policy of power – reflected the concern of the rulers with maintaining authority in their kingdoms. When, in the seventeenth and early eighteenth centuries, monarchs and ministers shared influence, dominant economic ideas and the practice of states reflected their concern to build up state power through state intervention. When, after the industrial revolution, the merchants and manufacturers became the dominant interest-groups, prevailing ideas, as exemplified in the writings of Adam Smith, reflected the interests of both classes in freer

254

trade, ideas which in time influenced the policies of governments. When, with the accumulation of wealth within industrial states, shareholders and financial interests became dominant towards the end of the nineteenth century, conceptions about international economic relationships came to reflect their interests, favouring a stable exchange rate maintained through the mechanism of the gold standard, conditions for safe investment in foreign lands and adequate assurance of a safe return on the investment. When, after the First World War, strong central governments became the most significant forces governing economic relations, the prevailing ideas, as seen for example in the writings of Keynes, advocated the use of the government machine to create an adequate level of demand at home to sustain full employment, while internationally governments attempted to manage their foreign trade, through strict controls on imports and other exchanges, for the same purpose. Finally, when the most important interest-group came to be the large international companies, now not only trading but producing in many nations simultaneously, the prevailing doctrine reflected their interests in calling for a liberalisation of exchanges between states, a multilateral non-discriminating system, and strict conditionality in return for credit. In each case, the system demanded by theory and established in practice conformed with the interest not only of the dominant interest-group in each age but of one or two major nations in which these interest-groups were powerful.

The *motives* of states even more obviously reflected the nature of the dominant interest-groups. Once the new ideas had become widespread, they came to be reflected in the thinking of those in power. Consciously or unconsciously, the motives of the interest-groups, reflected in the economic thinking of the day, were absorbed into the ideas of governments and so in their policy-making. Because of the power of dominant ideas, what benefited British manufacturers in the early nineteenth century was believed to benefit Britain as a whole, and even other countries too; just as, a century and a half later, in a different type of international economy, what was good for General Motors was seen (at least by some) as good for the US, and even the whole world economy. In consequence, the *means* adopted also reflected the interests of the dominant groups. Because the interests of a particular group had come to be seen as the interest of the state, states inevitably adopted means that promoted the interests of that group. Finally, the types of *domination and dependence* which resulted also derived from the character of the dominant groups: the type of economic domination acquired by particular states in each age depended on the type of economic domination acquired by the privileged group concerned, whether monopolistic traders in the sixteenth century, English manufacturers in the early nineteenth century, European investors in the late nineteenth century or US multinationals in the twentieth century.

What were the main differences between the dominant interest-groups in the various ages we have examined?

The first distinction to be made is between those ages in which the dominant groups were private economic forces and those in which they were official. Both official and private forces have existed in every age: in each, there have been some governmental agencies, though with varying objectives, and some private groups interested in the international economy, though equally differing in their character and aims. What is significant is the *balance* between them in different ages. In general, the governmental forces exercised the dominant control in the age of autocratic regulation in the late Middle Ages, in the age of state-building (though in one or two cases – in the Hanseatic League in the former period, and in the United Provinces in the latter – governments were themselves controlled or dominated by commercial groups), and again in the age of autarchy between the wars. On the other hand, during the age of free trade in the early nineteenth century and the imperialist age between 1870 and 1914, international exchanges were largely in the hands of private forces and were deliberately left so by governments (even the central banks, whose role was often so important, remained usually private institutions and the operation of the gold standard, for example, which was mainly automatic, was barely influenced by governments); in the post-1945 period likewise, though government regulation has continued in many forms, often more sophisticated than ever before, the prevailing liberal policy which determined government actions left a relatively free hand to private forces, especially the big banks and manufacturing companies, which have become the most dynamic force in the international economy. In general, where official forces play a major role, the direct interests of states will play the main part in influencing policy; where private interests do so, states' actions will reflect rather the interest of private forces (though, as we have seen, the two interests are always closely interlinked).

More important, perhaps, than this balance between private and public forces, has been the differing *character* of these forces, both public and private, at different periods. So far as governmental forces are concerned, their underlying purposes, and therefore their methods of intervening in the international economy, have varied widely in different ages. For example, in the later Middle Ages, the four most important single motives of governments were the desire for revenues, the desire to secure adequate supplies for the home population, the desire to conserve specie, and the desire to preserve the strategic interests of the nation (the policy of power): and it was these which determined international economic policy. None of these played such a large part in determining the international policy of governments in subsequent ages. In the next period, when the great ministers and other advisers came to play a dominant role, official motives were concerned with strengthening the economic power of the state, building up particular industries and securing a favourable balance of trade (rather than of bullion): accordingly altogether different methods were employed, involving now protection for industry on a major scale, various forms of subsidy and monopoly, but less direct control of the movement of specie. In the next age in which governments intervened on a major scale, after the First World War, motives were different again: the aim now was to protect or revive employment and the level of economic activity generally; and so once more a different set of strategies was brought into play, involving not only protection, but also intricate currency controls and other types of detailed intervention.

But the difference between the various private interests involved at different periods have perhaps been more significant. Though many of the same groups have existed in different ages – exporters, importers, manufacturers, bondholders, shareholders, bankers and international companies, for example – the character of each group, and above all the balance between them, has varied widely. In the first two or three periods, there was little international investment, and the significant private groups were all traders of different kinds, joined in the early nineteenth century by manufacturers. Among these groups, the main struggle therefore was between traders who benefited from foreign trade, whether importers (such as the Marseilles merchants denounced by Colbert) or exporters (such as the English Merchant Adventurers) and the merchants who had no interest in it, or who even suffered from it, who favoured protection. Especially where the imports were carried by foreign merchants, even though they might still be highly prized by consumers, and even by some merchants, they were resisted not only by domestic traders but also by colonial traders, who were often in direct competition, and by domestic producers, for example of linen, tobacco and other goods whose sales were threatened by cheap imports.

In later ages, this conflict of interests between traders and manufacturers became the most common situation. Each group was itself divided – between the traders interested in foreign and those interested in domestic trade, the manufacturers hoping to win sales abroad and those desiring to keep them at home. Which kind of policy was mainly advocated and mainly pursued by governments, depended often on which of each group was more powerful. In England until the industrial revolution, the manufacturers and the traders who feared foreign competition were more influential than those which sought new markets abroad – who anyway had ample protection in the colonial markets at their disposal. From the early nineteenth century, the traders who were concerned with winning *new* markets, and therefore with a general lowering of tariffs, became more numerous and more vocal, and they found eloquent spokesmen in parliament and elsewhere (see pp. 82–3): so it was their view which finally prevailed. In the age that followed, it was the investors, as well as the merchants, who sought opportunities abroad, and so urged their governments to pursue a forward policy – in the Near East, in south-east Asia, in China – allowing them more scope to seize those opportunities (see p. 88).

In each age, in other words, there have existed groups whose interests inclined them to demand an *expansionist* policy, which would maximise opportunities for profit; and others whose interest led them to demand a *defensive* position, enabling them to protect markets or other interests which were threatened. Those that were strong and efficient have usually been in the former category, those that were weak in the latter. The policy pursued by a particular nation will depend on the balance between the two types of force. Thus, in the early nineteenth century, when Prussia was still primarily an agricultural country and when Prussian wheat farmers were efficient producers, interested in selling their grain abroad, Prussia pursued a relatively liberal trading policy, in manufactures as well as in agriculture: this maximised the interests of the farmers, both by encouraging other countries to pursue liberal policies towards wheat imports and by allowing relatively cheap imports of agricultural equipment and consumer goods. Towards the end of the century, however, despite the fact that Prussian agriculture remained efficient (and that German policy was still largely Prussian policy), Germany adopted a defensive posture. By that time industry had become far more important in relation to agriculture, both economically and politically, and it was therefore more the interests of industry, demanding protection, which dictated policy. This alternation between expansive and defensive policies can be seen not only in the policies of particular states, but also in the trading practices of international society generally. While the age of state-building was essentially a defensive age, devoted to developing domestic trade and industry, that of the age of merchants and manufacturers was an expansive one, devoted to developing international trade. While the age of bureaucrats was once again a defensive age, concerned above all with maintaining domestic levels of employment, that which followed was again expansive (at least until the oil shocks), concerned with maximising exchanges between states. The change from one policy to another reflects partly the interests of the dominant interest–groups, but partly those of particular powerful nations.

The policy pursued by a nation may, however, depend not only on the importance of a particular interest within the economy but also on the special *influence* of particular groups. Though in most cases governments choose the policies which they believe maximise the interests of the country as a whole, they are susceptible to influence from particular quarters, and may therefore interpret national interests in particular ways as a result of that influence. This is seen, for example, in the last thirty years, in the degree of influence wielded by agricultural interests, despite rapidly declining numbers. Though far less numerous than consumers in every country, the interests of the latter have been consistently sacrificed for the advantage of the former. This is sometimes said to be undertaken for strategic reasons – to ensure adequate food supplies in time of conflict – or for social reasons – to avoid the depopulation of the countryside and the collapse of rural life. But these have every appearance of being rationalisations for policies pursued on simpler grounds: the desire of governments not to lose agricultural votes. And it seems more likely to be for that reason, therefore, that trade in agricultural products, almost alone in the commercial field, has not in recent years benefited from the trend towards liberalisation that has been otherwise pursued.

Other interest-groups have acquired influence over government policy not because they were numerous, but because they enjoyed privileged access to those in authority, or shared with them common interests or origins. We saw how parts of the ruling class in England in the late nineteenth century had close connections with the world of banking and finance (see p. 90); and how a relatively small group at that time, for example those connected with the Bank of England and the city of London generally, were able to exercise a powerful influence on the decisions of government (see p. 87). Similarly, in the recent period, governments have listened carefully to the representations made to them by major companies – for example the great steel corporations, motor manufacturers and oil companies. The influence of such groups is wielded either direct with those in authority or through intermediaries in congress and other parliaments. This influence is designed if not to acquire special favours for the groups concerned (and there are certainly cases where this is the aim), at least to make certain that government decisions concerning the international economy take careful account of their views and interests. The ideal is to ensure that the interest of the group concerned is seen as the interest of the nation as a whole, so that the government protects the interests of the group in question in the belief that it protects the national interest.

There is a final distinction between interest-groups that may be worth noting. In some cases, the object of such a group is to secure particular action by government to promote its interests – a new form of protection, the promotion of its exports, the negotiation of a contract. In other cases, however, the main object of the group may be, if it is powerful and successful, to secure the *absence* of any intervention, a freedom to pursue its own interests in its own way without interference from its own or other governments. So, for example, in the early nineteenth century, British traders generally were only too glad to be able to win trade or markets in their own way, with as little interference from government as possible (though even this sometimes required action by governments, for example negotiations with other states to remove barriers). In other periods, however, one of the main aims of the business interests involved has been to win the support of government in promoting their commercial or financial interests. So in the age of ministers merchants were highly dependent on the action of their own government in securing access to particular markets, through colonial conquest or the establishment and defence of trading posts, or in negotiating trade agreements with other states. So too at the end of the nineteenth century, financial interests in Britain and other countries were often highly dependent on government action in providing the political framework within which they could operate profitably, whether a sphere of interest arrangement in China, a protectorate in North Africa, or a new colony in Africa and the Pacific. In the inter-war period again, with high levels of protection almost everywhere, the opportunities available to businessmen abroad often depended crucially on the arrangements negotiated by governments – such as the US and German trade treaties with Latin American countries, for example, the Ottawa agreement, providing for preferences between countries of the British empire, or the foreign exhange arrangements of the gold and mark blocs.

The character and aims of interest-groups have therefore varied greatly from one age to another, as have the methods they have used to promote their interests. They have, in particular, enjoyed a wide range of different relationships with the governments of their own countries, and demanded different types of assistance from them. The willingness of governments to provide that assistance has varied from age to age and case to case. It is thus to the way governments have seen their own national interests in economic relations with other states that we should now turn.

GOVERNMENT INTERESTS IN INTERNATIONAL SOCIETY

In all ages, governments have had objectives of their own that were not identical with those of the leading private economic forces. These have included the need for revenues, the need for a balance in international payments, the need for exchange stability, the need for satisfying their own consumers, and the need to win the goodwill and respect of other states. Thus the need for revenues has caused governments to place on companies taxes and other burdens, abroad as well as at home. The need for satisfying consumers has caused governments to impose quality controls, to remove the protection of home manufacturers, or even to encourage imports at the expense of home producers. The need for balance of payments stability has caused governments to place restraints on overseas investment, even when this was financially advantageous to the individuals or companies involved, or to impede the import of particular goods. And the need for international goodwill has caused governments sometimes to avoid certain types of policy which could assist their own companies, and to grant special concessions to other countries (such as aid or the special preferences for developing countries granted in recent years), even though this caused net economic costs to some of their own manufacturers and workers.

For most governments, most of the time, nonetheless, the 'national interest' has seemed to require the support of powerful economic forces at home, whose success abroad was conceived to be a success for the nation as a whole. Governments have therefore protected trade routes for their merchants, acquired new colonies in which they could trade, negotiated new commercial agreements, helped exporters to win new markets, assisted companies to win contracts, or helped banks to expand their operations in other lands: on the grounds that this was in the interest not only of those individuals and enterprises, but also of the country as a whole. Governments have also consciously or unconsciously, sought the preservation or extension of the economic *system* which makes possible such gains, in the belief that this too serves the interests of the nation as a whole.

As this survey has shown, the methods used by governments to protect their economic interests have varied widely from one age to another. There have been variations, first, in the *degree* of intervention by governments in the relationships. At no time have governments been indifferent on such questions. But they have, at certain periods, concluded that the national interest was best served by leaving private forces to engage independently, and undisturbed by regulation from above, in trade, investment, banking, shipping and other activities, concluding that these were best able to promote their own interests if undisturbed, and that the profits thus secured were profits also, directly or indirectly, for the nation as a whole. We saw (see pp. 16–18) the arguments found by Adam Smith and Ricardo to show that a community of interests of this sort must exist: indeed, that allowing private profit-making would benefit not only the people of the country whose advantage was most obvious, but the people of all states, including deficit countries, equally. Not surprisingly, such arguments were not always accepted so readily by countries less economically powerful and so more likely to be in deficit, whether in that age (p. 81) or more recently (see p. 155).

The degree of intervention by governments in economic relationships has thus varied from age to age (being greatest in the first, second and fifth of our six periods, and least in the third and fourth). It has varied also according to the economic circumstances of each state in each period, with the weak states most concerned to permit intervention and the strong states most willing to leave things to be determined by the struggle of private economic forces. So it was that in the nineteenth century it was Britain, and to a lesser extent other industrialising countries, such as France and Germany, that were most willing to follow *laisser-faire* policies, abroad as much as at home. And thus it is that since 1945, developing countries mostly insist on the need for strong international institutions to regulate trade and investment between states, while most richer countries have upheld the merits of a 'liberal' system, with the least possible intervention, whether by international organisations or governments.

But apart from this difference in the *degree* of intervention, there have also been wide variations in the *type* of measure favoured by governments to promote their interests. These too have reflected the varying interests of governments in each age, as well as the prevailing doctrine (which, of course, itself usually reflects the interests of particular states or groups of states).

In all ages, the most widely adopted measures have been those designed to influence the direction of trade. Most commonly, these have been intended to influence imports rather than exports; and normally to restrain rather than to encourage them. Sometimes, they have taken the form of total prohibition (as at times in the Middle Ages for particular goods and in some countries in more recent times). Most often, in all periods, they have taken the form of taxes – that is tariffs – on imports, designed to increase their prices and so to reduce their volume. Sometimes, especially in the last two periods, they have been restrictions by quantity in the form of quotas. Recently, new devices have been used for the same purpose: non-tariffs, barriers, import surcharges, threshold prices, 'voluntary' restraints, and so on.

The purposes too, have varied. In the early days, the aim was mainly to raise revenues; later, to allow the development of infant industries; then to protect the balance of payments; more recently, to protect employment. What measures have, in fact, been adopted, has depended as much on the doctrine of the day, or even the fashion of the day, as on any clear assessment of economic rationality, or even economic interests. For example, for most of the aims just described, the subsidation of exports would have been an equally effective measure, and ultimately more rational (since it would have promoted the industries most likely to be competitive over the long term, rather than those least likely to be so). Yet, except in the age of state-building, that measure has been little used, and is now even prohibited as anti-social (though it is difficult to see why, provided it were internationally regulated, it should be thought more anti-social than import barriers which distort trade more crudely and directly).

The two converse policies – import promotion and export control – have been more rarely used, if only because concern for the balance of trade has usually been a major motive. Both, however, have been employed on occasion. Import promotion, as we saw (see p. 117), was widespread in the late Middle Ages, when a major motive of policy was the provision of adequate goods, especially food, to maintain the living standards of the population generally. Britain's cheap food policy from 1870 onwards – encouraging food imports at the expense of home production – was comparable in effect. In each case, these policies, apart from their advantage to local consumers, had the paradoxical long-term benefit of promoting efficient home industries to compete with the imports that were stimulated (while those industries which have had most protection, such as shipbuilding, steel, textiles and others, have usually become less rather than more competitive as a result). Export controls were also widely used in the Middle Ages, partly for strategic reasons, but also for reasons of provision – to preserve needed essentials for home consumption. The latter motive has occasionally promoted similar measures in recent times (for example the prohibition of soya bean exports by the US government in 1973). But in recent times, export controls have more often been instituted on political grounds; as in the case of the prohibition of exports to China and Cuba maintained by the US for many years, and its strict control of exports to the Soviet bloc as a whole, or the embargo placed by Arab producers on oil exports to the US and the Netherlands in 1973. Collective limitation of exports has also been undertaken to maintain prices, as under a number of commodity agreements.

Another common motive for government intervention has been the desire to promote self-sufficiency and reduce dependence on foreign sources of supply. This has often taken the form of deliberately subsidising or otherwise favouring particular types of domestic production, usually to promote exports or save imports. As we saw, this was a measure commonly adopted during the age of state-building, to promote self-sufficiency in particular fields; notably in the measures introduced by Colbert in France. It was used for strategic reasons in the Navigation Acts introduced in England and other countries from the fourteenth century onwards to stimulate domestic shipbuilding. And it has been used still more widely in the inter-war and post-war periods: for strategic reasons by Hitler in the development of synthetic products; for import-saving purposes by Britain in subsidising aluminium-smelting, the motor car, machine-tool, micro-processor and other industries; to protect employment (over the short term only) in measures to assist steel, shipbuilding and other activities in many Western states; and for most of these purposes by nearly all developing countries. Strictly speaking, these are domestic measures, but they have international consequences; and because they distort international trade (and are often specifically designed to do so), they are, in theory, disapproved of within the contemporary international economic system, so that measures have now been designed to restrict most of them.[1]

Another widespread motive for intervention by governments has been concern to preserve the balance of international payments. The simplest measures to that end were the bullionist edicts of the Middle

Ages, prohibiting the export of gold and silver, or demanding that they should be paid over to the authorities by all merchants returning to their home country. In more recent times, strict controls governing the use of foreign exchange have been almost as crude. It is, naturally, nations whose balance of payments is weak – most developed countries from 1945 to 1958 and at different periods since, and most developing countries today – that have been especially concerned to introduce measures of this kind. Over the past decade or so, marginally more sophisticated types of intervention have been used to that end: import-licensing and other restraints on imports, subsidies or preferences of various kinds for home producers and contractors, and many types of incentive to exporters.

Similar motives have lain behind government measures designed to ban or restrict investment abroad. In the late nineteenth century, as we saw, restrictions on foreign investment were designed largely for political purposes: access to the capital markets of Britain, France and other countries was controlled or strongly influenced by the government, to ensure it was reserved to approved governments and was denied to potential enemies. Political factors have still played a part in more recent times. Access to the London capital market was until recently guaranteed by Britain to all Commonwealth governments, but not to others; investment in communist countries is controlled by most western governments, especially if it involves transfer of technology. But the main reason why governments restrict or prevent foreign investment today is economic: usually balance of payments considerations. Thus the US, though it has remained the chief foreign investor of post-war years (indeed, because of this), has introduced progressive restraints on that investment: the 'equalisation tax' of 1963, voluntary restraints in 1965, mandatory controls in 1968, and other subsequent measures (though some relaxation took place in the 1970s). European governments likewise have fluctuated between strict control of foreign investment and freer capital movement over the last two decades. In some periods, governments have encouraged investment abroad, for either economic or political reasons. The British government was benevolent towards large British foreign investments at the end of the last century, restrained it after 1945 and now again welcomes it; the US government encouraged high foreign investment during the 1920s and 1950s, but later placed tight restraints on it. Today, so long as there are no immediate balance of payments considerations involved, many Western governments encourage the outflow of capital, considering the long-term benefits, to the balance of payments and the prosperity of the country, to outweigh the immediate foreign exchange costs; and have even sometimes thought such an outflow had immediate advantages, for example in lowering the exchange rate and reducing monetary pressures (this was one reason for the total freeing of foreign investment by the British government in 1979). This is a case where the interests of governments and private interests are quite different. While the latter will seek the investment opportunities that are most profitable, the former are concerned about the effects on the balance of payments and levels of investment at home.

Apart from strictly economic measures of this kind affecting trade or investment, governments undertake various types of *political* action to promote their economic interests. The most extreme type of measure has been the attempt to win political control or influence in foreign territories, as seen especially during the age of imperialism. Although economic ends were by no means the only motivation involved here, it usually played a significant part (see p. 31). Even if the desire was largely to pre-empt other Western powers, this itself was desired partly for economic reasons. Certainly, colonial conquest had economic *effects*: colonial powers often granted a monopoly of trade to their own nationals or at least substantial preferences (preserved until today in the special arrangements between the EEC and many former colonies, under the Lome Agreements). In other cases, dominant powers were able, during the nineteenth century and at the beginning of this one, to win 'spheres of influence' or other arrangements securing commercial pre-eminence: this was the case, for example, in the various areas of China and Persia in which explicit spheres were recognised, in the many 'protectorates' of the age (such as the French protectorates in North Africa, the German in Southern Africa, and the Pacific and the British all over the world), and in the US conquests in Cuba, Puerto Rico and the Philippines, which, though never designated as colonies, were treated as such for economic purposes. In recent times, economic domination has been enjoyed on a less explicit basis, as by the Soviet Union in eastern Europe, by the US in Latin America, or by Britain and France in their former colonial territories; here, there has been no outright exclusion of other powers, and little overt discrimination, but a type of political domination, or at least a tradition of doing business together, which preserves a dominant trading position. Political influence has also been used at various times to maintain monopolies for certain groups: as with the monopolies granted for particular types of import trade in the Middle Ages, those granted to the chartered trading companies in various parts of the world from the seventeenth to nineteenth centuries, or the monopolies created by commercial organisations, sometimes supported by their governments, in recent times – for example, in the shipping conferences, the rate-fixing agreements of the world's airlines, pricing and market-sharing agreements between oil companies and uranium producers, and the attempts at monopoly price-fixing by governmental associations such as OPEC.[2]

So governments have used a wide variety of measures over the years to promote the interests of their own nationals in relations with other states. The type of measure employed in each age will depend on a wide range of factors: the goals of governments, those of the main interest-groups, the degree of their influence over governments, as well as the conventions of the day.

The type of intervention that takes place in each period will depend partly on the economic doctrine of the day. Often, as we have seen in Chapter 2, the doctrine applied to the international economy reflects that which has been adopted for the domestic economy. So we saw that the system of autocratic regulation applied to international trade in the Middle Ages mirrored the ideas used at the same time in relation to domestic economic regulation; and many of the same motives – provision, power, bullionism and revenues – dictated the nature of each. Similarly, during the age of state-building, the interventionist principles applied to international exchanges – monopolies, bounties, high tariffs – were similar to those adopted by the same nations at home at that time. The principles of free competition and minimum government regulation in the following age were applied equally to economic relations at home and abroad. In the era that followed, the doctrine of marginal productivity which was said to determine rational investment decisions in domestic economies was applied equally to justify economic investment in other parts of the world. The principle of government intervention in the economy to match demand and supply at a level to create full employment, as propounded in the inter-war years, was used in the international field to justify managed international trade for the same purpose (as successfully achieved by Germany in the late 1930s, for example). Finally, the principles of the mixed economy, of a generally liberal trading system guided by discreet intervention to maintain stability, were applied in the post-war era, with more or less success for 30 years, to govern domestic and international economic systems alike.

Each of these doctrines were held at the time to be economically rational by those who propounded and those who practised them. But each, in practice, confirmed with the interests of particular groups within the domestic economy, and with particular nations in which those groups were especially powerful in the international economy. At neither the national nor the international level had an economic system been devised which was effectively operated and controlled in the interest of public welfare rather than private advantage.

CONFLICT OF INTERESTS IN THE CURRENT INTERNATIONAL SOCIETY

The interaction of pressures by private interests and by governments to create the type of system that favours them can be seen in the current international economic society. Here too, the basic ideas that have governed the system – liberalisation, non-discrimination, convertibility of currencies and free competition – reflected the ideology ruling within the domestic economic system: that of a 'liberal' private enterprise system with marginal regulation. Here too, their application to the wider system benefited particular states, mainly those already dominant, which were in a position to ensure that they were adopted by the world as a whole. And here too other states, possessing a different interest, have in time gradually sought to adjust the system and to transform it into one that was more consistent with their own differing interests (see pp. 158–9).

There are signs that the international economic system established in 1945 is now evolving into something different in kind. Though the basic features of that system have not yet been altogether destroyed there are increasing pressures working towards change.

The central feature of that system was the commitment to the liberalisation of exchanges between states: that is, the abandonment of the highly protective system of the inter-war years. In the field of trade, that commitment led to a progressive reduction of restrictions, especially between the industrialised states, and so to a rapid increase in the value of world trade. By the late 1970s there were strong pressures for opposite policies. The steep rise in the price of oil intensified balance of payments problems, for rich and poor countries alike. Many industrialised states, including the most powerful state of all (which had been responsible for the liberalisation programme), were suffering high unemployment and serious balance of payments problems. These were widely believed to result, at least in part, from the rapid increase in imports, often from countries with lower wage levels. A number of important traditional industries, such as textiles, footwear, consumer electronics, shipbuilding and others, were badly damaged by this competition; while others, such as steel and automobiles, were threatened. All this brought increasing pressures for protection everywhere. As we saw, new types of protective measures were widely adopted: 'voluntary restraints', threshold prices, in some cases new quotas, individual or collective. Though the momentum of liberalisation has not totally halted – the Tokyo codes of 1979 brought a further small step forward – the latest measures related almost exclusively to liberalisation of trade between the industrialised countries, while trade with developing countries has been further restrained. And even among the rich countries, there was increasing discussion of 'managed' trade: an organisation of trade to assure a wider distribution of employment opportunities than unrestricted free trade could provide.

A second feature of the post-war system was commitment to the principle of non-discrimination in trading relationships. But this was never achieved: earlier trading preferences, such as those existing within the British Commonwealth and former French empire, were never fully abandoned, though they became less significant within the world economy as a whole. They were later supplemented by other types which were ultimately more significant. There was discrimination on political grounds: as in the managed trade among the Comecon countries favouring other members of the bloc, in the embargoes placed on US trade with China and Cuba, and controls placed on trade with other communist countries, and in the periodic political embargoes imposed by Middle East and African countries for different reasons. There was a reincarnation of colonial preferences in the arrangements made between the EEC and the CAP countries under the Lome Convention and its predecessors. There was the deliberate and non-political discrimination in favour of poor countries made under the scheme for generalised special preferences. And at the end of the 1970s there were demands among the industrialised countries for the right to discriminate against exports from *particular* countries whose products were threatening to cause unacceptable damage to domestic industries. The general principle of total non-discrimination in trade proclaimed in 1945 was steadily eroded.

A third basic principle of the post-war economic system was the adoption of stable exchange rates to replace the rapidly changing parities of the pre-war era. In theory, these were to be 'fixed but adjustable': in other words, they could be changed in response to fundamental changes in price competitiveness – and even then international authority was required – but would otherwise remain constant. In practice, however, from the time convertibility was first established in 1958, this system lasted only a few years. The growing variations in rates of inflation brought increasing discrepancies between the parities that had been set. The huge and increasing volume of international mobile capital intensified instabilities, since all holders of such capital felt the need to switch currencies to guard against exchange losses. Successive devaluations therefore took place: of sterling in 1967, of the franc in 1969, and of the dollar in 1971 and 1973. This finally brought about the total abandonment of the fixed rate system in 1973, in favour of a system of floating rates which was expected to be more responsive to changes in competitive power. Since, however, governments continued to try to influence exchange rates, either upwards or downwards, by discreet interventions in the market, the new rates were not necessarily, any more than the old, 'market' rates, still less rates that would balance inward and outward payments (as was shown when the attempts by the British government to bid down the sterling rate in the early part of 1976 led to the virtual collapse of the currency and so to huge inflationary pressures; while in the following period of non-intervention the parity rose to a rate which, influenced by Britain's North Sea oil endowment, bore no relation to competitiveness and condemned her to prolonged deflation). Speculative pressure – for gold, or against the dollar – was higher than ever. So though the fixed rate Bretton Woods regime was finished, instabilities, caused by varying inflation and currency speculation, were no less severe under the floating regime which followed.

Another and related change to the system resulted from the increasingly powerful inflationary pressures at work all over the world. Quite apart from the strong inflationary pressures from domestic causes operating within most countries, resulting from the strong bargaining position of many unions and the reluctance of governments to risk unemployment through deflationary policies, there were a number of international factors increasing those pressures. The increasing scarcity of many important factors of production, including some vital raw materials such as oil, land and housing in industrialised countries, capital goods in developing countries, and particular types of technology and expertise, led to a rapid rise in the prices demanded and paid for them. These pressures led governments in turn to seek to counter them by placing a high price, in higher interest rates, on money itself (though this was a factor of production now rarely in short supply); but though this had only a slight effect on readiness to borrow (as the Radcliffe report 20 years earlier had forecast), it hugely raised the price of it – so adding to inflation at the same time as containing it. Meanwhile, the banks, national and international, the real centres of power within the new system (whose profits flourished with the high rates), multiplied their lending almost indefinitely, in both the industrial and non-industrial world. And since that banking system, above all the so-called Euro-market, was almost entirely free of controls, there was no mechanism for inhibiting this expansion of credit. International lending was now no longer mainly by governments, nor even by international organisations, as in the 1950s and 1960s, though these too expanded their operations, but by this flourishing private system, which multiplied credit many times, with huge loans to developing countries and to the Soviet bloc, over and above the inflated credit created within the rich countries themselves.

These various changes in the international economic system accompanied, and in part reflected, shifts in the power of individual nations and governments. There was a marked reduction in the capacity of the US, the main creator of the post-war system, to impose its will on the international economy. Though domestically her economy remained strong, despite a declining rate of productivity growth, her international influence was weakened by continuous balance of payments problems, by the consequent decline of the dollar, and by her dependence on the willingness of other states to continue to accept dollars of falling value as reserve assets. There was a corresponding rise in the influence of other states whose economic power had increased: West Germany, Japan and, for a time, Saudi Arabia. But there was also a change in the *interests* of the principal states involved. The US, for example, began to find its former commitment to liberalisation less attractive as its competitive power weakened. Conversely, she began to appreciate the value of sanctions against countries in persistent surplus and of some degree of liberalisation in agricultural products, both courses she had resisted strongly when her own economic situation had been different. Against this, countries such as Japan and South Korea, which had themselves been reluctant to accept significant liberalisation only a decade or two earlier, now became its most strident advocates as they began to be its principal beneficiaries.

There were also pressures for changes within the system from the poor countries, whose influence (though not their power) began to increase somewhat with growing numbers. Many features of the post-war economic system were unwelcome to these states. Given their unfavourable trading position, liberalisation was not necessarily favourable to them: especially when applied in the one-sided way favoured by the industrial countries. Attempts to apply the system led them often into severe balance of payments problems. This made them highly dependent on credit from elsewhere. One of their chief demands was therefore for greater availability of credit from the IMF; over longer periods; and on less rigorous terms. This would have been mutually beneficial, since it would not only relieve their own balance of payments problems and accelerate their development, but also help to ease world recession and stimulate employment in richer countries. Despite this, it was never conceded by the wealthier states, on the grounds that it could promote world-wide inflation. Similarly, poor states demanded price-support arrangements for commodities, similar to those maintained by rich countries for their own farmers, to be undertaken through commodity agreements. Though this could have benefited rich states, by increasing the capacity of producer countries to import their own goods, these demands too bore little fruit. Only three or four effective agreements came into operation (for tin, coffee, cocoa and rubber) and some of these ran into difficulties or had little effective influence on price; while the financing arrangements, even with the proposed common fund, were manifestly inadequate (even the tin scheme, widely regarded as the most effective, was unable to finance purchases to sustain prices). Likewise, the economically more rational schemes for compensating states which had suffered a loss of earnings from commodity sales (run by the IMF and the EEC) were on too small a scale to affect significantly the economic situation of countries which suffered from severe falls in export earnings. On debt problems, though the position of the poorest debtor states was marginally eased by the agreement for relief reached in 1978, less poor countries continued to bear a heavy burden of debt repayment, which in many cases exceeded all new finance being received, so that their ability to raise further loans from private sources would shortly be exhausted. The division of the world into creditors and debtors was one of the major features of the international class-system.

Another change in the international economy resulted from the growing role played by transnational corporations. While the economic power of the US as a country declined, that of its great companies increased. Of the ten largest transnational companies in the world in 1978, measured in terms of their total assets, eight were US companies. Of the five largest international banks, measured in terms of their total assets, three were US banks. As we have seen, these companies, both industrial and financial, were increasing their operations much faster than the rate of growth generally – perhaps twice as fast. The fear that most economic activities throughout the world would soon fall into the hands of a few companies was no doubt exaggerated; but it mirrored an emerging reality. Such firms disposed of huge power, both at home and abroad. At home, they were so important, in terms of foreign exchange earnings and employment, that their voice had to be listened to by their own governments with attention. Abroad, they could influence the industrial capacity, employment, exports, imports, technical level and other features of many poor states. They controlled technology and its availability through their patenting policies. The growing power of such companies, and their increasing independence of any government, represented a new feature which had transformed the economic system among states.

Each of these three major economic forces, therefore – rich states, poor states and transnational companies – would benefit from different types of change in the existing economic system. Rich states increasingly favoured some system of 'managed' international economy, in which trade flows were carefully controlled to insulate high-wage, high-unemployment economies from the effects of competition from elsewhere, access to raw materials was assured, and close co-operation was maintained among major states on import restraints, interest rates, money supply, and competition policy generally. Poor states demanded an irreversible shift in real resources and technology towards poorer countries, through increased aid flows, an opening of markets in favour of their exports, intervention to stabilise and sustain commodity prices, and better credit arrangements to assist countries in early stages of development, which had the greatest need of capital funds and the least attractions for them. Finally, the major transnational companies sought an economy that was, so far as possible, free from either type of control, where trade and investment could flow freely from one state to another, and where they were themselves, therefore, able to maximise the economic opportunities for profitable operations open to them throughout the world.

There are three major sets of possibilities resulting from these different sets of demands.

One possibility is that, as a result of the increasing pressures for protection, the world might increasingly break up into a set of regional economies, with considerable barriers, overt or concealed, between regions, but with each region containing both rich and poor areas. Thus western Europe and Africa might, for example, represent one regional block: already the greater part of African trade is with west Europe, and there exists discrimination in favour of this under the Lome Agreement. North and South America might represent another such grouping – and again much of the trade of Latin America already flows towards its wealthier neighbours to the north. A third block could include Japan, possibly China, and the countries of south-east Asia. A fourth block might be formed of the Middle East and southern Asia: already there is considerable complementarity between them, with large labour forces from southern Asia working in the former area, and advanced but under-financed industry requiring capital in the latter. The Soviet bloc, also linking a developed centre with less developed states, could represent a fifth economic region, though it might begin to gravitate towards the west European – African block. Each group, containing one advanced and one dependent area, might grow apart, becoming relatively autarchic economic entities.

A second possibility is of a different form of economic disintegration. The rich and poor sectors of the world economy could become increasingly detached from each other. As rich states place increasing barriers in the way of the exports of poor countries, the latter may increasingly look to trade with each other in compensation. Until recently, trade of this sort has been small, partly because the economies of such states were not complementary but similar – they are often both producing and exporting the same goods, and competing for similar imports from elsewhere. Today, with the 'newly industrialising countries' increasingly capable of producing more sophisticated goods, and a wider division of labour even among other types of product, developing countries are becoming more interested in trade with each other, and even in exchanges of technical co-operation.[3] Richer states, conversely, seem to show less interest in poor countries. Their trade with each other has already grown much faster than with poor states. They might now decide to concentrate on liberalising trade among each other even faster, while increasingly excluding over-competitive imports, especially those from the newly industrialising countries. Each group would then be forced into increasing internal interdependence, while economic contacts between them would be still further reduced.

The third possibility is that which would most accord with the aspirations of the increasingly dominant transnational companies. It would avoid both these types of disintegration: on the contrary, the world economy would become more than ever a single unified market. The momentum towards liberalisation would be maintained. Poor countries, perhaps convinced of their own overriding need for capital, technology and management skills, would be persuaded to lift, or at least not to intensify, their controls on inward investment. To enable them to finance repayments, rich countries would be persuaded to open up their own markets to imports from poor states in low technology goods (which are not mainly those in which the transnational corporations are interested). They themselves would concentrate on capital-intensive production of high technology goods in which they specialise (but which, requiring little labour, could leave much of the population in rich countries unemployed or semi-employed). Strict monetary policies would be used to contain inflation. The great international banks would remain the main source of finance for many poor and middle-income countries. Everywhere there would be greater tolerance for the large companies which were believed to have contributed to bringing about world growth (even if the growth was in production that left large parts of the population unemployed).

The third of these scenarios most closely corresponds with the interests of the most powerful economic forces in the world today. It also corresponds with prevailing doctrines which, as in earlier ages, reflect those interests. It is perhaps closest to the current reality. To see whether there is still another alternative development which may be possible, let us consider, finally, what arc the decisive factors determining fundamental changes in the structure of economic relations between states.

PUBLIC WELFARE AND PRIVATE INTEREST IN INTERNATIONAL SOCIETY

We have seen that at different periods, there have existed a variety of systems among states for conducting their economic relations with each other: economic international societies corresponding to the political societies existing at the same period we have examined elsewhere. Within each of these systems, certain rules and conventions have been established governing the conduct of economic relationships. Different types of interest-group, evolving with the changing character of productive forces, have sought to influence these rules and the character of the international economy as a whole. Governments, though they have usually had separate interests of their own, have reflected in their actions the aims and aspirations of these dominant interest-groups. A variety of means, that is of economic and political strategies, have been employed by both governments and interest-groups to promote their interests. The net outcome has been a variety of patterns of economic relationship among states, normally character-ised by some degree of domination by the economically more powerful states and some degree of dependence for those which were economi-cally weaker.

What has determined the characteristic structure of each of these societies? The structure has, of course, been partly determined by basic features of the economic and political environment, by the system of communications between states, by the level of technical development, by the volume and character of trade or investment, by the degree and type of government intervention, and by the level of international regulation or rule-making undertaken to influence inter-national economic relationships.

But the most fundamental factor seems to be the character of the leading economic groups *within* particular states. Even within the same state, the interests of these groups have never been homogene-ous. Some have benefited from imports, some have suffered; some have supported economic expansion abroad, some have resisted it. But usually there has existed one group which has been dominant, and has been able to impose its will on the nation as a whole. We saw how, for example, in Britain in the nineteenth century, the interest of a small group, the manufacturing classes, in increased exports abroad gradual-ly (and only after a considerable time lag) prevailed over the interests of the more numerous land-owners and workers on the land in continued protection; and how this led to the concept of 'free trade', not only as an instrumental good benefiting particular interests in particular nations, but as an absolute good benefiting mankind as a whole.

Interest-groups alone and unaided, however, are unable to establish a particular type of international economic system. The creation of such a system depends mainly on the action of governments. Only, therefore, when an interest-group has secured the support of its own government will it succeed in transforming one type of international economic structure into another. While, therefore, many English manufacturers had become supporters of free trade doctrine from the end of the eighteenth century, and while they had strong supporters in the British parliament, it was only when the British government adopted the principle – when first Huskisson in the 1820s and later Peel and Gladstone in the 1840s, were converted to the concept – that the ideas began being translated into reality. And even this was at first only a limited reality, confined to the actions of the British government alone. A further step was ultimately needed – action by the British government to bring about a change in the policy of other governments: as seen, for example, in the Cobden Treaty with France of 1860, and subsequent agreements among other European governments.

Three things are therefore needed for the creation of a new system: the establishment of a particular interest by a particular interest-group, the acknowledgement and support of that position by its government, and the success of the latter in bringing about the adoption of a new system internationally. Often, the process is more complicated. Frequently, there are similar interests in a number of different states, each of which comes gradually to adopt a new position – like the many groups which demanded, for example, higher levels of employment and lower levels of imports in the inter-war period – leading to governments collectively adopting a new policy. Sometimes there is no formal agreement between states about the adoption of a new system: one or a few states adopt new policies, leading to their gradual adoption by most or all other states (as in that same period). In other cases, the new system is formally adopted by inter-governmental agreement: as occurred when the system of regulated liberalism was adopted after 1945.

Whether or not a new system is adopted, however, will depend crucially on the relative power of the states concerned. Small and weak states seeking a different type of economic relationship will usually not succeed in this, at least if they are opposed by more powerful states seeking the maintenance of the *status quo*. This can be seen in comparing the effect of United Provinces in the late seventeenth century and of England in the nineteenth century in bringing about the adoption of a more liberal trading system. In the seventeenth century, the United Provinces was, just as much as England was to be a century and a half later, the dominant trading nation. There, equally, leading thinkers and statesmen proclaimed an economic doctrine for freer trade, one which in many ways foreshadowed that put forward by Adam Smith a century or so later (see p. 15). United Provinces accordingly, like England in the mid-nineteenth century, favoured a significant liberalisation of trading arrangements between states. This advocacy, however, had absolutely no effect on the policies of other states: on the contrary, the stronger states, France, England, Prussia and the rest, were all the *more* concerned, because of Dutch trading strength, to maintain the protectionist policies of that age. It was partly because Britain, when she proposed a similar transformation in the subsequent period, was the most powerful state of the European system that she was able to bring about the alteration in the prevailing pattern which United Provinces had failed to achieve. But it was perhaps even more because her thinkers, led by Adam Smith, were able to transform the *thinking* about such matters which prevailed in other countries that she succeeded where the Dutch failed. Similarly, it was partly because the US in 1945 was so powerful and influential that she could, almost alone, establish the new international economic system created at the time. But it was much more because the liberal thinking, the condemnation of pre-war protectionism, which she uttered was widely endorsed by economists and statesmen everywhere at that time, that she was able to succeed. For those reasons, Britain, the only other state which played any significant role, was willing to accept, at Bretton Woods, a system that was far closer to American concepts and American interests than those of herself and other European states. Today, a majority of the states of the world seek the establishment of an entirely new system, a 'new international economic order'. But because those states are mainly weak and poor, above all because they have so far failed to transform economic thinking in the Western world, they have been unable to bring that new order into being. On the contrary, because of the dominance of governments committed to monetarist, free market philosophies and distrustful of international regulation, the system – as applied by the IMF and similar institutions – has moved further from the goals the new order proclaimed.

Particular interests and particular governments favour different types of economic system because they can assist them in achieving particular goals. Each international society we have examined, and its underlying doctrine, has been based on certain presuppositions concerning the underlying purpose. In the later Middle Ages the main objective of the dominant elites was to safeguard supplies of food and other necessities for the population; and economic policy was dominated by that aim. In the age that followed – from the mid-seventeenth to late eighteenth centuries – the most important aim of the rulers of the dominant states was to maintain a trade balance and to build local industry; and policy was drastically modified to secure that end. In the early nineteenth century, as commercial classes became more dominant, the primary aim was trade expansion, first in Britain and later elsewhere. Later, with the increasing influence of financial interests the aim was to expand trade and investment further afield, in the areas outside Europe; and this too affected economic policy. During the inter-war period, the dominant domestic objective was to safeguard employment and national self-sufficiency, and the international system was once more transformed in ways that would assist, it was believed, in achieving those aims. After 1945, the primary goal was stable economic growth which, for developed countries at least, was held to demand the liberalisation of trade and investment under multilateral rules.

The character of each system is determined by the presuppositions that underlie it. Liberal economic systems, such as those that prevailed during the early nineteenth century and in recent times, are normally supported by economic writers as being economically 'rational'. They are held to be so, however, on the basis of the premise that the objective of economic arrangements must be the maximisation of wealth. If governments had other aims, they might find it equally rational to support a quite different type of economic system among states. If, for example, governments placed a higher value on creating employment than on creating growth, they would favour quite different arrangements. If they placed (as they sometimes do in relation to their domestic economies) a high value on a just income distribution, between states as well as within them, they would support an international system different from any which has existed so far. If they favoured a wider distribution of economic *power*, they would demand an international system which precluded the domination of the system by particular nations, or particular private corporations, even if the latter system could be shown to promote faster economic growth (in the same way that they might not necessarily wish to maximise their security by according unlimited power to a single super-power or super-state). In all cases, governments would subordinate the desire for higher national incomes to other ends: the desire for less workless-ness in the first case, for greater equality between states in the second, or greater autonomy for each state in the last.

In so far as nations cherish different goals, therefore, they will favour different types of international system. If the main aim is a balanced development between states and regions, a different set of principles would be required from that needed if the main aim is the efficient allocation of resources or growth at any price (and even the concept of 'growth' may be conceived in different ways – growth that is widely distributed or growth that is fast but uneven). Similarly, one system may maximise stability within the international economy, while another may favour innovation or change including, for example, the displacement of traditional industries. One may favour the reduction of inflation (for example, by reducing the volume of international credit, controlling raw material prices or stimulating imports); while another may be designed to sustain world growth (for example, by maximum trade liberalisation and the generous allocation of credit, even at the cost of high inflation rates). one may favour high employment, by promoting agriculture, rural development and labour-intensive industries behind protective barriers; while another may favour high investment, rapid technological advance and capital-intensive development at the expense of employment levels. One may favour strict conservation of the world's rapidly declining resources, even if it means slow or nil industrialisation; while another allows them to be rapidly depleted in the interests of the fastest possible rate of economic growth. Finally, one may promote a continual widening of the gap between rich states and poor, through the concentration of investment resources where skills are highest and markets largest; while another may favour justice between states, by stimulating the development of the poorest regions and countries even at the cost of slower absolute rates of growth.

Thus the essential problem is not simply whether there should be better 'management' of the international economy; but what kind of management there should be to achieve what purposes. There is one major change in the international economic system today from all earlier ages. This is that there exists today a far greater degree of international discussion and negotiation concerning the world economy, and a greater capacity to introduce radical changes through conscious choice. There is now the possibility of international as well as national policies. For the first time, an international economic system could be deliberately adopted in order to correspond to the needs and aspirations of mankind as a whole. International organisations have now been established which can undertake some regulation of economic exchanges. Large numbers of states participate in decisions made by those organisations. More than in any earlier time governments have the opportunity to make a conscious decision in favour of the type of system which best maximises their goals. For the first time, therefore, a different balance between the demands of private interests and those of public welfare could be struck, if so desired, in establishing such a system.

It would, for example, be possible, if this challenge were taken up, to conceive of a scenario for the future quite different from those sketched earlier – and one more welcome, probably, to many governments of the world today. An international economic system could be established which was subject to a far higher degree of regulation by international bodies that at present, bodies which would themselves be responsive to the wishes of a wider majority of governments and peoples represented in them. In the monetary field, for example, the IMF might be built up gradually into an effective world authority governing the international payments system, including the private international banking system where necessary. It could introduce arrangements under which SDRs would gradually be substituted for dollars in world reserves, and all such reserves held by governments within the IMF. The allocation of SDRs, and therefore of reserves, would then be undertaken as a result of joint decisions within the Fund, based on the world's credit needs, as well as the payment needs of each state; and the allocation to each state would be made individually, in accordance with its situation and the policies it pursues, rather than related automatically to the size of existing quotas, as today. The World Bank, with a larger capital base, could become the agent through which all development funds were distributed to developing countries. It would so be enabled to raise a far greater volume of funds than are available today, and would decide the needs of each receiving country on national economic criteria alone, rather than on partly political considerations. A more effective body to oversee trade matters might promote progressive liberalisation of these types of trade of special concern to developing countries, especially simple manufactures and agriculture, in return for a system of graduation, under which the protection imposed by developing countries would be progressiviely reduced as their economies developed. New international guidelines governing the conduct of transantional corporations could be framed to ensure that their operations accorded with the interests of all those countries within which they operate and were subject to adequate international supervision; and some body established to ensure compliance. An effective international resources commission could be set up, to keep under review the availablility of the world's natural resources and their rate of depletion, and to define the conservation measures among states, as found to be necessary. Particular resources – such as those beneath the seas, for example – might for the first time begin to be placed under international ownership, and to be managed and exploited under international regulation for the benefit of all mankind. And there could even be (as the Brandt Commission has recently recommended) a system of international taxation, whose proceeds could be used to bring about more even development among states.[4]

Unfortunately, such a scenario, though it would be welcome to many, cannot be regarded as more probable than those we sketched earlier. As we have seen throughout this study, the capacity of states to influence the international economic system varies widely. Poor and weak states, however numerous, have few effective means for securing acceptance of their views by those nations which are richer and more powerful. Powerful interest-groups in the richer states would undoubtedly seek to prevent such a radical change in the existing system. There is no means of revolution available within the world's economic system. States that rebel from the existing system may only be weakened still further by total exclusion from it; and a radical division of the world economy between rich and poor would only leave the latter worse off than ever. Only if *thinking* about the kind of world economy that is desirable – the underlying doctrine – is transformed, is any substantial change in the existing system likely to come about.

As we have seen many times in this volume, the type of international economy established depends not only on what states are dominant but on what elites within them exercise power (and on what kind of economic doctrine they therefore cause to prevail). The type of world economic system that prevails today conforms, like those of earlier ages, to the interests not only of a few dominant states but of particular interest-groups and economic organisations within them. It may even benefit particular interest-groups within disadvantaged states. A fundamental change in the character of international economic relations today may therefore depend, as in earlier ages, on a change in the economic, social and political relationships that exist *within* states.

If the economic systems that prevailed within states were less preoccupied with maximising growth even at the expense of serious inequalities, less concerned with liberalisation, deregulation and the magic of the market-place, so too – if the record of the past is a guide – might the international economy. If domestic economic management were more concerned with the equitable distribution of wealth and welfare, with a wider dispersal of ownership and economic power, so too might international economic management. Under such circumstances it might begin to be accepted that most people in most states shared an interest in the more effective international regulation of a world economy which is increasingly turbulent, unstable and unpredictable.

At the moment there is little evidence that the rich countries of the world, which extract most benefit from the existing economic structure, are willing to endanger that position by according an effective share in its management to the majority of states having totally different interests. Such a transformation is likely to be effected only in so far as the underlying doctrine determining people's vision of the international economy is adjusted, and a new image established. The new image would be that of a world whose economy was regulated by common action for the benefit of all, rather than ransacked by private interests, concentrated in a small number of richer countries, for the benefit of the few; of a world economy rationally ordered and controlled, like that of the individual states within it, in the interests of public welfare rather than private interests; to secure the greatest benefit for the greatest number, rather than to allow the continued concentration of wealth where wealth is already highest, and the increasing impoverishment of those states and individuals that are already poorest.

Notes

NOTES TO THE INTRODUCTION

1. For an analysis of the causes of war in recent times, see E. Luard, *Conflict and Peace in the Modern International System* (Boston, Mass., 1968).

NOTES TO CHAPTER 1: DOCTRINE

1. All this applied equally within self-governing cities. 'The evidence of the fourteenth and fifteenth centuries makes it quite clear that most town economies of that period were highly regulated economies and that this intense regulation normally issued from certain common features of late medieval policy. The external policy of most towns was the reflection of a struggle for prosperity, even for survival, in a competitive world ... The internal policy of towns also led to a high degree of regulation which secured the control of the majority by an oligarchical minority or maintained a nice and precarious balance between a variety of craft gilds' (A. B. Hibbert, 'The economic policies of towns', in *The Cambridge Economic History of Europe*, vol. III (Cambridge, 1963) p. 188).
2. C. M. Cipolla, 'The Italian and Iberian peninsulas', in *The Cambridge Economic History of Europe*, vol. III (Cambridge, 1963) p. 420.
3. E. Miller, 'The economic policies of governments', in *The Cambridge Economic History of Europe*, vol. III (Cambridge, 1963) p. 285.
4. 'Vital goods had not only to be brought into a town but had to be kept there. The most obvious way of doing this was to prohibit export. Permanent and complete restrictions of certain exports did occur in the staple towns of Germany and at Florence, for example, but partial or temporary prohibition was more common' (A. B. Hibbert, op. cit. p. 175). Sometimes treaties between two towns were undertaken to allow duty-free or tax-free trade between their territories on grounds of provision.
5. F. Heckscher, *Mercantilism*, vol. II (London, 1935) pp. 62–73. See also A. B. Hibbert, op. cit., p. 162: 'The staple system involved the power to make merchants pass through a given town where they could be taxed,

where their goods could be forced to sale on the local market, and where their further progress could be stopped or made conditional on terms imposed by local traders.'

6. The essential difference between the 'bullionism' of this age and the attitude to gold in the age that followed was that in the earlier age the stock of bullion was safeguarded by non-commercial means, rather than by securing a favourable balance of trade.

7. 'The direct use made of the policy of power was deliberately to influence the supply and accumulation of stores of goods in the desired direction and to cause corresponding changes in prices. The import of goods necessary for war was directly ordered or encouraged by premiums, while their export was forbidden or burdened with dues' (E. F. Heckscher, op. cit., vol. II, p. 31).

8. This period corresponds roughly with the period we have elsewhere named the 'age of sovereignty' (E. Luard, *Types of International Society*, New York, 1976). The periods do not exactly coincide. The 'age of religions' described there (1550–1648) is here divided between the 'age of autocratic regulation' and the 'age of state-building'.

9. C. W. Cole, *Colbert and a Century of French Mercantilism*, vol. I (New York, 1939) p. 343.

10. Colbert, Memorandum to Louis XIV, 1664.

11. *Letters de Colbert*, VI, 265.

12. Cf. D. C. Coleman in Coleman (ed.), *Revisions in Mercantilism* (London, 1969) p. 110.

13. Colbert, *Lettres*, VI, 264ff.

14. Ibid., VII, 230.

15. Colbert, *Lettres*, II, 660, quoted in C. W. Cole, op. cit., vol. I, p. 337. On another occasion he declared that to add to the stock of money in the country was to 'increase the power, the greatness and the plenty of the state' (ibid.).

16. Colbert, *Lettres*, II, 337.

17. J. Locke, *Some Considerations of the Consequences of the Lowering of Interests and Raising the Value of Money* (London, 1691).

18. P. W. von Hörnigk, *Oesterreich uber alles wann es nur will* (1684), quoted in E. F. Heckscher, op. cit., vol. II, p. 22.

19. Colbert, *Lettres*, VI, 260–70, quoted in C. W. Cole, op. cit., vol. I, p. 343.

20. Most modern writers doubt whether there ever existed any consistent doctrine that can be described as 'mercantilism'. There existed, on the one hand, a series of policies of different kinds adopted by governments to strengthen the economic and military power of the states; and on the other there existed a series of writings, equally incoherent and unrelated, setting out a theoretical justification for some of these policies. Both policies and theories tended to be lumped together by Adam Smith and his successors, largely for the purpose of attacking them. It is not necessary to embark on this heavily discussed topic here: for our purposes, we can, so far as is possible, avoid the term 'mercantilism', and be content with describing the policies themselves.

21. It is sometimes said that Colbert too reflected merchant interests because he was the son of a cloth merchant. But it is doubtful whether this

was a significant influence. Colbert fully identified himself with the interests and purposes of his royal master: thus he wished to expand French trade for the sake of France, not the merchants, and was frequently impatient with the representations of the merchant class (see C. W. Cole, op. cit., vol. I, p. 332).

22. T. Mun, *England's Treasure Through Forreign Trade* (London, 1664) p. 23.

23. Though in France the prohibition was reimposed from time to time (for example in 1662 and 1670), French ministers also recognised that the main way to maintain a favourable balance was through the balance of foreign trade. 'Though Colbert went through the motions – and sometimes they were vigorous ones – of attempting to stop the export of coin and bullion, he placed his reliance on the indirect method connected with the fostering of industry, agriculture, colonies, shipping and so forth' (C. W., Cole, op. cit., vol. II, p. 545).

24. C. Davenant, *An Essay on the East India Trade* (London, 1697).

25. Quoted in E. F. Heckscher, op. cit., vol. II, p. 116.

26. C. W. Cole, op. cit., vol. II, p. 475.

27. C. W. Cole, op. cit., p. 338.

28. Colbert, *Lettres*, VII, 230.

29. Colbert, *Lettres*, VII, 250.

30. E. Luard, op. cit., pp. 90–5.

31. C. H. Wilson, *Profit and Power* (London, 1957) pp. 16–17.

32. Eric Roll, *A History of Economic Thought* (London, 1938) pp. 149–50.

33. Adam Smith, *The Wealth of Nations*, book 4, vol. II.

34. D. Ricardo, address of 1822, quoted in B. Semmel, *The Rise of Free Trade Imperialism* (Cambridge, 1979) p. 71.

35. Even before Ricardo, the English writer Robert Torrens, in his *Essay upon the External Corn Trade*, held that England should import corn freely from those countries best equipped to grow it and to exchange for this manufactures, where England's main advantage lay. This would reduce the price of labour, and so the cost of English manufactures, and eventually even the cost of imports: if British capital, labour and skill could 'by working up cloth, obtain from Poland a thousand quarters of wheat, while it could raise, from our own soil, only nine hundred, then, even on the agricultural theory, we must increase our wealth by being, to this extent, a manufacturing, rather than an agricultural people' (R. Torrens, *Essay upon the External Corn Trade* (London, 1815) pp. 221–2).

36. This was based on the assumption that there could be no movement of labour or capital from one country to another which would cause production to be moved elsewhere.

37. It would, of course, be a gross over-simplification to suggest the new theories were simply put forward as a rationalisation of policies that would promote Britain's national interests. In so far as the new doctrines favoured the dismantling of a complex and irrational array of restrictions and distortions (the origins of which had often been forgotten and overtaken by events), they implied a rationalisation of policy equally in the interests of all states. In so far as they suggested that taxes on trade for revenue purposes might be self-defeating or illogical, they revealed a

truth which was equally relevant elsewhere. But in so far as they implied that the freeing of trade was *always* beneficial, they ignored differences in the circumstances of states which could crucially affect the benefits this could have for each.

38. Though Britain normally had a deficit in her overall visible trade, this was more than covered by invisible earnings from shipping, brokerage, insurance and investments.

39. Parliamentary Debates, 8 February 1810.

40. B. Semmel, op. cit., p. 134.

41. Cf. J. Ehrman, *The British Government and Commercial Negotiations with Europe, 1783–1793* (Cambridge, 1962) pp. 177, 178: 'The connexions between theory and practice are never easy to assess . . . [But] there can be little doubt that a changing intellectual climate had its effects on Government's attitudes to changing conditions . . . There was a greater disposition to acknowledge that commercial advantage need not be measured in bullionist terms, that trade could be more complex, its benefits more indirect, and its measurement more difficult, than official opinion had been used to admit, and that there were occasions when Government might appropriately enable exports to find their natural outlets rather than impose a pattern directly by legislation and decree.'

42. B. Semmel, op. cit., p. 164.

43. Adam Smith, op. cit., book 4, vol. III.

44. J. Ehrman, op. cit., p. 29.

45. Cobden, Letter of 26 December 1859, quoted in J. A. Hobson, *Richard Cobden: The International Man* (London, 1918) pp. 246–7.

46. Quoted in John Morley, *The Life of Richard Cobden* (London, 1910) pp. 23–4.

47. J. S. Mill, *Principles of Political Economy* (London, 1848).

48. H. S. Jevons, *Essays on Economics* (London, 1905) p. 211.

49. P. Leroy-Beaulieu, *De la Colonisation chez les Peuples Modernes* (Paris, 1874).

50. Quoted in D. K. Fieldhouse, *Economics and Empire, 1830–1914* (London, 1973) p. 23.

51. J. Ferry, *Le Tonkin à la Mere-Patrie* (Paris, 1890).

52. C. A. Conant, 'The economic basis of imperialism', in *North American Review* (September 1898) pp. 337–9.

53. P. Leroy-Beaulieu, op. cit., pp. 628ff.

54. J. Ferry, op. cit.

55. C. A. Conant, op. cit., pp. 339–40.

56. H. Feis, *Europe the World's Banker, 1870–1914* (New Haven, 1930) p. 14. Some estimates place the total as rather less: see A. K. Carincross, *Home and Foreign Investment 1870–1913* (Cambridge, 1953) p. 186.

57. Feis, op. cit., pp. 47–8.

58. Cf. ibid., pp. 13–14: 'The total of British foreign ownership and the income therefrom steadily augmented, and its place in the economic system in which the British people lived became ever more important. The satisfactory operation of the British economic system became more and more fully linked with the satisfactory development of the rest of the world.'

59. For example, Phillimore's *International Law*, published in 1885, de-

clared that 'reprisals', which could include the use of force, were justifiable when a state 'refuses to fulfil some obligation . . . like the payment of a debt' (vol. III, p. 22). Oppenheim's *International Law*, first published in 1905–6, quoting a number of cases when Western governments took military action to enforce debts as examples of the right of 'reprisal', declared that 'an act of reprisal may be preferred against everything that belongs to, or is due to, the delinquent state or its citizens' (vol. II, p. 159).

60. Quoted in P. T. Moon, *Imperialism and World Politics* (New York, 1927) p. 105.
61. Chambre des Députés, 31 October 1883.
62. P. T. Moon, op. cit., p. 80.
63. D. K. Fieldhouse, op. cit., p. 3.
64. J. A. Hobson, *Imperialism* (London, 1902) p. 18.
65. As one well-balanced judge has put it: 'It seems undeniable that growing competition for established markets in Europe and America, coupled with the cyclical but extended and recurrent downturn in the value of exports during the last thirty years of the century, stimulated most industrialised countries to look for new markets elsewhere. This search for markets generated greater interest than ever before in the commercial opportunities of little known regions of Africa and Asia, which had not hitherto been brought fully within the orbit of international trade and whose economic possibilities were commonly overestimated precisely because they were impossible to calculate. At the same time the growing demand for industrial raw materials and foodstuffs which could not be obtained within Europe or North America stimulated the search for new sources of supply. Together these factors ensured that Europeans would rapidly penetrate most parts of the less developed world and that these would quickly be absorbed into the capitalist economy of the West' (D. K. Fieldhouse, op. cit., p. 35).
66. 'By the end of the 1880s metropolitan opinion generally was coming to the view that existing colonies were economically useful only if their markets were reserved for French exports and consequently that new dependences might be desirable if they provided monopolistic outlets for French produce, (D. K. Fieldhouse, op. cit., p. 23).
67. By 1920, only 9 years after the protectorate was established, almost two-thirds of Morocco's trade was with France.
68. That belief was challenged by some: notably by J. A. Hobson in Britain.
69. Pamphlet issued by the Manchester Chamber of Commerce, 1884.
70. F. Lugard, *The Rise of Our East African Empire.*
71. Sir H. H. Johnston, *The Colonisation of Africa.* (Cambridge, 1899) p. 446.
72. For a description of the various measures adopted, see W. Ashworth, *A Short History of the International Economy since 1850*, 3rd edn (London, 1975) pp. 228–9.
73. cf. R. Skidelsky, *The End of the Keynesian Era* (London, 1977) p. 37: 'The Second World War . . . provided the laboratory for testing out the new theories of economic management [Keynesianism]' and 'created the social consensus for which Keynesianism proved the ideal ideology,

promising benefits to all groups, including government and bureaucracy.'

74. M. Keynes, *'The end of laisser-faire'*, in *The Collected Writings of John Maynard Keynes*, vol. IX (London, 1972) pp. 292–3.

75. For example, the US economist, W. T. Foster.

76. M. Keynes, op. cit., vol. IX, pp. 287–8.

77. 7 May 1933.

78. Quoted in A. M. Schlesinger, Jr, *The Coming of the New Deal* (London, 1960) p. 175. Schlesinger points out that 'the planning philosophy' had begun to take over the regulation of agriculture in March 1933, and two months later when 'Roosevelt called for the organisation of industry and commerce under Federal authority, the planners occupied the other vital sector. These decisions to seek central management of agriculture and industry, determined the shape of what came to be known as the first New Deal' (ibid., p. 173).

79. A return to the gold standard was recommended after the end of the First World War by a series of international conferences (as well as by the influential Cunliffe Committee in Britain in 1919).

80. Cf. J. B. Condliffe, *The Commerce of Nations* (London, 1951) p. 511: 'Keynes's suggestions were that monetary policy should be based on the necessity for sustaining the domestic price level and that pressures on the external balance of payments should not be allowed to interfere with that purpose.'

81. A. M. Schlesinger, op. cit., p. 211.

82. That agreement, involving the depreciation of the dollar by deliberate policy action, together with undertakings concerning how the monetary authorities of the three countries would operate in the future, has been said 'to mark the true beginnings of managed exchange rates' (F. Hirsch and P. Oppenheimer, *'The trial of managed money: currency, credit and prices, 1920–1970'*, in *The Fontana Economic History of Europe, The Twentieth Century*, vol. II (London, 1976) p. 621).

83. Cf. J. B. Condliffe, op. cit., pp. 433–4: 'The simple fact is that the dream of a worldwide trading and financial system in which national boundaries would have little economic significance came close to realization between 1870 and 1914 ... The nineteenth century trading system came to an end by reason of the resurgence of nationalism, just as the medieval trading system had ended with conflict between the city states.'

84. Again, some of the most extreme expressions of this idea were made by American New Dealers. Roosevelt's Foreign Trade Adviser, George Peek, did not believe that there would ever be a return to a free trading system, and felt that strict government controls over trade were here to stay: 'I believe.' he wrote, 'that this situation represents a permanent change in the character of international trade.... The whole problem is one of finding methods whereby mutually advantageous exchanges of goods may take place.' He believed the answer lay in a 'system of government-managed trading' in which reciprocal trade agreements could serve as the mechanism for bilateral balancing of accounts (in A. M. Schlesinger, op. cit., p. 246).

85. W. A. Lewis, *Economic Survey, 1919–1939* (London, 1949) p. 83.

86. W. A. Lewis, ibid., p. 48.
87. For descriptions of these controls, see C. Zacchia, *'International trade and capital movements, 1920–1970'* in *The Fontana Economic History of Europe, The Twentieth Century*, vol. II, p. 520.
88. W. A. Lewis, op. cit., pp. 70, 139–40.
89. As Cordell Hull reported to President Roosevelt at the time of the International Economic Conference of 1933, 'each country advocated the abolition or reduction of all barriers to its commerce ... except of kinds which it is itself practising to such a degree that it is stopped from urging the case, and each country defended its own practices as just or as necessary, or indicated its willingness to abandon such practices provided other countries did this, that or the other ... before or simultaneously'.
90. Since governments did not usually have overriding legal power, banks could sometimes defy their wishes: British banks defied the British government of the day in lending to China in rivalry to the four-power consortium which the government favoured in 1912.
91. Cf. W. A. Lewis, op. cit., p. 12: 'No period is so rich in plans for prosperity. Democracies and dictatorships alike resolved that society should no longer be at the mercy of economic events, and sought gropingly and in conflicting and contradictory ways to control events by government agency.'
92. One reason for the failure of these efforts between the wars was the incompleteness of the participation. Between the wars, the US was never a member of the League or its economic bodies, and played little part in the international conferences of the time. (She attended the World Economic Conference of 1933, but by abruptly devaluing the dollar at a depreciated rate at the outset of the Conference, she effectively destroyed the value of her participation.) Both between and after the wars, the Soviet Union and her associates were also outsiders, who, played little part in the deliberations of other governments. And the governments of the greater part of the developing world, including such huge entities as China, India and Latin America, likewise played little part in international economic discussion. So it was mainly the governments of the major European countries alone which came together from time to time to discuss the economic problems of this age.
93. Even Keynes felt that fiscal and monetary policy should now be undertaken on a national basis: 'Above all' he said, 'let finance be primarily national' (see A. M. Schlesinger, op. cit., p. 180).
94. G. Myrdal, *An International Economy* (London, 1956) p. 5.
95. R. N. Gardner, *Sterling–Dollar Diplomacy* (Oxford, 1956) pp. 282–3, 331–6, 361–4.
96. Ibid., p. 366.
97. R. E. Asher *et al.*, *The United Nations and Economic Social Cooperation* (Washington, 1957) p. 53.
98. House of Commons Debate, 2 February 1943.
99. Another element of doctrine adopted in the new monetary system was the ideal of 'convertibility': the equivalent of the idea of 'liberalisation' in the field of trade. The exchange control and special currency devices so

much used in the inter-war period were restricted. After a transitional period lasting till 1958, the principle was fulfilled by most developed countries, who adopted non-resident convertibility in that year. For a few years the system worked reasonably well, but even among the rich countries it was to lead to substantial instabilities. Large volumes of internationally mobile capital funds, including those used for legitimate trading purposes, could now move rapidly from one currency to another at the slightest hint of a forthcoming change in parities. And it was the US itself, which had maintained convertibility in the fullest possible sense – in undertaking to convert its currency to gold – which was eventually, in 1971, to be placed in the greatest difficulty of all. And just as, in the field of trade, an apparently liberal system could be maintained only by securing voluntary undertakings from the most competitive countries to restrict exports, so in the monetary field an apparently convertible system could in practice only be maintained by securing from central banks in surplus states voluntary undertakings that they would not in practice convert to gold the currency which was most widely used for trading purposes, which was continually in excess supply, and was most expensive to hold.

100. In any case, the multilateral system never worked as planned. Multilateral control of parity changes, or at least multilateral *influence* over them, one of the main innovations of the system, was never put into practice: from 1949 onwards, member-states continually changed their exchange-rates unilaterally, adopting new parities of their own choice (whether or not, as intended, within 10 per cent of the old ones), while doing no more than inform the IMF of the fact a few hours in advance; and the only genuinely multilateral decision concerning parities, the Smithsonian Agreement of December 1971, negotiated among several states, was reached entirely outside the framework of the IMF. Stability in exchange rates, intended to be one of the major objectives of the system, was never satisfactorily achieved; instead, varying rates of inflation caused periodic exchange crises in the time of the 'fixed but adjustable' rates before 1973, and dramatic rises and falls in the time of floating rates after that date. Thirdly, the hope that the Fund might be a means of allowing governments in deficit situations to maintain expansionary policies during the adjustment process was never fulfilled: in practice, the Fund was used to demand precisely the opposite, the same deflationary policies which the gold standard had been condemned for necessitating. Fourthly, though the founders of the system explicitly recognised that responsibility for imbalances would lie as much with surplus countries as with those in deficit, and a 'scarce currency clause' included as a sanction against such countries, in practice that clause was never used, so that the system remained without such sanctions (and ironically the US, the very country which had most resisted the creation of effective sanctions – in the fear that they might be used against her – became later the country most concerned to create such a pressure). Finally, though the purpose of the system was to internationalise decision-making on monetary questions and remove the system from dependence on unilateral decisions by national authorities, in practice the main component of reserves all over

the world remained the currency of a single state (a currency that became increasingly unstable); and the decisions that really mattered for the stability of the system were those reached unilaterally by that particular state, which other countries had little power to influence.

101. R. Vernon, 'Future of the multinational enterprise', in C. P. Kinderberger (ed.), *The International Corporation* (Cambridge, Mass., 1970) p. 374.

102. United Nations, *Transnational Corporations in World Development* (New York, 1978) pp. 288–99.

103. For the best discussion of the supranationality of such organisations, see R. Vernon, *Sovereignty at Bay* (London, 1971), and C. Tugendhat, *The Multinationals* (London, 1971).

104. For further discussion of these alleged benefits, see R. Vernon, in C. P. Kindleberger (ed.), op. cit., p. 383.

105 R. Prebisch, *Change and Development* (New York, 1971) p. 240.

106. The declaration on the establishment of the NIEO of May 1974 declared that 'in order to safeguard . . . its natural resources each state is entitled to exercise effective control over them and their exploitation with means suitable to its own situation, including the right of nationalisation or transfer of ownership to its nationals, this right being an expression of the full permanent sovereignty of the state'.

107. The same declaration emphasised the need to 'facilitate the functioning and further the aims of producers' associations, including to make joint marketing arrangements'.

NOTES TO CHAPTER 2: INTEREST-GROUPS

1. The means available to each group to promote its ends are not confined to pressure on governments. They are interested also in bargaining with similar groups elsewhere. For this reason, although they may be in part *pressure* groups – organised to pressurise governments – we use here the term *interest*-groups, classes which share a common interest in securing particular economic objectives and a particular type of economic system.

2. Notably by R. F. Bently in *The Process of Government* (Chicago, 1908), and by David Easton in *The Governmental Process* (New York, 1951).

3. G. Unwin, *Finance and Trade under Edward III* (London, 1918) pp. xxiii, 186–7, 192–4.

4. E. Miller, in *The Cambridge Economic History of Europe*, vol. IV (Cambridge, 1967) p. 327.

5. E. Miller, 'The economic policies of governments', in *The Cambridge Economic History of Europe*, vol. III (Cambridge, 1963) p. 289. See also M. Postan, *Medieval Trade and Finance* (Cambridge, 1973) pp. 246–7: 'The nobility of England were producers of wool and consumers of imported goods and their representatives on the Council were led by the interests of their class to oppose the monopolistic attempts of the English merchants to exclude foreigners from immediate contact with the English consumers and agricultural producers.'

6. E. B. Fryde and N. M. Fryde, 'Public credit with special reference to north western Europe', in *The Cambridge Economic History of Europe*, vol. III (Cambridge, 1963) p. 518.

7. Ibid., p. 439. The English kings frequently had to pledge leading subjects, prelates or magnates, as security.

8. Fryde and Fryde, op. cit., p. 436. The bankers often acquired an almost similar degree of control over the Church. 'In turn as bankers became more essential they became more powerful within the hierarchy of the church and more capable of manipulating ecclesiastical power for their own ends' (H. A. Miskinin, *The Economy of Early Renaissance Europe, 1300–1460* (Cambridge, 1975) p. 151).

9. The Lancastrian and Yorkist councils contained members with interests and investment in trade and shipping (see M. Postan, op. cit., p. 247).

10. 'The House of Commons was constantly prepared to voice the view of the urban middle classes, and this middle class bias was repeatedly exploited in the commercial interests of the merchants. The City of London had evolved in the 15th century an efficient machinery for propaganda in parliament' (M. Postan, op. cit., pp. 245–6).

11. E. Miller, op. cit., vol. III, pp. 289–90.

12. M. Postan, op. cit., pp. 259, 263, 269, 281. As he points out, the Hanseatic merchants, interested in foreign trade, 'had no need to be exclusive in the local markets of their towns. Their interests were flung far and wide ... their prosperity was based on their ever-growing foreign trade; and foreign trade, especially when it is growing, invariably favours free trade' (ibid., p. 237).

13. Ibid., pp. 281, 242, 262.

14. E. Miller, op. cit., vol. III, p. 313.

15. A. B. Hibbert, 'The economic policies of towns', in *The Cambridge Economic History of Europe*, vol. III (Cambridge, 1963) p. 174.

16. Quoted in M. Wolf, 'French views on wealth and taxes from the Middle Ages to the Old Regime' in D. C. Coleman (ed.), *Revisions in Mercantilism* (London, 1969) p. 201.

17. C. W. Cole, *Colbert and a Century of French Mercantilism*, vol. I (New York, 1939) p. 292.

18. C. Davenant, *An Essay on East India Trade* (London, 1697).

19. Sir J. Child, *New Discourse of Trade* (London, 1693) ch. 4.

20. See M. P. Ashley, *Financial and Commercial Policy under the Protectorate* (London, 1934) ch. XII.

21. See C. M. Wilson, *Profit and Power* (London, 1957) pp. 93, 124.

22. Ibid., p. 106. That Clarendon ignored this clamour, and shortly after concluded a Treaty of Peace and Alliance with the Dutch, shows that such pressure was not always successful; but governments tempted to make war themselves might be prodded by the powerful voices which proclaimed the commercial advantage in such a course.

23. He declared the entire system to have been contrived by 'the producers, whose interests have been so carefully attended; and among this latter class our merchants and manufacturers have been by far the principal architects'.

24. W. E. Minchinton, *The Growth of English Overseas Trade, in the Seventeenth and Eighteenth Century* (London, 1969) p. 103.

294 *Notes*

25. E. F. Heckscher, *Mercantilism*, vol. II (London, 1935) p. 29.
26. See Eric Roll, *A History of Economic Thought* (London, 1938) pp. 81–2.
27. See C. H. Wilson, 'The other face of mercantilism', in D. C. Coleman (ed.), *Revisions in Mercantilism* (London, 1969) pp. 122–5.
28. C. W. Cole, op. cit., vol. I, p. 334.
29. C. H. Wilson, 'Trade, society and the state', in *The Cambridge Economic History of Europe*, vol. IV (Cambridge, 1967) p. 572.
30. W. E. Minchinton, op. cit., p. 103.
31. *The Cambridge Economic History of Europe*, vol. IV (Cambridge, 1967) p. 240.
32. Ibid., pp. 242–4.
33. Ibid., p. 248.
34. J. B. Condliffe, *The Commerce of Nations* (London, 1951) p. 92.
35. See C. H. Wilson, 'The other face of mercantilism', in D. C. Coleman (ed.), op. cit., pp. 127–33.
36. C. H. Wilson, 'Trade, society and the state', in *The Cambridge Economic History of Europe*, vol. IV, p. 492.
37. J. S. Bromley, *The New Cambridge Modern History*, vol. VI (Cambridge, 1970) p. 15.
38. Eric Roll, op. cit., pp. 64–5.
39. C. H. Wilson, 'Trade, society and the state', in *The Cambridge Economic History of Europe*, vol. IV, p. 574.
40. C. H. Wilson, *Profit and Power*, p. 153.
41. French land-owners were protected, like those in Britain by a corn law, and French iron-masters by a heavy duty on iron. Cf. A. Birnie, *An Economic History of Europe, 1760–1939* (London, 1930): 'When in 1815 the conclusion of peace allowed the work of tariff reform to be resumed, it was found that the favourable time for it had passed. Under the restricted franchise which prevailed in France from 1815 to 1848, the great landowners and the industrialists enjoyed a monopoly of political power and both these classes had become strongly attached to protection. The government was prepared for a relaxation of the tariff but, in face of the determined attitude of the legislature, it could do nothing.'
42. J. B. Condliffe, op. cit., p. 210.
43. Cf. A. Birnie, op. cit., p. 69: 'Britain was now the only industrialized nation in Europe, her manufacturers were busy flooding the continent with their goods. Their interest no longer lay in securing the home market, where they had no competition to fear, but in capturing the foreign market, and they were eager to unite with the commercial classes in removing the chief legal obstacles to the expansion of overseas trade.'
44. P. Ashley, *Modern Tariff History* (London, 1920) p. 288.
45. 'Not the least part of the aristocratic supporters of Corn Law abolition fell into this grouping because they had sufficiently diverted their interests so that they might readily believe they had much to gain from the growing prosperity of an industrial England. By marriage and investments the aristocracy and the gentry had become connected with mercantile and industrial enterprise; moreover the gentlemen upon whose lands the cities of an industrial England were encroaching were anticipating a rise in values and rents which must result from industrial

development, and others who owned coal, or iron or lead mines, were in a similarly agreeable situation' (B. Semmel, *The Rise of Free Trade Imperialism* (Cambridge, 1970) p. 139).

46. J. Morley, *The Life of Richard Cobden* (London, 1891) p. 366.
47. The last was mainly a Peelite administration.
48. E. Stanward, *American Tariff Controversies in the 19th Century* (New York, 1904) quoted in P. Ashley, *Modern Tariff History*, p. 153.
49. *The New Cambridge Modern History*, vol. x (Cambridge, 1960) p. 40.
50. J. B. Condliffe, op. cit., p. 203.
51. R. L. Schuyler, *The Fall of the Old Colonial System* (Oxford, 1945) p. 99.
52. D. C. M. Platt, *Finance, Trade and Politics in British Foreign Policy, 1815–1914* (Oxford, 1968) p. xxxviii.
53. Equally disinterested arguments were found for the opposite viewpoint: 'Tariff history is largely a record of interested groups seeking a privileged position in the national economy and advancing patriotic reasons for so doing. Employment, living standards, national welfare, and national power are the stock in trade of the protectionist argument' (J. B. Condliffe, op. cit., p. 228).
54. J. Ehrman, *The British Government and Commercial Negotiations with Europe, 1783–1793* (Cambridge, 1962) p. 183.
55. Cf. H. Feis, *Europe the World's Banker, 1870–1914* (New Haven, 1930) pp. 1–2.
56. H. Feis, ibid., pp. 62–8.
57. H. Feis, ibid., pp. 114–16.
58. D. K. Fieldhouse, *Economics and Empire 1830–1914* (London, 1973) p. 396. This was part of a well orchestrated lobby and campaign: the Journal des Chambres de Commerce Françaises expressed similar sentiments in an editorial.
59. Ibid., p. 397.
60. Ibid., p. 297.
61. Quoted in Fieldhouse, op. cit., p. 216.
62. Ibid., pp. 405–6.
63. Ibid., p. 385.
64. 'The resulting political disorder provided the incentive for British economic interests based on Singapore to work for imperial control as a basis for their proposed enterprises on the mainland. There are few clearer examples of the way in which economic forces on the periphery could lay the foundations for imperial expansion' (D. K. Fieldhouse, op. cit., p. 197).
65. P. T. Moon, *Imperialism and World Politics* (New York, 1927) p. 99. Cf. also H. N. Brailsford, *The War of Steel and Gold* (Shannon, 1914) p. 57: 'This process of impressing foreign governments is clearly simplified when the venture has at its head some noted social or political figure. A British bank operating in Egypt chooses Lord Milner as its Chairman. A bank which aims at serving Turkey has as its head Sir Ernest Cassel, who was often King Edward's host. Lord Cowdray, battling in South America against the Standard Oil Trust for concessions, sounds out as his ambassador the late Whip of the Liberal Party.'
66. H. Feis, op. cit., p. 87.

67. Feis concluded that, in France, 'between the banks and the government exceptional intimacy, with mutual temptations, arose.... Doubts must remain as to the wisdom of creating so close an association between any set of private interests and the state' (ibid., pp. 158–9).
68. D. C. M. Platt, op. cit., p. 32.
69. H. Feis, op. cit., pp. 85–6.
70. Ibid., p. 88. Brailsford also noted the common sentiment and interests of government and finance: 'It would be as false to say that the diplomatist is the sordid tool of finance as it would be to say that the financier is the disinterested purse-bearer of patriotism. They belong to the same social world, they each submit to the vague influences which cause the world to turn its interest now to this corner of the earth, not to that. ... The financier knows that in pushing his business he is incidentally buying power for the empire. The diplomatist is convinced that he is serving the country by promoting trade' (Brailsford, op. cit., p. 220).
71. In one case, the individual responsible for colonisation was not a trader but a sovereign, King Leopold, who was mainly personally responsible for the establishment of effective Belgian rule in a huge area of Africa, the Congo.
72. See N. A. Pelcovits, *Old China Hands and the Foreign Office* (New York, 1948) for many such cases concerning China. For examples, see D. K. Fieldhouse, op. cit., pp. 184, 237, 322–4, 385–7 and *passim*.
73. Ibid., p. 265.
74. Ibid., p. 456; P. T. Moon, op. cit., p. 399.
75. D. K. Fieldhouse, op. cit., p. 31.
76. Joseph Chamberlain, speaking to a Birmingham audience of manufacturers and working men in 1893.
77. Speech at the Mansion House, 7 August 1881.
78. Sir Arthur Salter, *World Trade and its Future* (Philadelphia, 1936) p. 39.
79. F. Hirsch and P. Oppenheimer, 'The trial of managed money: currency, credit and prices, 1920–1970', in *The Fontana Economic History of Europe, The Twentieth Century*, vol. II (London, 1976) p. 619.
80. A. M. Schlesinger, *The Coming of the New Deal* (London, 1960) p. 239.
81. Among the wider public too, there was special anger against bankers, the dominant figures of the previous age, who were still seen as sources of power yet responsible for depression and defaulting: 'The best way to restore confidence in the banks,' Senator Wheeler of Montana declared in the US, 'would be to take these crooked presidents out of the banks and treat them the same as we treated Al Capone when he failed to pay his income tax.' And another senator, Senator Glass of Virginia, said of them equally caustically that 'One banker in my state attempted to marry a white woman and they lynched him.' Quoted in W. E. Leuchtenburg, *Franklin D. Roosevelt and the New Deal, 1932–40* (New York, 1963) p. 22.
82. Occasionally, politicians were prepared to stand up for liberal trading policies. In Britain, Attlee attacked the duties introduced by the national government in 1931 on the grounds that it would lead to increasing economic conflict without assisting the standard of living of workers: 'There is no protection for the consumer or the worker and there is nothing to ensure efficiency. What the scheme amounts to is a very large

dole for separate industries. I believe that the proposals will lead to industrial warfare.... Carried out to its logical conclusion it will lead to an attempt to set up an economic bloc of the British Empire and probably some allies. This will mean economic competition with some other bloc and that economic warfare will lead to political warfare' (House of Commons, 4 Feb. 1931). More often, parliaments represented a pressure in *favour* of protection.

83. Leuchtenburg, op. cit., p. 58.
84. 'New impetus was given to the trade association movement and to industrial agreements limiting the scope of competition and wherever possible eliminating redundant capacity. Voluntary limitation of output, price maintenance, combined marketing and research services, the pooling of patents and processes, standardization, comparative cost analysis, and similar attempts to reduce costs and secure the economies of large-scale production, were advocated by arguments stressing the views of cooperative effort and the disadvantages of unrestricted competition' (J. B. Condliffe, op. cit., p. 58).
85. Leuchtenburg, op. cit., p. 88.
86. 'Primarily this was a movement described as fair competition toward the abandonment of free competition and toward concerted action among producing groups. In the beginning it was a repudiation both of state control and of free competition – an attempt to obtain by agreement acceptance of industrial and trading practices that would limit destructive competition. But after the Depression of 1929–33 it led to state-supported and state-enforced monopoly organization in many countries.... Limited state trading monopolies made their appearance and ultimately the conduct of trade came under bureaucratic regulation in many countries' (J. B. Condliffe, op. cit., p. 461).
87. W. E. Leuchtenburg, op. cit., pp. 188–9.
88. Agricultural workers were in most countries, though a far larger section of the population, less powerfully organised to influence governments. And this too is reflected in governments' international policies: especially the failure of effective measures (outside the US) to maintain agricultural prices.
89. For a description of the methods used by US corporations in influencing the US administration, see E. M. Epstein, *The Corporation in American Politics* (Englewood Cliffs, N. J., 1969) pp. 74–8, 90–1, 197–203.
90. R. Vernon, *Sovereignty at Bay* (London, 1971) p. 228.
91. E. M. Epstein, op. cit., pp. 47–8.
92. 'The movement of funds within multinational groups, when several are following the same policy, can threaten and sometimes destroy national policies with regard to currency, exchange rates, balance of payments and the availability of credit' (C. Tugendhat, *The Multinationals* (London, 1971) p. 129).
93. R. Vernon, *Sovereignty at Bay*, pp. 168–9.
94. 'In international trades unions, it is recognised that worldwide collective bargaining remains a distant prospect. At present the bargaining autonomy within the trades union movement lies with the national organisations' (United Nations, *Transnational Corporations in World Development* (1978), p. 98).

NOTES TO CHAPTER 3: MOTIVES

1. Evan Luard, *Types of International Society* (New York, 1976) ch. 7.
2. 'The tendency of national currency to leak out and be replaced by inferior foreign coins, combined with the frequent complaint that there was a shortage of money current for day-to-day needs, led to a much closer government control of overseas payments. The export of bullion and coined money from England and France was forbidden with monotonous regularity. . . . Thus the direction of the flow of bullion was becoming a matter of prime concern for governments' (E. Miller, in *The Cambridge Economic History*, vol. III (Cambridge, 1963) p. 333).
3. Rot. Parl. II, 6.247.
4. Cf. C. M. Cipolla, in *The Cambridge Economic History of Europe*, vol. IV (Cambridge, 1967) p. 41: 'Whether for each of the three production factors (labour, capital and raw materials) separately, or for all three of them collectively . . . the aim was always to facilitate imports and discourage exports. So far as labour was concerned, the emigration of skilled artisans was generally prohibited while immigration was favoured . . . Similarly, measures were also taken to encourage the import and discourage the export of capital . . . Measures on the same lines were taken in far greater number in order to improve the supply of raw materials. Imports were actually facilitated by abolishing or reducing import duties while exports were discouraged by imposing export duties or even by absolute prohibitions.'
5. Cf. E. Power, *The Wool Trade in English Medieval History* (Oxford, 1941) p. 87: 'The English monarch had an obvious interest in the [wool] staple for he could employ it as a useful diplomatic lever. Foreign rulers and towns were always anxious to have it on their soil for the sake of the trade and revenues which it brought. Edward I used his embryonic staple as a bait for the alliance first of the Court of Holland, then of the Court of Flanders. Edward II employed it in his negotiations with France, Brabant and Flanders. Edward III bought with it the alliance of the Flemish towns at the beginning of the Hundred Years War'.
6. 'A desire to maintain stocks of mobilisable wealth available for government exploitation easily gave rise to measures of exchange control or a concern about the balance of trade. Thus revenue preoccupations, and the power preoccupations of which they were a manifestation, gave governments a specific interest in an expanding range of economic activities' (E. Miller, op. cit., p. 288).
7. E. F. Heckscher, *Mercantilism*, vol. II (London, 1935) p. 33.
8. Similar measures were introduced later by France and Denmark in the seventeenth century, and by Sweden in the eighteenth. The same strategic aim could be promoted by simpler means: towards the end of the Hundred Years War in 1449, a memorandum concerning the English war aims included the 'destruction of Breton and Norman shipping in order that the English merchants may have the shipping of the seas'.
9. C. M. Cipolla, op. cit., p. 415.
10. 'Very often . . . the tariff was not considered sufficient protection and public authorities resorted easily to absolute prohibitions to import and sell foreign manufactures on the home market' (ibid.).

11. 'These acts were neither permanent, nor effective but at least they showed that there were now many voices asking for protection and that in favourable circumstances their demands would be translated into government policy' (E. Miller, op. cit., p. 326).

12. In Guines, 'drapers were forbidden to have their weaving and fulling done outside the town or to export cloths which had not been made in it and inspected and sealed by the local authorities, while weavers, fullers and shearers were forbidden to go to work outside the town as long as they could find work within it. Restrictions on foreign merchants give clear evidence of the mentality of the townsfolk and are a salutory reminder of the humble level at which such grand forces as "protectionist policy" or "restriction of foreign imports" might operate, for strangers importing cloth were not allowed to have a stall in the market place but could deal only in what they could carry under their arms' (A. B. Hibbert, 'The economic policies of towns', in *The Cambridge Economic History of Europe*, vol. III (Cambridge, 1963) pp. 215–16).

13. The main purpose of the 'cameralists' in Germany was to point out the comparative effect of different taxation and other economic policies on the development of industry and trade.

14. Pepys, *Diary*, 2 February 1664.

15. C. W. Cole, *Colbert and a Century of French Mercantilism*, vol. I (New York, 1939) p. 345.

16. Colbert, memorandum to Louis XIV, 1664.

17. Quoted in E. F. Heckscher, op. cit., vol. II, p. 19.

18. J. Child, *A Treatise Concerning the East Indian Trade* (London, 1681) p. 29.

19. Lord Bolingbroke, *Letters on the Spirit of Patriotism* (London, 1752) p. 204.

20. Colbert, letter to the Intendant at Rochefort, 1666.

21. *The Cambridge Economic History of Europe*, vol. IV (Cambridge, 1967) p. 509.

22. Eric Roll, *A History of Economic Thought* (London, 1938) p. 81.

23. J. Locke, *Some Considerations of the Consequence of the Lowering of Interests and Raising the Value of Money*, quoted in E. F. Heckscher, op. cit., vol. II, p. 197.

24. Essai sur les Formes de Gouvernement.

25. *The Cambridge Economic History of Europe*, vol. IV (Cambridge, 1967) pp. 224–57.

26. 'As national statesmen beating together the ideas and the administrative machinery for a national economy, they appreciated the potential wealth to be derived from overseas territories which were being revealed. They incorporated such territories into their theories and into their practice. ... Overseas possessions fell easily and naturally into the context of a self-contained national economy which seemed so essential to the European statesmen of the fifteenth and sixteenth – and indeed subsequent – centuries' (*The Cambridge Economic History of Europe*, vol. IV (Cambridge, 1967) p. xv).

27. R. Hakluyt, *A Particular Discourse Concerning Western Discoveries* (London, 1589). G. L. Beer held that 'the desire to free England from the necessity of purchasing from foreigners formed the underlying basis

of English commercial and colonial expansion' (*The Origin of the British Colonial System* (New York, 1908) vol. I, p. 38).

28. Josiah Child, *A New Discourse of Trade* (London, 1693) pp. 212–20.

29. In a very few cases, however, domestic industry was weakened to assist colonial products: thus tobacco-growing was stamped out in England so that it should not damage the North American tobacco industry.

30. J. Ehrman, *The British Government and Commercial Negotiations with Europe, 1783–1793* (Cambridge, 1962) p. 194.

31. Already in 1807, Castlereagh, while renouncing any aim of territorial acquisition or even political dominance, proposed that Britain's main aim in South America 'should be depriving our enemy of one of his chief resources and the opening to our manufactures of the markets of that great continent'.

32. 'One of the strongest impressions left ... is indeed of the interdependence of foreign policy and matters of trade. This of course was true of all European countries, particularly when the trade of the Old World was concerned ... British foreign policy was conditioned largely by commercial interest, so that interaction was intimate, natural and continuous ... Trade was of the very stuff from which their diplomacy took form' (J. Ehrman, op. cit., pp. 184–5).

33. C. K. Webester, *The Foreign Policy of Castlereagh, 1815–1822* (London, 1825) p. 409.

34. Under the agreements of 1860 and 1828 respectively.

35. In such situations, those countries being wooed by both sides were well placed to secure the maximum economic advantage: the smaller German states were able to use Britain's fear that they would join the Zollverein to extract significant commercial concessions – though this did not prevent them nevertheless joining it not long afterwards.

36. Ward and Gooch (eds), *Cambridge History of British Foreign Policy*, vol. II (London, 1939) p. 469. One of the main objects of the treaty, according to the British Ambassador in Vienna, was to 'give to Bavaria and Wurttemberg a community of interests with Austria and counterbalance the ascendancy which Prussia had acquired over them' (p. 468).

37. In 1842 he wrote to a friend that free trade agitation and the peace movement were 'one and the same cause. It has often been to me a matter of the greatest surprise that the Friends have not taken the question of free trade as the means – and I believe the only human means – of effecting universal and perpetual peace' (John Morley, *The Life of Richard Cobden* (London, 1910) pp. 23–4).

38. Quoted in J. B. Condliffe, *The Commerce of Nations* (London, 1951) p. 222.

39. D. C. M. Platt, *Finance, Trade and Politics in British Foreign Policy, 1815–1914* (Oxford, 1968) p. 88.

40. H. Feis, *Europe the World's Banker, 1870–1914* (New Haven, 1930) p. 36.

41. 'The fundamental fact is the rapid accumulation of surplus capital. It grows in the hands of ... magnates, banks and ground landlords more rapidly than the demand for it at home. It tries continuously to get itself employed at home, and the result is that periodic over-production, which

shows itself in a "slump" of trade and a crisis of unemployment.... When rates of interest fall at home, it begins to look abroad for something at once remunerative and not too risky' (H. N. Brailsford, *The War of Steel and Gold* (Shannon, 1914) p. 79).

42. For example, 'buyers of Tunisian bonds in Europe were interested only in the relatively high rates of interest offered, well above those currently paid on European gilt-edged stock and made still higher by the bonds being bought at a discount. Bankers were out to gain substantial profits from commissions and less honourable devices' (D. K. Fieldhouse, *Economics and Empire, 1830–1914* (London, 1973) p. 113). Similarly, in Egypt, 'the total debts were grossly inflated by exorbitant commissions and other charges made by the bankers and by being sold below their face value' (ibid., p. 119). See also H. Feis, op. cit., pp. 4, 18, 36, 40.

43. The wages of Indian male mill operatives, working 13, 14 or 15 hours a day, varied from 15 to 20 rupees a month (from £1 to £1.6s.8d.) in 1908 (H. N. Brailsford, op. cit., p. 83).

44. Quoted in J. A. Hobson, *Imperialism* (London, 1902) p. 79.

45. *Britain's Industrial Future*, the Report of the Liberal Industrial Inquiry (London, 1928).

46. D. K. Fieldhouse, op. cit., p. 318.

47. The scheme 'had little connection with the practical needs of the French business world. Its economic rationale was a visionary belief in the commercial potential of large-scale communications. This was economic imperialism of a sort, but it had little in common with the imperialism of a European merchant or manufacturer' (ibid., p. 318).

48. Whatever the motives of governments might be, such contracts brought substantial advantage to those who financed and constructed them. In one or two cases they were covered by a so-called 'kilometric guarantee', which had the effect that the longer the route chosen, the greater the profit. Brailsford gives an account of a railway on which he travelled in Turkey which 'described enormous arcs' and 'did not seem to serve any visible town', because 'every unnecessary curve means so many miles added to the total length of the line, and so many hundreds of thousands of pounds to its annual guaranteed profits' (H. N. Brailsford, op. cit., p. 84).

49. Circular to British envoys abroad, 2 March 1849.

50. H. Feis, op. cit., p. 105.

51. Ibid., p. 150.

52. For further examples of action to protect investment see pp. 190–1.

53. H. Feis, op. cit., pp. 96–7.

54. Ibid., p. 96.

55. Ibid., pp. 98–9.

56. In Tunisia, for example, 'from 1870 the struggle between the consuls from Britain, France and Italy again became acute, and concessions were regarded as evidence of dominance at court, even if no European capitalist could be induced to take them up' (D. K. Fieldhouse, op. cit., p. 116).

57. H. Feis, op. cit., p. 126. The following pages list many examples of orders obtained as a condition of making a loan.

58. Ibid., p. 187.
59. Ibid., pp. 176–7.
60. It is true, as Fieldhouse points out (op. cit., p. 21), that the high point of colonial expansion, in the 1880s, preceded the highest point of tariff protection in Europe. But this does not invalidate the general point that it was the decline of trade generally in Europe, which was intensified by protection, which stimulated the search for markets abroad: as we saw above (p. 26–8), European statesmen certainly believed that the search for overseas markets was made more urgent by the decline of markets nearer home.
61. See p. 88. cf. D. K. Fieldhouse, op. cit., p. 154: 'In China and South East Asia, the characteristic pattern of European demands during the second half of the nineteenth century was for freedom of access to more ports, better conditions for expatriate residents, greater freedom of activity within the country and ultimately the right to build railways and establish enterprises inland.'
62. Sir H. H. Johnston, *The Colonisation of Africa* (Cambridge, 1899) p. 446.
63. Quoted in Fieldhouse, op. cit., p. 397.
64. Ibid., p. 320.
65. Ibid., pp. 326–8.
66. Ibid., p. 155.
67. Sir F. Lugard, *The Dual Mandate in British Tropical Africa* (London, 1922) p. 43.
68. P. T. Moon, *Imperialism and World Politics* (New York, 1927) p. 555.
69. A less frequent economic motive was the desire for land which could be used for plantations or other forms of agriculture: the 'speculative land-grabbing concern ... expressed neither the commercial nor the investment needs of the metropolis but the opportunism, and in some cases patriotism, of individual British or German subjects who were encouraged by the achievements of the explorers to believe that profits could be made by acquiring large areas of "vacant" land in those regions of darkest Africa where there were no established European commercial or other interests' (D. K. Fieldhouse, op. cit., pp. 369–70).
70. The money 'could not be raised within China, and Peking would therefore be compelled to borrow overseas. On the precedent of Mediterranean states during the previous quarter century foreign borrowing on this scale was almost certain to entail foreign influence over Peking' (ibid., p. 417).
71. In 1922, soon after this period ended, El Salvador had to agree, in return to a loan from a US bank, not only to accept that 70 per cent of customs revenue should be used to repay the loan, but also that, if necessary, the bank was to nominate the official who would become collector-general of the entire customs revenues.
72. H. Feis, op. cit., p. xvi.
73. The importance of financial factors in influencing political influence in Morocco is shown by the settlement of Algeciras, which demanded that control of the finances and customs in the country should be shared equally between France and Germany to safeguard equal political influence.

74. For a more detailed account of the relationship between political and economic motives in the granting of loan facilities, see M. Feis, op. cit., pp. 89–95, 122–43, 160–76.
75. Quoted in H. Feis, ibid., pp. 123–4.
76. A. M. Schlesinger, *The Coming of the New Deal* (London, 1960) p. 247.
77. House of Commons, 8 September 1931.
78. Quoted in *Documents on Nazism, 1919–1945* (London, 1974) p. 403.
79. Ibid., p. 409. The policy was pursued with remarkable success in Germany: reliance on agricultural imports was reduced from 25 per cent to 15 per cent between 1933 and 1939.
80. Neville Chamberlain, House of Commons, 4 February 1931.
81. House of Commons, 2 June 1933.
82. Quoted in A. M. Schlesinger, op. cit., p. 208. During the Conference, President Roosevelt sent Moley a message demanding that, before the US could be expected to implement the proposed decisions, 'a sufficient interval should be allowed the United States to permit . . . a demonstration of the value of price lifting efforts which we have well in hand' (ibid., p. 213).
83. Exceptions were the US, in the late 1930s, and Sweden. In Germany, Schacht introduced special bills of exchange (Mefo-bills), guaranteed by the Reichsbank and repayable within five years, which were used to expand credit in line with the rise of productive resources. This was one of the reasons why Germany was more successful than most other countries in restoring relatively full employment: unemployment was reduced from six million in 1933 to one million in 1935.
84. J. M. Keynes, *General Theory of Employment, Interest and Money* (London, 1947) p. 379.
85. Ibid., p. 378.
86. *Documents on Nazism, 1919–1945*, p. 405.
87. This aim was explicitly declared in the circular sent by the German Foreign Office to its embassies abroad in June 1934. This stated that Germany's treaties with Hungary and Yugoslavia, which were commercial as well as political, were 'designed to create in Hungary and Yugoslavia two points of support for German policy in the Danubian region, in order above all to counteract French and Italian policy directed against German policy in the region'.
88. Though not intended primarily for strategic reasons, the imperial preference system was certainly taken by some to indicate a tendency towards economic confrontation: Clement Attlee in the House of Commons denounced them as an attempt to 'set up an economic bloc of the British Empire and probably some allies' which could easily 'lead to political warfare'.
89. 'One element in the failure of nations to adopt policies that would have led to increasing economic interdependence was the fact that warning voices were raised against the strategic dangers of such interdependence. It began to be realized that trade carried with it an element of power and, in certain circumstances, of domination. The first breach in the British free trade tradition, for example, was made in favour of certain "key industries" deemed essential for national defence. The French, Czechs, and other nations were equally alive to the increased importance in

modern war of the chemical, optical, glass, steel and other industries' (J. B. Condliffe, op. cit., p. 483).

90. R. E. Baldwin and D. A. Kay, in C. F. Bergsten and L. B. Krause (eds), *World Politics and International Economics* (Washington, 1975) p. 113.

91. Quoted in R. N. Gardner, *Sterling–Dollar Diplomacy*, 2nd edn (New York, 1969) p. 9.

92. For reasons why this was necessary for developing countries, see G. Myrdal, *An International Economy* (London, 1956) especially pp. 275–98.

93. J. H. Dunning, *Studies in International Investment* (London, 1970) p. 1.

94. IMF, *Balance of Payments Yearbook* (1975).

95. J. H. Dunning, op. cit., pp. 1–2.

96. Cf. E. Penrose, in J. H. Dunning (ed.), *The Multinational Enterprise* (London, 1971) p. 232: 'Their size, international scope, political, managerial and technological expertise, and in general the apparently wider "options" open to them in determining their policies, all give rise to a feeling in the less well-endowed host countries that bargaining power is grossly unequal, with the result that the foreigner obtains a disproportionate gain from his activities in the country.'

NOTES TO CHAPTER 4: MEANS

1. 'The general economic regression of the early fourteenth century ... made paid service in the king's army, not to speak of the opportunity for booty and ransom, attractive. War with rich France was certainly more popular than war with poor Scotland, though the opportunity for romantic deeds of arms was the same.... The soldiers in Edward III's armies were men on the make and military considerations seldom clouded their selfish intentions. Bertrand du Guesclin was captured four times and on each occasion was released by his captors for ramsoms which steadily mounted' (D. Hay, *Europe in the 14th and 15th Centuries* (London, 1966) p. 158).

2. 'Strong towns dealing with the weak could use a thorough-going compulsory staple system to achieve their ends and could turn supply regions into private reserves. Thirteenth century Venice demonstrates the use of such overriding power. A treaty of 1234 made her the only city at which Ravenna merchants could sell corn and salt, and a 1236 settlement barred to Ragusa all trade in the northern Adriatic except for the carriage of foodstuffs to Venice: at the same time Venice claimed a monopoly of the export of corn in the lower Po Valley and the Mark of Treviso and a virtual monopoly further south' (A. B. Hibbert, *'The economic policies of towns'*, in *The Cambridge Economic History of Europe*, vol. III (Cambridge, 1963)).

3. 'The Hanse's chosen weapon was the blockade, that is the suspension of all trade.... Henceforward joint action was to be undertaken with the intention of forcing concessions from the town or country at fault' (P. Dollinger, *The Hanseatic League* (London, 1970) pp. 47–8).

4. E. F. Heckscher, *Mercantilism*, vol. II (London, 1935) pp. 81–4.

5. A. B. Hibbert, op. cit., pp. 166–7.

6. C. M. Cipolla, '*The Italian and Iberian peninsulas*', in *The Cambridge Economic History of Europe*, vol. III (Cambridge, 1963) p. 417.

7. Cf. D. C. Coleman, *Revisions in Mercantilism* (London, 1969) pp. 32–33: 'it was precisely this mercantilist conception of society which led statesmen to even greater ruthlessness than would have been possible without the help of such a conception'.

8. C. H. Wilson, '*Trade, society and the state*', in *The Cambridge Economic History of Europe*, vol. IV (Cambridge, 1967) p. 536.

9. Cf. *The New Cambridge Modern History*, vol. VI (Cambridge, 1970) p. 187: 'The upsurge in international economic activity and association did not signify that major political combinations were made, or wars fought from economic motives. For those who decided the issues of war and peace, or alliance, economic measures were instruments of policy, never its aim.'

10. In 1662, the Duke of York in England (the future James II) expressed his anger that Clarendon, the chief minister, should have expressed himself against a design 'so honourable in itself and so much desired by the City of London' as a further war against the Dutch; while Monck also gave his support for the war on the grounds that 'what matters this or that reason; what we want is more of the trade the Dutch now have'. See C. Wilson, *Profit and Power* (London, 1957) p. 107.

11. 'England saw in the war of 1744 an opportunity to ruin the French sugar colonies and eliminate their competition in the European market. The French West Indies interests likewise saw an opportunity to ruin a rival and enlarge France's share of the colonial foreign market for manufactured goods' (*The New Cambridge Modern History*, vol. VII (Cambridge, 1957) p. 39).

12. *The Cambridge Economic History of Europe*, vol. IV (Cambridge, 1967) p. 574.

13. The first attempt to rationalise tariffs to correspond with national interests was made in France, just before this period began, in 1576 by Bodin, who recommended duties on imports of manufactures and on exports of raw materials.

14. The English Navigation Act of 1651 specifically laid down that all salted fish, fish oils and whale fins were to be imported only in English ships, to cut off the huge Dutch trade in these products. The Staple Act of 1663, which replaced the Navigation Act, and which enumerated the particular goods which must be imported and exported in English ships, named primarily goods in which the Dutch had previously enjoyed a significant part of the trade. Most European goods were now to be shipped either in English ships or ships of the exporting country itself, so that the Dutch entrepôt trade might be largely eliminated.

15. R. Davis, *The Rise of the Atlantic Economy* (London, 1973) p. 242.

16. See R. W. K. Hinton, *The Eastland Trade and the Commonwealth in the Seventeenth Century* (Cambridge, 1959) p. 64.

17. *The Cambridge History of Europe*, vol. IV (Cambridge, 1967) p. 234. This company was reinforced in 1621 by a Dutch West India Company, which

played an important part in waging warfare in Brazil and which was even more closely tied to government.

18. 'The vetting and presentation of claims formed a major, if not *the* major preoccupation of British diplomacy in Latin America, whether at the legation or at the Foreign Office itself. Scarcely a day passed, Mr Layard complained to the Commons in 1863, when some such Latin American claim was not received at the Foreign Office, and there was not a single South American state against which there were no claims for redress outstanding' (D. C. M. Platt, *Finance, Trade and Politics in British Foreign Policy, 1815–1914* (Oxford 1968) p. 331).

19. The importance ascribed in Britain to the expansion of trade abroad, under all circumstances, is shown by the fact that Lord Grey, pointing out in the House of Lords in 1812 that 'the manufacturers of Yorkshire make the clothing of the French army' while the two nations were at war, saw this as a matter of congratulation rather than concern.

20. D. C. M. Platt, ibid., p. 143.

21. Ibid., p. 91.

22. D. C. M. Platt, 'British commerce and diplomacy in Latin America', Thesis (Oxford, 1962) pp. 28–30. In 1824, Sir James Mackintosh presented a petition of the City of London to the House of Commons and urged the government to act forcefully, if necessary, to secure the repayment of loans being made by English financial houses to South American governments, since it was a 'great national interest as well as duty to watch over the international rights of every Briton and to claim them from every government' (B. Semmel, *The Rise of Free Trade Imperialism* (Cambridge, 1970) p. 151).

23. H. Feis, *Europe the World's Banker, 1870–1914* (New Haven, 1930) pp. 166–7.

24. Ibid., p. 169.

25. Ibid., p. 140.

26. Hansard 10 July, 1914.

27. Sometimes, the concessions related to trade of all sorts, more often to the construction of railways, roads, ports, mines or other undertakings. Thus the British thought they were being very open-handed in agreeing with the Russians that in their Persian sphere of influence 'the concessions to be reserved might be limited to roads, railways, telegraphs, harbours and irrigation' (Sir C. Hardinge to Sir Arthur Nicholson, Ambassador in St Petersburg, quoted in D. C. M. Platt, *Finance, Trade and Politics in British Foreign Policy, 1815–1914*, p. 64).

28. Quoted in D. C. M. Platt, ibid., p. 410.

29. Ibid., p. 61.

30. Ibid., p. 104.

31. Parliamentary Debates, House of Lords, 16 June 1903.

32. H. Feis, op. cit., p. 144.

33. H. Feis, op. cit., p. 28. Governments supported their cable companies equally vigorously. Britain and Germany competed particularly intensively in this field, giving subventions and the support of government departments to their companies for the sake of the political advantages which such contracts were believed to provide.

34. Ibid., p. 126.
35. Ibid., p. 195.
36. Ibid., pp. 126–7.
37. Ibid., p. 127.
38. Ibid., p. 143.
39. 'The evidence taken before the Royal Commission on the Civil Service (1914) suggests that by the end of the period it was definitely considered to be part of the duty of British representatives to bring British merchants into touch with local commerce and officialdom' (D. C. M. Platt, *Finance, Trade and Politics in British Foreign Policy, 1815–1914*, p. 131).
40. Ibid., p. 134.
41. M. Feis, op. cit., p. 86.
42. 'First, the government acted to prevent the arrangement or emission of loans to countries whose political actions were deemed unfriendly or whose political alliance and interests seemed to clash with those of France. Second, admission to official listing was made conditional upon pledges, assurances, or compensations of a political order. Third, the government used its connections with financial circles, its influence over public opinion and press to facilitate the borrowing of states with which it was allied, or to arrange the sale of loans in return for which political advantages had been secured' (ibid., p. 134).
43. Ibid., p. 174.
44. 'The motives of agreeing to a charter were political; the bank was intended to rebuild Persian prosperity as a barrier to a Russian takeover. Though unsuccessful in its first aim, the Imperial Bank of Persia acted, in and after the late nineties, as the barely disguised medium through which the governments of Britain and India could forestall the Russians in the competition for "political" loans' (D. C. M. Platt, *Finance, Trade and Politics in British Foreign Policy, 1815–1914*, pp. 30–1).
45. Ibid., p. 31.
46. Ibid., p. 31.
47. The Royal Niger company equipped their agents with blank treaty forms beginning with the words: 'We, the undersigned chiefs of —————— , with the view of bettering the conditions of our country and people do this day cede to the Royal Niger Company (Chartered and Limited) forever, the whole of our territory, extending from —————— .' The blank treaty bound the chiefs not to have 'any intercourse with any strangers or foreigners except through the said Royal Niger Company (Chartered and Limited)'. The Treaty pledged the company to offer the chiefs protection and to pay a certain sum of money. In return, the company was given full powers to mine, farm and build in any part of the country.
48. For similar reasons, the Philippines, though held as a colony by the US for fifty years, was never named as such; and Hawaii, when it was taken over by the US in 1892 after the landing of marines, at the request of an American-led demonstration, was said to have asked for a union with the US and was formerly annexed, yet was not to become a state for another 60 years.

49. One of these concessions made a net profit of over 3m. dollars in six years on capital of 200,000 dollars. The shareholders received annual dividends averaging more than ten times the value of the stock, in addition to a huge capital appreciation (see P. T. Moon, *Imperialism and World Politics* (New York, 1927) p. 87).

50. M. Feis, op. cit., pp. 114–15.

51. Parliamentary Debates, Senate, 25 February 1901.

52. M. Feis, op. cit., p. 109.

53. For a fuller description of the growth of tariffs in this period see J. B. Condliffe, *The Commerce of Nations* (London, 1951) pp. 479–504.

54. *Documents on Nazism, 1919–1945* (London, 1974) p. 394.

55. Ibid., p. 394.

56. Quoted in A. M. Schlesinger, *The Coming of the New Deal* (London, 1960) p. 246.

57. *Documents on Nazism, 1919–1945*, p. 396.

58. Ibid., p. 395.

59. See W. A. Lewis, *Economic Survey, 1919–1939* (London, 1949) p. 66.

60. For figures for the principal countries see C. Zacchia, '*International trade and capital movements, 1920–1970*', in *The Fontana Economic History of Europe, The Twentieth Century*, vol. II (London, 1976) p. 578.

61. Ibid., pp. 579–82.

62. C. Zacchia, op. cit., p. 577.

63. C. F. Bergsten and L. B. Krause (eds.), *World Politics and International Economics* (Washington, 1975) pp. 9–10.

64. For a description of the political factors determining the distribution of aid, see John White, *The Politics of Foreign Aid* (London, 1974) pp. 38ff.

65. K. P. Sauvant and F. G. Lavipour, *Controlling Multinational Enterprises* (London, 1976) p. 71.

66. For a fuller account of such activities, see N. H. Jacoby, P. Nehemkis and R. Eells, *Bribery and Extortion in World Business* (New York, 1977).

67. Cf. UN, *Transnational Corporations in World Development*, p. 44: 'In order to maintain control of the complex flows of components and finished goods among scattered units in different countries, firms need to exert a degree of control at a level in the hierarchy above that of the national subsidiary.... In other words control can become embedded within the fabric of the firm without being readily apparent to the outside observer. The more national units become conditioned to indirect, harmonised control procedures, the more difficult it becomes for them to respond unilaterally to the needs of the local economy.' See also C. Tugendhat, *The Multinationals* (London, 1971) pp. 11, 25.

68. The Andean Pact demanded 51 per cent control by local shareholders, as did certain governments in the Middle East.

69. This was implemented in India and Nigeria, and was demanded within a time limit among the Andean Pact countries.

70. Especially power-generation, public utilities, transport, communications, wholesale or retail trade, oil and petrochemicals: see UN, op. cit., p. 21.

71. Ibid., p. 90.

72. The OECD and the International Chamber of Commerce also drew up

voluntary guidelines on the conduct of multinationals.
73. Ibid., p. 110: 'There is some evidence that financial returns to a transnational corporation ... under a service contract may even be higher than those derived from concessions. In such a case the financial risks are substantially reduced, while the structure of the legal arrangements meant the transnational corporation was less vulnerable politically.' For further examination of the power which can be exerted by large corporations in developing countries, see R. Vernon, *Sovereignty at Bay* (London, 1971) pp. 168–9; and L. Turner, *Multinational Companies and the Third World* (London, 1973) pp. 53–4.

NOTES TO CHAPTER 5: ECONOMIC DOMINANCE AND DEPENDENCE

1. For the study of different forms of stratification in different international societies in history, see E. Luard, *Types of International Society* (New York, 1976) ch. 9.
2. E. F. Heckscher, *Mercantilism*, vol. II (London, 1935) p. 63.
3. A. B. Hibbert, '*The economic policies of towns*', in *The Cambridge Economic History of Europe*, vol. III (Cambridge, 1963) p. 174.
4. 'A great part of the external history of the more important medieval cities can be written around their conflicts with one another to secure control of a trade route to dominate the source of a vital commodity and to monopolise access to a great market. Such contests are to be found in all regions and at all times.... A wholly successful policy meant complete monopoly of the trade in some commodity, unchallenged command over some vital route, sole access to some market, together with freedom from fiscal and other interference in the trade so monopolised' (ibid., pp. 165–6).
5. 'Hanse policy ... continued to be directed towards the conservation of its privileges: the political methods of realising this policy were alliances, embargoes, blockades, and in the last resort war' (E. Lönnroth, '*The Baltic countries*', in *The Cambridge Economic History of Europe*, vol. III (Cambridge, 1963) p. 392).
6. H. A. Miskinin, *The Economy of Early Renaissance Europe, 1300–1460* (Cambridge, 1975) p. 148.
7. G. Holmes, *Europe: Hierarchy and Revolt, 1320–1450* (London, 1975) p. 72.
8. Ibid., p. 73.
9. Colbert, *Lettres*, VI, 264; II, 610, VII, 250–4 (see E. F. Heckscher, op. cit., vol. II, pp. 17–18).
10. Quoted in ibid., vol. II, p. 19.
11. C. H. Wilson, *Profit and Power* (London, 1957) p. 118.
12. Quoted in C. H. Wilson, ibid., p. 96.
13. In the middle of the seventeenth century, three-quarters of the traffic in Baltic grain, nearly three-quarters of that in timber, and nearly half of that in Swedish metals were carried in Dutch ships, and thirteen times as

many Dutch ships as English passed through the Sound.

14. 'The burden of England's tale of complaint was, in brief, that the Dutch carried away from England and her dependencies little but raw materials and semi-manufactured goods, making large profits in the subsequent stages of manufacture and commerce. The skill of the Dutch in selling back manufactures, necessities and luxuries to their victim was only the second stage of a process plausibly represented as one of "double robbery"' (ibid., p. 144).

15. Since the Dutch had few raw materials of their own, they were particularly vulnerable to threats to their supplies. Their prosperity depended on their maintaining imports of wool from England and Spain, naval goods from the Baltic, precious metals from Spain (with which they paid for Baltic goods), and colonial products from the West Indies; as well as, of course, supplies of spices and other products from their own possessions abroad.

16. J. Tucker, *A Series of Answers to Certain Popular Objections to Separating from the Rebellious Colonies* (Gloucester, 1776).

17. J. Tucker, *Cui Bono* (London, 1782) pp. 16–19.

18. Quoted in B. Semmel, *The Rise of Free Trade Imperialism* (Cambridge, 1970) p. 34.

19. Pamphlet on the Funding System, in P. Sraffa (ed.), *Works of Ricardo*, vol. IV, p. 179.

20. B. Semmel, op. cit., p. 63.

21. Ibid., p. 156.

22. Including re-exports: A. H. Imlah, *Economic Elements in the Pax Britannica* (Harvard, 1958) pp. 190–1.

23. Ibid., p. 169.

24. Ibid., p. 163.

25. Ibid., p. 164.

26. Her industrial strength also gave Britain considerable power as a purchaser: in 1840, Britain was buying 36 per cent of the exports of all other countries, in 1860 31 per cent and in 1873 still 26 per cent (ibid., p. 167).

27. For a discussion of the different types of trade treaty at this period, see D. C. M. Platt, *Finance, Trade and Politics in British Foreign Policy, 1815–1914* (Oxford, 1968) pp. 86–92.

28. Ibid., p. 87.

29. House of Commons, 21 Feb. 1787.

30. Ibid.

31. H. Brougham, *Enquiry into Colonial Policy* (Edinburgh, 1803) pp. 217–18.

32. A. H. Imlah, op. cit., p. 163.

33. Ibid., pp. 70–5.

34. Ibid., p. 171.

35. Ibid., p. 175.

36. Ibid., pp. 70–4.

37. M. Brougham, op. cit., pp. 217–18.

38. Cf. H. N. Brailsford, *The War of Steel and Gold* (Shannon, 1914): 'Russia is sensitive because she depends as absolutely as any Latin American republic on her repute in Western markets. She must float by

far the greater part of her loans abroad. She cannot even provide from her own resources, for the municipal enterprise of her cities, her undeveloped coal and iron and petroleum fields; all await the fertilisation of foreign capital. If we can conceive for a moment what German opinion would mean to us if we had to float Consols to the Deutsche Bank, if Manchester had to go to Berlin for money to build her tramways . . . we shall be able to realise grimly why and how much the opinion of the English people matters to the Russian government.'

39. Arthur Lewis, *Growth and Fluctuations, 1870–1913* (London, 1978) p. 199: 'The imperial powers did not encourage and in a few cases actively discouraged industrialisation.'

40. H. Feis, *Europe the World's Banker, 1870–1914* (New Haven, 1930) p. 278.

41. F. Fischer, *War of Illusion* (London, 1975) p. 294.

42. Parliamentary Debates, Chamber of Deputies, 11 January 1912.

43. For a more extended account of these events, see H. Feis, op. cit., pp. 361–81.

44. China's financial dependence was increased after 1900 by large payments of compensation imposed on her by the Western powers after the Boxer Rebellion, as a result of which (as in Egypt and Turkey) a considerable part of Chinese revenues became mortgaged to paying off debts to the foreign powers. In 1909–10, a four-power consortium of British, French, German and US banks was formed to lend money to the Chinese government. The US interests demanded the appointment of an American to supervise the expenditure of the loans, a demand strongly opposed by Russia and Japan. Further taxes, including internal taxes and taxes on wine and tobacco, were assigned to the repayment of these loans. After the revolution of 1911, the new ruler, Yuan Shih-kai, turned again to the four-power consortium for a loan. In retaliation, Russia, demanding control of all undertakings north of the great wall, formed a rival syndicate to lend to China to ensure her interests would be protected. Eventually, to reduce competition and the weakening of their bargaining power all the six powers joined together to make a loan, and laid down strict conditions, which included the establishment of an audit system headed by their own representatives and the administration of particular taxes by foreigners (though there continued to be considerable dispute among them as to which foreigners should occupy which posts).

45. Imlah, op. cit., p. 191.

46. Ibid.

47. United Nations, *International Capital Movements in the Inter-War Period* (New York, 1948).

48. League of Nations, *Industrialisation and World Trade* (Princeton, N. J., 1945).

49. On the eve of the Second World War, about two-thirds of Europe's industrial output was produced by Britain, Germany and France, while income per head was highest in Britain, Sweden and Germany (D. H. Aldcroft, *The European Economy, 1914–1970* (London, 1978) p. 118). See also W. A. Lewis, *Economic Survey, 1919–1939* (London, 1949)

p. 139.

50. In 1929, US long-term investment was 40 per cent in industrial bonds and notes, 45 per cent in government and municipal loans, 5 per cent in ordinary shares, and 3 per cent in preference shares (W. A. Lewis, *Economic Survey, 1919–1939*, p. 49).
51. D. H. Aldcroft, op. cit., p. 74.
52. For figures of foreign investment in this period, see W. A. Lewis, *Economic Survey, 1919–1939*, p. 49.
53. D. H. Aldcroft, op. cit., pp. 139–40.
54. W. A. Lewis, *Economic Survey, 1919–1939*, pp. 42, 79.
55. D. H. Aldcroft, op. cit., pp. 112–13.
56. W. A. Lewis, *Economic Survey, 1919–1939*, p. 150.
57. From 1929 to 1930, the average price of wheat fell 19 per cent, cotton 27 per cent, wool 46 per cent, silk 30 per cent, rubber 42 per cent, sugar 20 per cent, coffee 43 per cent, copper 26 per cent, tin 29 per cent: the index of prices of all commodities entering world trade fell from 1929 to 1932 by 56 per cent for raw materials, 48 per cent for foodstuffs and 37 per cent for manufactures (W. A. Lewis, ibid., p. 56).
58. Ibid., p. 58.
59. 'The great fall in primary produce prices during the world depression enormously cheapened the imports of industrial countries, and though the subsequent increase of trade and the operation of restrictive schemes arrested this development, they reversed it only to a small extent. The relative prices of exports and imports remained more favourable to industrial countries than in the previous decade. . . . Because the imports of industrial countries were kept down by commercial policy and under-employment, the incomes of other countries were prevented from expanding much. And because the latter had for the time being little opportunity to increase their earnings from foreign trade, they seemed to be unfavourable fields for foreign investment, which might otherwise have helped to create bigger incomes there' (W. Ashworth, *A Short History of the International Economy since 1850* (London, 1962) pp. 262–3).
60. W. A. Lewis, *Economic Survey, 1919–1939*, p. 58.
61. 'The major destabilizing influence came with the collapse in American lending. . . . The dramatic curtailment of lending exercised a powerful deflationary impact on the world economy. . . . The position of the debtor countries deteriorated sharply between 1928 and 1929 as they experienced a hefty drop in their net capital inflow. . . . These countries faced a severe deterioration in their trade balances as export values fell faster than import values, while external interest obligations, which were fixed in terms of gold, rose sharply as a proportion of export receipts. . . . The way out of the impasse was sought through deflation, devaluation, restrictive measures and default on debts' (D. H. Aldcroft, op. cit., pp. 85–6).
62. Ibid., p. 95.
63. The defeated countries were expected to pay even for relief: 29 per cent was sold for cash, 53 per cent on credit, and only 8 per cent given away.
64. Ibid., pp. 60–4.

65. K. Moreton and P. Tulloch, *Trade and Developing Countries* (London, 1977) p. 34.
66. United Nations, *Transnational Corporations in World Development* (New York, 1978) p. 37.
67. J. Dunning (ed.), *The Multinational Enterprise* (London, 1971) p. 19.
68. Ibid., p. 20. These estimates were, however, strongly contested by others.
69. R. Vernon, *Sovereignty at Bay* (London, 1971) p. 17: 'in 1969 the US was receiving 7 billion dollars a year in interest, dividends, royalties and fees, while it invested and re-invested about 5.4 billion dollars a year'.
70. J. Pincus, *Trade, Aid and Development* (New York, 1967) pp. 55ff, 233ff.
71. United Nations, op. cit., p. 56.
72. Cf. ibid., p. 7: 'the transnational corporations have largely determined the location of mineral processing capacity according to their own needs, and not necessarily those of the producer nations'.
73. Ibid., pp. 104–5.

NOTES TO CHAPTER 6: CONCLUSIONS: PRIVATE INTERESTS
AND PUBLIC WELFARE IN INTERNATIONAL SOCIETY

1. For example, in the codes adopted during the Tokyo Round.
2. Though OPEC is nowhere near a monopoly organisation, it sufficiently dominates production to be able to set prices. Producer countries which do not belong (including Britain) show little disposition to engage in price competition and in practice conform with the prices set by OPEC.
3. India, for example, today provides technical assistance to a number of countries, including some with much higher income a head.
4. An attempt to describe the way such a system of international management might be operated in greater detail is made in the author's *The Management of the World Economy* (London, 1983).

Index